Praise for Muse

A primer for museum ... developing programs which take advantage of our culture's interest in using photography to document, experience, and share.
Jeff Gates, Lead Producer, New Media Initiatives, Smithsonian American Art Museum

A veritable cornucopia of the latest research. The essays are impressively frank and refreshingly free of opinion masquerading as fact. This book will become a standard reference on the topic. A great volume, really, really good work.
Ed Rodley, Associate Director of Integrated Media, Peabody Essex Museum

Provides much needed context to inform photography policies, practices, and programs in the 21st century museum. A comprehensive exploration of this timely and important topic, it is an essential resource for museum practitioners and scholars.
Dr Randy C Roberts, Deputy Director, Jan Shrem and Maria Manetti Shrem Museum of Art, University of California

This book breathes respect for the museum visitor, and charts new territories in the most insightful ways, opening many doors to better comprehend what visitors do when visiting.
Prof. Nico Carpentier, Department of Informatics and Media, Uppsala University

This up-to-the-minute collection offers fresh perspectives for both museum and photography studies, overturning conventional wisdom and sidestepping moral panics to examine the control and production of culture in the twenty-first century.
Dr Annebella Pollen, Principal Lecturer, History of Art and Design, University of Brighton

This book takes a fascinating, in-depth look at visitor interaction and photography within the museum setting, and will for us be a valuable resource from which to learn, enabling us to provide a richer experience for visitors to our future exhibitions.
Jeremy Sutton-Hibbert, Document Scotland

This wide-ranging volume brings together three key debates of the moment: the inexorable rise of imaging culture, the privileging of experience and the ownership of "heritage".
Prof. Elizabeth Edwards, Emeritus Professor of Photographic History, De Montfort University

MUSEUMS AND VISITOR PHOTOGRAPHY

MUSEUMS AND VISITOR PHOTOGRAPHY

Redefining the Visitor Experience

Edited by Theopisti Stylianou-Lambert

MUSEUMSETC | EDINBURGH & BOSTON

CONTENTS

INTRODUCTION

MUSEUMS AND VISITOR PHOTOGRAPHY

Theopisti Stylianou-Lambert

WITH THE DEVELOPMENT OF photographic technologies and mobile devices, an astonishing number of photographs are produced yearly throughout the world. It is estimated that in 2015 alone more than one trillion photographs were taken, with the number growing exponentially each year (Heyman, 2015) There is no way to calculate precisely how many photographs are taken in museums, but that number is bound to be a large one. With the rising popularity of online social networks and photo-sharing applications, vernacular photography, including visitor photography, has entered our economy of images dynamically and has a growing function to play in visually defining people and places.

Visitor photography has become a major part of the museum experience and many museums have or are reevaluating their policies on photography. Some museum professionals have reservations about its increasingly widespread use and the effects it might have on the museum experience. Others, acknowledging its popularity, embrace photographic practices and even encourage them in an effort to be more inclusive. Nevertheless, there is limited research related to visitor photography which can guide photographic policies and exhibition design. Furthermore, while more and more museum visitors use photography and accumulate personal photographs, their effect on the museum experience and its meaning, and the ways in which they are used, are also largely understudied. The use of photography is already redefining visitor experience both inside and outside museum walls. Since this is the case, we need to understand how photography is used, shared, distributed or displayed after a museum visit and even years later.

This book aims to fill this gap in the literature and to provide thought-provoking material to help museum professionals and academics begin to understand visitor photography and explore its potential as a research tool, its uses in connecting with audiences, its implications for marketing and promotion and, finally, its potential as a valuable source of exhibition material.

Recent debates: to ban or not to ban

There is not much academic literature dealing with visitor photography in museums; but there has been an animated debate in newspapers, magazines and blogs about whether or not photography should be allowed in museums. While visitor photography has traditionally been allowed without restriction in zoos, science museums and natural history museums, there is no consensus on photographic policies in art museums (Kiiler, 2011). Perhaps for this reason, the recent debates focus on the art museum. The opponents of photography in art museums usually offer three main arguments:

- legal restrictions due to different intellectual property agreements and the need or desire to maintain control of sales of official merchandize (posters, postcards etc.);
- conservation considerations and security issues;
- the detrimental effects photography might have on the aesthetic experience.

On the other hand, the supporters of visitor photography usually focus on these three main arguments:

- banning photography limits access, education and research and is against public interest;
- visitors have a "moral right" to use the images they encounter in museums;
- recent studies support the use of photography in museums as an inclusive and democratic tool of engagement with exhibits.

The following sections briefly discuss two main issues which emerge from these debates: *ownership* and *experience*.

Ownership: copyright restrictions vs. public access

The issue of copyright restrictions is perhaps the most cited argument for banning photography in museums. Even in museums where photography is allowed, more often than not it is still banned in galleries which exhibit contemporary art, or artworks on loan from other collections. Copyright restrictions are multiple and often confusing, usually stemming from the fact that the author, owner and exhibitor of an object have different rights and legal obligations. Furthermore, the exhibitor is not always the owner and the owner is not always the artist. It is often mentioned that photographic restrictions have to do with the desire of museums to control the distribution and sale of officially sanctioned images (Simon, 2009). But most importantly, museums, as the trustees of objects, see themselves as responsible for the integrity and reputation of the objects they house; they want credit for the work they are doing and have an obligation to respect and implement donor and artist requirements (Crews, 2012).

To add to the complexity, copyrights expire in a set number

of years, but this does not always mean that a museum object is copyright-free after the expiration of its copyright. For example, masterpieces by da Vinci, Rembrandt and others are in the public domain with no copyright protection (Crews, 2012). However, museums usually decide whether or not images of the artworks will be available to the public, in what form and how they can be used. More precisely, the practices and policies of a museum influence whether or not a researcher can receive permission to use an image (and the cost of doing so), whether or not a visitor can download a high resolution image from a museum's website or whether or not she can take a photograph of the artwork during a visit. As a result, further photographic restrictions may be imposed on copyright-free artworks. Despite the good reasons for restricting photography in museums, it is important to separate museum policies from legal copyright restrictions to understand the role of museums in setting photographic policies.

It seems that there is a conflict between the desire to maintain tight control of the representation and circulation of images of objects through restrictive photographic policies and the educational and public interest goals of a museum. Motivated by this conflict, Kenneth D. Crews, the director of the Copyright Advisory Office of Columbia University, examined the policies of 50 art museums in the USA and found that "museums have strained the limits of copyright claims and indeed have restructured concepts of ownership and control in ways that curtail the availability and use of art images far beyond anything that may be grounded in copyright law" (Crews, 2012: 797). Similarly, Petri (2014: 1) examined law cases related to photographic reproductions of two-dimensional works of art in the public domain and concluded that "current museum practice in view of copyright is to some extent unethical" because museums often claim copyright even in cases where photographic reproductions of artworks are in the public domain. Instead, the author encourages museums "to wake up to their mission" (Petri, 2014: 8).

Restrictive photographic policies do not appear to concur with the mission of museums to offer free and public access to their collections. This is especially true when it comes to visitor photography. The proponents of the museum as an open, democratic space which is people-, rather than object-centred, see the banning of photography as a step backwards (Mairin, 2014). Miranda (2013), at Artnews blog argues:

> For years, advocates of open-source culture and a growing chorus of art bloggers have lobbied for less restrictive photo policies on the grounds that our shared artistic legacy is intended to be, well, shared. Not to mention that there is no small irony in being forbidden to take pictures in cultural establishments that celebrate the work of artists like Andy Warhol, Sherrie Levine, and Richard Prince, figures whose work is based, to a large degree, on the photographs of others.

Miranda and other supporters of visitor photography see the act of taking photographs as democratic, a visitor "right" that is often denied.

A number of museums have recognized their ethical "obligation" towards their audiences and made important steps towards allowing and even encouraging photography in their spaces. For example, in an attempt to make as many shows as possible visitor photography-friendly, the Brooklyn Museum has incorporated text into its lender and artist agreements which allows photography (Bernstein, 2012). Furthermore, museums have started providing their own high resolution images available for download from their websites. For example, the Rijksmuseum has uploaded high resolution images of artworks which can be accessed for free . In an interview, Taco Dibbits, the Rijksmuseum's director of collections, commented:

> We're a public institution, and so the art and objects we have are, in a way, everyone's property... If they want to have a Vermeer on their toilet paper, I'd rather have a very high-quality image of Vermeer on toilet paper than a very bad reproduction. (Cushing, 2013)

Central to the argument to the right of public access is the notion that the public is a co-owner of the collection, should have some control over its uses and that reuse is inevitable. It is also argued that visitors have a right to record their experiences in museums for future use (Simon, 2009). As various chapters in this book argue, there are uses of this "experiential record" which can be educational, inspirational and which can create strong bonds with museum objects and the museum itself.

Experience: aesthetic vs. other kinds of experiences

The other main argument of the opponents of visitor photography in art museums is that photography has a negative effect on aesthetic experiences. More specifically, it is argued that the use of photography is superficial, intrusive and gets in the way of a unique aesthetic experience. According to Gibson (2013: 19):

> ...the museum that allows the indiscriminate use of smartphones and tablets in its galleries is one that has lost control of its collections. The first casualty is the art experience itself.

It is argued that allowing photography in museums creates an atmosphere which is not conducive to quiet contemplation and personal encounters with art (Lay, 2014; Rosenbloom, 2014). Visitor photography creates noise, confusion, disturbance and tensions between visitors. Interestingly, both the Van Gogh Museum in Amsterdam (in 2014) and the Musée d'Orsay in Paris (in 2011) reintroduced their bans on photography because of the tension created between those who wanted to look at the artworks and those who wanted a clear view in order to take a photograph (Bailey, 2014).

Even if we agree that photography may have negative effects on a purely aesthetic experience, there are several problems with this argument. First, Gibson (2013) and other opponents of visitor photography equate "art experience" with "aesthetic experience". As is well known, motivations for visiting an art museum vary. Apart from a craving for aesthetic and emotional experiences (art loving filter), other motivations might include a desire for knowledge and inspiration (professional filter), a wish to have new experiences (self-exploration filter), to experience a tourist destination (cultural tourism filter), socialization needs (social visitation filter) or a combination of these (Stylianou-Lambert, 2009). Furthermore, photography is part of a museum experience and provides just one layer of engagement. Using photographic equipment does not mean that other layers of engagement are not desirable or possible. For example, it is imaginable for a visitor to have an aesthetic experience with an artwork and then snap a picture to share with a loved one even though she acknowledges that the photograph cannot replace or reproduce her experience. As a result, the strict dichotomy between visitors using and not using photography is a false one.

As several chapters in this volume show, photography can facilitate many visitor functions, such as social interaction, physical and online sharing, education and inspiration, as well as encourage a deeper involvement with museum objects and memory-forming narratives. The limited research available has shown that visitor photography, with the help of smartphones, tablets and social media, is a powerful tool for enabling social interaction (Leighton, 2007; Weilenmann, Hillman & Jungselius, 2013), allowing visitors to engage with the exhibitions in different ways (Weilenmann, Hillman & Jungselius, 2013), stimulating the motivation to learn (Leighton, 2007; Vartiainen & Enkenberg, 2014) and providing continuity between museum content and the social life of visitors outside the museum (Sayre & Wetterlund, 2008).

Furthermore, the critics of photography in museums focus on the seemingly superficial behaviour of visitor photographers rather than the actual uses of visitor photography. It goes without saying that mobile phones and tablets have changed the photographic behaviour of visitors. Yet, this visible behaviour is only the tip of the iceberg. What is unseen, and arguably more important, are internal processes of meaning making and communication through sharing (Kiiler, 2011).

It is assumed that the only valid experience or "reality" is that of the unmediated viewing experience between visitor and object/artwork. Seeing an original artwork is not necessarily an unmediated process but a complex one which usually involves more than one person. According to Sontag (1977: 115):

> Photography *is* the reality; the real object is often experienced as a letdown. Photographs make normative an experience of art that is mediated, second-hand, intense in a different way. (My emphasis)

Visitor photography can be seen as another, different "reality" which is not necessarily inferior to that of the "naked" eye

Book contents

To explore the potentials of visitor photography, this book is divided into four sections:

- understanding visitor photography;
- researching: visitor photography as a research tool;
- connecting with audiences: audience development and advocacy;
- participating: visitors as contributors of content.

Understanding visitor photography

The chapters in the first section of the book attempt to examine and understand at a deeper level the photographically mediated "reality" of museums, both in the museum space and online. Patrick Van Rossem, in *Chapter 1*, provides a thoughtful discussion on how audiences are increasingly seen as active participants/actors in museum narratives both by museum professionals and artists and opens up the possibility that visitor photography can be used in museum education practices that encourage a more deconstructive and transformative visitor experience.

In *Chapter 2*, Tadashi Naito provides a detailed example of a personal photographic experience as well as the frustrations and revelations that came with it. He found that the impossibility of photographing a particular artwork actually led him to another way of seeing and a richer experience. Ellie Miles, in *Chapter 3*, analyzes the behaviour of visitors before and after the renovation of the *Sutton Hoo and Europe AD 300-1100* gallery at the British Museum and confirms what Naito intuitively and introspectively arrived at: that visitors who take photographs spend more time with the objects and are more engaged with the collection.

Visitors do not only photograph museum objects and spaces but often they turn their lenses on each other and themselves. In *Chapter 4*, Alli Burness argues that self-representational social photography is a new way of looking in the museum and that the "moral panic" created in the media comes mainly from distorted and exaggerated reports of extreme examples that come to be seen as typical. She urges museum professionals and researchers to side-step discussions about the value of self-representation (for example selfies) and focus on visitor *practices*, and further explore issues of identity formation and social communication.

One of the strengths of visitor photography is that it simultaneously exists in two interconnected "worlds": in the museum and in everyday life; in the physical world and in the virtual. Nowadays, mobile technology and other emerging technologies enable visitors to transfer their museum experiences online almost immediately. Alexandra Weilenmann and Thomas Hillman, in *Chapter 5*, discuss two crucial functions of online visitor photography. First, its role as a "social media souvenir" and second, its potential to re-curate exhibitions in an online environment.

Researching: visitor photography as a research tool

This section considers visitor photography as a research tool that can help researchers and museum professionals better understand visitors' experiences or answer specific research questions unrelated to the museum experience. For the past few years, Linda Henkel, Katelyn Parisi and Carey Mack Weber have been exploring the relationship between photography and memory by using the museum as a "psychology lab". In *Chapter 6* they discuss how taking photographs in a museum and retrieving them at a later point influences visitors' memory of museum objects. The authors usually instruct participants on how to use their cameras and use specific and highly-regulated psychological experiments to gauge the research participants' memory of objects.

In contrast, *Chapter 7* and *Chapter 8* explore how researchers can find ways to piggyback on the intuitive nature of visitor photography to create new ways of understanding visitors' experiences without disturbing the regular flow of a visit or a visitor's behaviour. Visitor photography, in the museum space or posted online, becomes a valuable source of data which can be analyzed to investigate interpretation, personal connection with objects, popularity of objects, or the flow of a visit. For example, in *Chapter 7*, Elee Kirk describes her experience with a research project which used children's photography to understand the experiences of young children in a natural history museum. In her research, photography provides a "natural", "seamless" research tool, and through photo-elicitation, a starting point for more meaningful discussions with a not-so-articulate group of visitors. Additionally, Mariruth Leftwich, in *Chapter 8*, analyzes visitors' photographs of Graceland posted on Flickr to illuminate the visitor experience at Elvis' home. It was evident from the photographs that visitors are attracted to the personal world of Elvis and often try to make connections between their own world and Graceland.

Of course, we need to keep in mind that the meaning of an object is shaped by its relationship with an individual. A photograph alone, or even a set of photographs from a museum visit, cannot tell us what people are thinking when taking a photograph or what it means to them. From a set of photographs we might be able to understand how people move around in an exhibition space and what objects attract visitors the most, but more qualitative methodologies (such as interviews with visitors, or ethnographic observation) are necessary to decode meaning making processes and the uses of photography. Johanna Barnbeck, in *Chapter 9*, used such mixed methodologies to examine how people relate to artworks at the Rijksmuseum. The research revealed the importance of social narratives and as a result the study helped researchers develop interfaces which socially augment selected masterpieces at the museum.

Connecting with audiences: audience development and advocacy

Visitor photography can also be used creatively for audience development and advocacy purposes. Kjersti Lillebø and Kirsten Linde, in *Chapter 10*, maintain that museums should speak the same visual language as the audiences they want to attract. They have analyzed marketing images of the Akershus Museum in Norway in order to understand how these may reflect visitors' photographic self-representations posted online. They discovered that nowadays both the museum and its visitors portray the Akershus Museum as a destination for family outings, togetherness and entertainment. Museums, using their visitors' photographs as "tips", can understand how a specific museum is imagined and experienced and can even redesign their promotional material to visually match visitors' photographs.

Chapter 11 tells the story of a public engagement project at the Portland Art Museum, #captureParklandia, which used the mobile photo-sharing and social networking service Instagram to connect the museum and its visitors with public parks in a variety of ways. In this chapter, Kristin Bayans and Justin Meyer offer a successful example of how photography can be used as a platform to discuss civic issues, engage diverse audiences inside and outside the museum, and forge new relationships with special interest groups.

The museum selfie has been at the heart of discussions about identity formation in museums. It is either seen as a superficial, narcissistic act or a visual embodiment of an experience and an identity marker. Mar Dixon, a London-based museum blogger and social media consultant, recognized the selfie's potential and in 2014 initiated the #MuseumSelfie Day;

a hugely popular yearly event which aims at spreading appreciation for museums and their objects. Dixon invited people to visit a museum on a specific day, take a museum selfie and share it. In *Chapter 12*, she talks about how #MuseumSelfie Day came to be and the momentum it created. In *Chapter 13*, Jeffrey Bowen presents a variety of examples of museums and other institutions which have successfully used selfies in an effort to engage with and attract new audiences, develop an institutional brand and increase donations. Bowen argues that museums should not hesitate to creatively use this popular photographic behaviour.

#MuseumSelfie Day and other similar initiatives have a clearly physical as well as digital presence and the visual results are usually playful images of visitors posing with museum objects. There are certain cases where sculptures or paintings appear to be taking their own selfies at arm's length or a visitor "becomes" a painting by posing in front of it. Nevertheless, all these cases require a physical presence. But what happens when the museum selfie does not involve an actual museum visit and editing tools can be freely used? In *Chapter 14*, Leslie-Jean Thornton provides such an example; a collaboration between museums and an Instagram editing community.

Participating: visitors as contributors of content

If we accept that visitors create their own realities through their photographs, then it is not a stretch to think about visitor photography as a database of potential exhibition material. The chapters in this section present projects that use photographs taken or owned by visitors as exhibition material with a discussion of what worked and did not.

Russell Dornan, in *Chapter 15*, discusses *An Idiosyncratic A to Z of the Human Condition* which took place at the Wellcome Collection in 2014. Half the exhibition was made up of historical objects from the collection and the other half displayed content generated by the museum's audiences, both physical and online. Dorman provides a detailed explanation of the development, design process and outcomes of the project and concludes that the success of the project was mainly due to the relatively simple call for action, which enabled audiences to respond creatively, and the participatory quality of the project

However, technology does not always guarantee creative responses or meaningful interactions. In *Chapter 16*, Jenna Ashton discusses the *Chandelier*, a large digital sculpture installed at the Museum of Science and Industry in Manchester, which circulates visitors' self-portraits, taken at computer stations nearby, along with photographs and key dates from Manchester's science and industry achievements. Ashton provides a critical analysis of the uses of the Chandelier and concludes that, at least in this case, technology fails to generate spontaneous digital interactions between the museum and its visitors or conversations with strangers as the museum originally aimed.

Another challenge for museums aspiring to engagement with diverse audiences in collaborative projects is how to generate public awareness and reach the right audiences. This requires strategic planning, collaboration among different museum departments, perseverance and flexibility to change strategies that do not work. Divya Rao Heffley, in *Chapter 17*, guides us through the inception, implementation, challenges, and evaluation of the successful project *A People's History of Pittsburgh*, an online, crowd-sourced photography album initiated by the Carnegie Museum of Art. The project focused on people's own photographs and narratives and worked well on several platforms: a dedicated website, a special exhibition, and an artist's book. Similarly, Marta Brunelli, in *Chapter 18*, offers several examples of how curators and educators can take advantage of people's narratives of school photographs in order to implement innovative projects in school museums online and offline. Both Heffrey and Brunelli see photographs as "social objects" which can facilitate participation and stimulate dialogue.

To conclude, the chapters in this book testify to the potential of visitor photography as a powerful tool for research, for connecting and attracting audiences, and for contributing to museum content. We collectively see visitor photography as a set of personal and social practices which can facilitate understanding and sharing and a democratic and empowering act which can provide access points to exhibitions and bring audiences closer to museums and their objects.

ACKNOWLEDGEMENTS

A part of the research for this book was completed while I was a Smithsonian Fellow in Museum Practice at the Smithsonian Center for Learning and Digital Access (SCLDA). I would like to warmly thank Stephanie Norby, Pino Monaco and Tracie Spinola from SCLDA and Rebecca Kasemeyer from the Smithsonian National Portrait Gallery for making my stay a smooth and productive one. Furthermore, I would like to thank all the authors of this book who, in their own ways, are actively exploring the possibilities of visitor photography and enthusiastically agreed to share their thoughts and experiences with us. Finally, thanks are due to MuseumsEtc and Graeme Farnell for making this book happen.

REFERENCES

Crews, K. (2012). Museum Policies and Art Images: Conflicting Objectives and Copyright Overreaching. *Fordham Intellectual Property, Media & Entertainment Law Journal*, 22, 795-834.

Cushing, T. (2013). Amsterdam's Rijksmuseum Does Digital Archives Right: Hi Res Downloads And A Suite of Online Editing Tools. *Techdirt*. Available at: https://www.techdirt.com/articles/20130529/19425723249/amsterdams-rijksmuseum-does-digital-archives-right-hi-res-downloads-suite-online-editing-tools.shtml.

Gibson, E. (2013). The Overexposed Museum. *New Criterion*, 32(4), 19-21.

Kiiler, E. (2011). Circulation of Museum Visitors' Photographs: from art museums to collaborative archives. *Spaces of Creation*, 15 (Nov.), 58-66.

Leighton, D. (2007). In the frame: investigating the use of mobile phone photography in museums. *Int. J. Nonprofit Volunt. Sect. Mark.*, 12, 308-319.

Petri, G. (2014). The Public Domain vs. the Museum: The Limits of Copyright and Reproductions of Two-dimensional Works of Art. *Journal of Conservation and Museum Studies*, 12(1), 1-12.

Sayre, S. & Wetterlund, K. (2008). The Social Life of Technology for Museum Visitors. *Visual Arts Research*, 34(2), 85-94.

Simon, N. (2009). What Are We Hiding? *Museum, Nov.-Dec.*, 29-31.

Sontag, (1977). *On Photography*. New York: Farrar, Straus and Giroux.

Stylianou-Lambert, T. (2009). Perceiving the Art Museum. *Journal of Museum Management and Curatorship*, 24(2), 139-158.

Vartiainen & Enkenberg (2014). Participant-Led Photography as a Mediating Tool in Object-Oriented Learning in a Museum. *Visitor Studies*, 17(1), 66-88.

Weilenmann, A., Hillman, T. & Jungselius, B. (2013). Instagram at the Museum: Communicating the Museum Experience through Social Photo Sharing. In *CHI'13 Proceedings of the SIGCHI Conference on Human Factors in Computing Systems* (pp. 1843-1852). New York.

Bernstein, F. (2012). At Galleries, Cameras Find a Mixed Welcome. *The New York Times*, (14 March). Available at: http://www.nytimes.com/2012/03/15/arts/artsspecial/art-museums-photography-policies-vary-widely.html.

Miranda, C. A. (2013). Why Can't We Take Pictures in Art Museums? *Art News*, 13 May. Available at: http://www.artnews.com/2013/05/13/photography-in-art-museums/.

Bailey, M. (2014). To Ban or Not to Ban Photography. *The Art Newspaper*, 12 March. Available at: http://theartnewspaper.com/articles/To-ban-or-not-to-ban-photography/32000.

Mairin, K. (2014). The Value of Museum Selfies. *Edgital* 29 August. Available at: http://www.edgital.org/the-value-of-museum-selfies/.

Rosenbloom, S. (2014). The Art of Slowing Down in a Museum. *The New York Times*, 9 October. Available at: http://www.nytimes.com/2014/10/12/travel/the-art-of-slowing-down-in-a-museum.html?_r=0.

Heyman, S. (2015). Photos, Photos Everywhere. *The New York Times*, 29 July. Available at: http://www.nytimes.

com/2015/07/23/arts/international/photos-photos-everywhere.html.
Lay, P. (2014). From the Editor. *History Today*, 2 October.

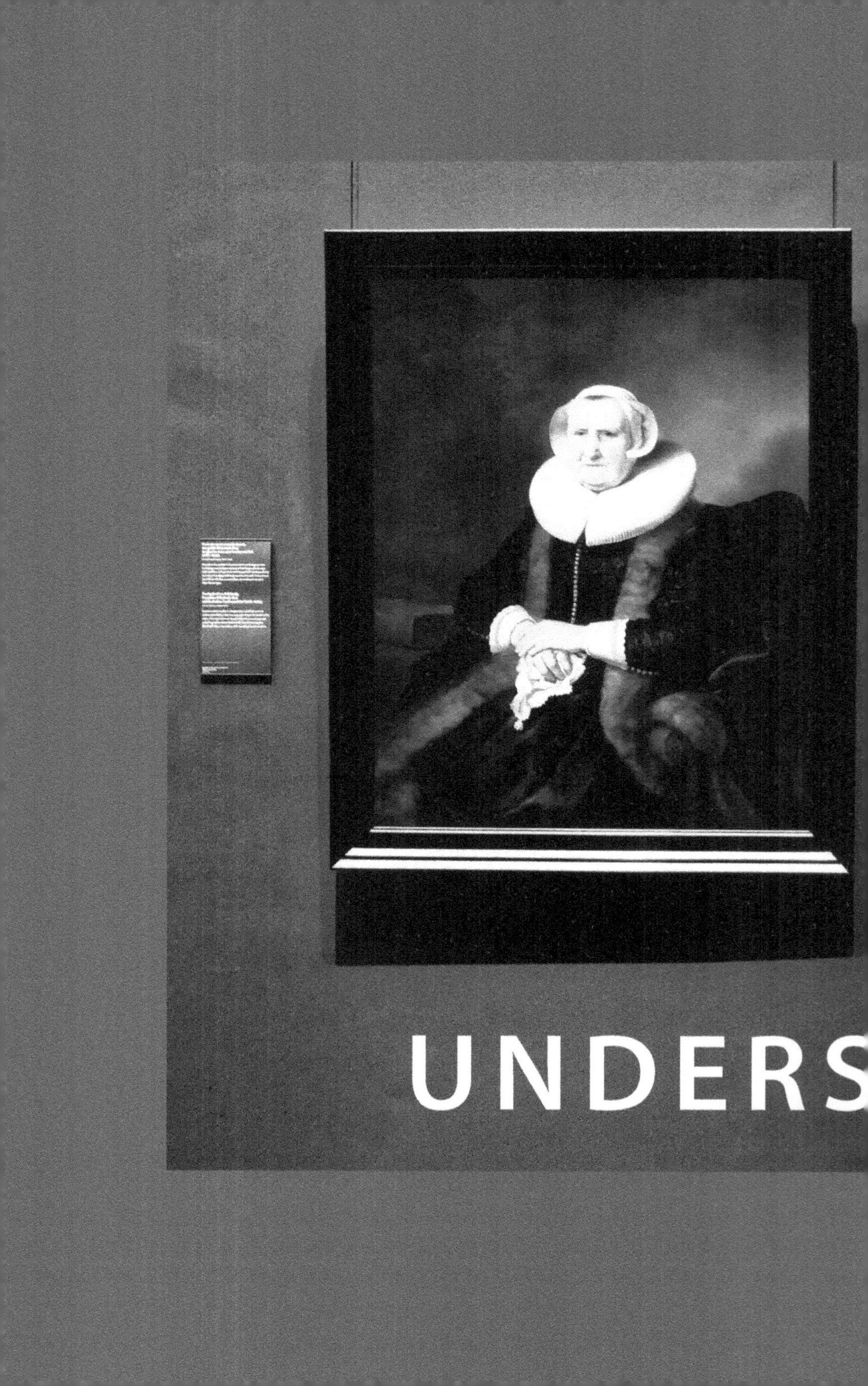

UNDERS

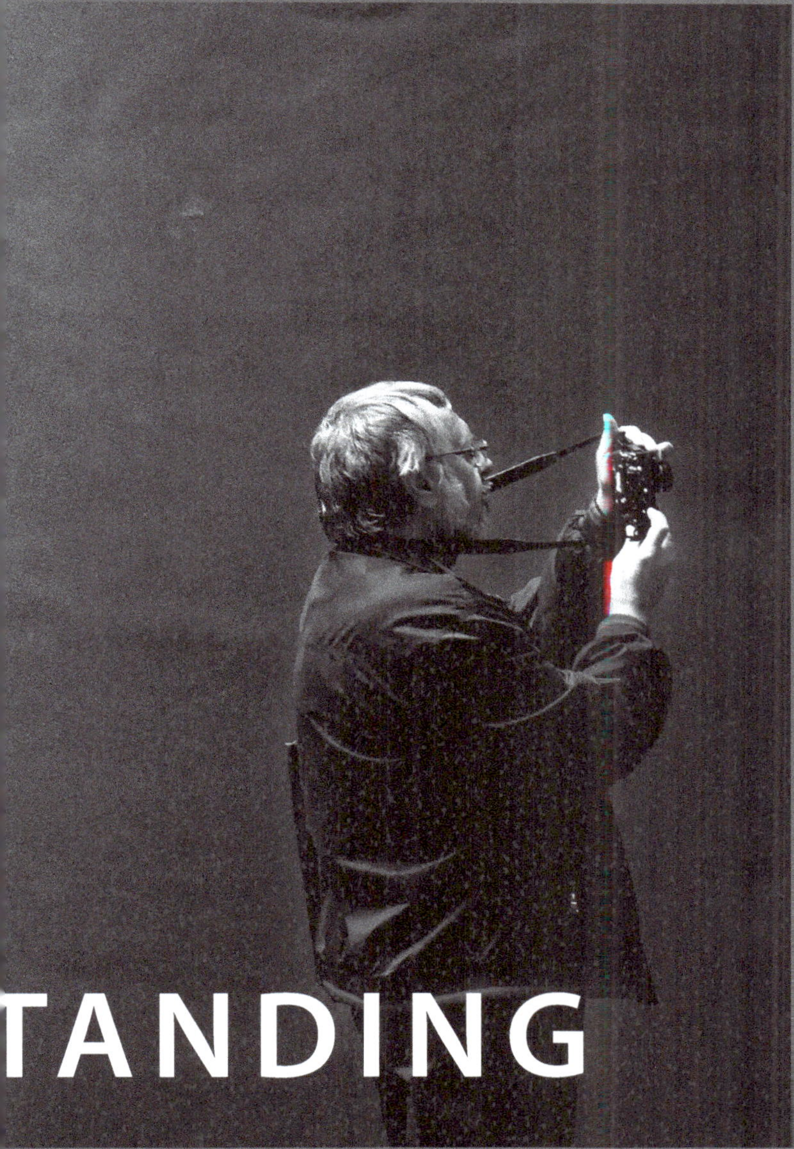
TANDING

CHAPTER ONE

BEYOND EXPERT VISION: VISITOR PHOTOGRAPHY AS INSPIRATION

Patrick Van Rossem

WHEN YOU VIEW A PAINTING, take particular care not to go, like ignorant people, excessively near; but rather, beginning far off, approach gradually, till it appears rough; then recede a little, till it looks sweeter: it is what connoisseurs call finding the proper light of a painting.
– Cosmetti, 1767

How to behave in a museum? What is a proper way of looking at art? What knowledge is required in order to experience and understand a work correctly? These are some of the questions museum professionals, critics, art historians and others have asked themselves ever since public exhibitions became customary in the second half of the eighteenth century. With a public now increasingly finding its way to art museums, art professionals, via channels such as books, newspapers and magazines, have started to advise people how to look at art properly. In order to avoid the "destructive" effect of uneducated perception, advice has been given (Brewer, 2013) on how to evaluate works of art. Ideals, however, need examples or models and what better than to propose the connoisseur himself as model. The above quoted advice of Cosmetti (1767: 16), stands as a clear example. Not behaving like a connoisseur makes you look ignorant in the eyes of other viewers. Brewer (2013) remarks that the advice also shows us that visiting an exhibition was considered a social act. You had to fit in. Social mechanisms such as being subordinated to a controlling, social gaze made sure that one conducted oneself with decorum.

This idea has been thoroughly explored by both Carol Duncan and Tony Bennett. In *Civilizing Rituals* Duncan (1995) characterized museums as ritual sites, where visitors engage themselves in performance-like behavior. The museum and its codes, the architectural environment, and elements such as the signage become both stage set and script. According to Duncan, this makes visitors adjust their behavior in a manner befitting the importance of the site. It legitimizes in turn their own presence in the museum. This ritualistic behavior is necessary, for, as Duncan argues, it is required in order to successfully engage with the museum's transformative aims: enlightenment, spiritual nourishment and aesthetic pleasure. The museum, in other words, produces ritualistic behaviour which in turn gives visitors the authority to engage with the art. In 1995, sociologist Tony Bennett published *Birth of the Museum*. He situated the rise of the public museum in the nineteenth century within an ideological economy of order used by the state to display both power and knowledge for the benefit of the people. The exhibitionary complex, Bennett argues, places people on the side of power and it regulates both their behaviour and knowledge. Winning the hearts and minds of the visitors required, however, that everyone should see. It produced a visualising technology – the exhibition – which regulated the crowd and made it visible to itself. The audience became a kind of spectacle in its own right. It also turned the audience, Bennett argues, into a controlled and surveyed entity. The audience ultimately regulates itself through interiorizing ideas and images of how an ideal visitor should behave in order to attain proper decorum. The ideal visitor, in other words, copies the behavior of experts and connoisseurs who know how to approach works of art. Visitors are also expected to read the texts found in the exhibition spaces. These contain the knowledge deemed necessary for understanding. Viewers will also ideally look and contemplate quietly so they can successfully experience the enlightenment the art brings as well as the aesthetic pleasure it promises.

The viewer under consideration in these studies is of a generic kind. Over time, as museology and museum pedagogy developed, differences amongst members of the audience became more important. Considerable progress has been made when it comes to identifying and analysing different kinds of audience groups. Today museums and art organisations no longer think of viewers as passive visitors but rather as active and motivated museum-goers. Museum pedagogy welcomes ideas such as “the emancipated spectator”, developed by French philosopher Jacques Rancière (2009). He argues that spectators can no longer be seen as passive philistines and that one should stop seeing and treating them as such. Being a spectator, he argues, is something we all already are. Spectators know and recognize visual codes and are critical actors who know how to find the realities behind appearances. In this, we are all equal – there are no experts and no uneducated people – because we are all actors in our own story. And it is from these multiple starting points, these stories, that different stories intersect. No starting point should be privileged and both “territories” – for example fields of expertise – and any fixed distribution of roles should be avoided, argues Rancière.

But the acceptance of approaches such as Rancière’s and the widespread recognition of viewers as active actors does not necessarily imply that gallery education has become more critical and self-reflective. Is there a shift within art education towards activating viewers’ existing knowledge, accommodating critique and discussion, or designing ways to facilitate feedback? In her research into art mediation in Flemish museums, Inge Van Reeth (2009) records the existence of perspectives which do regard viewers as active. Museums, however, also tend to categorize and divide their audiences. In many cases a group of informed viewers is differentiated from a more broad and general audience. Distinctive activities and educational tools have been developed for both groups. The audience division and the type of categories these museums work with – informed and less informed – significantly contradicts the idea of an "emancipated spectator". The general audience is in most cases offered information which reproduces expert ideas. A self-critical gallery approach which does indeed work with the idea of a more active viewer in a more constructive and critical way is rare or even absent according to Van Reeth (2009). The view is shared by educator and theorist Carmen Mörsch (2011) who stated that, notwithstanding valuable exceptions, gallery education as a critical practice is still a minority activity. Her involvement as exhibition educator in Documenta 12 in Kassel in 2007 led her to distinguish four institutional functions within art education. Art education is *affirmative* when it directs itself towards an already interested and specialized audience. It is *reproductive* when it tries to bring in families, schools, younger people and other, "uninitiated" visitors. It becomes more critical when it adopts a *deconstructive* perspective in which visitors become participants. Education, the institution and those addressed as participants work together in order to question the museum as authority. The goal of education is that people develop and express personal judgments and that they get an awareness of themselves as active interpreters rather than "passive" onlookers. Gallery education can, finally, also become *transformative* when it seeks to influence rather than merely question things. Here, education aims for real institutional change and social impact.

These four functions can overlap and coexist. Mörsch, however, notices that both the deconstructive and transformative function are rare in both gallery education and curatorial practice. The idea that viewers are already emancipated; that they are in fact participants and should be treated as such and that they are capable of forming opinions and developing stories based on their personal experiences is infrequent. An exception is the Van Abbemuseum in Eindhoven. This museum of modern and contemporary art experiments widely with projects in which viewers are offered the chance to become participants, giving them the opportunity to develop more personal relations to both the art and the institution. The boundary between the curatorial and educational is often blurred or non-existent. In the exhibition project *Play Van Abbe 4*, organized in 2011, the audience was offered the opportunity to visit and experience an exhibition in different roles. Because, as the museum states (The Pilgrim, the Tourist, the Flaneur, 2011), there is no single way to look at an artwork, visitors were invited to play a role: they could be pilgrim, tourist, flaneur or worker. Each role had tools which made the visit distinctive and different. Roles were not fixed and players could swap. Game masters assisted those playing in the museum. A multiplicity of stories – both initiated by the museum and/or invented by the participants – came into being. One of the underlying goals of the role-play was that visitors would become more conscious of their own behaviour, perception and ideas in relation to art; and appreciate that changing roles can bring about different insights and understandings. *Play Van Abbe 4* avoided the monolithic idea that there is only one valuable story – the expert's story – to be told. It favoured the idea that different kinds of comprehension can be at play simultaneously and that knowledge and experience can be both produced and triggered in a critical and subjective manner rather than solemnly presented and gained contemplatively. The flaneur listening to a soundscape on her earphones made associations which differed enormously from the pilgrim's investment in art history and aesthetics.

Exhibitions built around ideas of multiplicity and difference are rare. Those which actively promote polyphonic readings and responses even more so. With Mörsch's categories in mind it is easy to qualify *Play Van Abbe 4* as an exhibition which deliberately tried to achieve both deconstructive and transformative effects. Since *Play Van Abbe*, the museum has continued along similar lines. It keeps on questioning, in experimental projects and exhibitions, every single aspect of the museum as a public institution. Particular attention is paid to the presence of the audience. The museum tries to be open, welcoming ideas and feedback from visitors, and inviting them to contribute to the curatorial and educational program. A good example is the ongoing project *Storylines* which started in 2013. For us, this project is extremely relevant, because it shows that an open, receptive attitude can generate ideas proposed by visitors – now participants or even users – who co-construct curatorial and educational aspects of the museum. The museum also makes the feedback and visitor ideas received visible to other members of the audience. In the third section of this chapter, I will argue that photographs taken by visitors can have similar effects if museums are indeed open and receptive to the messages evoked in them. *Storylines* starts from the idea that narratives are by definition incomplete. The museum invites people – via an open call on the web and in the museum itself – to propose new storylines about the art collection and new ways to experience it. So far, four proposals have been realized. One focuses on the architecture of the museum. Another invites people to experience the collection through the eyes of children. The olfactory sense claims center stage in a tour called *Inhaling Art – Scented Art*. A fourth tour invites visitors to adopt different physical positions in relation to both art and architecture. It explores relations between body, object and space. The storylines disrupt visitor expectations. Children's experiences are not art historical stories which explain and contextualize art. Standing on your head or lying down can hardly be called classical decorum. Smelling boxes which contain certain aromas disrupts the focus on the ocular and adds an often overlooked sense to the visit.

In the *Toolshop* – a space where visitors choose a particular mediation tool – participants are also offered the opportunity to give feedback about the experiences they had with the chosen tool(s) by responding to questions. For example, *What feedback do you want to give the creator of the storyline?* Or *The offer of Storylines has surprised me because…*

When I visited the museum, 26 answers were displayed by visitors in the *Toolshop*, all very positive and enthusiastic about *Storylines*. Visitors appreciated the social interaction. People who follow similar storylines interacted and exchanged experiences – a clear difference from more traditional visits in which social interaction is limited to the people who know each other. Participants praised the fact that they have to be active and supported the museum's choice to create more interactive relations between the museum, the art and its audience. One visitor wrote that, "normally you stand, look and move on. But now it is OK to act a little bit crazy."

For others, the *Storylines* helped them avoid the tendency to go through the museum too quickly. It made them stop and experience works of art differently. The idea that it was alright to create your own stories about art was deeply appreciated. Of course, these few remarks do not give us a full insight into what people thought. They do, however, tell us that for some visitors-turned-participants the experience was more than worth it because it brought about changes in the ways they perceive and experience art.

I would like to relate the museum's preoccupation with the dialogical, social interaction, feedback, self-consciousness and critical reflection, to an idea put forward by theorist Irit Rogoff (2008) in her essay *Turning*. Here the author asks herself what the so-called educational turn in curating might mean? To answer the question Rogoff turns to Michel Foucault's evocation of the Greco-Roman term "parrhesia", which, according to him, means something like free speech, understood in terms of speaking truthfully, frankly, or critically. At the core of "parrhesia" is the idea that speakers express their own, personal and subjective relation to truth. Rogoff relates the Aramaic meaning of the term – speaking "openly, blatantly, in public" – to Foucault's characterization of "parrhesia". She subsequently relates it to the educational turn in curating, which, she believes, becomes "the moment when we attend to the production and articulation of truths [...], but truth as that which collects around it subjectivities that are neither gathered nor reflected by other utterances." (Rogoff, 2008: 9). For Rogoff, creating opportunities for people to express their personal relation to truth – in other words, their subjective understanding of truth, in a free, uninhibited and even blatant way, is what the educational turn could be about. Now is this not partly what the Van Abbemuseum offers to its players, users and participants? It creates spaces – by being vulnerable, explicit and openly self-critical – and opportunities in which one can express subjective truths. The museum invites and hosts proposals which add meaningful multiplicities to the ones already shared, or to those which are in the process of becoming. It creates room for dialogue, exchange and commitment and most of all it welcomes dissident views, alternatives and criticism. Players become experts in a museum where visitors are indeed treated as "emancipated spectators". The museum no longer stages itself as the ultimate expert; the keeper of a superior truth. On the contrary. It welcomes parrhesia and reminds viewers that particular stories – truths – are of equal importance as those created by "real" experts who supposedly "know".

Dialogical relations and the creation of a space wherein true parrhesia is possible can, however, only be achieved if art institutions and those who work in them recognize that the idea of an emancipated spectator – a spectator who is already an expert of his or her own story and the relations which exist between them and the outside world – can only exist if we move beyond the division between specialized and general. Passive reception, induced by autocratic formulae needs to be supplanted by a philosophy which favors difference and active dialogue.

Both Van Reeth (2009) and Mörsch (2011) remind us that there is still a lot left to do in order to achieve this. A look at some of the pictures taken by museum visitors is, I suggest, a good place to start thinking of the spectator as emancipated, enthusiastically inventing and/or elaborating stories; claiming parrhesia by posting pictures on the internet.

First, we will look at some works made by artists who have taken a particular interest in the presence of the audience. They too are bringing us closer to the "real" spectator; moving us slowly away from an ideal one, who is often but a mirror image of the expert and connoisseur herself.

Artists and spectators

> Aunt May and Uncle Jim do not always fit the philistine costume history has assigned them. Attracted to art by its promotion in mass media, they come to an artist enthusiastically but with little grasp of what that artist is doing. Disconcertingly they pose as hippies-ready-for-anything and want to be shocked over and over... (Kaprow, 1964: 49)

In 1964, American artist Allan Kaprow pointed out that audiences were changing. Observation showed (Kaprow, 1964) that mass media had negative effects on their thoughts about art. Spectators come to art, he argued, in order to be shocked by it and not as so-called philistines or even as genuinely interested and open-minded people. This development worried the artist since the understanding – and approval or disapproval – of art was no longer a matter of educated perception. Educating people about art was also hampered because of the strong, formative impact of mass media's sensational preoccupation with art. Visitors misjudge or misunderstand art because, Kaprow seems to suggest, they no longer know what the artist is doing. Is Kaprow advocating an ideal visitor? Did he long for an audience which could be educated in order for it to understand what artists were trying to do and say? Suffice to say that an artist in the sixties started to worry about the presence of the audience and that he described it in terms of unknowing and knowing the wrong things. Kaprow was not the only one who noticed the presence of the audience. Henry Sayre (1989) wrote that an important shift occurred in the sixties. He believed that, "The shift from object to audience has had profound effects on art generally. It has opened art up to the plurality of interpretation" (Sayre, 1989: 5). But can we really presume that plurality is something artists like or even strive for? What do artists think of having an audience? And what do they think about having an audience which possibly experiences their art very differently from their own intent or experience? I would like to look at the work of some artists who muse in their art on the presence of the audience. I will begin at the end of the sixties, for it is then that artists started to realise that they were confronted with an institutionalised, museum and gallery going audience which consciously decides that it wants to see and actively seeks art.

The insight, so it seems, was not always met with great

enthusiasm. American artist Bruce Nauman found its presence rather difficult: "It is difficult to address yourself to an anonymous public" (Cordes, 1989: 350). His reservations were partly informed by the fact that he realized that he was caught up in a production logic; producing works for anonymous consumers that might turn his work into theirs:

> I mistrust audience participation. That is why I try to make these works as limiting as possible... It has more to do with me not allowing people to make their own performance out of my art. I don't like to leave things open so people feel they are in a situation they can play games with. (Sharp, 1970: 113)

> I didn't want to present situations where people could have too much freedom to invent what they thought was going on... I wanted it to be my idea, and I did not want people to invent the art. (Van Bruggen, 1988: 19)

Nauman (Van Rossem, 2012: 171) clearly mistrusted spectators because they could misunderstand him or narcissistically embody his work, turning it into their own performance, their idea and property and thus ending his desire to represent his ideas. MAKE ME THINK ME[1] and EAT ME FEED ME[2] are like shouts written down by Nauman in black, capital letters. These works on paper speak of the viewers' presence and their consummating interpretative act. It seems that when confronted with the spectator, the work of art can only act out its own dependency on the spectator and testify about her devouring "understanding". The mistrust motivated the artist to beg:

PLEASE PAY ATTENTION PLEASE[3] for the audience's attention. In the videotaped performance *Stamping in the Studio*[4] the artist is seen running around. By turning the camera upside down he takes up an anti-ocular stance. His running produces a monotonous rhythmic that sounds like a military march. The sound ruptures the screen; showing us – via the ear – an intentional subject, persisting in his activity and self-control. If anything, it positions us as what Mikhail Bakhtin (1986: 126) called a "superaddressee", a kind of witness whose understanding is presumed. And Nauman does move us in a direction he is sure we will comprehend: "you can feel that tension, you can feel that foot" (Sharp, 1971: 148). These works point in the direction of an artist who has not yet come to terms with the presence of the audience. Questions arising from this communication and representation debacle, are I think: Who are you? What do you want? Can you understand what the work is about? How can I make you feel what I feel? Nauman was not the only artist who asked himself such questions. The general impression is, that "the shift from object to audience" (Sayre, 1989: 5), brought about discomfort and unease amongst many artists. Their work speaks of it.

A certain type of work, one could even call it a genre, stands out: works which represent the audience for the audience itself. In 1975, American artist Dan Graham appeared before a live audience in the happening *Performance/Audience/Mirror*. He paced up and down before the seated crowd; at times facing it or looking at the large mirror behind him which reflected the audience and himself. While doing so, he described his actions and behaviour. In turn he also described the behaviour and carriage of the audience or its individual members as well as their sounds and facial expressions. They could verify what he said about them by looking in the mirror. The performance has a vulnerability that differentiates it from the sometimes rather hostile approach of Nauman. Rather than appearing confused because of the audience's presence and proximity, Graham moved closer to it in order to make it more self-conscious of its presence and behaviour. He also highlighted the fact that they are audience members who want to be entertained and that he as an artist is forced to cater to their desires. Graham also performs his own performance anxiety (Van Rossem, 2012). He stumbles, misspeaks, and coughs. The presence of the audience seemed to be an imposing one and the encounter between artist and audience speaks only of the fact that both artist and audience are caught up in a reciprocal dependency which can bring about discomfort, unease and anxiety.

Let's now jump to the end of the eighties. But not without first highlighting a degree zero in the relation between artist and audience. German artist Anselm Kiefer, whose work was included in *Play Van Abbe 4*, did not believe that people could understand his work. "Art is difficult," he said, "there are only a few people who can actually say something about it" (Needham, 2011). Another German artist, Martin Kippenberger, went much further when he made cynical reason the core of his relationship with the audience (Van Rossem, 2007). For him, making art was an activity which could only mean something to himself. He was the ultimate expert and he was convinced that the audience had absolutely no real interest in art. Kippenberger also thought that consumerism made audiences numb. The cynical attitude however did not dominate. At the end of the eighties, German artist Thomas Struth looked more closely at audiences. His decision to do so was informed by the artist's observation that tourists increasingly visit museums (Tuchmann, 2003). It was his intention to photograph them, in order to capture their reactions to the artworks on display and to reveal the impact which behavioural codes, ways of presentation and museum architecture have on the audience. His large photographs are layered works which muse on time, idolatry, ideology, history painting versus photography, and mediation. My interest here lies in the shift from photographs which show audiences photographed from the rear and standing in front of works, to the *Audiences* series, which shows the faces and postures of visitors looking at art. These pictures show us spectators who demonstrate pensive behaviour, contemplation, dreaming, searching for detail and souvenirs; they show attention, seriousness, glances and adoration. When exhibited, these large photographs reveal to spectators that art can become an object of mass consumption. The photographs also confront the audience with its own structured behaviour; showing it what it does, but also how unfree and conditioned it is. We recognize ourselves in the behaviour, carriage and expressions of these spectators. The question seems to be: is this who you want to be? Is this who you are? Spectators are made aware of their act of looking. They are made aware of the fact that they are amidst a crowd of spectators. The artist himself, however, is no longer present to show us his own anxiety about the audience's presence. Struth is the quiet observer; moving closer to the real audience as if to familiarize himself with it.

The last work I find compelling in the debate on how artists experience the presence of a museum audience, is

I See a Woman Crying (2009), by Dutch artist Rineke Dijkstra. The video can be traced to Dijkstra's interest in the uninhibited moments between childhood innocence and adult awareness. We see a group of schoolchildren looking at and talking about a work of art. Just as in Struth's *Audiences* series, we do not see the work of art itself. At first, the children mainly describe forms and colours. After a while they attribute emotional states to the image: serious, sad, lonely, scared, abandoned... Stories start to develop: "she looks like she just disobeyed someone"; "she bites her nails because she is nervous", "she cries because she is lonely"; "people are jealous of her"; "nobody wants to be her friend"... The stories mix and diverge; the children agree or disagree with each other. The video clearly functions as a trigger for narratives built around children's typical anxieties and realities. The stories they tell are based on subjective reactions to what they see, filled with experiences and feelings common to their age. Dijkstra's work not only speaks of these children's imagination, but also of the potential which art has in triggering a polyphonic richness in minds which are not yet conditioned. The work is compelling when we compare it to the often encountered defeatism amongst artists when it comes to what art is capable of. Do we encounter here a renewed trust amongst artists in the potential of art? Maybe. But the fact remains that these are children and not the grown-up and "conditioned" museum visitors we encounter in Struth's works. Maybe Dijkstra is reminding us of something we have lost: an uninhibited attitude, a willingness to approach art with our own history and subjectivity in order to build up a more personal connection to it and develop more individual stories about it. The question remains whether we as grown-ups are still capable of doing so. Does the work indicate a shift in the direction of an increased acceptance of more personal and polyphonic readings of artworks? Possibly. But the "history" we have sketched is but a construction. Other readings will bring different insights. My reading of these works, together with my observations of younger generations of artists, suggests that artists are indeed coming closer to the real audience rather than longing for a more ideal and "understanding" one. That they, slowly, are "allowing" difference; that is, accepting that visitors are often players who make up their own stories about the art they encounter. But, do we really need the artists' permission? Visitor photography, posted on the internet, seems to tell us that visitors are already inventing their own stories. Whether artists like it or not.

Beginners and expert-players

A young girl is standing before a large white screen showing two monumental hands at both her left and right. The hands look as if they are about to grab her and the girl is screaming loudly. We are looking at a photograph, taken and posted on Flickr by a father and his daughter during a visit to the Los Angeles County Museum of Art (LACMA). The picture, entitled *Screaming Kate with Hands* (Figure 1) shows us daughter Kate in front of the projected art video *For Beginners (all the combinations of the thumb and fingers)*, a video installation (2010) by Bruce Nauman. The picture of the installation alters the work considerably. In reality, it consists of two superimposed screens both showing Nauman's hands while they are enacting all the combinations of the four fingers and thumb. The artist's voice, in a commanding, loud and often directive way

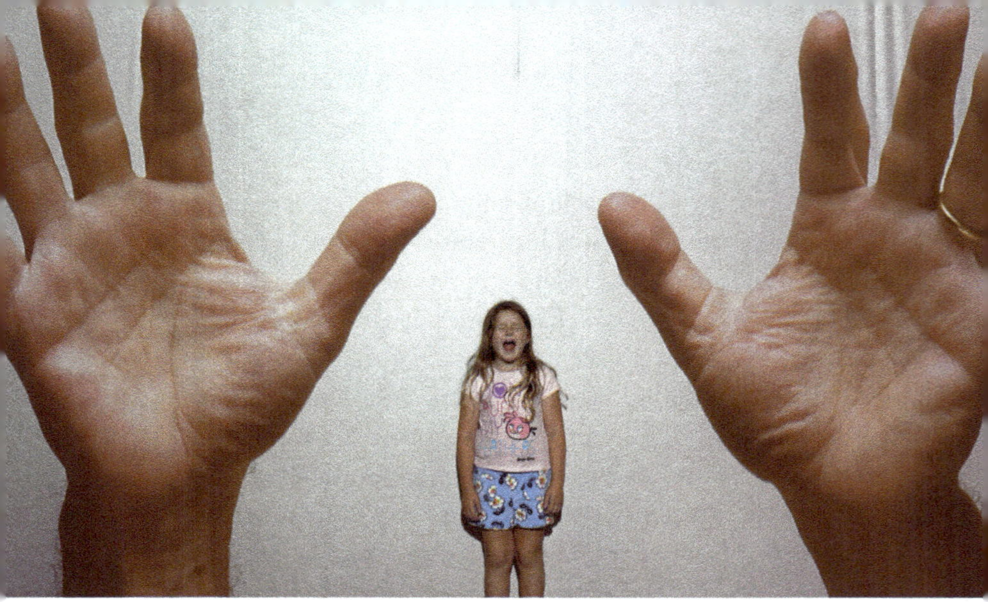

FIG. 1: *Screaming Kate with Hands*. Taken on May 19, 2013 and posted on Flickr. Photograph: Simon Watt.

– provides the verbal instructions. They echo throughout the large exhibition space. By cutting the work photographically at a specific moment, the visitor-photographer interprets and restages the work in such a way that it becomes a kind of horror-comedy scene. A girl is about to be grabbed by two monstrous hands. In the art historical reception of Nauman's art, a work like *For Beginners* is often understood within the artist's preoccupation with the performativity of language (Kraynak, 2003), his play with the presence of the audience (Van Rossem, 2012) or his interest in performance and video art (Van Rossem, 2009). Another theme present here, and one often encountered in his oeuvre, is failure. The idea of failing at something – doing something, understanding someone – but keeping on trying, is a thread which runs through his work. Here, the hands cannot always keep up with the verbal instructions. But they keep trying. The museum label explains that the piece "forces us to look at the simplest of our gestures, in time and space". But whether or not the work truly "forces" us is something which experts in language and performativity are welcome to discuss. It is certainly a story worth telling.

But the work does not only "force" people. Observation of visitor photography posted to the internet teaches us that it also moves spectators in ways which are more unexpected. Remember Nauman's "fear"? "It has more to do with me not allowing people to make their own performance out of my art. I don't like to leave things open so people feel they are in a situation they can play games with" (Sharp, 1970: 113). Whether or not Nauman still hopes that people will not play games and make performances out of his art I do not know. But that people are turning *For Beginners* into their own

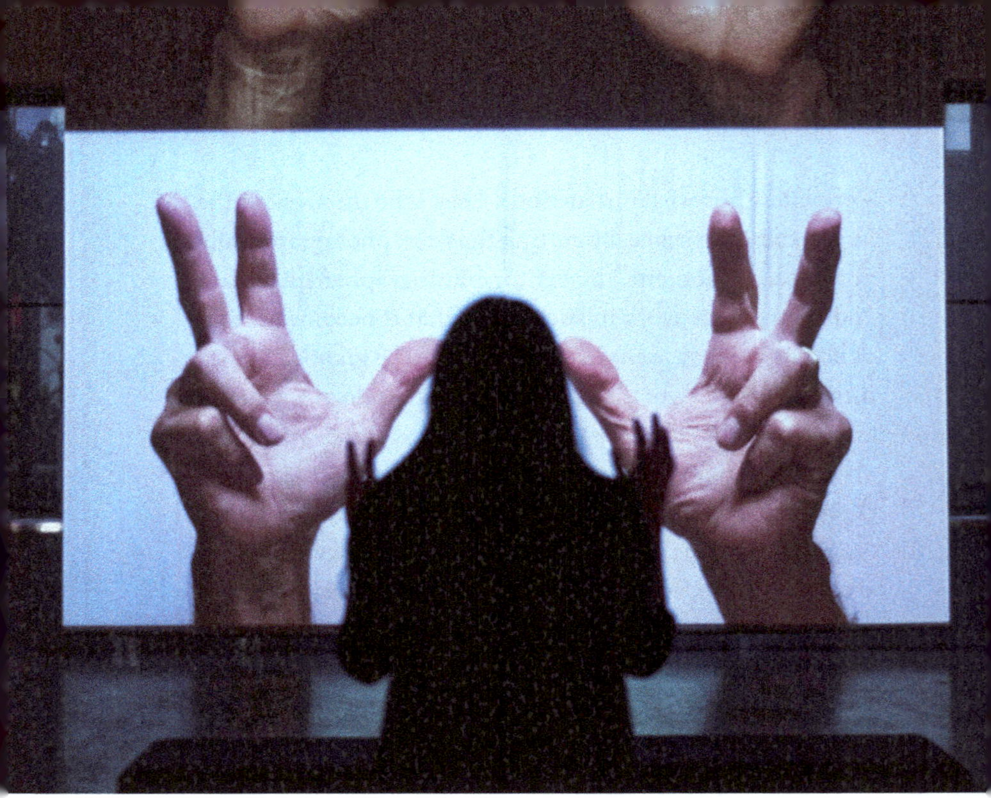

FIG 2: *people@lacma6*. Taken on March 13, 2012 and posted on Flickr. Photograph: xtnsgo.

performance is something Flickr, blogs and other social media websites prove. Apart from *Screaming Kate with Hands* other photographs also show visitor performances in front of or behind the screen. Some engage in shadow play. The performances relate the work to dance, fashion and even to the multiplicity of arms often found in the representation of eastern deities. Other people edit part of the projected image and relate their body to the hands. Visitors often try to capture a specific moment in the video so they can relate the hands to their own body. A man standing in front of the work is photographed in such a way that the hands in the video become "his" antlers. A girl is photographed in front of the work at the very moment when the video projection shows the hands, positioned left and right of the girl, with only their middle fingers raised. It looks as if someone is flipping her the bird. Some of the pictures are funny. Some are more serious and poetic: a couple holding hands. Some visitors follow the verbal commands, or at least seem to (Figure 2).

Many of these pictures can be seen as moments of parrhesia, in which traditional museum decorum is abandoned, and the art is lived, decoded, interpreted, associated and subjectively acted out in photographed performances. They speak of stories that are no longer only those of the artist; they create a layered multiplicity of meaning. Visitors become expert-players; experts of their own subjective truth, digitally shared with the world at large. Pictures such as these should be of interest to all those dealing with the curatorial, art mediation and gallery education, for they remind us of the fact that spectators, when given room, often want to be expert-players, emancipated spectators and participants who both deconstruct and transform the works exhibited. They permeate the work with stories which can be recycled and staged within the art mediation of a particular work. Here, the photographic performances are the starting point for stories which relate *For Beginners* to aggression, humor, intercultural dialogue, film genres (comedy, horror, romance) theater genres and many other narratives not directly suggested by the work itself.

Visitor photography can be used as an inspiration for gallery education practices which aim to be more deconstructive and transformative. This is an example of how personal stories and experiences can be acted out in active and social behavior which opposes the concept of the museum as authority and as the ultimate guardian of knowledge. I am not suggesting that the more traditional affirmative educational function should be abandoned. But it would be strange to overlook the desire amongst at least a part of our audience to add stories other than those created by connoisseurs. Visitor photography can become a powerful ally for those seeking a more emancipated approach to gallery education because it often opposes the traditional view of audience behavior. In the past, the behavior depicted in many visitor photographs would have been the subject of caricature. Today, our failure to look at, listen to and learn from these visitors will only result in we ourselves becoming caricatures.

NOTES

1. *MAKE ME THINK ME.* Graphite and tape on paper, 142 x 97.2 cm, 1994.
2. *EAT ME FEED ME.* Oil stick, charcoal, graphite and tape on paper, 112,4 x 161,9 cm, 1990.
3. *PLEASE PAY ATTENTION PLEASE.* Artwork, collage and letraset, 27, 5 x 27,5 inch, 1973.
4. *Stamping in the Studio.* (Videotape, black and white, sound, 60 min., 1968).

REFERENCES

Bakhtin, M. (1986). The Problem of the Text. In Emersen, C., Holquist, M. (eds.). *Mikhaïl M. Bakhtin. Speech Genres & Other Late Essays.* Austin: University of Texas Press.

Bennett, T. (1995). *The Birth of the Museum: History, Theory, Politics.* New York: Routledge.

Brewer, J. (2013). *The Pleasures of the Imagination: English Culture in the Eighteenth Century.* New York: Routledge.

Cordes, Ch. (1989). Talking with Bruce Nauman: An Interview. In Kraynak, J. (ed.) (2003), *Please Pay Attention Please: Bruce Nauman's Words –Writings and Interviews,* Cambridge: The MIT Press.

Cosmetti (1767). *The Polite Arts, Dedicated to the Ladies* (Vol. 1). London: Roach & Dell.

Duncan, C. (1995). *Civilizing Rituals: Inside Public Art Museums.* New York: Routledge.

Kaprow, A. (1964). The Artist as a Man of the World. In Kelley, J. (1993). *Allan Kaprow - The Blurring of Art and Life.* Los Angeles: University of California Press.

Kraynak, J. (2003). *Please Pay Attention Please: Bruce Nauman's Words – Writings and Interviews,* Cambridge: The MIT Press.

Mörsch, C. (2011). Alliances for Unlearning: On gallery education and institutions of critique. *Afterall, 26* (Spring). Available at: http://www.afterall.org/journal/issue.26/alliances-for-unlearning-on-the-possibility-of-future-collaborations-between-gallery-educa.

Needham, A. (2011). Art is difficult, it's not entertainment. *The Guardian,* December 9. Available at: http://

www.theguardian.com/artanddesign/2011/dec/08/anselm-kiefer-art-white-cube.

Rancière, J. (2009). *The Emancipated Spectator*. London: Verso.

Rogoff, I. (2008). Turning. *e-flux*. Available at: http://www.e-flux.com/journal/turning/.

Sayre, H. (1989). *The Object of Performance – The American Avant-garde since 1970*. Chicago: The University of Chicago Press.

Sharp, W. (1970) Nauman Interview. In Kraynak, J. (ed.) (2003), *Please Pay Attention Please: Bruce Nauman's Words –Writings and Interviews*, Cambridge: The MIT Press.

Sharp, W. (1971). Interview with Bruce Nauman. In Kraynak, J. (ed.) (2003), *Please Pay Attention Please: Bruce Nauman's Words –Writings and Interviews*, Cambridge: The MIT Press.

Storylines. once upon a time... the collection now (2013). Available at: http://vanabbemuseum.nl/en/programme/detail/?tx_vabdisplay_pi1%5Bptype%5D=24&tx_vabdisplay_pi1%5Bproject%5D=1242.

THE PILGRIM, THE TOURIST, THE FLANEUR (AND THE WORKER) play van abbe part 4 (2011). Available at: http://vanabbemuseum.nl/programma/detail/?tx_vabdisplay_pi1%5Bptype%5D=19&tx_vabdisplay_pi1%5Bproject%5D=756.

Tuchmann, Ph. (2003). On Thomas Struth's Museum Photographs. *Artnet*. Available at: http://www.artnet.com/magazine/features/tuchman/tuchman7-8-03.asp.

Van Bruggen, C. (1988). *Bruce Nauman*, New York: Rizzoli.

Van Reeth, I. (2009). *Bemiddeling tussen kunst en publiek in hedendaagse beeldende kunst*. Gent: Instituut voor beeldende, audiovisuele en mediakunst. Available at: http://www.bamart.be/files/BAM_publieksbemiddeling.pdf.

Van Rossem, P. (2007). Het schilderij als geschonden lichaam. Over Martin Kippenbergers onderhuids en 'bovenhuids' picturaal debacle (Painting as wounded body. On Martin Kippenbergers subcutaneous and epidermal pictorial debacle). In Van Damme, C., Van Rossem, P., Van Eeckhaut, M. (eds.), *Touch Me Don't Touch Me - De Toets als Interface in de Hedendaagse Kunst*. Gent: Leerstoel Karel Geirlandt Universiteit Gent and Academia Press.

Van Rossem, P. (2009). Performing the impossibility of painting and the near-impossibility of sculpture. Creativity, inhibition and doubt as performed in the photography, film and video art of Bruce Nauman. In Van Damme, C., Van Rossem, P., Van Eeckhaut M., Scherlippens, B. (eds.), *Behind or Beside You*. Gent: Leerstoel Karel Geirlandt Universiteit Gent and Academia Press.

Van Rossem, P. (2012). The audience as an authorial presence in the creative act. Considering authorship and the performative turn in the 1960s and 1970s. *Kunstgeschichten der Gegenwart*, 10, p. 171.

CHAPTER TWO

DIGITAL PHOTOGRAPHY AND THE MATERIALITY OF OBJECTS AND IMAGES

Jonathan Tadashi Naito

JUST INSIDE THE main entrance of the British Museum, across the hall from the coat check, there is a small exhibition space: Room 3. On a visit to the museum on a rainy January afternoon, I decided to step in, only because I had rarely, if ever visited it before. The temporary exhibition housed three pots produced in Japan during the Jomon era (c.14000-500 BCE). The object which immediately captured my attention was the pot placed in the center. Like the others, it featured the familiar rope-inspired design of Jomon ceramic art, yet in this case the pattern playfully exploited the sculptural potential of its material, bending and climbing beyond the lip of the main body of the vessel. Were these figures? Flames? Organic details? Embellishments rooted in the pure pleasure of making ceramic art? I could neither decide nor look away, especially after I discovered that these extensions were two-sided, in stark contrast to the smooth surface of the pot's interior. I took a digital camera from my pocket, photographed the label, verified that it was legible, and then turned my camera to the pot itself.

Later that night, I downloaded the photographs to my laptop and gave them a closer look. I had realized that the light in Room 3 was far from ideal, so I wasn't surprised to find that the pots in my photographs were less sharp than I would have liked. On the screen of my computer, it was also easier to see the degree to which the photographs were marred by the reflections I had unintentionally captured, such as the all-too-familiar reflection of myself taking the photo (Figure 1). The only other patron in Room 3 during my visit also made several surprise appearances. I was disappointed, but not overly so. My collection of photographs would serve the purpose of enabling

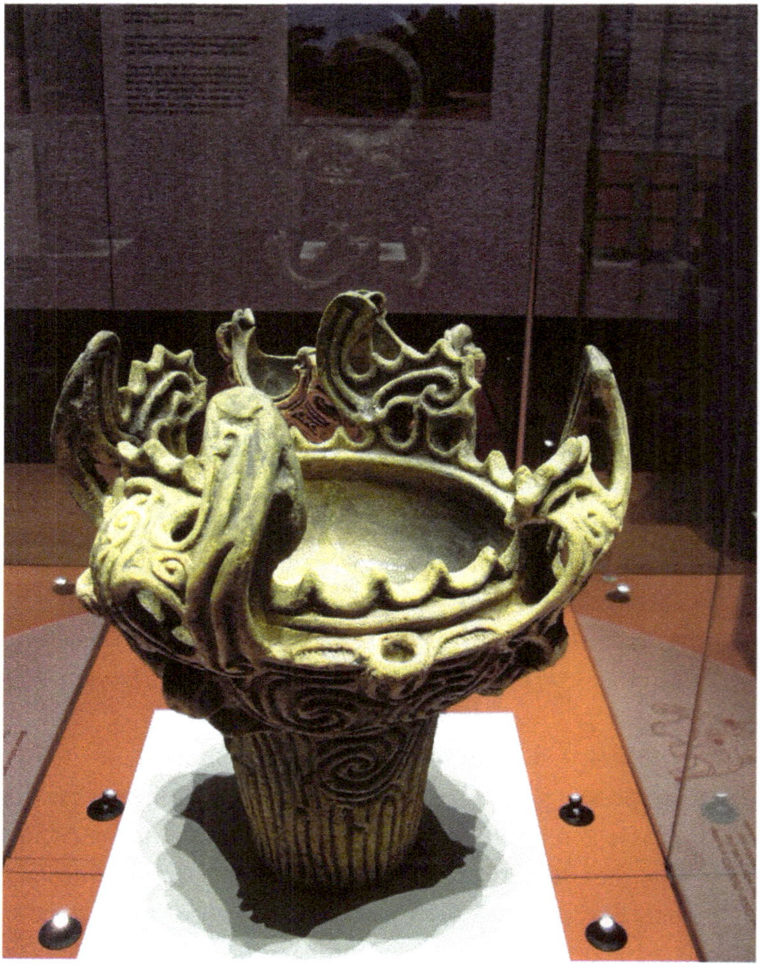

FIG. 1: A Jomon pot on display at the British Museum. Photograph: Jonathan Naito, 2013.

me to recall my initial fascination. I had no plans to create prints from them or to show them to others, except perhaps in a casual conversation in which their shortcomings would hardly receive notice. In any event, I suspected that the British Museum's website would have a better photograph of the same pot – which turned out to be the case. Given the circumstances, the photographs I had taken were about the best that I could expect; they were also likely to be the best that I would need.

The second half of Roland Barthes's *Camera Lucida* opens with the author contemplating photographs of his recently deceased mother. His disappointment, or, more properly, his sense of loss, is palpable. None of the photographs before him seem to adequately recall her:

> According to these photographs, sometimes I recognized a region of her face, a certain relation of nose and forehead, the movement of her arms, her hands. I never recognized her except in fragments, which is to say that I missed her being, and that therefore I missed her altogether. It was not she, and yet it was no one else... Photography thereby compelled me to perform a painful labor; straining toward the essence of her identity, I was struggling among images partially true, and therefore totally false. (Barthes, 1981: 65-66)

For Barthes, all but perhaps one of the many photographs of his mother is "merely analogical, provoking only her identity, not her truth" (Barthes, 1981: 70-71). In the eyes of the person who knew her best, her essence has evaded capture and subsequent recovery. While there are clear differences between the encounter which Barthes describes and my own anecdote, there are important similarities. Indeed, I would argue that his words speak with particular urgency to the nature of the photograph in the age of digital photography and the opportunities it offers for today's museums. In what might seem a paradox, the proliferation of photographs taken with digital cameras has made the limitations of the photograph more apparent, especially when they concern objects and images housed in the charged space of the museum. Even if I couldn't claim a "painful labor," I nonetheless strained to capture the essence of the pot – a straining that continued after I left the museum. A short time later, I went back to Room 3 to encounter the Jomon pot again.

For a variety of reasons, the rise of digital technology has coincided with an increasing sense of the photographic image as provisional. If the unit cost of a photograph is virtually zero, why hesitate to take a hastily conceived and likely mediocre picture? Rather than skill in the operation of a camera, why not rely on a combination of camera technology and chance to capture an adequate image? With the ubiquity and ease of use of editing software, why worry about framing an image at all? Particularly in its mundane, everyday aspect, it is hard to deny the association of digital photography with both abundance and a disregard of craft – at least as traditionally understood.

This is clearly true within the walls of the museum. While in the film age the earnest, camera-toting patron might have dedicated several minutes to the production of a handful of photographs of an admired object, in the digital age a visitor is likely to take many more photographs of the same object or a quick photograph or two of many more of the objects on view.

Yet this larger pool of images is not any more likely to produce a definitive image or collection of images. This failure, which is likely to be repeated countless times in the life of an individual, points directly to a more general phenomenon: what Barthes aptly described as the "merely analogical" achievements of photography itself.

At the same time, there are situations in which advances in camera technology have enabled digital photography to rise above the merely analogical. One need only consider the use of the digital camera as a pocket-sized photocopier. Indeed, I produced one such copy during my visit to the Jomon exhibition: a copy of the object label. Institutions are beginning to recognize and adapt to this new reality. In early 2015, the British Library announced a change in its policy on "self-service photography": individuals are now allowed to use their personal devices to photograph many items in the library's collection. As the name of this policy suggests, the high resolution of the digital photograph has erased many of the differences between the photograph and other forms of documentation. In the digital age, the photograph is simply another data file produced, processed, stored, and analyzed alongside other digital files of the same and other varieties.

Soon after my trip to the British Museum, I visited the Saatchi Gallery. As crowds swarmed the special exhibitions, I sought out a quieter space, and found one in the room designed specifically for the Saatchi Gallery's only permanent installation: Richard Wilson's *20:50* (1987). Wilson's installation is a pool of recycled engine oil with a surface so still and so reflective that it challenges the eye's ability to recognize reflections as reflections. With the illusion that one is suspended

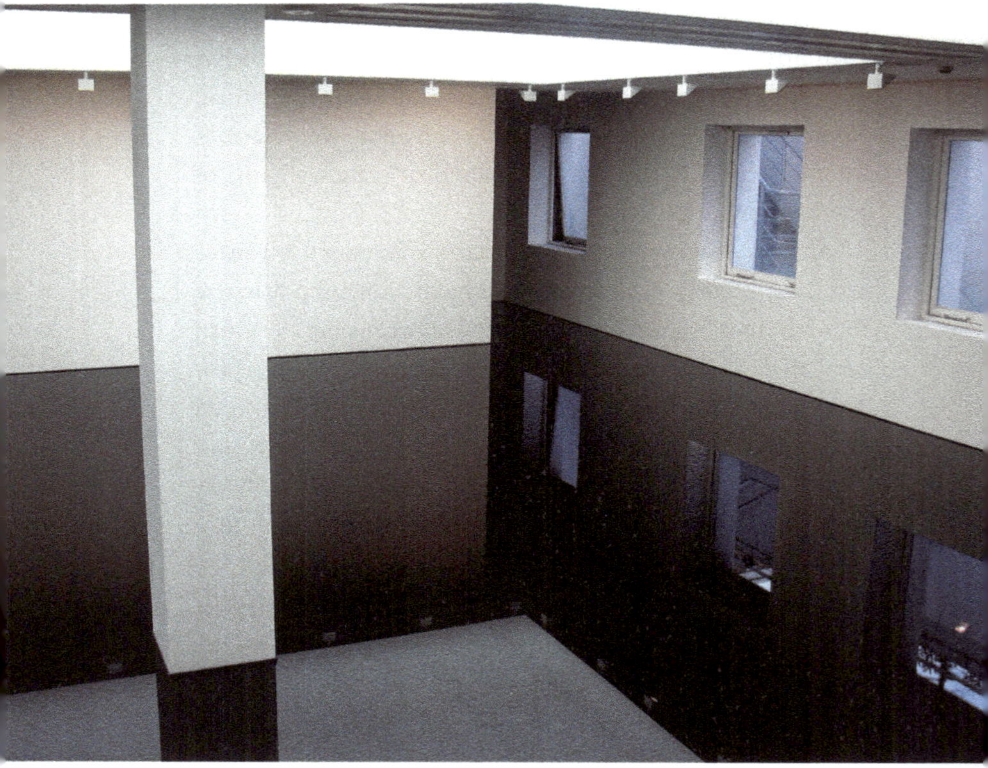

FIG. 2: Richard Wilson, *20:50*. Photograph: Jonathan Naito, 2013.

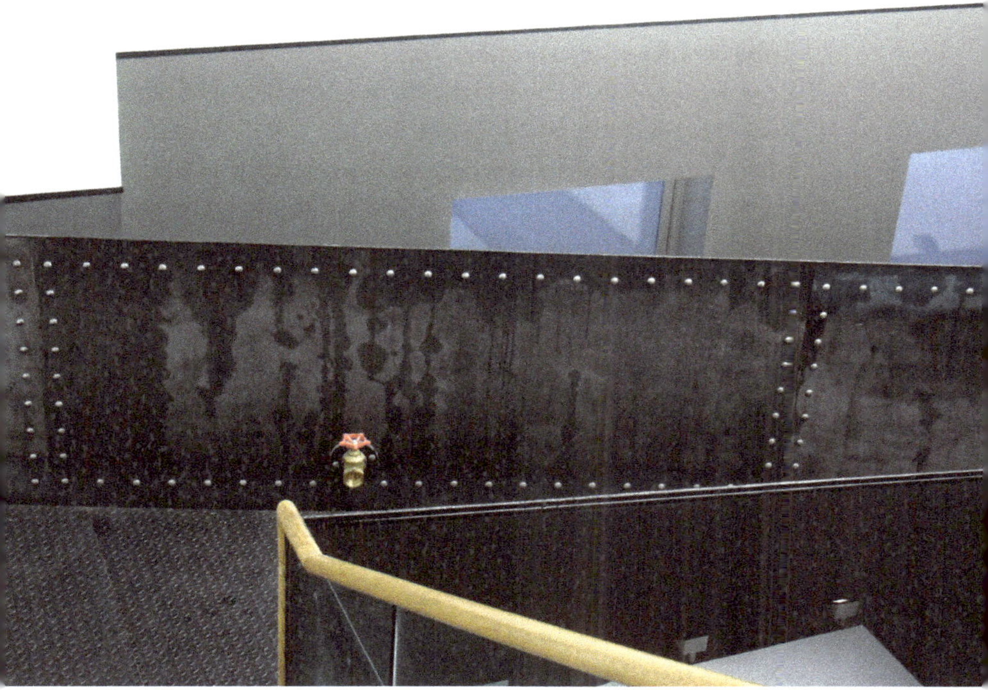

FIG. 3: Richard Wilson, *20:50* (detail). Photograph: Jonathan Naito, 2013.

in a room that is two-stories tall (Figure 2), a sense of vertigo takes hold.

I took out my camera, but immediately recognized the impossibility of my task. Black oil fills virtually the entire floor, leaving only a small platform for observers at one end and a narrow path that juts out into the pool. No matter where I positioned my camera, there was simply no way to capture the work as a whole in a single image, nor was it possible to mentally reconcile the fragments I had produced. In several cases, a photograph that I took with the intention of capturing an illusion on the surface of the pool instead ended up emphasizing the guardrail, the metal walls, the rivets, a spigot, the non-slip floor – everything other than what I had intended (Figure 3). Moreover, as I contemplated the various angles from which I might shoot, and strategies for capturing different aspects of the installation, the light outside began to shift. I became aware of the windows as contributing more than geometric interest and a mundane institutional anonymity; they were also important light sources. So much of Wilson's installation is a product of the careful manipulation of light, as I was reminded by the changes which came over it with the approach of evening: a sharpening of the reflection, a slight tonal shift on the surface of the pool and the white walls of the room. All of this was far too subtle to capture with my camera. It was as if Wilson and the Saatchi Gallery had discovered a copy-protection technology for visual art. Yet I was thankful. The impossibility of photographing 20:50 led me into a richer experience. I entered a cycle of taking a photograph, examining the resulting image, learning more about the work, and repositioning my camera. With each turn of this cycle, I became more aware of the installation's materiality and what it meant to be in its presence in that particular place, at that specific time.

There is another, rather obvious, reason why Wilson's installation resisted photographic capture. *20:50* is a three-dimensional work of art, and in photographing it I was compressing it, attempting to translate it into a two-dimensional image. However, it would be a mistake to overemphasize this point. My camera also influenced my encounter with flat – or flatter – objects in the museum. Valery Koshlyakov's *Grand Opera, Paris* (1995) was another work which drew me in, and another work which resisted my attempts to photograph it. From across a large room, as I encountered it that day, the frenetic activity of Koshlyakov's painting only slowly emerges. While it never fully disguises its materials – tempera on cardboard – its faded browns, yellows, and pinks make the painting surface appear softer and more stable from afar (Figure 4). Up close, the image of the Grand Opera dissolves into a mess of drips, stains, and swirls which barely mask a pockmarked painting surface that has been thoroughly ripped and scraped (Figure 5). In trying to photograph it, I found myself moving backward and forward, but never at the proper distance to take it all in, let alone capture it with my camera. It is a painting which attracts, teases, and frustrates the attention of the viewer, particularly when the encounter with the work is mediated through a camera.

This, though, suggests an opportunity for the museum. László Földényi (2001: 59) has observed that the patrons of an art museum often resemble "blind creatures," as they struggle to see what lies before them. A similar claim could be made

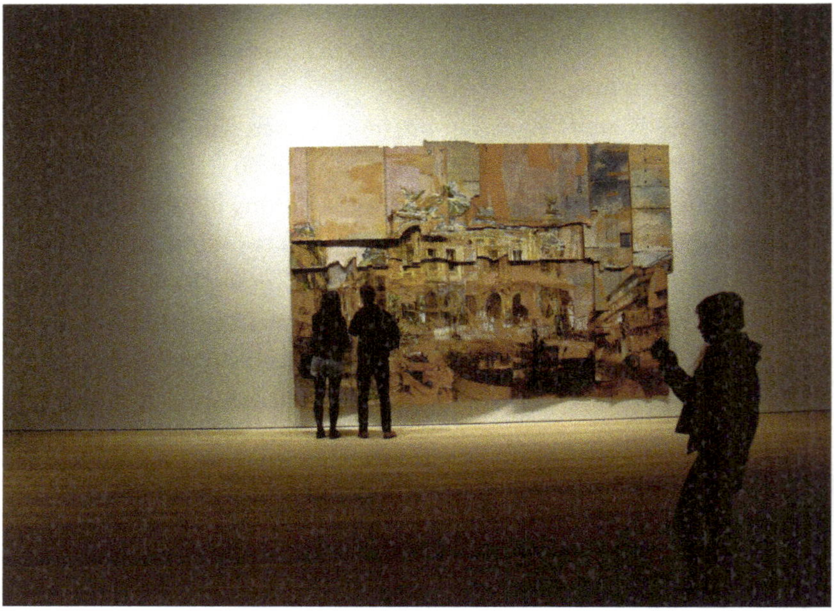

FIG. 4: Valery Koshlyakov, ***Grand Opera, Paris*****.** Photograph: Jonathan Naito, 2013.

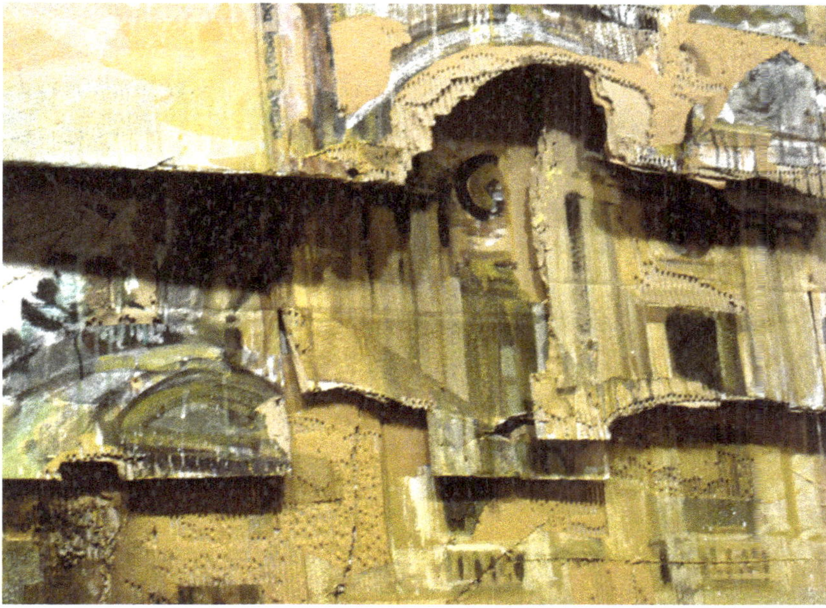

FIG. 5: Valery Koshlyakov, *Grand Opera, Paris* (detail). Photograph: Jonathan Naito, 2013.

about all museums: they provoke a rarely practiced way of seeing. This is a phenomenon which the digital camera is uniquely positioned to catalyze as an aid to the newly blind. If the impulse to photograph an object implies a desire to carry it away, the immediacy with which a digital image becomes available and its high resolution enable a different sort of experience in the museum as well.

I imagine a museum which actively encourages its patrons to use their cameras to discover and explore the unphotographable, which transforms the digital camera into a device which exposes the many things that the camera cannot do. I imagine the straining towards objects and images, and the useful records of that straining which would result. I imagine what visitors might take away from such a museum, and what might draw them back into it. Or, rather than imagining, perhaps I am simply describing what is already happening in museums today.

REFERENCES

Barthes, R. (1981). *Camera lucida* (Richard Howard, Trans.). New York: Hill and Wang. (Original work published 1980).

British Library. (n.d.). "Self-service photography in the reading rooms." Available at: http://www.bl.uk/reshelp/inrrooms/stp/copy/selfsrvcopy/reading_room_photography_guidelines_st_pancras.pdf. [Accessed 29 January 29 2015.]

Földényi, L. (2001). In Noever, P. (ed.), *The discursive museum*. New York: Hatje Cantz.

CHAPTER THREE

VISITOR PHOTOGRAPHY IN THE SUTTON HOO GALLERY AT THE BRITISH MUSEUM

Ellie Miles

EVERY YEAR MORE than six million visitors come to the British Museum, and for the first time in 2013–14, more than half (54%) of these people reported that they took a photograph during their visit (Morris Hargreaves McIntyre, 2014). With more than three million people taking photographs at the museum's site in Bloomsbury, it is no surprise that when the image-sharing social media service Instagram announced the top ten geo-tagged photo locations in the UK, the British Museum was fifth on its list (Furness, 2014a). A quick search of the photo-sharing site Flickr reveals that every day more than 50 images are uploaded by its users and tagged with the text *british museum*. Although newspaper columnists have voiced concern at the behaviour of visitors taking photographs in museums, even suggesting photography in museums should be banned (Christiansen, 2014), we know relatively little about visitor photography in the context of a museum visit.

This chapter examines visitor photography behaviour and its relationship with visitor engagement in one of the British Museum's recently redeveloped galleries: *Sutton Hoo and Europe AD 300–1100*. This part of the collection includes the well-known objects excavated from the Sutton Hoo ship burial, including a mysterious helmet. Photography has the capacity to make objects and moments iconic, and for many the helmet has become the face of the Anglo-Saxon world. Before the 2014 gallery opened, the helmet was displayed in a different arrangement in the same space at the museum. Room 41 is a large, cross-shaped gallery on the museum's first floor, with a floor space of 389.5 square metres. Whilst work was carried out to redevelop the gallery, parts of the collection were temporarily displayed elsewhere in the museum, which gave the museum the opportunity to test and evaluate some of the ideas proposed for the redisplay.

The British Museum's interpretation team use a variety of visitor research methods when working on new exhibition and gallery projects. This includes front-end, formative and summative evaluation of projects, often undertaken by students on placement as part of a postgraduate course. Examples of these evaluations can be seen on the British Museum's website (British Museum, 2015).

Using tracking methods adapted from the work of Serrell (1998) and others, the museum can gain insight into the attracting power, holding power and dwell time of visitors, and find out about the different ways that visitors behave, as well as evaluate different interpretation approaches. The tracking process involves recording the flow of visitors around the museum's spaces on a map, including noting the time spent at each case, so we can build up patterns of visitor behaviour, and use this insight when developing our interpretation (Francis *et al*, 2011). As part of the tracking and observation process volunteers record whether visitors take photographs, consult the museum's multimedia guide, and whether they enter into discussions with other visitors.

This data was collected twice in Room 41, both in 2010 before the gallery was redisplayed, and in 2014 when the new gallery had opened. Both these studies include tracking information, questionnaire data and data about discussions, the use of guides and whether visitors took photographs. Although this raw data has been collected, it has never been the focus of a more detailed analysis focussing on photography before. This chapter uses the datasets from Room 41 in 2010 and 2014 and investigates how visitor photography corresponds to other visitor behaviours that were taking place before and after the gallery redevelopment. These quantitative findings, gathered by volunteers, are used to give a snapshot of visitor photography in the museum.

Both the 2010 and 2014 studies tracked 200 visitors around the Sutton Hoo displays in Room 41. This figure includes visitors who stopped to look at part of the gallery for at least ten seconds (Davidson & Locsin, 2010; Moffat, 2014; Newbury, 2014). Visitors who did not stop in the gallery were categorized as "walkthroughs" and were not included in this sample. The 2010 project was carried out in September, during weekdays. Two volunteers, Julia Davidson and Kara Locsin, collected, entered and analysed the data (Davidson & Locsin, 2010). The 2014 research project was carried out in two phases: the first phase of data collection, entry and analysis was carried out by Amy Moffat in May and June 2014 (Moffat, 2014); the second by Anna Newbury from October to November 2014 (Newbury, 2014).

Findings

In 2010, the tracking data show that 101 photographs were taken by the 200 gallery visitors who were tracked. These photographs were taken by 40 people, suggesting that one in five visitors took a photograph during the time they spent in the gallery. In 2014, the total number of photographs taken in the gallery by the sample had risen by nearly 10%, to 110. This time the photographs were taken by 49 visitors, suggesting that now nearly a quarter of visitors took at least one photograph during their visit to Room 41. This increase was surprisingly modest, given that from the period 2010 to 2014 smartphone ownership in the UK rose from around 25% to around 75% of the adult population (Arthur, 2014). Perhaps the rate of increase reflects the British Museum's long-standing photography policy, which is reasonably permissive and stipulates that:

> Hand-held cameras, including cameras fitted with flash bulbs or electronic flash units, may be used for private purposes in the galleries unless otherwise indicated. Private photography in the galleries requiring the use of a stand, special lighting or other equipment is only permitted by prior arrangement... (British Museum, 2003)

This approach, which institutions such as the National Gallery have adopted more recently (Furness, 2014b), may account for the comparatively slow rate of increase, as photography was already an established feature of the average British Museum visit. Further research might compare behaviour in institutions with a history of different policies.

Even if more people took photographs, the data show that although the small number of very keen photographers (who took more than eight photographs) remained constant, there was an increase in the number of visitors taking just one or two photographs.

Although the tracking research did not record the devices used to make these images, it does record the group composition that visitors were part of (for example, if they were visiting as a group of two adults and one child). The number of lone photographers almost doubled, from 11 in 2010 to 20 in 2014. Despite the rise in the solitary activity of photography in the museum, more photographs were also taken as discussion took place. In 2010, six visitors took photographs whilst having discussions with other visitors. In 2014, this number rose to 15. This rise in the number of more casual photographers taking a few images reflects the way in which these images were taken. The increase suggests that photography is becoming part of the social museum visit behaviour pattern, and although photographs are shared on social media, the social sharing of photographs often actually begins when the photograph is taken.

Looking at the overall sample from 2010 and 2014 provides a bigger dataset to see how visitor behaviour breaks down across the visitor behaviour categories that the British Museum uses. Visitor behaviours are segmented into categories of meaning making:

- *single object*: a visitor who spends the majority of their time in the gallery looking at one object;
- *follower*: a visitor who appears to follow the narrative of the exhibit by moving from case to case or section to section;
- *browser*: a visitor who browses the exhibition, and will wander until they find an object which catches their attention;
- *completist*: a visitor who stops at almost everything in the gallery;
- *Sutton Hoo completist*: a special category for this project, for visitors who spent time looking at every object in the central Sutton Hoo part of the gallery

The chart in Figure 1 shows the viewing strategies of visitors who took photographs. There is a lower number of visitors

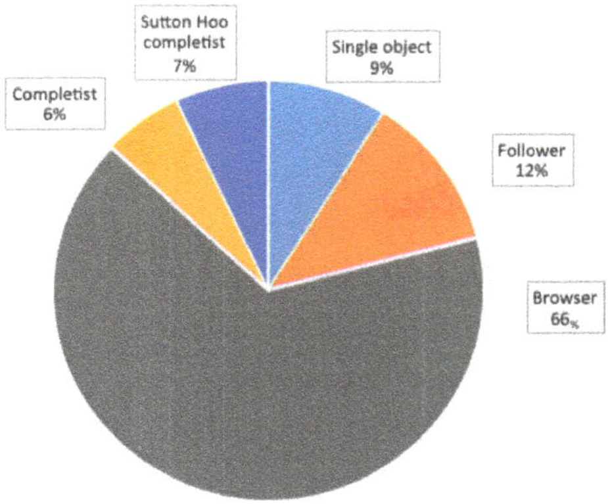

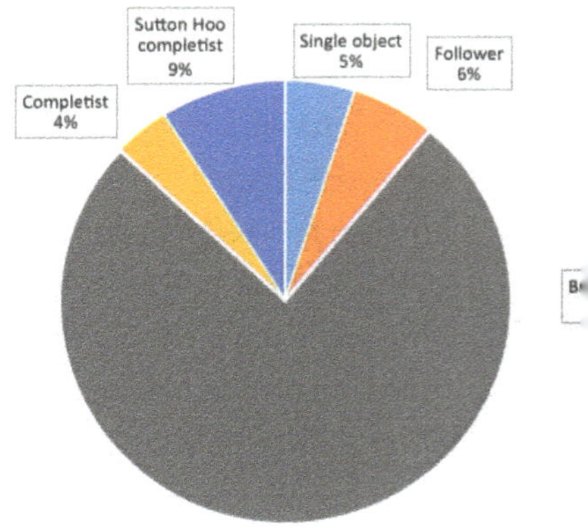

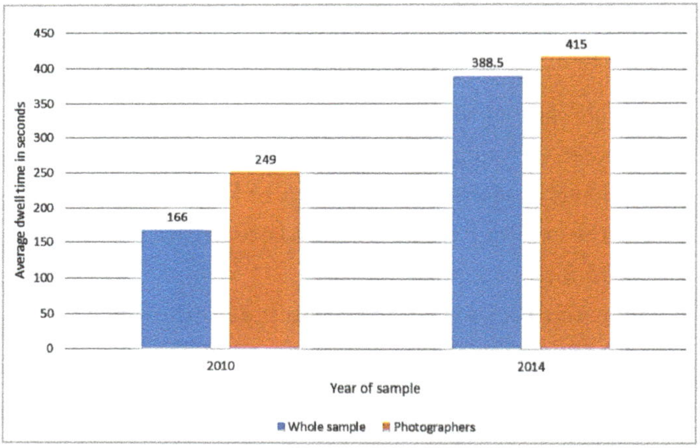

FIG. 1: TOP LEFT | Viewing strategies of visitors who took photographs.
FIG. 2: TOP RIGHT | Viewing strategies of visitors who did not take photographs.
FIG. 3: BOTTOM | Median dwell time (in seconds) of visitors to Room 41.

displaying a *browser* strategy when compared to Figure 2 (visitors who did not take photographs in the gallery), suggesting that the photographers were more methodical in their movement around the gallery. There is also a higher proportion of visitors whose visits were dominated by a single object, when compared to the visitors who did not take photographs. The proportion of *completists* remains the same, although the photographers were weighted towards *Sutton Hoo completists* suggesting a deeper level of engagement with the gallery as a whole.

The average dwell time for visitors in 2010 was 166 seconds (Davidson & Locsin, 2010). When looking at the average dwell time for visitors who took photographs, this figure rises substantially, to 249 seconds (Figure 3). The gallery redevelopment improved the median dwell time in the gallery from 166 seconds to 388.5 seconds, putting it amongst the most engaging galleries in the museum. However when broken down, the data suggests that visitors taking photographs still had a significantly higher dwell time than visitors who did not take photographs. Visitors who took photographs stayed on average 415 seconds. Although the redesign increased median dwell time, neither the redisplay nor the proliferation of smartphone ownership has dramatically changed visitors' photographic behaviour.

This suggests that visitors who take photographs are more engaged with the objects, reflecting the findings of Henkel's research into human and camera memories, which points to a link between engagement, memory and free-choice photography in museums (Henkel, 2013).

The case which most visitors chose to photograph (both

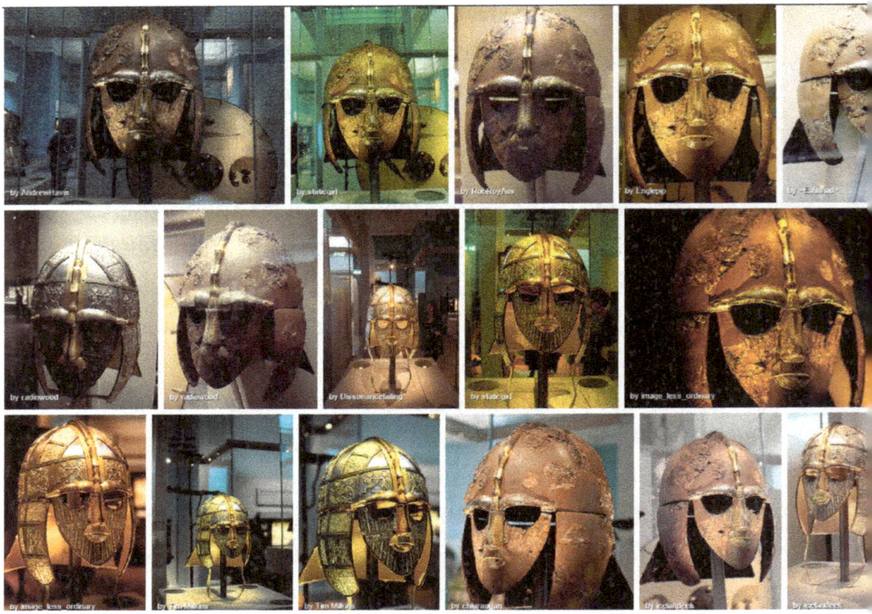

FIG. 4: Photographs of Room 41 shared on Flickr, 2014–15.
Photographs: Andrew Havis, staticgirl, Rob Roy, Englepip, ~Ealasaid~, radiowood, Dissonancefalling, Steve Cottrell, Tim Milkins, Chiara Ogan, and Icelandeek.

before and after the gallery redevelopment) was the Sutton Hoo helmet case. In 2010 the case was photographed by 20 visitors, and in 2014 this rose slightly to 24. In 2014, 48% of visitors stopped to spend time with the Sutton Hoo helmet, dwelling for an average (mean) of 51 seconds. One in four of the visitors who looked at the Sutton Hoo helmet in 2014 photographed it. The median dwell time for people who photographed the helmet was slightly longer – 53 seconds compared with 50 seconds for visitors who stopped but did not take any photographs.

The Sutton Hoo helmet is an iconic image, and it is this photograph which is most commonly shared online through Instagram and Flickr (Figure 4). The fragments of the helmet have been carefully mounted and the helmet (Figure 4, top left) is displayed prominently in the redisplay, facing the doorway through which most visitors enter the gallery. To the left of the helmet (Figure 4, bottom right) is a silver replica of how the helmet would have looked when new and whole. As the most-photographed case it is not surprising that these are the images from the gallery which are shared most often online. Although it is difficult to produce a definitive sample (due to the non-standard description and tagging of user-generated content on these services), by searching key tags it is clear how certain characteristics emerge in these photographs. Both before and after the helmet and replica were redisplayed the eye holes of the helmets are often centred, sometimes in three-quarter profile. This approach is also used to show the replica helmet. Some users upload comparable images of both helmets. As the most popular object for photography it is not surprising that it is the most often shared object from Room

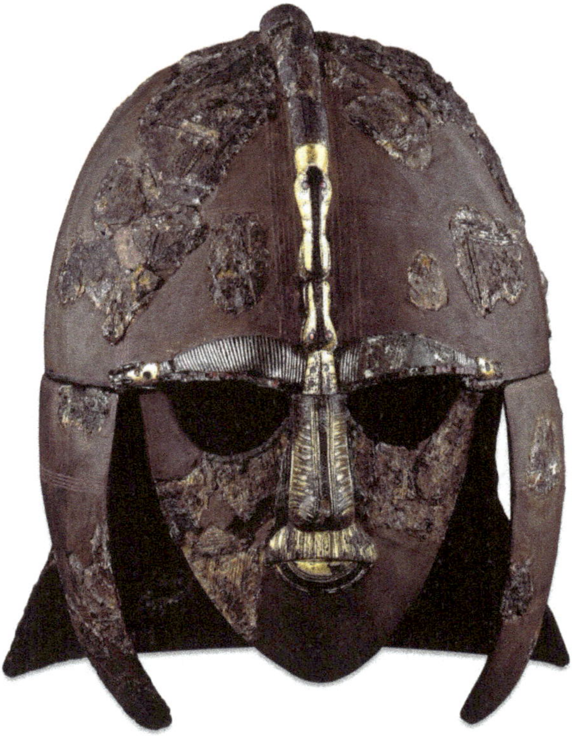

FIG.5: The professional photograph used in press and marketing by the British Museum to promote the gallery. Digital photograph, 2014. © The Trustees of the British Museum.

41 online (as far as we can tell), but the emergence of a formula that reflects the British Museum's official photography is interesting (Figure 5).

Outcomes and further research

The museum is an essentially visual medium (Alpers, 1991), so it is understandable that people want to take and share photos. The growing function of museum photography as part of a social visit, not just an intellectual style of visit, has huge potential for permanent galleries, as research shows that 54% of visitors to the British Museum have a social motivation for visiting (Francis, Slack & Edwards, 2011). Visitors who take photos are often part of social groups, so visitors who aren't taking photos in one gallery are likely to be accompanied by visitors who are taking photos, and vice-versa.

The Sutton Hoo helmet has been a popular museum exhibit since it was first on display, and its popularity in the pre-2010 gallery "encouraged the project team to move the Sutton Hoo exhibits to the heart of the new gallery physically and conceptually, and to ensure that all visitors come face-to-face with the helmet" (Frost, 2014: 8). The British Museum uses a "gateway object" approach to introduce visitors to collections. This approach means identifying a number of key objects around which to structure the display, which are then highlighted using design and interpretation techniques. The interpretive text for these gateway objects should start with what visitors can see, and then work out from there to tell the bigger story (Frost, 2014). In this way the gateway objects become gateways to the gallery's narrative, as a way to engage visitors more deeply. This research suggests that the gateway object approach works well for those visitors who both do and do not take photos.

Gateway objects usually meet four criteria: they must have narrative relevance; have a degree of importance; be iconic; and be visually attractive (Francis, Slack & Edwards, 2011). In meeting these criteria the Sutton Hoo helmet became "the ultimate gateway" object (Frost, 2014: 7). In this sense the British Museum, and its visitors, promote what Burch (2002) has called a process of "sacralisation" by encouraging a process of replication: the practice of photographing the helmet and circulating the images of it reinforces the object's status as iconic. Sacralisation in this way is a participatory process, as photographers participate in a pattern of filming or photographing (see Anton *et al* discussing their filming of the London's Olympic Park, 2012). Visitor photography reinforces the object's status as imagery circulates through social networks.

The findings from this modest case study suggest that what can seem like a "moral panic" over visitor photography is not justified in terms of observable visitor behaviour, which at the British Museum has remained relatively constant. Instead, the research has shown that visitors who take photographs are more engaged with the collection, and spend more time with the objects than visitors who do not take photographs.

ACKNOWLEDGEMENTS

The author would like to thank Julie Carr, Julia Davidson, Claire Edwards, David Francis, Nicola Freeman, Stuart Frost, Kara Locsin, Amy Moffat, Anna Newbury, Rebecca Penrose, Sascha Priewe and Luke Taylor for their help with this research.

REFERENCES

Alpers, S. (1991). The museum as a way of seeing. In Karp, I., and Levine, S. (eds.) *Exhibiting cultures: the poetics and politics of museum display*. Washington: Smithsonian University Press.

Anton, M., et al. (2012) London's Olympic waterscape: capturing transition. *International Journal of Heritage Studies*, 19(2): 125–138.

Arthur, C. (2014). The death of the featurephone in the UK – and what's next. *The Guardian*, 30 April. Available at: www.theguardian.com/technology/2014/apr/30/featurephone-smartphone-uk. [Accessed 19 January 2015]

Burch, S. (2002). Shaping symbolic space: Parliament Square, London as a sacred site. In: A. Phelps, G. J. Ashworth and B. O. H. Johansson, (eds.) *The construction of built heritage: a North European perspective on policies, practices and outcomes*. London: Ashgate.

British Museum. (2003). *The British Museum Visitor Regulations*. Available at: https://www.britishmuseum.org/PDF/Visitor_Regulations_Mar03.pdf. [Accessed 18 May 2015.]

British Museum. (2015). *Visitor research: evaluating exhibitions*. Available at: www.britishmuseum.org/research/

research_projects/all_current_projects/visitor_research.aspx. [Accessed 19 January 2015.]

Christiansen, R. (2014). Should we ban photography in museums and galleries?" *The Telegraph*, 8 March. Available at: www.telegraph.co.uk/culture/museums/10682442/Should-we-ban-photography-in-museums-and-galleries.html. [Accessed 19 January 2015.]

Davidson, J. & Locsin, K. (2010) *Visitor evaluation of gallery 41: Early Medieval Europe*. British Museum Internal Report.

Francis, D., Slack, S., & Edwards, C. (2011). An evaluation of object-centred approaches to interpretation at the British Museum. In J. Fritsch (ed.), *Museum and gallery interpretation and material culture*. London: Routledge.

Frost, S. (2014). The gateway to understanding? Evaluation and visitor research. *Legacy: The magazine of the National Association for Interpretation*, 25(4), 6–8.

Furness, H. (2014a). Poppies and pop stars: most popular Instagram posts of 2014 revealed. *The Telegraph*, 3 December. Available at: http://www.telegraph.co.uk/news/11270597/Poppies-and-pop-stars-Most-popular-Instagram-posts-of-2014-revealed.html. [Accessed 19 January 2015.]

Furness, H. (2014b). National Gallery relents over mobile phones. *The Telegraph*, 12 August. Available at: http://www.telegraph.co.uk/culture/art/art-news/11028015/National-Gallery-relents-over-mobile-phones.html. [Accessed 19 January 2015.]

Henkel, L. (2013) Point-and-shoot memories: the influence of taking photos on memory for a museum tour. *Psychological Science*, 25(2), 396–402.

Morris Hargreaves McIntyre, (2014). *British Museum rolling survey Q1 2014/15: research findings from April-June 2014.* Manchester: Morris Hargreaves McIntyre.

Moffat, A. (2014) *Summative evaluation of Room 41: Early Medieval Europe*. British Museum Internal Report.

Newbury, A. (2014) *Gallery 41 evaluation: Sutton Hoo and Early Medieval Europe*. British Museum Internal Report.

Serrell, B. (1998) *Paying attention: visitors and museum exhibitions*. Washington DC: American Association of Museums.

CHAPTER FOUR

NEW WAYS OF LOOKING: SELF-REPRESENTATIONAL SOCIAL PHOTOGRAPHY IN MUSEUMS

Alli Burness

WHEN WE GO TO MUSEUMS we do not just look,
we make a definite response to the work.
(Agnes Martin, 2005)

In early 2013, I visited the Thyssen-Bornemisza Museum in Madrid and saw Rembrandt's *Self-portrait Wearing a Hat and Two Chains*. A couple were the only others also looking at the painting at this time. As I moved away, the man turned and gave his digital device to his companion. Clearly excited and moved, the man posed within the visual space of the object standing with his body overlapping it as if it were a new friend His companion captured the moment with a photograph. The man examined the image on the digital screen and, with a few instructions, passed the camera back for another attempt. Although there was no one else in the gallery, I sensed a larger audience to this moment. This method of experiencing a work of art was new to me. Why do people take photographs of themselves with museum objects? What do these images and their associated behaviours mean? How do these images speak, and how can we understand what they are saying?

Echoing the sentiment of Agnes Martin that opens this chapter, I argue that self-representational social photography is a definite response to, and a form of self-expression inspired by, museum objects. By creating these images, visitors are expressing their sense of self, using museum objects and including these objects within their social community. Drawing on research by identity and communication theorists as well as museum audience literature, I will demonstrate that the creation of these images represents a new way of looking within the museum. Studying self-representational social photography in museums can reveal the "*experiences* that individual people can have with objects as a way of seeing" (Wood & Latham, 2013). This chapter will explain why the selfie, or self-representational social photography, is a natural fit within the museum visitor experience. Both the museum experience and these images are personal, embodied and felt practices.

This chapter is guided by the practices of museum visitors. I am using the term "self-representational social photograph" to refer to images of a subject that are broadcast online by that subject. These photographs may be taken by the subject but may also be taken by another person, usually under the direction of the subject, as in the example that opened this chapter. The two important elements of this behaviour for the purposes of this chapter are, first, that the image depicts a subject and, second, that the image is published online by that subject. The use of this term, instead of *selfie*, allows us to be guided by museum visitor practices rather than restricted by formal definitions.[1] Besides artworks, museum visitors represent themselves in social photography with a wide range of museum objects. I will use the term "museum object" to refer to "any physical, tangible thing that is part of the museum experience" (Wood & Latham, 2013). This incorporates art, artefacts and specimens as well as practical items such as tickets, vitrines and the museum building itself.

Moral panic and the *Mona Lisa* argument

Self-representational social photographs have attracted largely negative media reports (see O'Shea, 2014; Petri, 2013; Ryan, 2013; Audley, 2015). Reporting on these images has followed the process of a "moral panic," a concept originally outlined by Stanley Cohen (1972).[2] One feature of a moral panic is exaggerated or distorted media reporting about a new behaviour, focusing on extreme examples that come to be seen as typical (Critcher, 2003). Media reports highlight extreme impacts of self-representational social photography by amplifying specific negative examples or ill-founded claims.[3] Popular reports have linked these images to conditions such as psychopathy (Fox & Rooney, 2015) and the spread of head lice (Keeling, 2014). One hoax report, believed to be factual by many, claimed that they indicated mental ill-health (Sturt & Nordstrom, 2014). Other reports have questioned the value of self-representational social photography on the basis of their creation at Holocaust memorial sites (Margalit, 2014) or as motivation for individuals to take their own lives (Aldridge & Harden, 2014). These reports assert that behaviours associated with these images indicate self-orientated, obnoxious, socially dysfunctional behaviour or narcissism. Anne Burns (2015: 1720) characterises these claims as accusations that reflect "a poor understanding of the complexities of narcissism" and instead are intended to discipline and police those who take these photographs.

A second and related feature of a moral panic is disproportionate media anxiety around a behaviour relative to its actual impact (Marwick, 2008). Google claims that 93 million self-representational social photographs were taken each day on Android devices alone during 2014 (Brandt, 2014). Yet the predominantly negative media reporting about these images does not acknowledge that the vast majority are taken without incident, nor did they incur negative or destructive consequences. This type of reporting polarises debate, constructing a dichotomy between their perceived damaging impacts and their potential benefit as an empowering tool for self-expression (see Ryan, 2013; Simmons, 2013). Theresa Senft and Nancy Baym (2015: 1597) have pointed out that celebrating all these images "as empowering makes as little sense as denigrating them all as disempowering, and yet this polarizing rhetoric persists". In reality, self-representational social photography is a tool that can be applied to various and nuanced social ends. The current method of reporting reduces space for public conversation about how to read these images and their function as a communication tool with which to perform identity.

A third feature of a moral panic is the presence of "moral entrepreneurs" who "pronounce upon the nature of the problem and its best remedies" (Critcher, 2003: 17). In the case of self-representational social photography, these moral entrepreneurs include editors and cultural critics operating within the media. Individuals fulfilling these roles have positioned these images as antithetical to the physical world and pronounce that we should refrain from the practice. Chris O'Shea (2014) argues that posting these images to social media develops shallow and inauthentic relationships with others.[4] Sherry Turkle (2013) describes them as an "interruption," positioning digital communication as separate from, and less authentic than, physical experience. These claims falsely assume that the digital and physical realms are separable and that the digital is virtual. This assumption of a "digital dualism," a term coined by Nathan Jurgenson (2011, 2015), is at the heart of Turkle and O'Shea's pronouncements that self-representational social photography (as a type of digital communication) is less valuable than other modes of communication.[5]

The digital dualist assumption has featured in media reports and editorials about visitors' use of self-representational social photography in museums. These reports have focused on examples that occur around iconic museum destinations, particularly Leonardo da Vinci's *Mona Lisa*. Kenneth Goldsmith (2013) asserts that iconic works have "become wallpaper for selfies" (01:05:00) and that visitors using social media are in fact absent from the museum. Jonathan Jones (2009) suggests that visitors taking photographs with mobile technology are "killing the Mona Lisa" with "destructive camera abuse". When London's National Gallery relaxed a prohibition against photography, media reports centred on concerns that visitor photography (particularly of the self-representational kind) would prevent all visitors from deep engagement or extended looking at objects (Bland, 2014). Eric Gibson (2013: 20) remarks upon visitors "turning their backs" on the *Mona Lisa* to take self-representational social photographs. He feels that this behaviour demotes the art object from being the focus of an art experience and is a motivation to damage artworks by touching them.

Criticism of the kind outlined above has established a dominant narrative in the media that argues against museum visitors taking self-representational social photographs. I call this narrative the *Mona Lisa* argument. It involves media representatives focusing on these images with iconic works, denying the practice as a valid museum experience based on a misinterpretation of bodily practices and making unfounded connections with the destruction of objects. Indeed, a report of a student breaking a plaster cast replica of a statue at the Brera Academy in Milan during an effort to take a self-representational social photograph attracted heightened media attention (Trianni, 2014; Steinhauer, 2014). This incident continues to be referenced in media reports despite significant misreporting (Eler, 2014; Munro, 2014; Sutton, 2015).[6] As a specific type of moral panic, the *Mona Lisa* argument drowns out discussion about the social function of these images in museums. It negates the efforts of museums to learn how self-representational social photography may be leveraged as an engagement opportunity and denies the legitimacy of this type of museum experience for visitors.

It is worth noting that elements of Gibson's article unwittingly foreshadow research into the social role of self-representational social photography by communication theorists such as Katie Warfield (2014a; 2014b; 2014c) and Jill Walker Rettberg (2014). Gibson determines that a sustained focus on an object and emotional response are central to a meaningful museum experience. He describes an art experience as being "a direct, personal, revelatory encounter" (Gibson, 2013: 20).[7] He calls for museums to take on the role of moral entrepreneur by policing visitors with mobile devices to ensure that they have experiences of this type. He also describes his discomfort at being a "voyeur" and feeling like an intruder as visitors around him take self-representational social photographs. He mistakes the creation of these images as being motivated by narcissism. However, communications theorists Rettberg (2014), Jurgenson (2014) and José van Dijck (2008) have determined these are highly personalised moments of communication. Like Gibson's ideal art experience, research by Warfield (2014a, 2014b, 2014c) has revealed that taking a self-representational social photograph is an embodied, personal and felt experience.

Identity, performance and performativity

Across the museum audience research literature, a growing body of evidence places identity at the centre of the visit experience. Jay Rounds speculated that "identity work is a latent psychological function" (2006: 135) of the museum experience with "identity work" defined as "the process through which we construct, maintain, and adapt our sense of personal identity, and persuade others to believe in that identity" (2006: 133). In 2009, John Falk placed identity at the centre of a museum visitor experience model, outlining audience segments based on identity-related visitor motivations. Studies examining the role of visitor photography within the museum experience have yet to emerge; however, a strong theoretical connection exists between the increasing use of self-representational social photography and identity work in the museum.

In this chapter, I use a concept of identity defined as a sense of self that is continuously constructed through the performance of everyday life. It is shaped by performative gesture while being contingent on place, communicating different messages to different audiences and influenced by surrounding environments and discourses. To deepen and clarify this concept, I will expand this definition by drawing on the work of American sociologist Erving Goffman and British cultural critic Stuart Hall.

In 1996, Hall declared that an essentialist notion of identity had been deconstructed across a range of disciplines and that various "anti-essentialist" theories had been advanced in its place (1996: 1). While this shift is now well-established in academia, we continue to see essentialist notions of identity, or a sense of self as unified, applied in mainstream media. This essentialist concept of identity struggles to accommodate the everyday requirement to continually present ourselves to a multitude of audiences and in many roles, a process now made explicit by social media. This is the process that Turkle (2013) and O'Shea (2014) cannot incorporate within their understanding of authentic experience and relationships. To build this into our understanding of social reality, we must apply a concept of identity which recognises the ever-changing nature of self as well as the influence of both individual agency and broad, ideological discourse.

Individual agency takes centre stage in Erving Goffman's theory of performance of self in everyday life. Goffman (1959) explored identity as a sense of self created by continuous performance within the social interactions of everyday life, emphasising dramaturgical elements.[8] Theatrical features in the presentation of self include the "front" or the "the expressive equipment intentionally or unwittingly employed during a performance" (1959: 23). "Setting" or location is one element of the front in which a performance takes place. A natural history museum, for example, presents different subject positions than a contemporary art museum as settings for identity performance. A second element of the front is the "personal front," which includes the bodily practices, features, clothing and accessories of a person (1959: 24). A visitor may choose to adopt behaviours condoned by museum regulations for looking and walking as part of her personal front during her time in a museum, or she may elect to behave in ways that subtly or explicitly resist accepted practices (Figures 1 and 2). By taking a self-representational social photograph with a particular object in a museum, a visitor performs her identification with the subject positions it offers.

Drawing on Goffmanian theory, Rounds (2006) outlines the impact of social discourses which manifest as commonly recognised behaviours. He applies the term "enactments" to socially recognised bodily practices that, when performed, enable others to understand and respond to a social role (2006: 142). To illustrate, we may see the emphasised surveillance behaviours of museum docents as enactments, with uniforms and deliberate attention to people rather than objects used as identifiers for visitors to recognise their role. Rounds describes these enactments as "playing to the moment," and "featuring the same kind of intensification that museums convey upon objects" (2006: 142). We may observe this in museum visitors taking self-representational social photographs as they "play to the moment" by enacting their role to a digital community. In this way, we see that in addition to an individual's performance of self, identity is *performative* as a social role is selected from a range of available roles.

Hall's definition of identity is comparable to Goffmanian theory in being ever-changing, temporary and constantly mobile. However, Hall has described identity as a "meeting point," a "point of suture" or "temporary attachment" between social discourses that hail individuals to subject positions on the one hand and individuals who agree to invest in subject positions on the other (1996: 5-6). These large, ideological discourses such as "history, language and culture" (in which we can include museums) create and call us to subject positions (1996: 4).[9] The influence of an individual's agency in her performance of identity is balanced with roles offered by social discourse. This suturing of individuals with discourses is

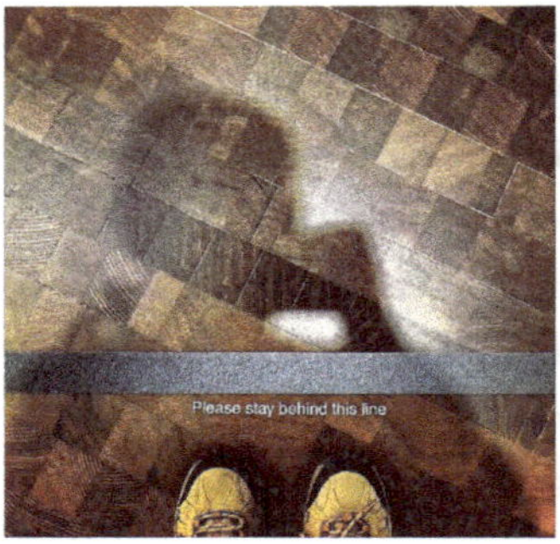

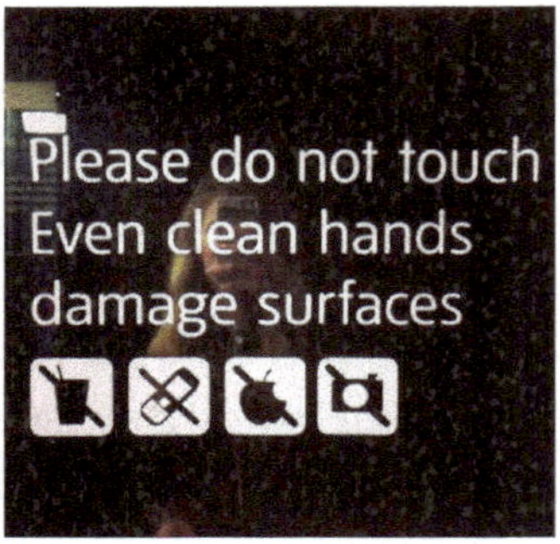

FIG. 1: LEFT | Photo taken by @agustinpolanco at Denver Art Museum, posted to Instagram on 15 September 2013.
FIG. 2: RIGHT| Photo taken by @colleendilen, posted to Instagram on 25 July 2014.

reflected in museum audience literature. According to Falk, identity is "the combination of both internal and external social forces," a process to which both cultural and individual agencies contribute (2009: 72).

With social media now a prevalent presence for many, the performance of self is explicit and communally acknowledged with the use of tools such as self-representational social photography. These images are one method to communicate the performance of everyday life both in the moment of their creation and when they are broadcast online. As we play to the moment during the creation of self-representational social photographs, these moments can be considered as a Goffmanian enactment, an everyday moment made a little bit larger than life. They are performative gestures because they express ourselves as "sutured" to larger social discourses in any given moment, whether that be in a museum, a bathroom or taking part in a protest. The logic of identity performance and performativity enables us to authentically exist in many roles simultaneously, to exist in physical and digital spaces with our identity in each of these informing our sense of self in the other.

Identity in the museum

The idea of the visitor as an active agent in the museum experience has been a recent development relative to media audience research. Eilean Hooper-Greenhill (1995) points out that "media studies in the 1950s proposed the active audience... long before we had even begun to study our audiences in museums" (1995: 9). Research into how media messages are used by audiences as active agents with individual motivations originated in the

1940s (Abercrombie & Longhurst, 1998). However, until the late 20th century, the voices of curators, directors and artists were presumed to dominate the meaning-making process in the museum. Since then, museum audience research has built a strong case for the central role of personal experience and memory in visitor meaning-making, defined by Dipesh Chakrabarty as "embodied knowledge" (2002:11). Within this term, I include emotion and creative imagination because they too are borne of personal or social context rather than rational or academic reasoning. Whereas embodied knowledge has always shaped the museum visit, the museum sector has now begun to seek out engagement techniques with which it can be leveraged.

Some staff in museums are familiar with the powerful role embodied knowledge plays in the museum because it is consistently expressed by onsite visitors and through visitor-generated social media content. The Metropolitan Museum of Art reflects this awareness in an online interpretive resource in which neuropsychiatrist Eric Kantor and neuroscientist Edward Vessel (n.d.) detail a connection between looking, emotion and the perceived meaning of specific objects. The Director of the National Museum of Australia, Mathew Trinca (2013), incorporates embodied knowledge when arguing that memory and the senses are as central to the museum experience as academic reasoning. A brief survey of recent museum audience research further demonstrates this rapidly rising awareness of the visitor as an active agent in the meaning-making process. Falk (2009) touches on embodied knowledge by examining the function of the limbic system in the human brain and concludes that cognition and emotion are inseparable. His conclusions are demonstrated by detailed visitor interviews, which illustrate the role of emotion in forming long-term memories of a museum visit. Similarly, Gaynor Bagnall (2003) concludes that rational aspects of a museum visit work in conjunction with visitors' emotions and imagination.

A study by Leinhardt et al. (2000) uses the diary, a private and written form of self-representation, to assess the role of embodied knowledge in the visitor meaning-making process. In their study, 40 diary entries were created by eight people who visited five exhibitions. The study focuses on the "private and interior" narratives conducted by the diarists as they experienced and expressed their museum visit (2000: 2) While these diaries depict the self in writing rather than photography, the two mediums are equally "authored, edited, and selected," reflecting how a "unique and special experience [in a museum] is folded into, and becomes a part of, the visitors' larger sense of self" (2000: 3). They also maintain the features of performative identity critical to the active visitor, namely "an awareness of social context, self-monitoring and reflection". Examples from the diaries demonstrate that objects which are selected for consideration depend on visitors' personal memories, imagination and experience.

The diary study also demonstrates aspects of Goffman and Hall's identity theory evident in each visitor experience. Reminiscent of Goffman's aspects of performance, Leinhardt et al. note that some diarists saw the museum "as frame and setting for the objects within," with recognition of the tone, mood and ambience this created for the objects and their display (2000: 12). Hall's "suturing" of a sense of self is apparent when visitors "deliberately blurred the lines between the exhibit and themselves, developing a personal meaning for the object, or exhibit, or drawing an interpretation out into their own lives" (Leinhardt et al., 2000: 26). Both the diaries and self-representational social photography illustrate how visitors weave their personal identity and emotion into the visit experience. In addition to showing bodies and objects overlapping or interacting, comments, emoticons and hashtags included with self-representational social photographs detail the application of emotions and personal experience. Like the diaries, these images record the process of blurring the lines between the lives of visitors and a museum object.

The visitor's body plays an important role in applying embodied knowledge within the museum experience. Figure 3 shows museum signage which reflects the inherently active and felt nature of the museum visit by listing verbs as a method of outlining condoned behaviours. The first verb, under which all others are listed, is the French word "voir" meaning "to look." Helen Rees Leahy has observed that the eye of the visitor is always active. She unpacks the dynamic, multi-focal relationship among the body, its actions and objects (2012: 5-6). Moments of sustained gazing in the museum are punctuated by glancing, a look associated with distraction, "a furtive or sideways look whose attention is always elsewhere" (2012: 47). These different types of looking combine with the ways visitors feel and use their bodies to position themselves in the museum space and in relation to objects. The relationship between looking and the action of the body is, as Leahy notes, "central to the social life of the museum" and has the capacity to "integrate the inner and outer worlds" of the visitor (2012: 78-79).[10]

Self-representational social photographs can be seen

as evidence of the application of embodied knowledge by emplaced and active visitors who are suturing museum objects within their identity. To apply Falk's words, these images in museums exist in "that unique and ephemeral moment when both of these realities become one and the same – visitors are the museum and the museum is the visitor" (2009: 36). Laurajane Smith has argued that museums exist through the "multi-layered performance" of visitors and staff. They are "not so much a 'thing'" but are the result of "a cultural and social process" (Smith, 2006: 2).[11] By taking self-representational social photographs, visitors perform their sense of self using museum objects and, in so doing, create their own identity *as well as the identity of the museum.* By actively forging and continually creating identities during their museum experience visitors are engaging in the social process of place-making in the museum – or, more simply, making the museum. As such, these images can be seen as evidence of a meaningful visit experience, one in which both the visitor and the museum are enacted.

Seeing through the selfie

The embodied museum experience finds a parallel in the experience of taking a self-representational social photograph, as articulated in the work of some communication theorists. Through phenomenological interviews with a group of young women, Warfield has investigated the motivations of those who take selfies, how those motivations influence the image-making process and how that process provides insight into emerging digital identities (Warfield, 2014a; 2014b; 2014c). Warfield (2014b: 2) has advocated for examining selfies by speaking

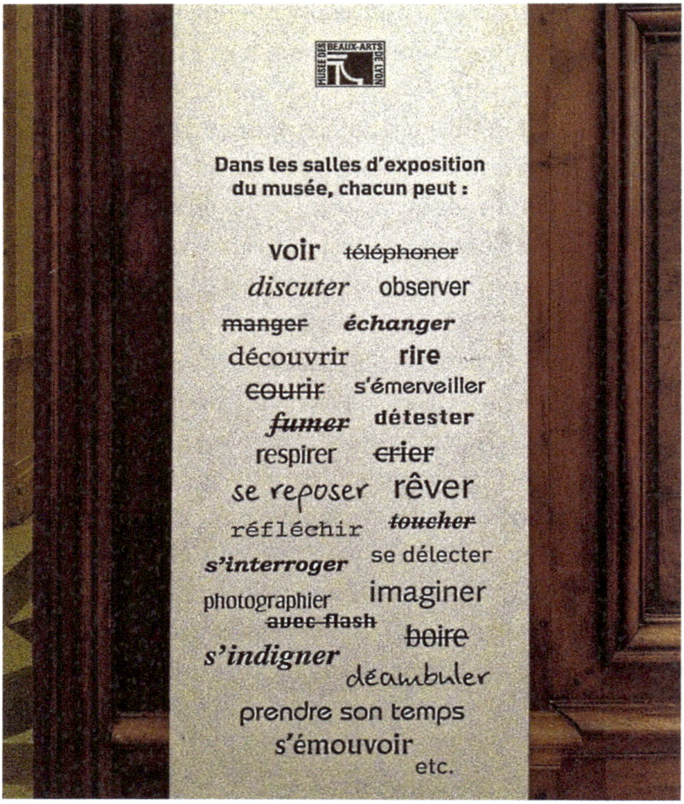

FIG. 3: Signage at the Museum of Fine Arts, Lyon, France, August 2013.
Photograph: Alli Burness.

to the producers of these images – by stepping into the image-making process and "talking with the embodied and emplaced image-makers themselves".

Warfield's (2014a; 2014c) research suggests that selfie takers seek an element to their image which is intangible and intrinsic to their sense of self in that moment. This element is felt and embodied and is the result of a "connection to the image from within" (Warfield, 2014c, 20:43). It is also a performance of an evolving sense of self in everyday life. The selfies broadcast by subjects of Warfield's (2014c) study are both "authentic to the eye as well as the girl's sense of self" (21:05). They are authentic to how the selfie taker feels and sees herself to be in that moment. This momentary and fleeting sense of authenticity is not confined by faithfulness to a physical appearance. In the words of Warfield's subjects:

> I often take them when I feel the need to stop and see myself *for* myself. (Anonymous, age 23)
> I like having the camera in my own hands. I like seeing my face in the camera. I like being in control of the image and what I'll look like. (Anonymous, age 18)
> (2014a, 34:32)

Excerpts from Warfield's interviews invoke embodied knowledge in the capturing of emotions, feelings and personalised communication. Warfield believes that this intangible sense of authenticity comes from an "affecting and emotional place within" (2014c, 19:50). She describes these images as "felt and experienced, owned and embodied" (19:55). As a result of her research, Warfield proposes that selfies encourage us to feel the process of looking at ourselves and each other by seeing "through different sets of eyes" (2014a, 31:33). This statement echoes the work of Jurgenson (2014), who describes these images as "less making media and more sharing eyes". Sarah Hromack (2014) applies this concept when describing how "the museum selfie enables museums to 'see' themselves... the 'self' in museum selfies becomes a collective 'we' " (05:25). Warfield concludes that selfies are, in their proliferation and sense of communal looking, challenging the traditionally disembodied eye of the camera.

Extending the insights from Warfield's work, self-representational social photography can be understood as a type of embodied language or speech act. Warfield (2014a) describes those who take these images as "using the lens to talk" (35:10). José van Dijck (2008: 62) describes them as "a visual language conveyed through the channel of a communication medium". As a type of language, these images are "the image-speak that is uniquely yours, it is your own voice-as-image and is thus especially intimate and expressive" (Jurgenson, 2014). It is the highly personal nature of this method of communication that caused Gibson (2013) to feel like a voyeur when watching others at the Louvre. However, Senft and Baym (2015) point out that "rather than inviting voyeurism, selfies show a "self enacting itself" and invite spectators to reflect on the "very instability of the term 'self' " (quoting Paul Frosh, 2015: 1595). This idea can feel destabilising and threatening. The highly personal nature of these images insist that we consider all of their aspects to understand their meaning. This includes the personalised, communicative gesture as they are created as well as the image, its broadcasting and response from audiences.

Another contextual element that shapes the meaning of a self-representational social photograph is the location in which it is taken. Elizabeth Losh (2014) argues that proximity helps digital audiences recognise the subject and the intended meanings of these images. She determines their place-making function is an activity which correlates the subject of this type of image "with a background that can communicate copresence by transmitting elements of the rhetorical scene to others in an imagined social network". In his exploration of selfies taken in politically sensitive heritage sites, Paul Mullins (2014) concurs with Losh, arguing that such a self-representational social photograph "visually invokes a heritage without articulating its meaning". He concludes that such an image "essentially writes its subject into history" (or sutures an individual to larger social discourses) and that the meaning and authenticity in these images is borne of an emplaced personal experience. The heart of a self-representational social photograph is in the "personal imagination" of what a specific place means to its subject. The work of both Losh and Mullins about the place-making function of these images resonates with Smith's concept of visitors creating museums as significant social places through an active and performative social process.

The intentions of those who create self-representational social photographs and the location and conversations within which these images are embedded are intrinsic to their meaning. To understand how these images speak, Rettberg (2014), a media theorist and researcher, urges us to remember that selfies "aren't simply texts published from a distance. They are images and words that are part of a conversation". Similarly, Jurgenson (2014) describes them as "merely a by-product of communication rather that its focus". It is perilous to read self-representational social photographs as isolated acts or objects; we must be careful not to ignore their contexts as well as intended meanings and audiences. While we may be allowed to leave these elements out of our reading of an artwork in a museum, self-representational social photography is rarely created to function outside the intended relationship between a subject and her digital community.

Leveraging self-representational social photographs

Self-representational social photography has the potential to reveal insights into the museum experience. Synergies between the embodied and emplaced museum experience and the taking of self-representational social photographs suggest that these images may be leveraged to foster personal connection and meaning-making in the museum. To do so, museum staff can learn to read these images not as texts, from the outside looking in, but by speaking to their creators. This will occur via deeper engagement with visitors who take these images and by igniting reflection and conversation about the motivations behind them and their role within the museum experience.

Nina Simon's (2010) well-known participatory model suggests techniques with which to reflectively discuss taking self-representational social photographs with visitors in museums. Using these techniques, "institutions can tap into pre-existing stories and connections" between visitors and objects. She coins the term "social objects" to indicate those that lend themselves to conversation, pointing out that these are objects which also inspire visitors to "snap photos of each other". Simon persuasively argues for the use of questions as a method for conducting dialogue around social objects. Rather than asking leading questions, she recommends the use of open questions which elicit answers that museum staff are genuinely interested in hearing. Using this technique to explore this type of image, education programs can touch on all three areas of evaluation methodology by inspiring reflective thought and feedback. Such programs leverage what visitors *do* while taking these images, what they *say* about the activity in response to questions and what they *leave behind* in the form of images online. This combination of participatory questioning and evaluation has the potential to act as a form of three-dimensional audience research built into programming.

Can museum staff apply this type of insight during the planning and development of exhibitions and programs? Wood and Latham (2013) offer a potential strategy with their "object knowledge framework," which attempts to intentionally work in the intersection where visitors and objects meet. To apply this framework, questions are raised at strategic points during the development process. These questions seek to determine how an object mobilises emotions and shapes the personal identity of visitors or, in other words, how an object taps into the embodied knowledge of visitors. Research in social networks is suggested as one method to identify answers, and, in so doing, visitor self-representational social photography is incorporated into this strategy. Like Simon, Wood and Latham's strategy encourages museum staff to listen and incorporate the personal insights of visitors into museum programming as revealed in self-representational social photography.

Some museums are beginning to incorporate self-represen-

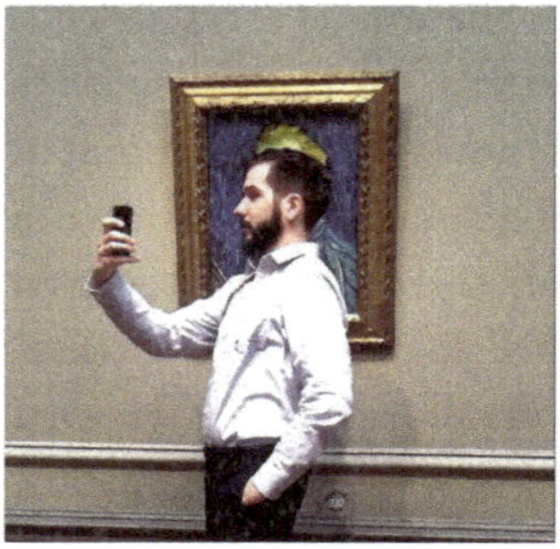

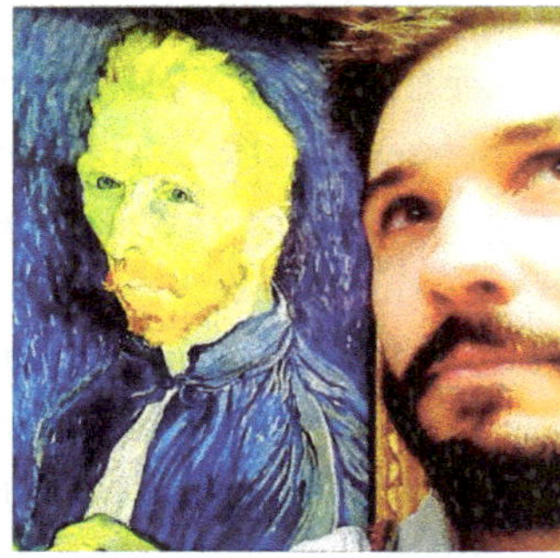

FIG. 4: LEFT | Image of @shawnlenker taken by @patrickbenko at the National Gallery of Art, Washington, DC. Posted to Instagram 25 October 2014.

FIG. 5: RIGHT | Image by @shawnlenker at the National Gallery of Art in Washington, DC. Posted to Instagram 25 October 2014.

tational social photography into programming, and excellent case studies can be found in other chapters of this volume. At the National Gallery of Art in Washington, DC, a series of semi-regular meet-ups with members of the local Instagram community, otherwise known as Instameets, provides a good example. Prompts that request self-representational social photography have been included as part of the programme at the Instameets. These events have included discussion between educators and participants about the use of social photography, igniting reflective thought and creative response to the museum experience. Evaluation of the Instameets is conducted in multiple ways. It is obtained visually through the images that participants create in response to prompts, verbally in the form of conversation during the meet-up and written in response to surveys. The gallery's Instameets are rich opportunities for audience research and reflect an application of Simon's technique.

Images taken during the gallery's Instameets demonstrate how self-representational social photography functions as communication. Figure 4 was taken by an Instameet participant of a fellow participant taking a selfie, and Figure 5 is the selfie taken by the fellow participant. These images were created spontaneously and simultaneously in response to a prompt. Together, they indicate a camaraderie between these visitors and an awareness of being within the same imagined digital community. The images were created while the visitors were at the museum, yet the conversation within which these images were intended to operate was situated primarily online. Figure 5 was posted with an accompanying comment by the subject, "spending some quality time with my good friend

Vincent" (National Gallery of Art, 2014). This comment extends the imagined digital community to include the museum object and, it could be argued, its creator, Vincent van Gogh. As this communication pivots around a museum object, the digital experience blurs with and influences the emplaced and embodied experience in the museum. These images together reveal that the two realms are entangled.

Feedback from the gallery's Instameet participants also provides insight into the connection between the visitor and the object as fostered through the act of taking a self-representational social photograph. Instameet participants regarded the museum as an environment within which to experiment with this practice and were enthused that the events were "vital hands-on brain activity for understanding and implementing uses of new digital media" (National Gallery of Art, 2014). Participants also understood that their images are "real-time data-making opportunities," indicating a recognition that their input was valued by the museum (National Gallery of Art, 2014). Tellingly, one participant reflected that "the simple act of physically imitating a work gave me a new connection and understanding of it" (National Gallery of Art, 2014). While imitating the object to create her self-representational social image, this participant was developing a physical understanding of the object and gaining new embodied knowledge. Statements such as these speak to the value of using self-representational social photography as a way to both initiate the creation of and communicate the application of embodied knowledge in the museum.

Conclusions

Images and feedback from the gallery's Instameet events indicate that self-representational social photography is a new way of looking in the museum. By side-stepping media narratives about the value of these images and focusing on visitor practice and feedback, we can begin to see how these images function as social communication as well as a way to express embodied knowledge and perform identity. In essence, visitors engaging in self-representational social photography are paying the ultimate compliment to museums by weaving museum objects into their identity. These images are borne of the meeting between visitors and objects and from the enmeshed nature of the digital and physical realms. They point to the social role that objects play in the lives of our visitors and the important role that museums have in facilitating those relationships.

This chapter is intended to provide a starting point for applying self-representational social photographs as a tool for gaining insight into the museum visitor experience. For museum staff to understand how and why their visitors take self-representational social photographs, speaking with visitors who create these images is crucial as is enabling them to think reflectively about this practice. In this way, museum staff can develop a body of evidence that will help them answer questions about segments of their visitor cohort and learn how they experience museums. These photographs provide a way to continue developing our understanding of how identity drives the museum experience and learn to see when these motivations are manifested in visitor behaviours.

ACKNOWLEDGMENTS

The author would like to thank Dana Allen-Greil for the opportunity to learn from the National Gallery of Art's first Instameets as well as Dr Narelle Lemon for reviewing and advising on the development of this chapter.

NOTES

1. The *Oxford English Dictionary* (OED) (2013) defines "selfie" as "a photograph that one has taken of oneself, typically one taken with a smartphone or webcam and shared via social media." The term enjoys a wider application by the media and the public than the OED definition recognises. This broad use of the term cannot be sufficiently explained by click bait news headlines and opportunistic use of hashtags. In order to understand the selfie as a "cultural artefact and social practice" (Senft & Baym, 2015: 1589), we require a more nuanced definition. In this chapter, I have chosen to apply an alternative term while other theorists have proposed an alternative definition. Katie Warfield (2014a) points out that the OED definition provides the basic details of their creation but leaves us without insight into their meanings or social function. Theresa Senft and Nancy Baym (2015: 1589) offer an alternative definition that incorporates their complex nature, proposing that a selfie is "a photographic *object* that initiates the transmission of human feeling in the form of a relationship" and "also a *practice* – a gesture that can send (and is often intended to send) different messages to different individuals, communities, and audiences".
2. Various authors have defined a list of features that indicate a moral panic (Crichter, 2008; Goode & Ben-Yahuda, 1994;

Marwick, 2008). Media reporting of self-representational social photography meets many, if not all, of the steps outlined across the literature.

3. Regarding claims connecting self-representational social photographs with narcissism, Senft and Baym (2015) assert that, at the time this chapter was published, "we have not seen a single peer-reviewed piece of scientific literature that convincingly demonstrates that selfie production and mental illness are correlated" (p. 1590). In the cases cited in this chapter, conclusions were based on studies with small sample sizes, research that is not peer-reviewed or is implicated with companies who have vested interest in the outcome.
4. This concept appears frequently in popular media. The most high-profile may be the 2014 television series *Selfie*, broadcast by the American Broadcasting Company. Focusing on a young woman who feels that her friendships are not authentic because they are maintained through a presentation of herself using social media, an acquaintance attempts "an analog civilizing" (Senft & Baym, 2015) to alter her behaviour, which is perceived as narcissistic.
5. It is worth noting at this point that we can further contextualise the media response to these images as a "technopanic" and "hype cycle" (Marwick, 2008; Garber, 2014). A technopanic understands an extreme media response to a popular new media technology as an anxiety about modernity (Marwick, 2008). Technopanics "focus on new media forms" and their predominant use by young people (Marwick, 2008). Reporting about these images follows common media patterns around new experiences afforded by technology, such as those that have occurred around video games and violent behaviour. Disproportionate concern about the negative impacts

of self-representational social photography sits within "a historical continuum which includes panics over other types of technologies and signs of modernity" (Marwick, 2008). A hype cycle, in comparison, is a larger process that may encompass technopanic. It is the process by which a new technology initially triggers "excitement, anxiety or disillusionment" before eventually the heightened attention plateaus as the behaviour in question becomes accepted as ubiquitous (Garber, 2014).

6. The sculpture in question was, in fact, a plaster cast replica located in the communal area of the associated art school and not the museum at the *Brera Academy*. These facts were not included or were misreported in media accounts about the incident. Public comments which update this information were ignored by media outlets (Steinhauer, 2014). It is also worth noting that one other case of a sculpture being broken in an attempt to create a self-representational social photograph occurred in an unregulated public space and not within a museum institution (Sutton, 2015). Media reports were quick to link the two unrelated incidents as indicative of a trend (Cascone, 2015; Sutton, 2015).
7. Some art historians and theorists have argued persuasively for the centrality of the object in the art museum experience and are considered foundational in some contemporary museum interpretation strategies. These include John Dewey (1934) and James Elkins (1996) as cited by Rika Burnham and Elliot Kai-Kee (2011). I accept the value of these strategies. However, I do argue that they are only one way to validly experience the museum and that self-representational social photography is one of many ways to apply mobile technology to meaningfully experience these spaces and the objects they contain.

8. Goffman's ideas laid the groundwork for contemporary theorists in feminist and queer scholarship who have reconceptualised gender as a performative rather than biological production (Butler, 2011).
9. This aspect of Hall's definition reflects the influence of Louis Althusser's (1970) concept of interpellation, or the capacity of dominant ideologies to hail or call individuals to subject-positions. By intuitively recognising and responding to a call, individuals come to constitute subjects of larger ideologies. Althusser's concept is notable in that it asserts individuals are always and already subjects created by ideology, implying that the agency of the individual is extremely limited, if not negated.
10. Whereas Leahy makes this statement in specific reference to walking in the museum, I would argue it applies equally well to other physical activities.
11. Smith (2006) includes museums within her examination of heritage, which is the primary concept deconstructed in her research.

REFERENCES

Abercrombie, N., & Longhurst, B. (1998). *Audiences: A sociological theory of performance and imagination.* London and New Delhi: SAGE Publications.

Aldridge, G., & Harden, K. (2014). Selfie addict took two hundred a day – and tried to kill himself when he couldn't take perfect photo. *Daily Mirror,* 23 March. Available at: http://www.mirror.co.uk/news/real-life-stories/selfie-addict-took-two-hundred-3273819.

Althusser, L. (1970). Ideology and the ideological state apparatus. In Althusser, L. *Lenin and philosophy and other essays*. New York: Monthly Review.

Audley, A. (2015). Prince Harry is right - selfies need to stop. *The Telegraph*, 8 April. Available at: http://www.telegraph.co.uk/news/health/children/11519666/Prince-Harry-is-right-selfies-need-to-stop.html.

Bagnall, G. (2003). Performance and performativity at heritage sites. *Museum and Society*, 1(2), 87-103.

Bland, A. (2014). Camera phones at the National Gallery stoke fears that technology is leaving us incapable of deep engagement with anything. *Independent*, 17 August. Available at: http://www.independent.co.uk/arts-entertainment/art/news/cameraphones-at-the-national-gallery-stoke-fears-that-technology-is-leaving-us-incapable-of-deep-engagement-with-anything-9673776.html.

Brandt, R. (2014). Google divulges numbers at i/o: 20 billion texts, 93 million selfies and more." *Silicon Valley Business Journal*, 25 June. Available at: http://www.bizjournals.

com/sanjose/news/2014/06/25/google-divulges-numbers-at-i-o-20-billion-texts-93.html.

Burns, A. (2015). Self(ie)-discipline: social regulation as enacted through the discussion of photographic practice. *International Journal of Communication*, *9*(2015), 1716–1733.

Burnham, R., & Kai-Kee, E. (2011). *Teaching in the art museum: interpretation as experience*. Los Angeles: The J. Paul Getty Museum.

Butler, J. (2011). *Bodies that matter: on the discursive limits of sex*. London and New York: Routledge.

Cascone, S. (2015). Selfie-taker smashes priceless historic Italian statue of Hercules. *Art Net News*, 4 May. Available at: https://news.artnet.com/in-brief/tourists-smash-italian-statue-while-taking-selfie-294167.

Chakrabarty, D. (2002). Museums in late democracies. *Humanities Research*, *IX*(1), 5-12.

Cohen, S. (1972). *Folk devils and moral panics: the creation of the mods and rockers*. London: MacGibbon and Kee.

Critcher, C. (2003). *Moral panics and the media*. Buckingham, UK: Open University Press.

Dewey, J. (1934). *Art as experience*. New York: Perigree.

Eler, A. (2014). Ancient statues pose for selfies. *Hyperallergic*, 12 August. Available at: https://hyperallergic.com/143180/ancient-statues-pose-for-selfies/.

Elkins, J. (1996). *The object stares back: on the nature of seeing*. New York: Simon and Shuster.

Falk, J. (2009). *Identity and the museum visitor experience*. California: Left Coast Press.

Fox, J., & Rooney, M. C. (2015). The dark triad and trait self-objectification as predictors of men's use and self-presentation behaviors on social networking sites." *Personality and Individual Differences*, *76*, 161–165. Available at: http://www.sciencedirect.com/science/article/pii/S0191886914007259.

Frosh, P. (2015). The gestural image: the selfie, photography theory, and kinesthetic sociability. *International Journal of Communication*, *9*(2015), 1607–1628.

Garber, M. (2014). The end of the selfie hype cycle. *The Atlantic*, 1 October. Available at: http://www.theatlantic.com/technology/archive/2014/10/selfies-are-boring-nowand-thats-why-theyre-finally-interesting/381001/.

Gibson, E. (2013). The overexposed museum. *The New Criterion*, *32*, December, 19–21.

Goffman, E. (1959). *The presentation of self in everyday life*. United Kingdom: Penguin.

Goldsmith, K. (2013). *"Poet laureate" lecture 2013: my career in poetry, or how I learned to stop worrying and love the institution* [video file], March 20. Available at: http://original.livestream.com/momatalks/video?clipId=pla_6580e2d0-8645-4a5c-8d2e-729a7b07dec2.

Goode, E. and Ben–Yahuda, N. (1994). *Moral panics: the social construction of deviance*. Oxford: Blackwell.

Hall, S. (1996). Introduction: who needs identity? In Hall, S. and du Gay, P. (eds.), *Questions of cultural identity*. London: SAGE Publications.

Hooper-Greenhill, E. (1995). Museums and communication: An introductory essay. In Hooper-Greenhill, E. (ed.). *Museum, media, message*. London and New York: Routledge.

Hromack, S. (2014). *The museum selfie* [video file],

January. Available at: http://whitney.org/WatchAndListen?play_id=916.

Jones, J. (2009). These tourist snappers are killing the Mona Lisa. *The Guardian*, 9 March. Available at: http://www.theguardian.com/artanddesign/jonathanjonesblog/2009/mar/09/mona-lisa-tourist-snappers-louvre.

Jurgenson, N. (2011). Digital dualism versus augmented reality [web log post]. *The Society Pages*, 24 February. Available at: http://thesocietypages.org/cyborgology/2011/02/24/digital-dualism-versus-augmented-reality/.

Jurgenson, N. (2014). The frame makes the photograph [web log post]. *Snapchat blog*, 7 January. Available at: http://blog.snapchat.com/post/72561406329/the-frame-makes-the-photograph.

Jurgenson, N. (2015). Q&A on digital dualism [web log post], January. Available at: http://nathanjurgenson.com/post/107219758205/q-a-on-digital-dualism.

Keeling, B. (2014). "Are selfies causing head lice infestations among teens?" *sfist*, 24 February. Available at: http://sfist.com/2014/02/24/are_selfies_causing_head_lice_infes.php.

Leahy, H. (2012). *Museum bodies: the politics and practices of visiting and viewing*. London: Ashgate.

Leinhardt, G., Tittle, C., & Knutson, K. (2000). Talking to oneself: diaries of museum visits. *Museum Learning Collaborative Technical Report # MLC-04*. Available at: http://www.lrdc.pitt.edu/mlc/documents/mlc-04.pdf.

Losh, E. (2014). Beyond biometrics: feminist media theory looks at *Selfiecity*. Available at: http://selfiecity.net/#theory.

Margalit, R. (2014). Should Auschwitz be a site for

selfies? *The New Yorker*, 26 June. Available at: http://www.newyorker.com/culture/culture-desk/should-auschwitz-be-a-site-for-selfies.

Martin, A. (2005). Response to art. In Martin, A. & Schwarz, D. (eds.), *Agnes Martin: Writings*. Ostfildern-Ruit: Hatje Cantz.

Marwick, A. (2008). To catch a predator? The MySpace moral panic. *First Monday*. Available at: http://firstmonday.org/article/view/2152/1966.

Metropolitan Museum of Art. (n.d.). Viewpoints: body language. Available at: http://www.metmuseum.org/collection/viewpoints.

Mullins, P. (2014). Imagining heritage: selfies and visual placemaking at historic sites [web log post], 20 June. Available at: https://paulmullins.wordpress.com/2014/06/30/imagining-heritage-selfies-and-visual-placemaking-at-historic-sites/.

Munro, C. (2014). 'Statue selfies' are the next great internet art trend. *Art Net News*, 13 August. Available at: https://news.artnet.com/art-world/statue-selfies-are-the-next-great-internet-art-trend-76865.

National Gallery of Art. (2014). [#atnga_lookingtogether Insta-meet participant feedback]. Unpublished raw data.

O'Shea, C. (2014). Science confirms that selfies are the worst. *The Daily Lounge*, February. Available at: http://dailylounge.com/the-daily/entry/science-confirms-that-selfies-are-the-worst.

Oxford English Dictionary. (2013). Oxford dictionaries word of the year 2013. *OxfordWords blog*. Available at: http://blog.oxforddictionaries.com/press-releases/

oxford-dictionaries-word-of-the-year-2013/.

Petri, A. (2013). President Obama takes a memorial selfie. *The Washington Post*, 10 December. Available at: http://www.washingtonpost.com/blogs/compost/wp/2013/12/10/president-obama-takes-a-funeral-selfie/.

Rettberg, J. W. (2014). *Seeing ourselves through technology: how we use selfies, blogs and wearable devices to see and shape ourselves*. New York, NY: Palgrave Macmillan.

Rounds, J. (2006). Doing identity work in museums. *Curator*, 49(2), 133–150.

Ryan, E. G. (2013). Selfies aren't empowering. They're a cry for help. *Jezebel*, 21 November. Available at: http://jezebel.com/selfies-arent-empowering-theyre-a-cry-for-help-1468965365.

Senft, T., & Baym, N. (2015). What does the selfie say? Investigating a global phenomenon. *International Journal of Communication*, 9(2015), 1588–1606.

Simon, N. (2010). *The participatory museum*. Available at: http://www.participatorymuseum.org/chapter4/.

Simmons, R. (2013). Selfies are good for girls. *Slate*, 20 November. Available at: http://www.slate.com/articles/double_x/doublex/2013/11/selfies_on_instagram_and_facebook_are_tiny_bursts_of_girl_pride.html.

Sturt, D., & Nordstrom, T. (2014). The selfie: mental disorder or insight to getting better results? *Forbes*, 29 April. Available at: http://www.forbes.com/sites/davidsturt/2014/04/29/the-selfie-mental-disorder-or-insight-to-getting-better-results/.

Smith, L. (2006). *Uses of heritage*. London and New York: Routledge.

Steinhauer, J. (2014). Man breaks statue in quest for selfie. *Hyperallergic, 19 March*. Available at: http://hyperallergic.com/115340/man-breaks-statue-in-quest-for-selfie/.

Sutton, B. (2015). Selfie snappers smash baroque sculpture in herculean feat of stupidity. *Hyperallergic*, 2 May. Available at: http://hyperallergic.com/204167/selfie-snappers-smash-baroque-sculpture-in-herculean-feat-of-stupidity/.

Trianni, F. (2014). Student breaks 19th century Greco-Roman statue while taking a selfie. *Time*, 18 March. Available at: http://time.com/28679/student-breaks-statue-selfie/.

Trinca, M. (2013). History in museums. In Clark, A. and Ashton, P. (eds.), *Australian history now*. Sydney: University of New South Wales Press Ltd.

Turkle, S. (2013). The documented life. *The New York Times*, 15 December. Available at: http://www.nytimes.com/2013/12/16/opinion/the-documented-life.html?_r=1.

van Dijck, J. (2008). Digital photography: communication, identity, memory. *Visual Communication*, 7(1), 57-76.

Warfield, K. (2014a). *Why I love selfies and why you should too* [video file], 2 April. Available at: https://www.youtube.com/watch?v=aOVIJwy3nVo.

Warfield, K. (2014b). *Making selfies/making self: digital subjectivities in the selfie*. Paper presented at the Image Conference Berlin, 30 October. Available at: http://www.academia.edu/8991582/Making_Selfies_Making_Self_digital_subjectivities_in_the_selfie.

Warfield, K. (2014c). *The treachery and the authenticity of images* [video file], 4 November. Available at: https://www.youtube.com/watch?v=Jho-2IZ_tnE.

Wood, E., & Latham, K. (2013). *The objects of experience: transforming visitor-object encounters in museums*. Available at: http://www.lcoastpress.com/book.php?id=483.

CHAPTER FIVE

SOCIAL MEDIA SOUVENIRS: EXPANDED EXPERIENCES THROUGH VISITOR PHOTOGRAPHY

Alexandra Weilenmann and Thomas Hillman

THE PRACTICE OF everyday photography has exploded to the point where it has been widely estimated that as many as 10% of all the photos ever produced were taken in 2011. A major factor in this dramatic increase in photographs is that many of these photos were taken with mobile phone cameras and shared on social media. The phenomenon of readily available cameras, carried almost all the time and in many cases constantly connected to the internet implies significant changes for the practice of photography. The kind of "Kodak culture" of everyday snapshots that Chalfen (1987) described in his seminal work on amateur photography has given way to a culture of "social photography" where everyday moments are captured and shared often and instantly for a potentially enormous online audience of friends and family, but also strangers. Cultural institutions such as museums, science centers and zoos have long been sites where visitors have taken photographs as souvenirs of their experiences, but the convenience of mobile phone cameras and opportunities for editing and sharing that they afford can only serve to grow the practice.

While making photography more available and convenient, mobile phone based cameras also prompt new possibilities for capturing and collecting our experiences which allow for new forms of everyday visual storytelling (Okabe, 2004). The increasing amount of photography and sharing, along with new forms of storytelling and interaction, have forced many museums and cultural institutions to reevaluate their roles. When visitors become co-creators of content, new opportunities to engage in, around and with exhibitions arise. Figure 1 shows an example of a classic souvenir from a visit to a museum or zoo nearly a century ago, a family photograph.

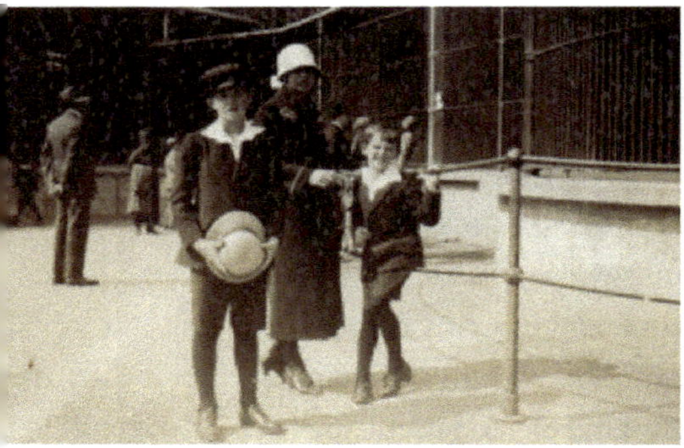

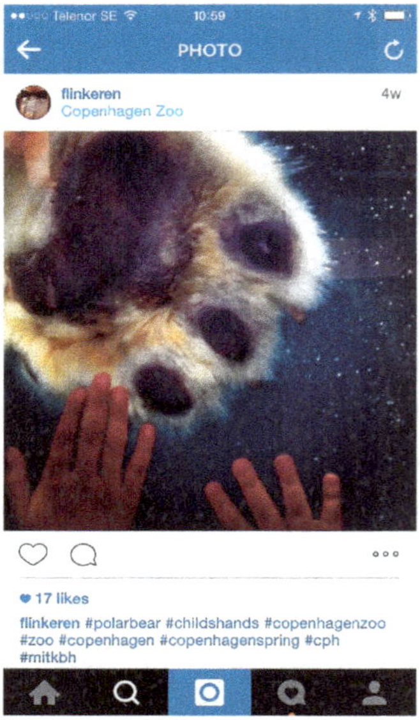

FIG. 1: ABOVE | A classic souvenir photograph from 1925.

FIG. 2: RIGHT | Instagram image from Copenhagen Zoo, 2015.
Photograph: @flinkeren.

Figure 2 shows a souvenir from a visit today, a picture which a visitor has taken and shared on Instagram.

In this chapter we summarize and discuss a number of trends we have seen in our empirical studies of the use of social media and mobile phones at cultural institutions (cf. Hillman, Weilenmann, Jungselius, 2012; Weilenmann, Hillman & Jungselius, 2013). Our results suggest that alongside a cultural institution's own curatorial processes another trend has emerged where visitors increasingly re-curate exhibitions outside the physical institution in online environments through their own representations and interactions on social media. We will offer several examples of the types of social media souvenirs visitors collect and share. We discuss how visitors re-curate content, create collections, create photographic opportunities and engage with those provided by the institutions they visit as well as how they present themselves as part of that context by performing or placing themselves in the images. First however, we briefly outline our methodological approach for studying visitor photography.

Our situated social media approach

Over the past few years we have undertaken studies of the use of mobile technology and social media in cultural institutions. In this chapter we focus specifically on visitors' photographic practices in two types of cultural institutions: natural history museums and zoological gardens. We have carried out fieldwork in several such institutions, including Gothenburg Natural History Museum and Borås Zoo, both in Sweden, where we have done extensive fieldwork, and one day studies at Copenhagen Zoo in Denmark, Smithsonian National Zoo in the USA, and Seoul Zoo in South Korea.

Methodologically, we have approached visitor social media use as a located practice-taking place in the cultural institutions. This means that we take as our point of departure the setting and the space within which social media posts are created and shared. This approach can be contrasted to conducting a similar study as an entirely online or virtual ethnography (Hine, 2000; Leander and McKim, 2003) where social media posts as finished products are analyzed apart from the physical space in which they were created. We have developed a framework for situated social media use which combines detailed ethnography with the analysis of online activities (Hillman & Weilenmann, 2015). In the field, this involves video-recorded observation, tracking of visitor movements and stimulated recall interviews where participants discuss their own social photography during a visit. Online, our approach involves both computational and manual content analysis of large corpora of social photography posts along with detailed analysis of the social media interactions of individual visitors.

While visitors to cultural institutions use their smartphones to access a wide variety of social media while visiting, the particular application chosen as a focus in this chapter is Instagram. Unlike earlier photo sharing services such as Flickr, for the first few years of its existence Instagram was only accessible through smartphones and had no official web presence. While other services such as Flickr and YouTube have followed Instagram's lead by creating mobile apps which support manipulation and live sharing, its introduction combined with higher quality cameras in mobile phones marked a shift toward exploiting the affordances of touch-screen internet connected smartphones. Although we focus on the Instagram application in this chapter, the processes we are describing are to a large extent present across other social media platforms.

In our work, we have chosen to examine the phenomenon of social photography specifically in relation to visits to cultural institutions. This context offers advantages to a study of ways that people collect and share aspects of their experiences. In particular, spaces such as museums, science centers and zoos are planned environments which are explicitly structured through curated exhibitions. Since visitors photograph and share aspects of these highly planned spaces, their choices in terms of ways of collecting, manipulating and sharing content from exhibitions can be readily compared to the structures instantiated in the exhibitions themselves. This renders visitors' work to curate photographic artifacts from their experiences on social media more visible than in the case of other less explicitly structured environments.

Social media souvenirs

By focusing on visitors' practices with their own devices and applications, we have examined a number of practices which visitors engage in outside those planned for them as part of exhibitions or programs. One such practice is the ways in which visitors *re-curate* exhibitions through their use of social photography (Hogan, 2010). In their social media productions, visitors create new themes, add their own interpretations, and create stories around the exhibits that are beyond the control of the institution. In investigating re-curation practices, our research has illuminated how visitors capture and create what we have called *social media souvenirs*. Drawing an analogy

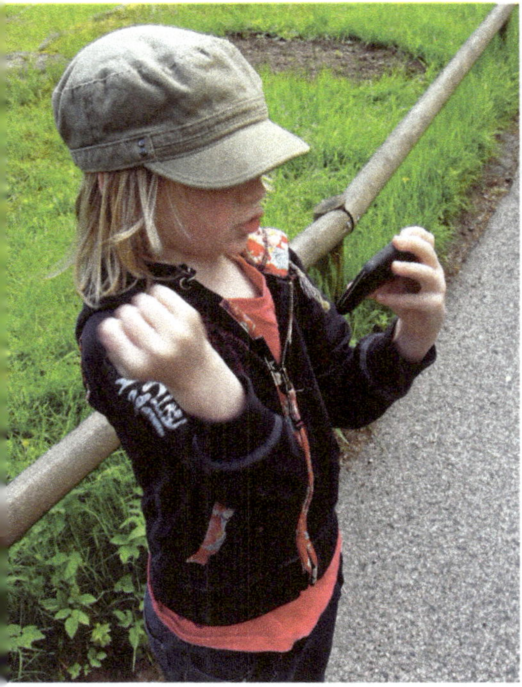

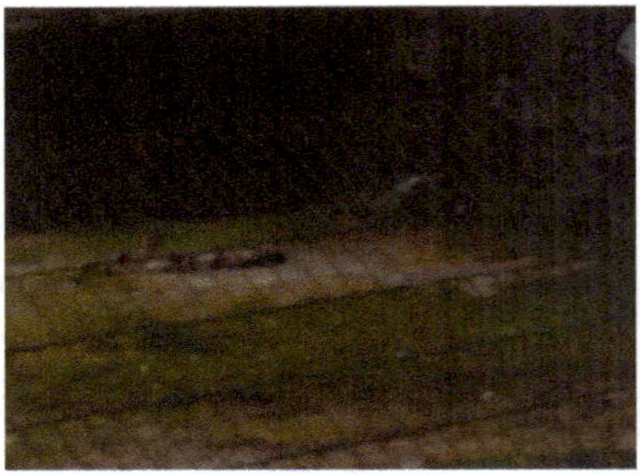

FIG. 3: LEFT | A young zoo visitor celebrates a successful photograph of a cheetah at Borås Zoo.

FIG. 4: ABOVE | The resulting photograph.

between how 19th century trophy hunters looked for exotic animals to bring home from their travels, visitors are now often capturing and sharing their own photographic trophies on social media, capturing the spirit of the animal as alive and as a hunter might encounter it. Indeed, photography and taxidermy shared the power to fabricate nature in new spaces; to capture animals in their supposedly natural attitudes and display their form to audiences eager for glimpses of exotic wilderness and knowledge of natural history (Ryan, 2000).

Both zoos and museums of natural history provide people with close access to exotic animals that they normally would not encounter or get near to. As Ryan has argued, these institutions are diminishing the distance between the wild animal and the hunter-photographer.

One of our participants, an eight year old boy, talked about how while visiting Borås Zoo in western Sweden he was looking to photograph animals that were noteworthy in some way: by being big, scary, ugly, or cute. These characteristics made the animals interesting to him and something worth taking a photo of. In Figure 3, we see this boy doing a gesture of victory when he had managed to take a photo of a cheetah. While the photo he took (see Figure 4) is not of high quality from a standard viewpoint of photographic quality, for him it had value as something he had taken as part of his visit. This theme of ideas of quality which deviate from more traditional notions of photographic quality (such as sharpness, contrast and classical composition) also emerged in our interviews with Instagram users at a museum of natural history. Several participants discussed the importance of features such as a clever or funny caption when producing a photographic post for social media.

These findings imply that taking photos is not just about getting a high quality image in the traditional photographic sense. In fact, taking photographs and sharing some of them is part of the experience of visiting a cultural institution. With the advent of the camera came the opportunity to bring back personally captured photographic souvenirs from a visit to a museum or zoo. The internet-connected camera phone has added new opportunities by allowing visitors to edit and share their experiences in the moment, and allowing for instant feedback from friends and the wider social networking communities.

Creating collections

Much like the trophy hunters and taxidermists who helped fill the great halls of natural history museums, many social photography practitioners are also collectors of sorts. Their collection and re-curation activities depend on mobility within the museum space and build on the characteristics of camera phone hunting in a setting with mounted or captive animals that allow for unusually close viewings of exotic animals:

> Both animal photography and taxidermy depended upon a sense of physical closeness of human and animal, eroding the distance between the wild animal (and its habitat) and the hunter-photographer (and "his" homelands). Such spatial encounters were the very basis of the thrill for both the hunter-photographers and the viewers of their photographed and stuffed trophies. (Ryan, 2000: 218)

The creation of collections of social media posts, i.e. more than one from the same museum or zoo visit, is one way to tell a story. In our material from Gothenburg Natural History Museum, we have seen series of Instagrams ranging from two to seven posted by the same user. The corpus we worked with consisted of 344 Instagrams taken by 86 different users. Of these 86 social media users, 48% posted more than one Instagram from their visit to the museum. By creating collections, visitors to museums and zoos are taking the exhibits and rearranging them. In our work (Weilenmann, Hillman & Jungselius, 2013) we have examined how visitors work to post a series of Instagrams. Some visitors offered quite elaborate reasoning for how they chose to present their visits online. The first Instagram in a series of Instagrams often included what we called a cover page for the visit. In this way, the first Instagram set the scene for the story to be told in subsequent Instagrams. Many times these series included images that did not have a discernable theme visible to us as researchers, other than being images from the museum visit. One visitor could post a couple of images of animals in the exhibit and then add an image of their child having a snack in the museum café. Other times the Instagrams posted had a more easily discernable theme: one of our study participants put together a cabinet of curiosities, adding filters to give the images a particular look. Another put together a collection of feline specimens from around the museum. What was interesting here was that none of these collections consisted of objects or animals which were physically grouped together in exhibition spaces, but by placing them together in their own informal online galleries these users re-curated the museum collection and created their own.

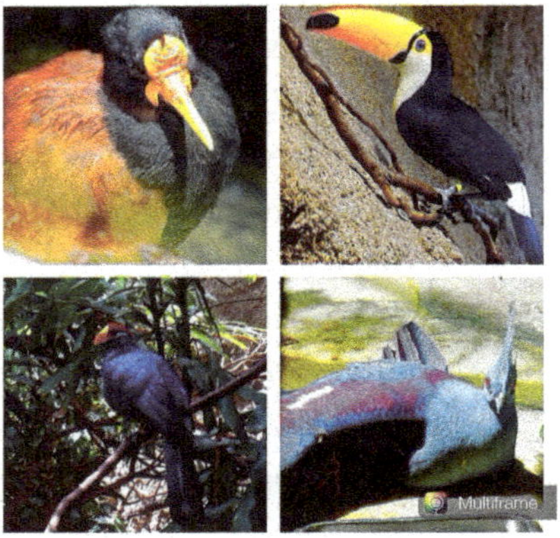

FIG. 5: Instagram collage taken at Barcelona Zoo, 22 May, 2015. Photograph: @clonvc.

When Instagram was originally released in 2010 there were no easily available applications which could edit several images into a single Instagram directly on a phone. In recent years, however, a number of such applications have appeared including PhotoGrid, InstaFrame and Multiframe. These applications allow a user to tell a story in just one Instagram instead of posting a series. In Figure 5, we see an example of one such collage created by a visitor to Barcelona Zoo.

A technical feature which adds to a visitor's ability to create collections is the hashtag function. By selecting one or several hashtags, social media users can direct their posts into certain streams or conversations. The participant who created a gallery of cats for example, added #cats to each of these Instagrams thereby making them part of a larger collection of images. Adding hashtags can be a technique for reaching an audience beyond one's own immediate followers and for attracting views, likes and new followers, but it comes with the risk of being unfollowed if hashtags are not used in a way seen as appropriate by the community (Jungselius, Hillman & Weilenmann, 2014).

Designing photographic opportunities

Cultural institutions design spaces to encourage photography in certain locations and discourage it in others. They attempt to enforce certain viewpoints and by doing so have a profound role in deciding what is photographed and how. Sometimes this is manifested as plainly as signs telling visitors what should and should not be photographed. At other times exhibitry such as life-size images which visitors can stand behind with their faces showing, or backdrops with costumes

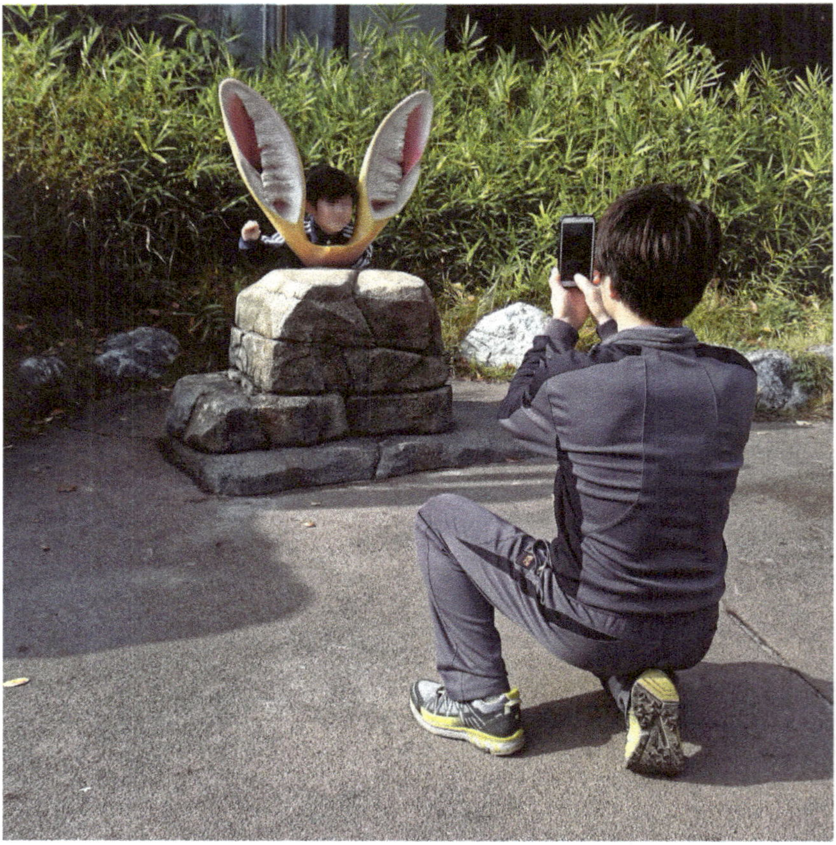

FIG. 6: A visitor poses with large animal ears at Seoul Zoo.
Photograph: Alexandra Weilenmann and Thomas Hillman.

for visitors to wear, provide clearly identified photographic opportunities (Figure 6).

More often than not, however, ideas of what parts of and how exhibitions should be captured are inscribed more subtly in the design of the spaces themselves. A simple example of this is the short barriers placed in front of the *Mona Lisa* at the Louvre. These direct the visitor not to touch the painting; but they are further away from the wall than arm's length would require and the *Mona Lisa* is displayed within a glass case. Very often, the barriers are supplemented by a temporary set even further from the painting. Both barriers create semicircular spaces in which visitors can stand, look and take that almost obligatory souvenir of the most famous work in the museum.

Another classic example is the viewing platform commonly found at zoos. In much the same way as the barriers at the Louvre, these bound the area from which to observe and photograph – but since the exhibits in zoos are live animals, creating photographic opportunities requires that both animals and visitors are encouraged to visit specific locations. Viewing platforms are often designed to work in concert with locations of enrichment activities for the animals, and are placed to offer reasonable viewing opportunities to large groups of visitors while also taking into account factors such as the size of the animals. Platforms for viewing large animals, for example, are often set back from the enclosure so that a whole animal can easily be framed within a photograph.

While cultural institutions provide photographic opportunities through the design of their spaces that often encourage a relatively limited range of photographic locations, all photographs taken of a particular exhibit are not the same. In fact,

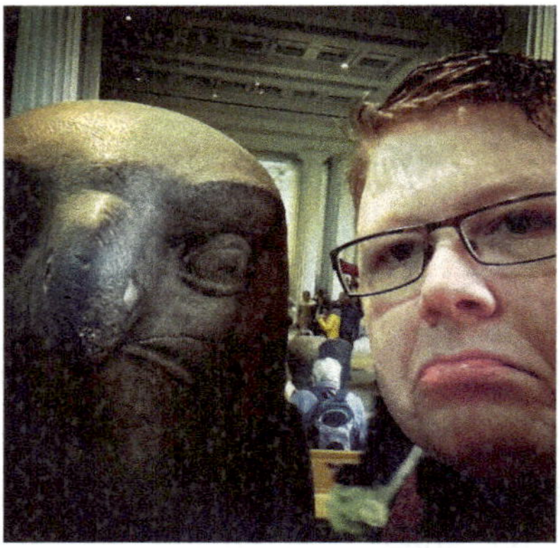

FIG. 7: Performing with an exhibit at the British Museum, 7 February 2015.
Photograph: @jbowleresquire.

our work has shown distinct variations in both the exhibits chosen for photography and the treatment of those exhibits.

In interviews, visitors have talked about their desire to deviate from a perceived "standard" image and to avoid taking the same photograph as everybody else. With mobile access to social media and immediate sharing of photographs online, visitors can easily view the images taken of a particular exhibit before taking their own and often orient to an audience which gives praise (in the form of likes and follows) for unusual or remarkable photographs (Jungselius, Hillman & Weilenmann, 2014). In many cases where an exhibit is particularly popular and the places it can be photographed from are limited, creating a unique photograph is no easy task and visitors put significant effort into taking them. This requires not only working within the constraints of the exhibition space, but also judging the uniqueness of an image in comparison with the many other images of the same subject already posted on social media.

Placing yourself in the exhibit

We have discussed how museums and zoos create photographic opportunities, encouraging visitors to take certain types of images in certain locations. Related to this practice is another type of behavior we have observed. In both zoos and natural history museums, it is popular to take pictures of your co-visitors or yourself with the animals displayed also featuring in the image. This type of photograph effectively places a person in a specific location. Here will focus on two such types of images.

The first is when visitors play with anthropomorphic elements and ascribe to animals human characteristics,

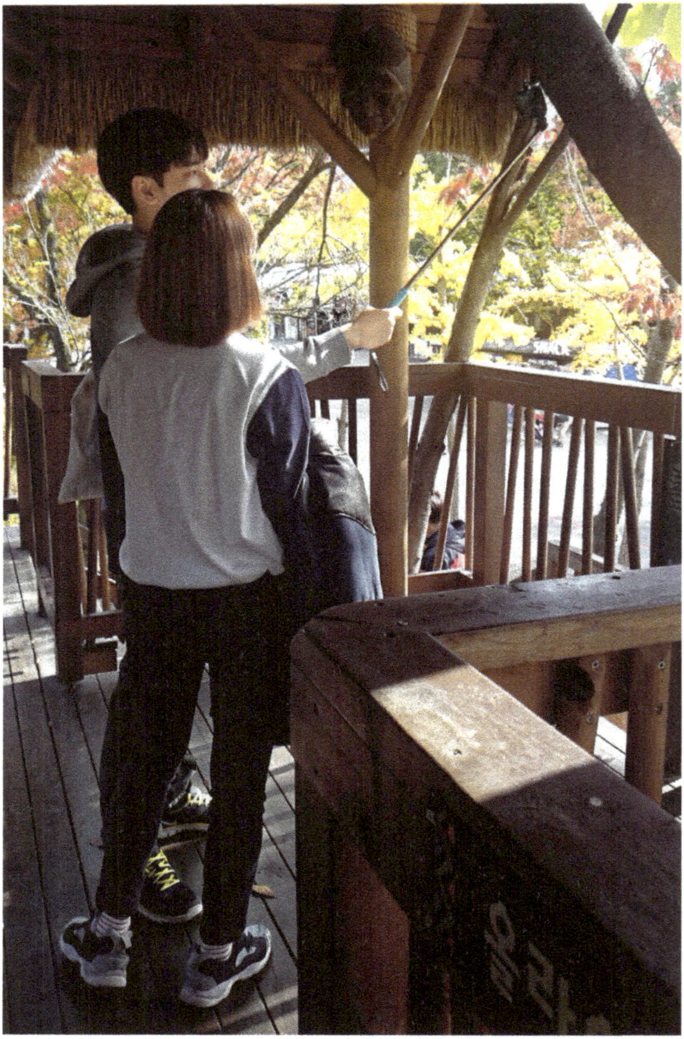

FIG. 8: Seoul Zoo visitors use a selfie-stick. Photograph: Alexandra Weilenmann and Thomas Hillman.

sometimes staging activities in which the animals play a part. It is quite common to stand close to an animal and mimic its face (Figure 7).

This type of photography draws on resemblances between humans and animals in a way that is also seen in so-called anthropomorphic taxidermy (Poliquin, 2012). In the natural history museum that we studied, the taxidermy is not designed to emphasize human characteristics in any way, but visitors still perform with the animal to add or emphasize such features.

Selfies form another somewhat overlapping category of images in which the visitor places herself in the picture. Selfies taken within cultural institutions often include parts of the exhibit. On Instagram (and on Twitter) hashtags such as #museumselfie, #zooselfie, #artselfie, or #galleryselfie are used for images that place oneself in a certain space. Thousands of visitors all over the world have used these tags particularly in relation to museum selfie day, held on January 21st each year (see Dixon in this volume).

At Seoul Zoo the practice of selfie-taking was particularly noticeable. While we do not want to make any generalizable claims about cultural differences, since more data is required to make such claims, we did observe many more visitors taking selfies in the Korean zoo than we have observed in European and North American zoos. There might be several explanations for this that are not necessarily related to differences between populations. One is that our fieldwork in Seoul was the most recent undertaken, and photographic practices and social media behavior can change rapidly. Related to this is the use of the so-called selfie-stick which has become particularly popular in Asia (Figure 8). Examining how visitors draw on their environment when documenting their experiences needs more study, and the selfie phenomenon is an area where we need more ethnographic fieldwork to fully understand what visitors are doing and how they are using this genre to communicate their experiences.

Conclusions

In this chapter, we have offered several examples of the types of social media souvenirs visitors collect and share as part of their visits to cultural institutions. Our findings suggest that alongside the museums' own curatorial processes we see another trend, in which visitors are increasingly re-categorizing and re-configuring the exhibitions in their presentations on social media. We have approached this phenomenon by adapting existing techniques for studying social media use as a located practice, including both analyses of online activities as well as visitors' local behavior and interaction.

Our findings have a number of implications for how we think about visitor-driven technology use in cultural institutions. Today, it is possible for visitors to communicate their experiences using mobile technology in a variety of ways, something that affects and extends the scope of the institution beyond its physical location. Emerging technologies will continue to enhance the promise of the participatory museum to a greater extent than has been possible before. Portable devices such as wearables and objects connected to the internet-of-things will increasingly create opportunities for linking visitors' technology with content in exhibitions. These technologies will also create opportunities for visitors to remodel and reorganize exhibition content regardless of whether the institution endorses or encourages this or not. This development enables a form of cross-boundary dialogue between cultural institutions and other environments. As this trend continues, we must find new ways to identify and address issues that arise when visitors bring their own technologies into exhibition environments, and vice versa, when cultural institutions can be moved out to new places and contexts. Especially in relation to photography and video, recent technological developments mean that visitors are given powerful new tools to communicate and engage with exhibitions in new ways, creating new opportunities for enjoyment, experience and learning. As digital, mobile technology becomes more powerful, these opportunities for the creation of social media souvenirs are likely to increase.

REFERENCES

Chalfen, R. (1987). *Snapshot versions of life*. Bowling Green: Popular Press.

Hillman, T., & Weilenmann, A. (2015). Situated social media use: a methodological approach to locating social media practices and trajectories. *Proceedings of the SIGCHI conference on human factors in computing systems*, Seoul: ACM Press.

Hillman, T., Weilenmann, A., & Jungselius, B. (2012). Creating live experiences with real and stuffed animals: the use of mobile technologies in museums. In *Proceedings of The Transformative Museum*. Roskilde: DREAM.

Hine, C. (2000). *Virtual ethnography. The Sage handbook of research methods. London: Sage Publications.*

Hogan, B. (2010). The presentation of self in the age of social media: distinguishing performances and exhibitions online. *Bulletin of Science, Technology & Society*, 30(6).

Jungselius, B., Hillman, T & Weilenmann, A. (2014). Fishing for followers: using hashtags as like bait in social media use. *Proceedings of the 15th conference of the Association of Internet Researchers*. Daegu, South Korea.

Leander, K. M. & McKim, K. K. (2003). Tracing the everyday "sitings" of adolescents on the internet: a strategic adaptation of ethnography across online and offline spaces. *Education, Communication & Information*, 3, 211–240.

Okabe, D. (2004). Emergent social practices, situations and relations through everyday camera phone use. In *The proceedings of the International Conference on Mobile Communication and Social Change*. Seoul.

Poliquin, R. (2012). *The breathless zoo: taxidermy and the culture of longing*. University Park: Pennsylvania State University Press.

Ryan, J. R. (2000). Hunting with the camera: photography, wildlife and colonialism in Africa. In Philo, C. & Wibert, C. (eds.), *Animal spaces, beastly places: new geographies of human-animal relations*. London: Routledge.

Weilenmann, A., Hillman, T., & Jungselius, B. (2013). Instagram at the museum: communicating the museum experience through social photo sharing. In *Proceedings of the SIGCHI Conference on Human Factors in Computing Systems*. Paris: ACM Press.

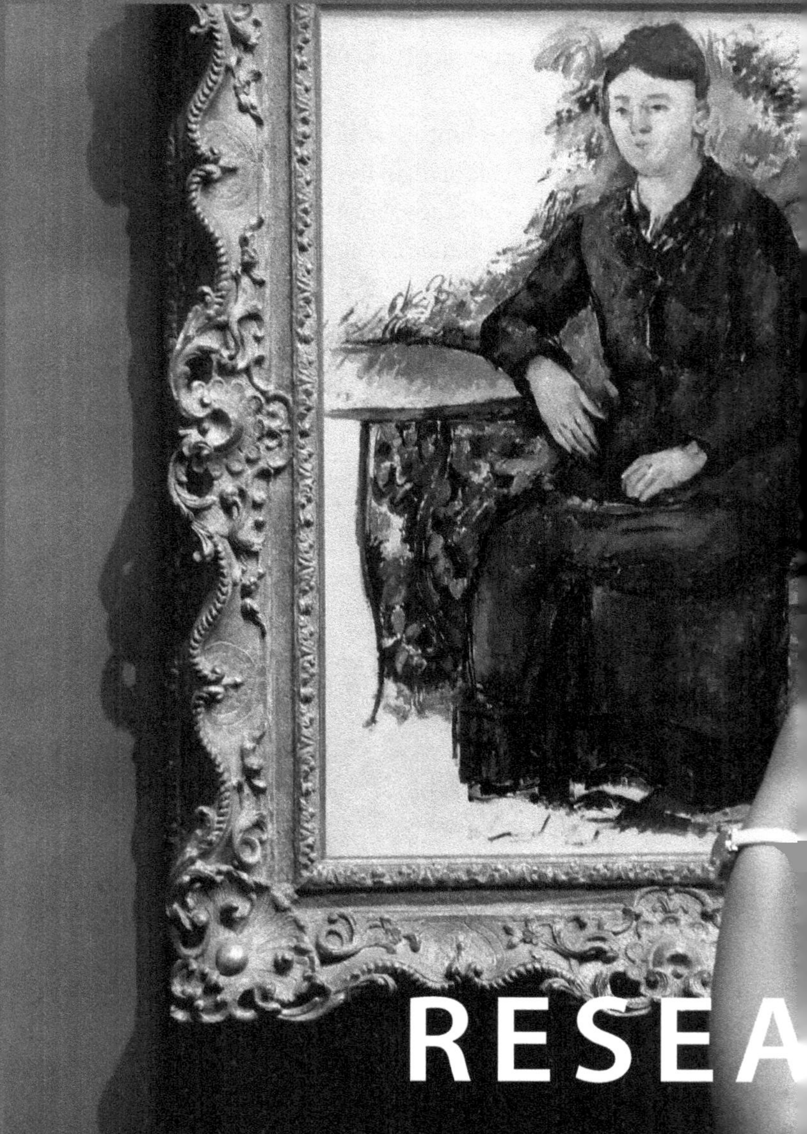

RESEA

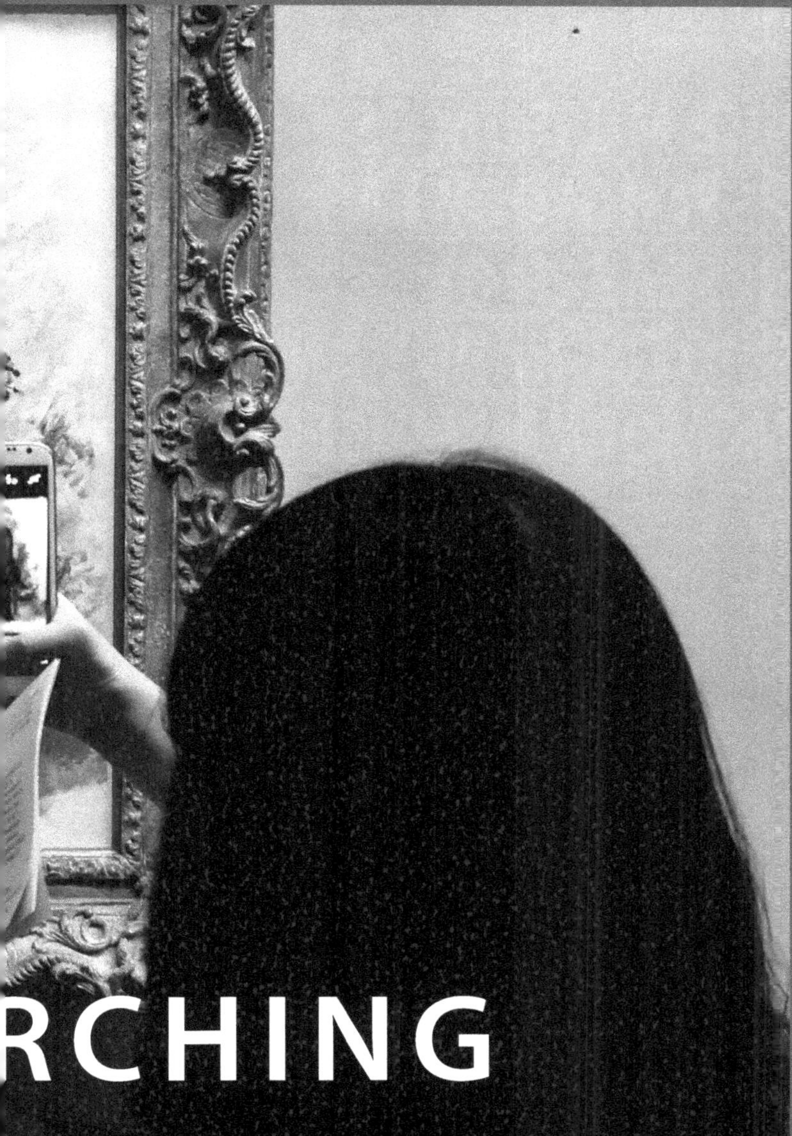
RCHING

CHAPTER SIX

THE MUSEUM AS PSYCHOLOGY LAB: RESEARCH ON PHOTOGRAPHY AND MEMORY IN MUSEUMS

Linda A Henkel, Katelyn Parisi and Carey Mack Weber

MUSEUMS SERVE MANY different functions to individuals and to society. They display and preserve the collections entrusted to their care and are involved in many educational programs and partnerships with the community. One often overlooked and underused function for museums is as a site for conducting psychology research studies. They provide a unique setting for psychological scientists to explore people's memory in a naturally engaging and rich environment, and for studying memory processes in a wider cross-section of the population than the "convenience samples" of undergraduates used in many studies conducted in the traditional laboratory setting. Field settings such as museums are especially appealing to researchers because although there is great value and much has been learned about people's memory in carefully controlled laboratory settings over the past century (see Banaji & Crowder, 1989), our understanding of memory and cognition is incomplete without studying the practical issues and problems of memory in everyday life in their natural settings (Neisser, 1978). Over the past several years, a small but growing number of studies has explored how museum visitors' memory for their experiences in the museum are influenced by taking and later reviewing photos of these experiences. In this chapter, such studies are discussed in the context of other work on why people take photos, how it affects their memories, and research on memory for museum visits in general.

How many photos are we taking and why do we take them?

The first photograph was taken less than 200 years ago in 1826; the first documented photo with a person in the shot was in 1838. By 1930, approximately a billion photos were taken each year worldwide, and the numbers increased steadily over the next 60 years. But that growth is dwarfed by the explosion of photographs taken with the advent of digital photography and then camera phones (Good, 2014). It is estimated that people took 86 billion photos worldwide in 2000, 300 billion in 2010, and 880 billion in 2014 (Good, 2014). Changes in technology have enabled people to have cameras readily available throughout their daily lives, and there is minimal cost to taking photos.

The use of photography in museums has grown over the years. Museums have differing policies on the use of photography on their premises, with some allowing it and others forbidding it. A prime reason for not allowing photography is that the low lighting found in many museums requires the use of a flash or a tripod. The flash could potentially damage fragile works, and tripods are a hazard for people walking through crowded or tight areas (Bielstein, 2010). However, the development of digital cameras and smart phones which can produce quality photographs in dim lighting without the use of flash has made photo taking during museum visits much more common. This has given rise to incidents of "camera rage" – tensions between the people looking at the displays and those preoccupied with photographing the displays and themselves, prompting *The Van Gogh Museum* in Amsterdam to reintroduce its ban on personal photography after a short trial period in which they allowed it (Bailey, 2014).

Although no studies have focused specifically on the reasons for taking photos in museums, people do report that the main reason they take photos and videos in everyday life is to help them remember events in their lives (Chalfen, 1998; Harrison, 2002; Shutterfly, 2014). And research has confirmed that looking at photos provides valuable retrieval cues which help people reactivate and remember their experiences (Berry et al., 2007; Deocampo & Hudson, 2003; Finley, Brewer, & Benjamin, 2011; Hodges, Berry, & Wood, 2011; Hudson & Fivush, 1991; Loveday & Conway, 2011; Milton et al., 2011; St. Jacques & Schacter, 2013; Galluccio, 1999; Koutstaal, et al., 1997, 1998; Schacter, et al., 1997).

What do people remember about their museum visits?

Several studies have examined what people remember about their museum visits. Although these studies do not specifically examine the use of photography, they are briefly discussed here because they raise important issues about the museum as a psychology lab. The studies are often conducted by psychological scientists affiliated with a university, and although the studies are conducted at a museum, the focus is not on understanding the museum experience in itself. Instead, the focus is on answering research questions about psychological issues such as how parent-child conversations facilitate children's learning and memory (Benjamin, Haden, & Wilkerson, 2010; Jant, et al., 2014; Tare, et al., 2011; Tessler & Nelson, 1994). One study examined whether memory and cognition of older adults with dementia can be improved by immersion in a historically authentic environment laden with artifacts and furnishings from their childhood and early adulthood years (Miles, et al., 2013). Another study examined the role of emotions and interpretation when people reconstruct their memories to create coherence and meaning (Medved, Cupchik, & Oatley, 2004).

Some studies conducted in museums do so as a means to obtain a larger sample size and broader age range and backgrounds than are easily obtainable in laboratory-based studies, and this was the motivation for using a museum to study individual differences in eyewitness memory (Loftus, Levidow, & Duensing, 1992). Although the purpose of such research is on testing hypotheses and developing theoretical models about memory over the lifespan, the museum is more than just a convenient location that happens to have rich, engaging, and plentiful stimuli and a wide range of people. Such work allows researchers to study memory in ways that are difficult to capture in the traditional laboratory setting, such as by observing spontaneous, naturally occurring family conversations, and so greatly contributes to our understanding of learning and memory (Callanan, 2012; Haden, 2010; Winerman, 2014).

A small body of work has focused directly on the museum setting itself, and what people's recollections of visits are like. Interviews with adults and children about their recollections of visits showed that people remember social aspects, such as who they were with; affective responses, such as their emotional reactions overall and to specific elements; and some details about the exhibits and artwork they viewed and the physical characteristics of the museum, such as its appearance and layout (Falk & Dierking, 1995; Wolins, Jensen, & Ulzheimer, 1992). When children wrote reflective journals after a visit to a historic house as part of a school trip, they frequently recalled information about the time period (such as the use of outhouses and chamber pots) and about the family who had lived in the house (Leach, 2011). The majority of children remembered various hands-on activities such as making a toy, or touching and playing with historic objects, and remembered their emotional responses to the site visit.

In fact, in one of the studies on children's memory for museum visits, the authors recommended encouraging school teachers "to bring a camera to create a visual record of the children engaged in the experience" (Wolins, Jensen, & Ulzheimer, 1992: 26). How might photographing what one encounters in a museum impact what one subsequently remembers? Does taking and later reviewing photos help memory, hurt memory, or have no influence on memory?

Is memory influenced by taking and reviewing photographs of a museum visit?

A small but growing body of psychology studies has examined people's memory of museum visits in relation to photos taken during the visit. Pathman examined developmental differences in two related but different aspects of memory known as episodic memory and autobiographical memory (Pathman, et al., 2011). They note that making direct comparisons between these two memory processes is difficult because of methodological differences in how they are typically studied, and that a museum setting allows control over some of the important variables necessary for meaningful comparison. They recruited 17 young children aged 7-9, 18 older children aged 9-11, and 20 young adults aged 18-27, and each individual took a tour of the Fernbank Museum of Natural History in Atlanta, Georgia. Some participants were asked to use a digital camera to photograph 30 objects or exhibits that the experimenter specified, with five photographs in each of six categories: fish/shells, dinosaurs/fossils, contemporary animals, characters, signs, and architectural features. Other participants were asked to photograph 30 objects or exhibits of their own choosing, from the same categories. After the tour, participants went to a quiet area in the museum and viewed 60 photographs of objects and museum exhibits that were not part of the tour and therefore were not taken by them. For both the photo-taking and photo-viewing task, they were told explicitly to pay attention to the objects and photos because their memory would later be tested. One or two days later, they were shown the 60 photos they took, the 60 photos they looked at, and 60 new photos, and had to indicate which ones they remembered taking, which ones they remembered viewing on the computer, and which were new. Results showed that all three age groups (young children, older children, and young adults) remembered more of the photos that they took than the photos they just looked at, though the relative differences between each age group varied depending on the type of memory task. These differences allowed the researchers to draw conclusions about the developmental trajectory of these different types of memory processes and which develops earlier, noting that autobiographical memory appears to develop earlier than episodic memory and suggesting that typical laboratory-based episodic memory tasks may underestimate children's memory abilities.

Another study examined children's memory of a visit to an archaeology museum on a class trip on which the researcher accompanied them and took photos of the different activities they engaged in: walking to and from the museum, climbing the museum steps, listening to the museum guide, digging for artifacts in the sandbox, and making clay models (Fivush, Hudson, & Nelson, 1984). The children were kindergarteners who were led on a guided tour of the museum, with several hands-on activities (such as digging for artifacts in a sandbox, or making clay models of the artifacts). They were interviewed to see what they remembered about the trip immediately after returning to the school that day, six weeks later, and then again one year later. The study focused on the children's general knowledge about events and their detailed personal memories (autobiographical memories) and how the two interact over time. After the interviews at six weeks and one year, the children viewed the photos and were asked if they remembered what was happening in each photograph and then had to place the photos in the order in which the events occurred. Six weeks after the museum visit, on average the children recognized 5.6 of them out of the six photographs, and the majority were able to correctly arrange all the photos in the correct temporal order. One year after the museum visit, children still recognized almost all of the photos (M=5.3) and were able to correctly order the photos as well as they did at the six-week interval. In a follow-up study with the same children six years later, they were asked about what they remembered and then shown the photos and were encouraged to recall additional information cued by the photos (Hudson & Fivush, 1991). Results showed that children required more specific verbal cues at the six-year interval to recall the event, and the amount of information recalled declined over time. Nonetheless, at all three time intervals when photos were shown (six weeks later, one year later, six years later), the photos triggered a fair amount of what was recalled, with 39% of the information recalled at six weeks being in response to the photos, 27% of information recalled at one year, and 37% of information recalled at six years. Thus when given these "highly specific cues" of photos

(Salmon, 2001: 354), children were able to recall as much about the event six years later as they were able to recall six weeks after the event. These findings are consistent with work in other settings showing the power of photographs and other visual props in getting an accurate understanding of young children's memory abilities (Salmon, 2001).

Other work has looked at the impact of taking photos on people's subsequent memory of their experiences in a museum by asking whether they better remembered art objects they photographed compared to art objects they merely looked at (Henkel, 2014). Taking photos could conceivably boost later retention by focusing the person's attention on the scene, but it could also harm later memory by distracting the person and focusing their attention on the camera instead of the scene being photographed. Numerous studies have attested to the detrimental impact of divided attention on memory caused by multitasking with cellphones or laptops while interacting with the environment (Hyman, et al., 2010; Fried, 2008; Hembrooke & Gay, 2003; Smith, et al., 2011). In addition, people may pay less attention to a scene when they take photos because they are mentally counting on the camera to remember for them. Past work has shown, for example, that when people rely on external storage devices such as a computer, or expect to have future access to information via the internet, they actually remember less (Sparrow, Liu, & Wegner, 2011).

To examine this, 27 college students visited 30 art objects at the Bellarmine Museum of Art in Fairfield, CT (Henkel, 2014). They were given a list of the objects (such as sculptures, paintings, pottery, jewelry) to read aloud and were brought to each object by the experimenter. They viewed each object for 20 seconds and then were told either to take a photo of the object or to continue viewing the object. They took the photo with a digital camera which allowed them to see what they were photographing on the rear screen of the camera. Ten additional seconds were allotted to take the photo or continue looking at the object, before the next object on the tour was visited. The next day, they went to the research lab on campus and were given a memory test consisting of the names of the art objects from the museum tour randomly intermixed with names of new items, and they had to judge which ones they encountered on the tour. For ones they remembered, they were asked about a visual detail of that object and given four multiple choice options (What did the Tang Dynasty warrior have in his hands? A shield, a spear, his helmet, nothing). They also did a second recognition test in which the photos were shown with the names of the objects and they had to remember which had been on the tour and which were new.

Results showed a photo-taking impairment effect: people remembered fewer objects and remembered fewer details about the objects when they had photographed them than when they had just looked at them on the tour. Recognition accuracy increased when photos were given as cues on the memory test, but even so, there was no memory advantage for photographed objects and, in fact, taking photos hurt memory rather than enhanced it.

These findings suggest that people's reliance on a camera to remember for them can lead to impairments in memory and, as noted, this is consistent with other work showing that outsourcing memories to external storage devices such as computers or the internet can have detrimental effects

(Sparrow, Lin, & Wegner, 2011). However, it is important to note that there are inherent trade-offs between internal and external memory storage (Schonpflug, 1986, 1988) and that externalizing memory is not new to the digital age and has concerned people for centuries (Nestojko, Finley, & Roediger, 2013). In a recent study comparing these trade-offs and potential adaptive functions to the costs incurred by offloading memory onto technology, participants studied the contents of a computer file containing word lists, not knowing if they would be asked to save the file or not (Storm & Stone, 2015). Results showed that saving one computer file before studying a new file increased memory for the new file. This "saving-enhanced memory" did not occur if the saving process was viewed as unreliable though, which suggests that people can strategically offload memory onto external storage devices so that they can move on from the no-longer-needed information and more efficiently focus their attention and cognitive processing on newer information.

Furthermore, it is not always the case that taking photos in museums has detrimental effects on memory. Henkel (2014) also examined whether focusing attention on the art object by zooming in with the digital camera on one part might have a different impact than just lining up the shot and taking the photo. A total of 46 undergraduates visited various art objects, some of which they looked at and then photographed as a whole, some of which they looked at and then zoomed in on a specified part (such as the feet of the statue, or the basket on the street in a painting), and some of which they just observed without taking a photo. The next day, they had to remember the objects visited on the museum tour, answer questions about visual details of the objects (including features that were zoomed in on and features that were not zoomed in on), and indicate on a map which rooms the object had been located in.

The results replicated the photo-taking impairment effect when comparing objects that were photographed as a whole versus those that were just looked at but not photographed: people remembered fewer objects and remembered fewer details about the objects, and they also remembered fewer of the objects' locations. But, interestingly, when people zoomed in on a specific part of an art object, subsequent recognition and detail memory accuracy was not impaired relative to just looking at the object. Furthermore, zooming in on one aspect of an object served not only to protect memory for the part that was zoomed in on, but also for the part that was not zoomed in on. This highlights key differences between what cameras can do and what the human brain is capable of. The camera captures an image of what is in front of it; a person can be looking at one part of an object and perceptually registering that in their brain, but their brain is simultaneously processing information about the object as a whole, creating a mental representation for the entirety rather than just for the part that they captured with the camera. This finding is consistent with research on what is known as "boundary extension", where people observing a scene activate and remember the larger context of the scene (Hubbard, Hutchinson, & Courtney, 2010; Intraub, Bender, & Mangels, 1992), and it shows that it is not always the case that we offload our memories onto our cameras and forget about them – the type of attention and the mental representations we create while photographing objects in different ways appears to matter.

The two studies in Henkel (2014) had people take photographs while on a tour of a museum but did not give them the opportunity to later review those photos prior to having their memory tested. This was done purposefully to model the increasingly familiar everyday life situation of people taking a large number of photos but not spending time to look at them afterwards. People report being overwhelmed by the amount of digital photos they have amassed and the daunting task of organizing them, and this discourages many people from reviewing and reminiscing about their photos (Bowen & Petrelli, 2011; Nunes, Greenberg, & Neustaedter, 2009; Shutterfly, 2014).

A series of studies by St. Jacques and colleagues addressed the impact of reviewing rather than taking photos on people's subsequent memory (St. Jacques, Montgomery, & Schacter, 2015; St. Jacques, Olm, & Schacter, 2013; St. Jacques & Schacter, 2013). As in the other psychology studies of photos and memory in museums, the primary purpose of the research was testing hypotheses and theories about memory and cognition, with the museum serving as a natural laboratory in which participants could encounter rich stimuli and have meaningful everyday life experiences. A major goal of this line of research was to explore the adaptive memory processes by which people update their memories by activating and strengthening existing memory representations while incorporating new information and experiences, and how this can contribute to both accurate memories as well as memory distortions. For example, in two studies, 83 people took a self-guided tour at the Harvard Natural History Museum and Peabody Museum of Archeology in Boston, MA while wearing a camera on a strap around their necks which automatically took photos every fifteen seconds (St. Jacques & Schacter, 2013). The use of such a camera meant that individuals were not dividing their attention between the camera and the exhibits they visited. Two days later, they viewed photos of scenes from their museum tour intermixed with photos from a tour that they had not been on. The researchers manipulated various aspects of the content of these photos (the temporal order, the angle or perspective in the photo). Two days after reviewing the photos, participants took a final memory test in which they judged which photos had been part of the museum tour. Many aspects of the data presented in the research report are beyond the scope of the present chapter, but key findings showed that reviewing photos taken during one's visit to a museum provides strong retrieval cues which enable people to reactivate and subsequently better remember their experiences there, with a greater sense of reliving the experience when viewing photos which matched their experience.

An additional study examined the neural mechanisms involved when people update their memories while reactivating prior experiences through remembering and how this contributes to both true and false memories (St. Jacques, Olm, & Schacter, 2013). Thirty-five people took a self-guided audio tour of the museum wearing a camera which automatically took photos at fixed intervals. The tour took around four or five hours. Two days later, each participant's brain activity was assessed while they looked at and rated photos of the museum tour in an MRI scanner. Two days after that, they took a final memory test in which they viewed photos from the museum tour intermixed with photos of events that were not part of the tour and they had to indicate if the photos showed a stop on their personal tour or not. Again, although numerous aspects of the data fall beyond the scope of this chapter, results nonetheless did show that reactivation by reviewing photos benefitted subsequent memory accuracy for the events that were actually experienced. The stronger people rated their subjective sense of reliving the experience when viewing photos, the stronger the improvement in memory retention was.

The most recent study in this series made comparisons between young and older adults and examined how their memories were shaped by having earlier reactivated their experiences by viewing photos of their museum tour (St. Jacques, Montgomery, & Schacter, 2015). As in the prior studies, reactivating memories by reviewing photos of the museum tour led to higher rates of correctly remembering the experiences later. Older adults showed benefits from photo review as did young adults for correctly remembered museum events but the memory boost for older adults was smaller.

A recent study also looked at how reviewing photos of a museum visit can impact subsequent memory, but did so with an interesting twist (Parisi & Henkel, 2015). Given the widespread use of selfies, this study examined how different types of photos which museum visitors take (ones which focus on the work of art, or ones which show the person in the photo next to the work of art) can influence objective (factual) elements of people's memories as well as subjective elements (the quality and how the memory feels). Can seeing oneself in photos shape the perspective from which people re-experience the events while remembering? Can it influence other phenomenological qualities of the memories or memory for factual details? To answer this, 32 undergraduates took a tour of Fairfield University's Bellarmine Museum of Art and observed various works of art in three different exhibits as the experimenter/tour guide told them factual details about the exhibits and the works of arts they looked at (paintings, sculptures, and pottery). In one exhibit, the guide took photos of the objects with the participant standing next to the object. In another exhibit, the guide took photos of just the objects, without the participant in the photos, and in the remaining exhibit no photos were taken at all. Three days later, participants went to the psychology lab on campus and were asked to think about and remember their experiences in the different exhibits while either viewing the photos which were taken in that exhibit or reviewing just the names of the art objects. One week later, participants returned to the lab for a third and final session at which time they answered questions to assess their memory about which objects had been visited on the museum tour, visual and factual details about the objects and exhibits, as well as the phenomenological qualities of their memories (How vivid is your memory? How much visual detail do you remember? How clearly do you remember the spatial layout of the exhibit? How strong and what types of emotions and feelings do you remember experiencing at the exhibit?). A key focus of interest was the perspective of their recollection – did they remember the exhibit as if they were seeing it through their own eyes (known as a field perspective) or more as if they were an observer watching themselves with them in the scene (known as an observer perspective) – and whether this was influenced by the type of photos which were taken and reviewed?

Results showed that reviewing photos of an exhibit

enhanced people's ability to later correctly remember details about the objects they had seen in that exhibit relative to when photos were not reviewed. The type of photos reviewed – whether the person was in the photo next to the art object or the photos showed just the art object – did not impact memory accuracy, however: people's memory was boosted just by seeing photos of their experiences, regardless of whether they were in the photos or not. For the objects which were in an exhibit where photos were taken, memory for details was improved only for the specific objects of which photos were taken and reviewed, but not for the objects in that exhibit that were looked at and not photographed or reviewed. Thus whereas prior work showed that just taking photos – but not reviewing them – impaired subsequent memory (Henkel, 2014), this study showed the selective benefits that come from reviewing photos of one's experience on later memory.

In addition, having reviewed photos of a given exhibit influenced the perspective of people's memory for that exhibit. Regardless of whether the photos showed the person in them next to the object or just showed the object, after having reviewed photos compared to having not reviewed photos people had more of an observer perspective in their memories in which they felt they were seeing the exhibit with them in the scene.

Research summary

Taken together, this growing body of studies shows that people's memory for museum exhibits can be influenced by whether or not they took photos of the exhibits and whether or not they reviewed those photos. Taking photos can impair memory, but reviewing the photos helps. The type of photos taken (photo of the whole object vs. photo zooming in on a specified part) influences what is subsequently remembered, though so far evidence suggests that memory is not impacted by whether the person was in the photo or not. These findings have practical value when considering the use of photography in museums. While it may be distracting to other patrons, it does potentially serve valuable functions for the individuals taking the photos, at least if done in ways that are not counter-productive. People's awareness of such findings may encourage more effective photo taking strategies.

A host of other findings important for psychological theory were obtained in the various studies as well, addressing issues such as developmental differences in memory processes across the lifespan, and cognitive and neural mechanisms of memory updating. For example, photos appear to be valuable retrieval cues for young children, whose memories of their museum visits might otherwise be relatively impoverished. Museums as an extension of traditional research labs allow memory researchers to deal with the complexities of memory in everyday settings that are rich, detailed, meaningful, and emotionally evocative, and in doing so allow for greater ecological validity. Museums allow researchers to test theories that would be difficult to test in traditional lab settings, and so make major contributions to psychology's understanding of memory and cognition. In addition, they can provide access to broader representations of the population, which increases the generalizability of the research findings.

Some advice on conducting museum-based research

Some museums have long-standing partnerships with outside

researchers, such as the Boston Museum of Science, which even created a lab space on its premises, with an "explicit focus on research participation as an opportunity visitors can choose as part of their museum experience" (Callanan, 2012: 144). The Living Laboratory Initiative began there in 2005 and now has sixteen sites around the country (Winerman, 2014). Much can be learned from these well-developed partnerships, and we refer interested readers to Callanan's discussion where she emphasizes the importance of researchers finding overlapping goals with museums, getting to know these organizations, and giving something back.

The research described here on photos and memory for museum visits seems to have stemmed from new collaborations between researchers and museums. These studies were conducted by cognitive and developmental psychologists, and the main goal was addressing research questions whose answers make clear contributions to psychological science and its understanding of memory processes. This might sound like a very one-sided relationship, but there are many benefits to scientists, museums, and the public at large when museums open their doors to outside researchers. For instance, Callanan notes that research conducted in museums has actively engaged people of all ages who might not otherwise participate in and learn about scientific research; that museums provide unique training opportunities for students interested in science and education; and that museums get benefits such as publicity and an increased air of credibility afforded by association with institutes of higher education and occasionally funds from researchers using space in their facilities when they are large-scale projects funded by external grants.

Museum professionals interested in drawing on research findings to inform their policies on taking photos should consider the following issues. The research presented in this chapter shows ways in which photos can both help and hurt people's memories, and these findings may be especially important when considering educational programs in museums such as those designed to help children learn. For example, viewing and discussing the photos at the end of the museum visit may help strengthen their memories. Museum visitors may not realize how their memories are impaired by taking photos when they do not spend time to review those photos. When people outsource their memory to the external storage of a camera, expecting the camera in essence to remember for them, this can be counterproductive. Instead of experiencing the work of art in front of them, they are dividing their attention by documenting what they are seeing and potentially having a less rich experience as a consequence. Furthermore, they do not engage in the kind of additional mental processing that would benefit later memory, such as noticing the use of shadow and light in a painting and commenting to a companion about it, thinking about their reaction to the solemn expression on the face of a statue, or relating what they see to other experiences by noting how an artist's skills changed during different periods. While museum visitors no doubt have the best of intentions of looking at their photos later, the volume of photos people take overwhelms their willingness to organize and review them. As with children, encouraging people to review and organize their photos at the end of their visit might help.

The research reviewed here has shown that photos of

museum visits serve as valuable retrieval cues for later memory when people take the time to look at them. In fact, reviewing photos creates a stronger sense of reliving the experience. Psychologists have long since shown that people's memories for photos they have seen are remarkably accurate and long-lasting (Shepard, 1967). Museum professionals might wonder if those same benefits of looking at photos after an experience can be achieved by having museum visitors look at commercial products, such as postcards, books or catalogues. After all, these illustrations will have the benefit of professional lighting and angles, without the backs of other people's heads in the shot. However, people may prefer a photo which is more personal, one which they took themselves or one with them in it. This notion is consistent with psychological research on the "endowment effect", which shows that people tend to overvalue objects which they own and which they perceive as being theirs, due in part to associations between the object and the self (Dommer & Swaminathan, 2012). The subjective feeling of ownership is more important in creating this inflation of value than physical possession (Reb & Connolly, 2007), and this may make photos which one has taken – especially photos that one was in – seem more valuable to the museum visitor than photos in commercial products. Furthermore, the research reviewed in this chapter shows that people better remember photos which they took themselves rather than photos they just looked at.

Might museums encourage photography in situations in which it is less obtrusive? One of the studies described earlier used a wearable camera to take photos at random or timed intervals. The photos are not as good as when the user has control over lighting and angle, and people do not get to choose which objects are photographed or not. And, of course, a wearable camera would make taking selfies difficult. Nonetheless, the trade-off gained by being able to fully concentrate on the museum experience without being distracted by a camera may be worthwhile for some people. While the cost of some wearable systems is expensive for individuals, museums might consider loaning or renting them to visitors and providing a web address for them to access the photos later.

People take photos for many different reasons. A key reason for teenagers and young adults taking photos is to communicate what they are doing via social media, and this sharing serves to maintain social relations (Hunt, Lin, & Atkin, 2014). So saying "Hey look at me in front of the *Mona Lisa*!" may be more important to some people than saying "I am really impressed with the rich texture and blending of colors in the *Mona Lisa*." Opportunities staged to enhance such shots at select places in the museum might satisfy this desire and might successfully confine such activities to an area where they will be less disruptive to fellow museum visitors.

It might also be worthwhile identifying the different functions which photography plays in different types of museums. People may take different kinds of photos in science museums than in art museums, for example, and knowing what visitors' goals are will help researchers design studies to determine if those goals are being met.

Clearly, more research is needed to understand what functions the taking of photos in museums serves and how best to balance individual wishes with the safety, enjoyment, and education of other patrons (while protecting the objects).

However, museum professionals may have some concerns when researchers approach them about conducting studies at their facilities, such as disruption to visitors, issues of privacy, undue responsibility placed on their own staff, or risks to the museum visitors. Psychology studies conducted on human subjects by university researchers must undergo review by their organization's Institutional Review Board (IRB). IRBs review proposed studies to assess the risks and benefits to participants and ensure that participation is voluntary and informed consent obtained. This process ensures that participants are treated ethically and not exposed to unnecessary risk without their awareness or willingness to participate. Additional safeguards are in place when research participants are minors.

We recommend that museum staff have a contact person available with whom researchers can discuss practical issues ahead of time. What times are optimal for conducting the study, what exhibits are available, when exhibits are going to change, and where photography is and is not allowed are all issues that should be discussed in advance.

When researchers approach a museum about conducting research on its premises, both parties should also consider the fact that there may be some things that are obvious to the museum professionals that are not as obvious to the researchers. One of the authors of this chapter had selected objects of art for a study which were part of the museum's permanent collection, assuming that those objects would be on display for the duration of the study, only to discover that "permanent" means "permanently owned" and not "always on display." Likewise, things that are obvious and important to researchers may not always be apparent to museum professionals. For example, researchers generally prefer having control over their environment, including how far away from the exhibits participants stand from the exhibits and how much time they spend at a specific location. So knowing that a large group of excited children will be in attendance that day may prompt the researchers to reschedule.

Another issue to consider is who is participating in the study. Sometimes researchers recruit participants from their own subject pools, and other times they recruit from the people who are visiting the museum or from the museum's membership list. Different museums may have different policies on participant recruitment, which should be discussed at the outset. Callanan helpfully points out that in her experience, approaching potential participants while they were already in the museum for a while came across as "off-putting and intrusive" (2012: 144) and that her research team had more success in approaching people near the admission area of the museum instead.

We suspect that more researchers would conduct studies in museums if museums actively promoted the institution as a research-friendly space. When developing ideas for research on how taking photos shapes memory, one of the authors required a much richer environment than was possible in her lab space, but was concerned that if she approached the museum on her college campus about running the study, they would find it too disruptive. She was thrilled that they not only welcomed such a study, but that they were also extremely helpful when it came to practical considerations.

In fact, museums on university campuses are in a unique

position to invite researchers onto their premises, and we encourage them to reach out to a broad range of disciplines on campus. The Bellarmine Museum of Art at Fairfield University provides an excellent example of this. The museum opened in 2010 with a small but encyclopedic art collection, and since then has been used as a teaching museum for many faculty members. Two studies on photography and memory for museum trips have been conducted there (Henkel, 2014; Parisi & Henkel, 2015). In addition, a program called *The Art of Seeing* was created by the museum director, a museum educator, and a member of the nursing faculty, and a study was undertaken in the museum to see if the program increased the visual literacy and observational skills of nursing students (Grossman, Deupi, & Leitao, 2014). Showcasing this work alongside educational exercises (such as increasing visual literacy through the targeted analysis of art objects, or using art to enhance cultural and historical context) developed by faculty in a wide range of disciplines will attract more researchers to make use of the museum (Milkova & Stinebring, 2011).

Museums are an ideal setting for psychology researchers to explore psychological phenomena in a natural environment and they can help expand the scientific understanding of important issues in memory and development. Greater communication between researchers and museum professionals will facilitate even more research, especially with regard to the ways in which taking photos during the museum visit can increase learning and understanding, and enhance the enjoyment of the experience.

ACKNOWLEDGEMENTS

We would like to thank Peggy St. Jacques and Marice Rose for their helpful comments on this chapter.

REFERENCES

Bailey, M. (2014). To ban or not to ban photography. *Museums International: The Art Newspaper*, March 2014, Number 255.

Banaji, M. R., & Crowder, R.G. (1989). The bankruptcy of everyday memory. *American Psychologist*, 44, 1185-1193.

Benjamin, N., Haden, C. A., & Wilkerson, E. (2010). Enhancing building, conversation, and learning through caregiver–child interactions in a children's museum. *Developmental Psychology*, 46, 502-515.

Berry, M., et al. (2007). The use of a wearable camera, SenseCam, as a pictorial diary to improve autobiographical memory in a patient with limbic encephalitis. *Neuropsychological Rehabilitation*, 17, 582-601.

Bielstein, S. M. (2010). *Permissions, a survival guide: blunt talk about art as intellectual property*. Chicago: University of Chicago Press.

Bowen, S., & Petrelli, D. (2011). Remembering today tomorrow: exploring the human-centered design of digital mementos. *International Journal of Human-Computer Studies*, 69, 324-337.

Callanan, M. (2012). Conducting cognitive developmental research in museums: theoretical issues and practical considerations. *Journal of Cognition and Development*, 13, 137-151.

Chalfen, R. (1998). Family photograph appreciation:

dynamics of medium, interpretation and memory. *Communication & Cognition*, *31*, 161-178.

Deocampo, J., & Hudson, J. (2003). Reinstatement of 2-year-olds' event memory using photographs. *Memory*, *11*, 13-25.

Dommer, S. L., & Swaminathan, V. (2012). Explaining the endowment effect through ownership. *Journal of Consumer Research*, *39*, 1034-1050.

Falk, J., & Dierking, L. D. (1995). Recalling the museum experience. *Journal of Museum Education*, *20*, 10-13.

Finley, J. R., Brewer, W. F., & Benjamin, A. S. (2011). The effects of end-of-day picture review and a sensor-based picture capture procedure on autobiographical memory using SenseCam. *Memory*, *19*, 796-807.

Fried, C. B. (2008). In-class laptop use and its effects on student learning. *Computers & Education*, *50*, 906-914.

Fivush, R., Hudson, J., & Nelson, K. (1984). Children's long-term memory for a novel event: An exploratory study. *Merrill-Palmer Quarterly*, *30*, 303-316.

Good, J. (2014). How many photos have ever been taken? [Web log post]. 15 September. Available at: http://www.Blog.1000memories.com.

Grossman, S., Deupi, J., & Leitao, K. (2014). Seeing the forest and the trees: Increasing nurse practitioner students' observational and mindfulness skills. *Creative Nursing*, *20*, 67-72.

Haden, C. (2010). Talking about science in museums. *Child Development Perspectives*, *4*, 62-67.

Harrison, B. (2002). Photographic visions and narrative inquiry. *Narrative Inquiry*, *12*, 87-111.

Hembrooke, H., & Gay, G. (2003). The laptop and the lecture:

The effects of multitasking in learning environments. *Journal of Computing in Higher Education*, 15, 46-64.

Henkel, L. A. (2014). Point-and-shoot memories: the influence of taking photos on memory for a museum tour. *Psychological Science*, 25, 396-402.

Hodges, S., Berry, E., & Wood, K. (2011). SenseCam: a wearable camera that stimulates and rehabilitates autobiographical memory. *Memory*, 19, 685-696.

Hubbard, T. L., Hutchinson, J. L., & Courtney, J. R. (2010). Boundary extension: Findings and theories. *Quarterly Journal of Experimental Psychology*, 63, 1467-1494.

Hudson, J. A., & Fivush, R. (1991). As time goes by: sixth graders remember a kindergarten experience. *Applied Cognitive Psychology*, 5, 347-360.

Hunt, D. S., Lin, C. A., & Atkin, D. J. (2014). Communicating social relationships via the use of photo-messaging. *Journal of Broadcasting and Educational Media*, 58, 234-252

Hyman, I., et al. (2010). Did you see the unicycling clown? Inattentional blindness while walking and talking on a cell phone. *Applied Cognitive Psychology*, 24, 597-607.

Intraub, H., Bender, R. S., & Mangels, J. A. (1992). Looking at pictures but remembering scenes. *Journal of Experimental Psychology: Learning, Memory, and Cognition*, 18, 180-191.

Jant, E. A., et al. (2014). Conversation and object manipulation influence children's learning in a museum. *Child Development*, 85, 2029-2045.

Koutstaal, W., et al. (1999). Facilitation and impairment of event memory produced by photograph review. *Memory and Cognition*, 27, 478-493.

Koutstaal, W., et al. (1998). Post-event review in older and younger adults: Improving memory accessibility of complex everyday events. *Psychology and Aging*, 13, 277-296.

Leach, D. B. (2011). Children's recollections of a historic house visit: Recall of experiences and use of cognitive tools. *Visitor Studies*, 14, 34-47.

Loftus, E. F., Levidow, B., & Duensing, S. (1992). Who remembers best? Individual differences in memory for events that occurred in a science museum. *Applied Cognitive Psychology*, 6, 93-107.

Loveday, C., & Conway, M. A. (2011). Using SenseCam with an amnesic patient: accessing inaccessible everyday memories. *Memory*, 19, 697-704.

Medved, M. I., Cupchik G. C., & Oatley, K. (2004). Interpretive memories of artworks. *Memory*, 12, 119-128.

Miles, A. N., et al. (2013). Turning back the hands of time: autobiographical memories in dementia cued by a museum setting. *Consciousness and Cognition: An International Journal*, 22, 1074-1081.

Milkova, L. & Stinebring, A-C. (2011) *Academic Programs*. Allen Memorial Art Museum, Oberlin College.

Milton, F., et al. (2011). An fMRI study of long-term everyday memory using SenseCam. *Memory*, 19, 733-744.

Neisser, U. (1978). Memory: what are the important questions? In Gruneberg, M. M., Morris, P. E. & Sykes R. N. (eds.), *Practical aspects of memory*. London: Academic Press.

Nestojko, J. F., Finley, J. R., & Roediger, H. L. (2013). Extending cognition to external agents. *Psychological Inquiry*, 24, 321-325.

Nunes, M., Greenberg, S., & Neustaedter, C. (2009). Using

physical memorabilia as opportunities to move into collocated digital photo-sharing. *International Journal of Human-Computer Studies, 67*, 1087-1111.

Parisi, K., & Henkel, L. A. (2015, May). "Here's looking at me!": Viewing photos of our experiences alters the perspective in our memories. Poster presented at the 27th annual convention of the Association for Psychological Science, New York, NY.

Pathman, T., et al. (2011). A "snapshot" of declarative memory: differing developmental trajectories in episodic and autobiographical memory. *Memory*, 19, 825-835.

Reb, J., & Connolly, T. (2007). Possession, feelings of ownership, and the endowment effect. *Judgment and Decision Making*, 2, 107-114.

Salmon, K. (2001) Remembering and reporting by children: the influence of cues and props. *Clinical Psychology Review*, 21, 267-300.

Schacter, D., et al. (1997). False recollection induced by photographs: a comparison of older and younger adults. *Psychology and Aging*, 12, 203-215.

Schopflug, W. (1986). The trade-off between internal and external information storage. *Journal of Memory and Language*, 25, 657-675.

Schopflug, W. (1988). Retrieving texts from an external store: the effects of an exploratory context and of semantic fit between text and address. *Psychological Research*, 50, 19-27.

Shepard, R. N. (1967). Recognition memory for words, sentences, and pictures. *Journal of Verbal Learning and Verbal Behavior*, 6, 156-163.

Shutterfly, Inc. (2014, October). Photos and storytelling:

Report on survey conducted by Edelman Berland.

Smith, T. S., et al. (2011). Effects of cell-phone and text-message distractions on true and false recognition. *Cyberpsychology, Behavior, and Social Networking*, 14, 351-358.

Sparrow, B., Liu, J., & Wegner, D. M. (2011). Google effects on memory: cognitive consequences of having information at our fingertips. *Science*, 333, 476-478.

St. Jacques, P. L., & Schacter, D. L. (2013). Modifying memory: selectively enhancing and updating personal memories for a museum tour by reactivating them. *Psychological Science*, 24(4), 537-543.

St. Jacques, P. L., Olm, C., & Schacter, D. L. (2013). Neural mechanisms of reactivation-induced updating that enhance and distort memory. *PNAS Proceedings of the National Academy of Sciences of the United States of America*, 110, 19671-19678.

St. Jacques, P. L., Montgomery, D., & Schacter, D. L. (2015). Modifying memory for a museum tour in older adults: reactivation-related updating that enhances and distorts memory is reduced in ageing. *Memory*, 23, 876-887.

Storm, B. C., & Stone, S. M. (2015). Saving-enhanced memory: the benefits of saving on the learning and remembering of new information. *Psychological Science*, 26, 182-188.

Tare, M., et al. (2011). Explanatory parent–child conversation predominates at an evolution exhibit. *Science Education*, 95, 720-744.

Tessler, M., & Nelson, K. (1994). Making memories: the influence of joint encoding on later recall by young children. *Consciousness and Cognition: An International*

Journal, 3, 307-326.

Winerman, L. (2014). A beneficial partnership. *Monitor on Psychology*, 45(9), 38-41.

Wolins, I. S., Jensen, N., & Ulzheimer, R. (1992). Children's memories of museum field trips: a qualitative study. *Journal of Museum Education*, 17, 17-27.

CHAPTER SEVEN

BUDDING PHOTOGRAPHERS: YOUNG CHILDREN'S DIGITAL PHOTOGRAPHY IN A MUSEUM

Elee S Kirk

THESE DAYS, A WALK around a family-friendly museum will frequently show that photography is not just an activity for adult visitors, with many children borrowing cameras or phones, or even using their own, to take snapshots of their visit. This chapter will discuss a research project which used children's photography as a method to explore the experiences of particularly young children, aged only four and five years, visiting a natural history museum.

The initial aim of the research was to understand what is going on when these children spend time in museums. But a further aim was to discover effective ways of carrying out broad, rich and experiential research with this age group, as the majority of researchers who study young children in museums are interested first and foremost in the children's learning, rather than their personal perspectives and experiences (for example Melber, 2007; Palmquist & Crowley, 2007; Synodi, 2014; Tunnicliffe, 2000). This means that, while there is a substantial amount of information about young children in museums, what is less in evidence is research which sees the children as visitors in their own right, and which is interested in everyday children's visits beyond their potential for learning. My research therefore made use of children's photography as a means of gaining their own perspectives on museums (for a full account, see Kirk, 2014). Because this research focused beyond children's learning, it has been possible to pay attention to the varied and unexpected elements of their visits, and this chapter will specifically focus on the relationship between the children and the camera itself within the museum context.

The research was carried out during 2011 in the Oxford University Museum of Natural History and involved recruiting families with children aged four or five years as they entered the museum, and asking the children if they would use my digital camera to photograph things they liked or found interesting. They were then left to enjoy their visit as they would normally. At the end of the visit, the family re-joined me, and the children and I looked together at their photographs on a laptop as I recorded our conversation about the museum, using the pictures as a starting point. In total the project included 32 children – an equal mix of girls and boys – who produced between them 1,597 photographs – an average of 50 photographs per child, ranging from a minimum of seven photographs, to a maximum of 219.

I had not initially intended to use a method based solely on children's photography. There is a growing trend, stemming from methods such as the Mosaic Approach (Clark & Moss, 2001) for researchers to make use of multiple child-friendly methods when carrying out research with young children in museums (Carr et al., 2012; Kelly et al., 2006; Marcus, Burke, & Dobel-Ober, 2009; Piscitelli & Anderson, 2001). During the early stages of this research I piloted other methods for collecting data, including asking the children to draw whilst being interviewed, and asking them to give me a tour around the museum, but I found that both of these methods led to unsatisfactorily didactic and shallow conversations with the children, and were not effective for giving their personal perspectives. The children's photography, on the other hand, prompted an astonishing flow of conversation, giving rich and varied data about their visits to the museum. This data included both spoken words and photographs, as well as the interjections of family members.

Using the resulting visual and verbal data, the research explored many aspects of children's experiences in this museum. Here I focus on the ways in which children interacted with cameras and photography. This provides an ideal discussion point around the ways in which this methodology has provided rich data on the children's experiences, without the overriding concern with their education which is present in so much childhood research.

The advantages of children's photography

In spite of the popularity of mixed methods for research with young children, like me, a growing number of researchers are discovering that photography works particularly well with this age group in the museum setting. In a museum consultation in Australia, Dockett, Main and Kelly (2011) found that, when given a range of ways to express themselves, young children showed a distinct preference for photography compared to other creative methods such as drawing. Both Cook and Hess (2007) and Dunn (2012) carried out successful research with young children in museums based largely on the children's photography, and other museum researchers have used photography with slightly older children (Lemon, 2013; Marcus et al., 2009).

There may be a number of reasons for this success. Before beginning the research, I knew that I had to find data collection methods that were *both* suitable for use with young children *and* suitable for use in a museum. What I didn't fully appreciate until I had piloted several different approaches, was that the method had to be suitable for the people that children *become* when they are in the museum, which is *not the same* as the people they are when they are at home or in school. This means that an activity (such as drawing) which is intuitive to children in a setting such as a school, may not make as much sense to them in a museum.

Childhood scholars maintain that research methods need to "resonate with children's own concerns and routines" (Christensen & James, 2000: 7). In a museum, children have particular expectations about what will happen during their visit – based both on their previous experience and on what is happening around them at the time. By watching those around them, children are also discovering how to *be* in a museum, and what sorts of activities they should expect to enact. One type of behaviour which children are likely to see around them (assuming it is not forbidden) is visitors taking photographs of both the museum objects and of each other. Given the "everydayness" of photography in museums, it is unsurprising that all the children who participated in my research easily and willingly picked up this behaviour for themselves with very limited instructions, even if they had rarely or never used a camera before (sometimes to the surprise of their parents).

But it is not just the act of *taking* photographs that is an "everyday" activity in relation to museum visiting. I would also suggest that the reason people take photographs in museums is to remember, share and discuss their experiences and the things they saw, and this is exactly what the children were being asked to do with their photographs. The children easily understood and settled into the format of the photo-elicitation interview, and the discussions felt natural and productive as a way of communicating with them.

Photography also helped overcome one of the serious

problems with researching young children – their often poor memory of past events (Loftus, Levidow, & Duensing, 1992). The relationship between visitor photography and memory is complex, as suggested by research from Henkel (2014) that photographing objects in museums may actually inhibit memory formation in adult visitors, possibly because the act of photography distracts from concentrating more fully on the objects being viewed. However, for the purposes of my own research it seemed that viewing and discussing their photographs soon after taking them acted as an extremely effective *aide mémoire* to the children. This is because the children were not only taking photographs, but also looking back at them, allowing the pictures to "'slow down' activity and provide a static and visible 'moment' available for repeated reflection" (Fasoli, 2003: 43).

It is, of course, unsurprising that seeing a photograph reminds the children about that part of the museum. However, the fact that the children themselves took the photographs also appears to be significant for a number of reasons. First, by scrolling through the grouped thumbnails of their complete set of photographs, children had an overview of the whole of their visit (or at least all the parts they photographed). This made their memories of the visit less abstract, and meant they could revisit the parts of the museum they had seen and reflect more effectively on which of these had been the most enjoyable or interesting to them. Second, the photographs did not just remind children of what they had *seen*, but went beyond the visual to remind them of what they had said, done or touched: they were a visual route into wider sensory memories. Third, the photographs reminded the children of what had happened when they had taken the pictures *during the time* of their visit, whereas when children gave me a "tour" of the museum, they interacted with exhibits in new ways, with me as an audience, and so were less able to demonstrate what their original visit had been like. Fourth, as well as being reminded of things in the museum by looking at the photographs in question, children could also remember things that they had photographed without actually having those particular images in front of them: where a thumbnail was not visible, they would sometimes search for pictures they knew they had taken. This suggests that the act of photographing is memory-forming in itself, which is unsurprising, as taking a photograph is both an embodied and an intentional action.

The photographs were useful not only as prompts for the children's spoken interviews, but also as data in their own right, powerfully putting forward the children's perspectives. This did not require particular skill on the children's part, but only to be able to take photographs that were identifiable. Mizen (2005) states that the camera puts the viewer visually in the children's shoes, and within this research some photographs certainly showed how children viewed elements of the museum differently from adults. In addition, the photographs also allowed the children to discuss aspects of their visit that were unknown to their parents. However, the photographs were also important as data because they provided a visual voice for children who had difficulties in expressing themselves verbally. While some children were chatty and confident, others were more reticent. For example, the four-year-olds Ally and Rhys (all children are referred to by pseudonyms) both spoke fewer than 100 words in their interviews, but each took 34 and

35 photographs respectively, which allowed for a more oblique interpretation of their experience. Alison Clark (2001: 336) quotes Rob Walker as referring to this as "the silent voice of the camera": a means for participants to express themselves without the need for verbal language.

One of the key advantages of photography is that it appears to be a particularly appealing activity for young children (Stephenson, 2009): in other words, it is *fun*. When piloting the drawing and tour-based methods, I had to constantly cajole the children with the offer of small treats, whereas photography was rewarding in its own right. Many parents thanked me for letting their child take part in such an enjoyable activity, and many siblings fussed to borrow their parents' cameras or smartphones so that they could take photographs too. Photography was also empowering to the children, who enjoyed having control over this piece of "grown-up" equipment (Einarsdottir, 2005). Because the camera was digital, they had the freedom to take as many or as few photographs as they chose (Dockett, Main & Kelly, 2011), although this freedom was not so great as to be baffling: as stated by Finnerty (2005: 12), photography allows children "choice within reasonable parameters". And as has been found previously, the children found it gratifying to see their photographs on the computer screen, to the extent that none of them actually showed a desire for printed copies of their pictures (Stephenson, 2009).

Children's photographic behaviours

Having discussed the advantages of photography as a method for working with young children in museums, I will discuss some of the research findings. I will not go into the types of

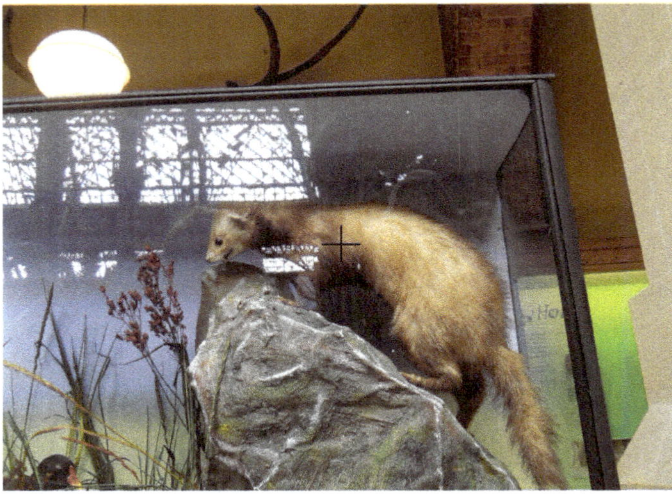

FIG. 1: Karen's photograph of a polecat, 2011.

objects that children chose to photograph, other than to say that on the whole this research backs up other research showing that they are drawn to things that are brightly coloured or sparkly, such as crystals, and to things that are already familiar and interesting to them, such as dinosaurs (Anderson et al., 2002; Danko-McGhee, 2006; Weier, 2004). That said, it is worth briefly noting that the photographs also highlighted children's interests in the less charismatic, small and seemingly insignificant objects, which rarely make it into the research literature, such as small shells, insects, eggs and ammonites (Kirk, 2013). However, what is more significant here is evidence for how children went about being photographers in the museum. And while the children's use of the camera was as idiosyncratic as their museum visits, certain patterns of camera use emerged which appeared to stem particularly from the age of the children participating, and to reveal their developing photographic skills.

One of the most basic decisions made in taking a photograph is choosing the subject. However, a review of the children's photographs suggests that their perceptions of what a photograph is *of* differ subtly from those of an adult, which leads to subsequent differences in the unspoken rules of how to compose a photograph. See, for example, four-year-old Karen's photograph of the polecat (Figure 1). At first, her photograph appears to have been poorly framed, with her picture looking rather lop-sided and missing the bottom and left-hand edges of the case. It might be assumed that this is due to her lack of skill in manipulating the camera; however, a closer look reveals that the polecat is positioned in the middle of the picture (shown by the cross). I suspect that in this way Karen's composition

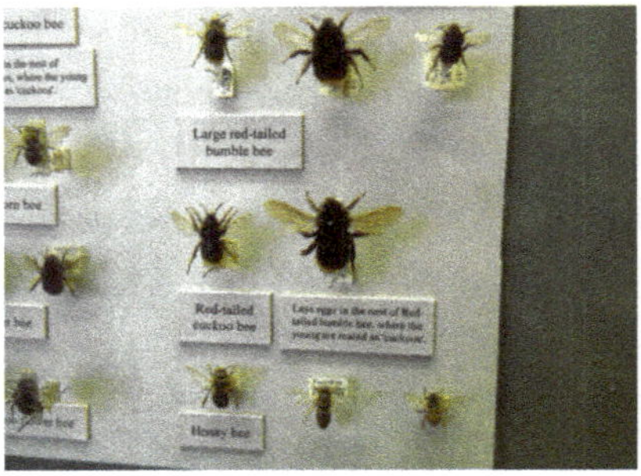

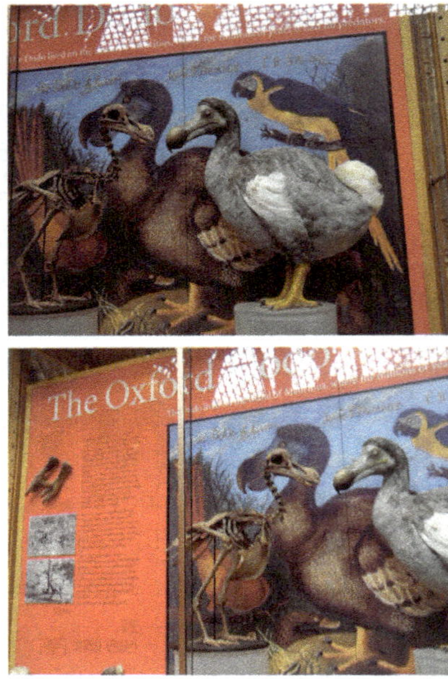

FIG. 2: ABOVE | Jack's photograph of bees, 2011.
FIG. 3: RIGHT | Karen's photographs of dodos, 2011.

was intentional, and that, because her choice of subject was the polecat itself, she did not see the need to include the whole of the rest of the case. Karen's photograph brings to mind Eskelinen's assertion that: "For children the value of an image does not lie in its technical merits. Instead, children capture items or moments they deem important." (Eskelinen, 2012: 175).

Not only does the subject tend to be in the centre of the children's photographs, but it seems a further unspoken rule is that their photographs tend to each have only a single intended subject. This was apparent from their descriptions of the subjects when compared to the framing of the photographs. It was particularly noticeable in five-year-old Jack's pictures, in which the single subjects are often carefully positioned in the centre of the pictures. This was even the case where the photograph included more than one object: when Jack and I talked about his picture of some bees, he told me that he was most interested in the large bee in the centre (Figure 2). Similarly, four-year-old Amy explained that a photograph she took of the lower half of a museum case was supposed to be of an ammonite, but that the surrounding objects also appeared in the photograph, stating: "I was mainly taking that picture but by mistake I got the other bits". And where a child wanted to photograph two things next to each other, they would often photograph them individually, with the intended subject in the middle of the picture, even when both specimens could easily have fitted into one picture. The most striking examples of this were Karen's two dodos, which each appear in both of her photographs, even though she explained that each picture is only *of* one of the dodos (Figure 3).

For Jack, his rule of centring the subject of the photograph

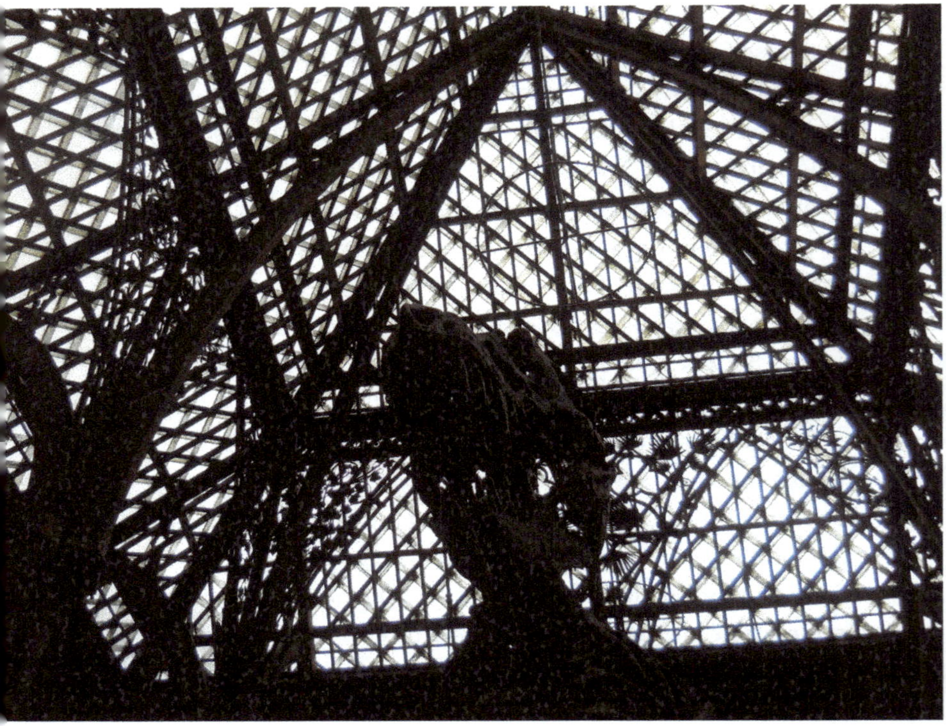

FIG. 4: Greg's photograph of a T. Rex, 2011.

often extended to requiring the subject to fit within the frame of the picture. In fact, Jack was so fastidious in framing his subjects that, when he found he couldn't fit the giant Japanese Spider Crab into the picture, he photographed a smaller crab in its place, as explained by his father:

> Elee: Ok, and what did you take a photograph of here?
> Jack: A crab.
> Elee: And why did you take a photograph of this crab?
> Father: You liked the spider crab, didn't you?
> Jack: Yeah.
> Father: There was a big crab next to it... But he couldn't get that in the camera... So because he could only take a photo of part of the, um, the big crab... He wasn't happy with that, so he had to take the picture of the smaller one because it could fill the whole frame.
> Elee: Oh, OK. So you had a look through the camera at the spider crab, did you?
> Jack: Yeah.
> Elee: And it didn't work as a picture.
> Jack: Yeah.

The thoughtfulness of Jack's approach to photography is striking here, particularly as children can be considered to be careless and snap-happy photographers.

In many other photographs of larger animals, children framed the image around the head, effectively taking portraits of the animals in question, for example in the photograph of the T. Rex, by four-year-old Greg (Figure 4). Indeed, Jack, who had been unhappy photographing only part of the spider crab, was happy to photograph the head of the beaver, suggesting that for him, the head was a legitimate representation of the whole animal in this case, where the animal could be considered to have a face (presumably unlike the spider crab). It is not clear how much this rudimentary animal portraiture occurs because the images of animals and people that children encounter in their everyday lives are often centred around faces, so that they are familiar with the conventions of portraiture, or whether the children are particularly drawn to the animals' heads and faces, as they are, from infancy, to human faces (Slater & Kirby, 1998).

It may also be that what appears to be rudimentary portrait photography partly occurred because the children tended to be quite close to their subjects when they took the photographs. One technique that the children certainly seem to lack (although the same can maybe be said for many adult photographers) was the realisation that they could reframe their photographs by changing their own distance from the subjects. This was apparent in a conversation with five-year-old Clara:

> Elee: So what's this a photograph of?
> Clara: Um, iguanodon's tail.
> Elee: Why did you photograph its tail?
> Clara: Because it was a bit big.
> Elee: Because the whole thing was too big to fit in the camera, was it?
> Clara: Yes.
> Elee: So you just photographed its tail?
> Clara: Yes.

While the instruction to photograph "things you like or find interesting" was generally interpreted by the children to mean museum objects, twelve of the 32 children also took photographs of family members. Fidler et al. (2011: 42) likewise found that young children were keen to take pictures of people in the museum, and suggest that this was in part because taking photographs of each other is a "familiar use of cameras" that the children would see on other occasions carried out by adults. Some of the family portraiture seemed to be at the suggestion of family members, who posed to be photographed; for example in four-year-old Karen's case she told me that a photograph of her father with the T. Rex had been his suggestion. Many more pictures were of family members simply looking at things in the museum, rather than of them posing. For four-year-old John, this family photography was particularly gratifying, and he laughed as he told me that he took a picture of his brother.

Two of the children, Rhys and Nina (both aged four), even turned the camera on themselves to take selfies – which, again, the children are likely to have seen being enacted by other people (Figure 5). In Rhys's selfie it is possible to see the camera strap, which shows that he is definitely holding the camera; however, either because of the length of his arms, or because of the camera strap, he struggled to hold the camera far enough away to fit his whole face into the picture. Nina's selfie was equally close, although more successfully framed and surprisingly well focused! It was interesting to note, however, that, even in cases where children's photographs included themselves or other family members, this did not prompt either them or their families to request copies of the pictures.

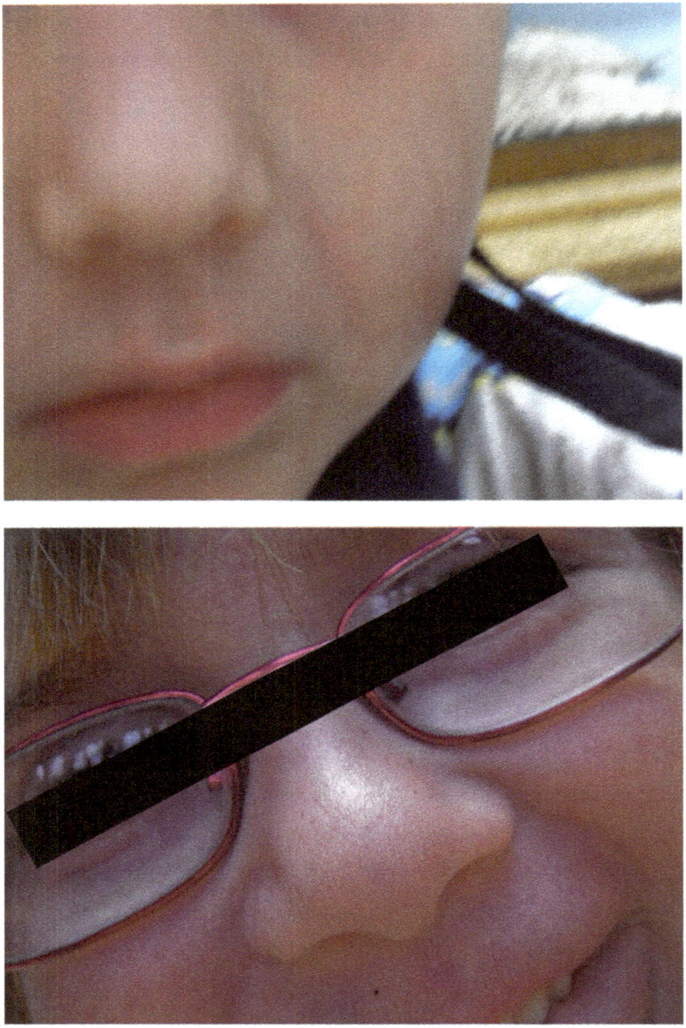

FIG. 5: Rhys' and Nina's selfies, 2011.

By looking at the photographs, it is also possible to see how children were learning to physically handle the camera. Nearly 99% of the pictures were taken in a landscape format, with only nine of the 32 children turning the camera to reframe their pictures, and these only taking a small number of pictures in portrait format. It appears that in at least some of these cases this was a technique that the children were not "inventing" for themselves, but that was instead being suggested to them by family members. This is particularly clear in the case of four-year-old Anna, whose father made her share the camera with her eight-year-old sister, Jenny. In the two pictures of the bee hive (Figure 6), we can see from the reflections and camera angles that older sister Jenny is taking the first photograph, and younger sister Anna the second, copying her sister's technique (although what can not been seen in the printed pictures is that Anna turned the camera in the opposite direction to her sister).

What is not clear is the degree to which children's preference for landscape photography was because they were not aware of the option of turning the camera to produce an upright image, and the degree to which the absence of the upright technique is due to a lack of motor skills when it comes to manipulating the camera: it may well be a combination of the two. Children's photographic skills more generally must depend on both their ability to hold and handle the camera and also on their discovery, either through observation or through being shown by others, of various aesthetic and physical techniques.

As already stated, it was not one of the initial aims of this research to investigate children's photography. Even so, the

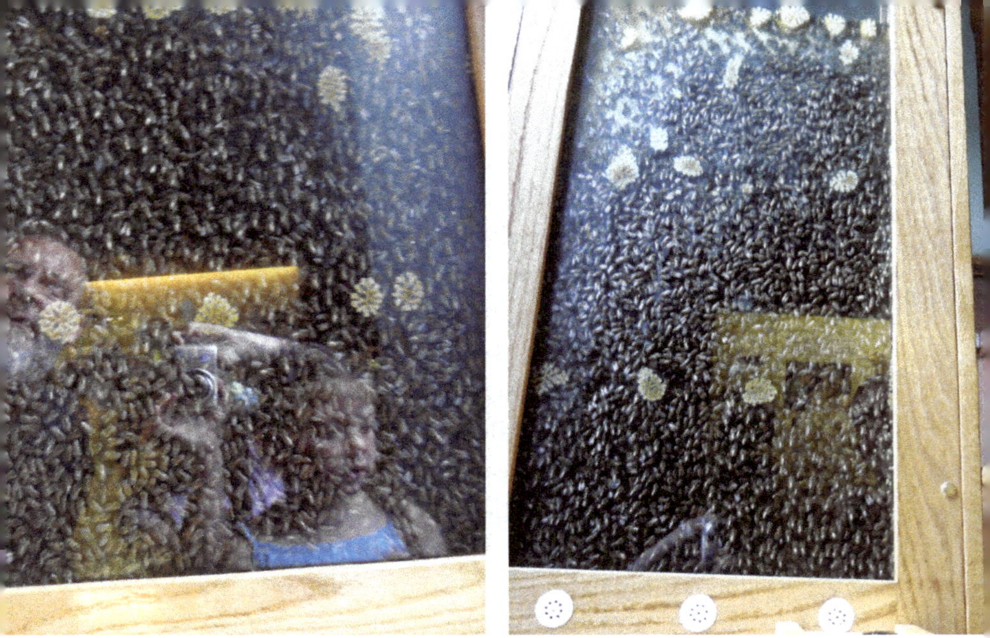

FIG. 6: Jenny and Anna's beehives, 2011.

rich data provided by the children through their words and pictures has revealed the beginnings of various photographic conventions and techniques emerging in these young children. The variations between children hint at the different levels of sophistication between these young children's techniques, and at the variety of ways in which they learn how to become museum photographers.

The impact of the camera

As a research tool, one aspect of children's photography which cannot be ignored is that the camera clearly had a significant impact on each child's visit. By participating in the research, the children's museum visits were not what they would otherwise have been, although it is difficult to judge the extent of this difference. For children who were familiar with cameras, the impact may have been smaller than for those for whom using a camera was a novelty. Arguably, because photography is an "everyday" activity for people visiting museums, it was less likely to have a significant impact on the children's visit than in studies in which photography is more intentionally used as a means of education and engagement (Lemon, 2013). An acknowledgement of the impact of cameras on the children participating in this research can also hint at the ways in which cameras might have an effect on the everyday visits of children who are not participating in research.

In spite of the uncertainty about the effect of the camera, it did seem that its impact was mainly in certain key areas. So, for example, the potential disruptive social impact of the camera on the group is demonstrated in the case of five-year-old Imogen, whose family chose to split up so that her older brothers did not try to take the camera from her. This contrasted with four-year-old Anna's father, who, without another adult to help look after his daughters, made the two girls take turns with the camera, "otherwise they just fight over it". In other cases, the family seemed to have enjoyed the fact that the child was taking photographs, joining in making suggestions and, as we have seen, posing for photographs.

There was also some evidence of the effect of the camera on children's engagement with the museum. In particular, it seemed that the children sometimes chose to photograph objects from the handling collection rather than touch them. This is suggested in the following conversation with five-year-old Kyle and his mother, about the stuffed pheasants in the handling collections:

> Elee: Did you just look at them or did you touch them?
> Kyle: I didn't touch them.
> Elee: You just looked at them?
> Kyle: Yeah.
> Elee: Why didn't you touch them?
> Kyle: Because...
> Mother: Because he was probably too busy taking pictures, wasn't you?
> Kyle: Yeah.

It may be, however, that some of the children were already less motivated to touch objects than others – during subsequent observations, it was clear that some children without cameras were choosing to look at, rather than touch, the handling collections. And it should also be noted that many of the children who took part in the research *did* touch objects, so that if the camera was a barrier to touch, it was certainly not an insurmountable one. More generally, it may be that the camera provides an alternative, but equally active, way of interacting with objects. This suggests an exploration of the impact of cameras on children's interactions with museum objects would be a fruitful area for further study.

One unexpected social impact of photography was on the research itself, and specifically on the ways that the children related to me as researcher. When piloting other methods of data collection, I found that children were often cautious of me and therefore unwilling to speak extensively. However, with photo-elicitation, the children were much more confident and willing to speak. I suspect that this is jointly because of time, trust and reciprocity. First, the children had the length of their visit to get used to the idea of talking to me, whereas with other methods I approached them at the end of their visit and asked them to immediately speak to me. Second, I lent them a piece of equipment, which must have demonstrated a level of trust that I had in them, thus helping them to trust me (Barker & Weller, 2003; Marcus et al., 2009). And third, I gave them the opportunity to carry out an enjoyable activity, and so they reciprocated by talking to me openly and trustingly about their pictures.

The potential of children's photography

The success of photography in this research project with young children strongly suggests that photography has wider potential for work with this age group in museums. Indeed, many museum educators, and as shown above, researchers and evaluators, are already starting to make use of this technology.

One of the advantages of photography as a tool for museum engagement is that it can allow young children to direct their own and their family's attention to the exhibits. Museum consultant Jo Graham (2009) promotes the provision in museums of objects such as toy cameras, torches and magnifying glasses for use by young children and their families. She refers to these as "explorer tools", and suggests that these tools "seemed to act as a non-verbal indication of children's interest for parents" and that they "tended to focus the family interaction on the museum collections or buildings with both parents and children talking about what they could see" (Graham, 2009: 7). While the toy cameras to which Graham refers cannot actually take photographs, there is no reason why real cameras cannot achieve the same end of focusing children's and their family's attention, whilst also allowing the children to take something away from the museum that they can discuss later with their families.

Because cameras are so easy and appealing for young children to use, Fidler et al. (2011) have suggested that they may even provide a way for this age group to engage with galleries that have not been designed with children in mind. This was not something my own research tested, as the children were generally already very engaged with the natural history collections in this family-friendly museum. However, it was apparent that the act of photographing museum objects was highly satisfying to the children, and allowed them to return to the objects during our conversation and to continue their personal meaning-making in relation to these objects.

This gives cameras a huge amount of potential for work

with more formal education groups in museums, "to support student-centered inquiry and curiosity" (Lemon, 2013: 356). Tomkins and Tunnicliffe (2007) have used children's photography as a way of encouraging them to focus on objects which they found particularly interesting, noting that taking a photograph is an act of possessing something that one wants to keep. However, within my research, a small number of children also took photographs of objects that they did not understand, such as unfamiliar animals, or artworks that piqued their interest. This suggests that cameras have the potential to go beyond "collecting" objects that are already meaningful, and allowing children to connect in new ways to museum objects.

The research project I have described in this chapter was deliberately very light-touch, with the intention of allowing the children's visits to be as unaffected by their participation in the research as possible. However, photography has much potential to be used in different styles of research and also with different audiences. For example, visitors could be given more direct instructions, or could be accompanied during their visits and involved in further research after the visit. Instructions for the participants could, for example, be directed at specific elements of the museum, as did Marcus, Burke and Dobel-Ober (2009), who asked older children to photograph the parts of the Whitworth Art Gallery in Manchester that helped or hindered their learning. Cameras can also be used alongside other technology or research tools. Dockett, Main and Kelly (2011) video recorded children as they took photographs, and then later incorporated the photographs into journals for the children to add to. This latter element was also used in photography-based research by Dunn (2012).

The ages of visitors and the settings in which the photography takes place may make a difference to the possibilities of photography. It would be interesting to explore further the usability of this research method with teens or adult visitors. It may be that part of the success of working with younger children is that they are not self-conscious about taking photographs for a stranger and are not possessive of the pictures once they have taken them.

Conclusions

One of the most important lessons I have drawn from this project is that the success of research (and education, evaluation and visitor engagement) can be increased by working with visitors in ways that make sense to them. Cameras, rather than being an exciting new technology, are an everyday piece of equipment in museums, with existing "scripts" to dictate their use. The challenge for the researcher, educator or museum interpreter is to find imaginative ways of "piggybacking" on these scripts to create new ways of understanding and expanding the visitor's experiences.

But by seeing children as visitors in their own right, as well as being learners, we can also become interested in what goes on when they visit a museum uninterrupted by researchers or educators. It is likely that for young children on everyday visits, digital photography will become an increasingly popular way for them to engage with museums. By focusing on the form of children's existing and developing photographic practice, we can expand our own understanding of how contemporary children go about making meaning in museums.

REFERENCES

Anderson, D., et al. (2002). Children's Museum Experiences: Identifying Powerful Mediators of Learning. *Curator: The Museum Journal*, 45(3), 213–231.

Barker, J., & Weller, S. (2003). "Is it fun?" developing children centred research methods. *International Journal of Sociology and Social Policy*, 23(1/2), 33–58.

Carr, M., et al. (2012). Young children developing meaning-making practices in a museum: the role of boundary objects. *Museum Management and Curatorship*, 27(1), 53–66.

Christensen, P. M., & James, A. (2000). *Research with children*. London: Routledge.

Clark, A. (2001). How to listen to very young children: the mosaic approach. *Child Care in Practice*, 7(4), 333.

Clark, A., & Moss, P. (2001). *Listening to young children: the mosaic approach*. London: National Children's Bureau Enterprises Ltd.

Cook, T., & Hess, E. (2007). What the camera sees and from whose perspective: fun methodologies for engaging children in enlightening adults. *Childhood*, 14(1), 29–45.

Danko-McGhee, K. (2006). Favourite artworks chosen by young children in a museum setting. *International Journal of Education through Art*, 2(3), 223–235.

Dockett, S., Main, S., & Kelly, L. (2011). Consulting young children: experiences from a museum. *Visitor Studies*, 14(1), 13–33.

Dunn, R. (2012). A vision of history: young children's perspectives on a museum. In Whiteman, P. & De Gioia, K. (eds.), *Children and childhoods 1: perspectives, places and practices*. Cambridge Scholars Publishing.

Einarsdottir, J. (2005). Playschool in pictures: children's photographs as a research method. *Early Child Development and Care*, 175(6), 523–541.

Eskelinen, K. (2012). Children's visual art and creating through photographs. *Procedia - Social and Behavioral Sciences*, 45, 168–177.

Fasoli, L. (2003). Reading photographs of young children: looking at practices. *Contemporary Issues in Early Childhood*, 4(1), 32–47.

Fidler, Y., Marcus, R., Burke, C., & Edwards, J. (2011). *In the gallery: children, young people and families co-researching their experience in museums*. London: MLA.

Finnerty, K. O. (2005). Celebrating the creativity of the young child. *The Journal of Museum Education*, 30(1), 9–13.

Graham, J. (2009). *"Which way shall we go? OK, I'll follow you..." Providing resources that help parents and carers support pre-school children to engage with museum collections and buildings*. Renaissance South West. Available at: http://www.learning-unlimited.co.uk/page4/files/PAFE.pdf.

Henkel, L. A. (2014). Point-and-shoot memories: the influence of taking photos on memory for a museum tour. *Psychological Science*, 25(2), 396-402.

Kelly, L., et al. (2006). Listening to young children's voices in museum spaces. *Conference of the Australian Association for Research in Education*.

Kirk, E. S. (2013). Gaining young children's perspectives on natural history collections. *Journal of Natural Science Collections*, 1, 38–43.

Kirk, E. S. (2014). *Crystal teeth and skeleton eggs: snapshots of young children's experiences in a natural history museum.* Leicester: University of Leicester.

Lemon, N. (2013). Voice, choice, equity and access: young children capture their art gallery education experiences. *Journal of Museum Education*, *38*(3), 349–363.

Loftus, E. F., Levidow, B., & Duensing, S. (1992). Who remembers best? Individual differences in memory for events that occurred in a science museum. *Applied Cognitive Psychology*, *6*, 93–107.

Marcus, R., Burke, C., & Dobel-Ober, D. (2009). *Creative spaces: children as co-researchers in the design of museum and gallery learning*. Renaissance North West. Available at: http://www.capeuk.org/wp-content/uploads/2010/06/Children-as-Co-researchers-in-the-design-of-museum-and-gallery-learning.pdf.

Melber, L. M. (2007). Maternal scaffolding in two museum exhibition halls. *Curator: The Museum Journal*, *50*(3), 341–354.

Mizen, P. (2005). A little 'light work'? Children's images of their labour. *Visual Studies*, *20*(2), 124–139.

Palmquist, S., & Crowley, K. (2007). From teachers to testers: how parents talk to novice and expert children in a natural history museum. *Science Education*, *91*(5), 783–804.

Piscitelli, B., & Anderson, D. (2001). Young children's perspectives of museum settings and experiences. *Museum Management and Curatorship*, *19*(3), 269–282.

Savva, A., & Trimis, E. (2005). Responses of young children to contemporary art exhibits: the role of artistic experiences. *International Journal of Education & the Arts*, *6*(13).

Slater, A., & Kirby, R. (1998). Innate and learned perceptual abilities in the newborn infant. *Experimental Brain Research*, 123(1-2), 90–94.

Stephenson, A. (2009). Horses in the sandpit: photography, prolonged involvement and "stepping back" as strategies for listening to children's voices. *Early Child Development and Care*, 179(2), 131–141.

Synodi, E. (2014). Verbal communication in museum programs for young children: perspectives from greece and the U.K. *Childhood Education*, 90(2), 116–126.

Tomkins, S., & Tunnicliffe, S. D. (2007). Nature tables: stimulating children's interest in natural objects. *Journal of Biological Education*, 41(4), 150–155.

Tunnicliffe, S. D. (2000). Conversations of family and primary school groups at robotic dinosaur exhibits in a museum: what do they talk about? *International Journal of Science Education*, 22(7), 739–754.

Weier, K. (2004). Empowering young children in art museums: letting them take the lead. *Contemporary Issues in Early Childhood*, 5(1), 106–116.

CHAPTER EIGHT

STEP INTO MY HEART: ANALYSING ONLINE VISITOR PHOTOGRAPHS FROM GRACELAND

Mariruth Leftwich

VISITOR PHOTOGRAPHS PROVIDE a glimpse into the visitor experience, sharing moments of resonance that may not be captured in any other way. This chapter addresses the use of online visitor photographs as a tool for recording and analysing the impact of an interpretive experience, using research conducted as part of a study into the Graceland visitor experience. Tours of Graceland, the home of Elvis Presley, begin with visitors hearing Elvis sing *Welcome to my World*, encouraging them to "step into my heart," a feat rendered possible as they are immersed in his home, and one captured through visitor photographs. These images are used as documentary evidence to examine the tour elements visitors find most compelling. Photographs were selected as a data source because of their ability to reflect how tourists "take possession of space" (Sontag, 1977: 9). Photographs also serve as mediators between places and the viewer's perspective (Van Gelder & Westgeest, 2011), providing a valuable means of understanding how visitors relate to the site.

The chapter focuses on how these "snapshots" of experience can be analysed to assess meaning and impact. The content analysis framework devised for the study is described using samples of photographs taken on the Graceland tour, providing an example of how to distil meaning from spontaneous visitor photos. The coding scheme employed consists of a number of categories, ranging from the basic content of setting and subject matter to image/object distance and the relationship of objects. The source of the images used in this research was Flickr, which houses non-solicited visitor photographs which document the Graceland experience, adding an important dimension to understanding the experience through the visitor's eyes.

Visitor photography methodology

Photographs are used as evidence and testimony, being "mobilised as witness" (Price & Wells, 2004: 58) in a range of academic fields. The growth of cultural studies has seen an increased use of visual images, but the vast majority of these studies have focused on commercially produced images, such as advertisements, leading to a "relative neglect of research on how everyday participants use the visual" (Silverman, 2006: 264). There has been even less analysis of travel and holiday photographs, despite the fact that "most collections of personal pictures are, in fact, dominated by time spent *away* from home" (Robinson & Picard, 2009: 8). Images have the potential to reveal insights that may not be accessible by other means, allowing researchers to glimpse how individuals frame the world around them.

Photographs document what is important to us, where we have been, and what we possess, acting as reminders of the important events, things, and people in our lives and providing rich sociological data (Banks, 2007; Lester, 2003; Sontag, 1977). These photographs, particularly in tourist studies, can help "understand the processes by which people engage with and make sense of the world" (Crang, 1997: 370). Waterton and Watson (2010: 2) explore the importance of this visual culture within heritage tourism, noting that the visual is a central component in the engagement between heritage objects and visitors and that "the processes that constitute meaning, that frame, reveal and construct the past that we see around us, are essentially visual". Given the role that visuality and photographs play in tourism and heritage, an examination of visitor photographs should reveal key aspects of the visitor experience.

The source of photographs used in this study is Flickr, an online photo-sharing platform which includes an extensive collection of Graceland photographs. These images also consist of text and annotations made by the photographers and subsequent viewers to this social platform. The combination of text and image provided a rich source of data which illuminates visitor meaning-making. Online photo sharing sites, such as Flickr, provide unique unmediated access to visitor photographs. The only mediation is on the part of the visitor, constituting its value in research terms, as it details how visitors literally framed their time at the site. This provides a lens for understanding the visitor experience, prioritising the "tourist gaze" (Urry, 1990) as a means for exploring the impact of the site.

The value of tourist snapshots

Visitor photographs are valuable avenues of exploration, as they document interest in the objects, settings, and the juxtapositions which visitors select to document during their tour experience. The vast majority of Graceland photographs on Flickr are "snapshots", images taken by amateur photographers as casual photos to document their tour. Even "snapshot" photos are usually conscious acts that are deliberate and self-reflective, with photographers paying attention to what is included in the scene they photograph. The selective nature of the photographs is evident in the images published by Flickr users, who often couple broad snapshots with more closely focused images.

When visitors frame their photographs they are establishing "a hierarchy with regard to the potentially visible", making the decision that "this content within this space at this time was interesting or worthy of attention" (Schirato & Webb,

2004: 22). Garrod (2009) acknowledges that visitor photographs are often prompted by an emotional response to the subject, providing useful data when exploring the affective dimension of the tourist experience. The ability for photographs to reveal a hierarchical representation of what appeals to visitors and to capture emotional connections makes them an important source of data for understanding the visitor experience.

Urry asserts the role of photography is "intimately bound up in the tourist gaze", citing central characteristics of its use for tourists. These characteristics include: that photographing is a way to appropriate the object being photographed, and that these photographs provide evidence that something did indeed happen – that someone really was there. Far from simply transcribing reality, photographs are the "outcome of an active signifying practice in which those taking the photo select, structure and shape what is going to be taken" (Urry, 1990: 139). Tourist photos on Flickr advance both iconic images of Graceland, like the shag carpeting of the Jungle Room, and unsuspecting personal details, such as a desktop photo of Elvis holding his young daughter. As Urry suggests, photographing Graceland is part of the act of being a tourist and bound in the need to document the experience and selecting what was meaningful. The photographs of Graceland allow visitors to negotiate their tour experience and provide a source of documentary evidence that can be used to explore how visitors perceived the experience.

Building a framework for analysing visitor photographs

Visual data is frequently treated like any other form of text, with procedures of interpretation for verbal and written data being used to analyse these texts. The evaluative decision made when taking a photograph, whether careful and deliberate or spontaneous, constitutes a visual text that is a product of the acts of selection, omission and framing (Schirato & Webb, 2004). Photos, after all, tell stories and these stories can be broken down using analysis similar to the way more traditional written stories may be coded. Just as with all qualitative data, there are different approaches to analysing photographs, with the most common being content analysis and visual semiotics. The challenge with both of these analytic frameworks in the context of this study is that they were formulated primarily to analyse images constructed for public consumption, rather than the more casual snapshots that document the Graceland experience.

The traditional framework for content analysis is too restrictive for the type of analysis that needs to be conducted with the Flickr images, where the world of social media collides with the "visitor's gaze". The ability for visitors to curate their own content, tag that content, and for others to respond to their photos and captions produces a modality of text that extends beyond traditional visual content analysis. While the nature of the analysis is more focused on the content of the images and text, rather than semiotic signs, there are elements of "reading images" that do prove useful as well. The content coding scheme developed encompassed a wide range of variables, beyond the typical frequency analysis of content analysis, to ensure that a full picture of visitors' interaction with the site was developed.

The sheer volume of visitor photographs of Graceland on Flickr required initial criteria for selecting images for analysis prior to the creation of content codes.[1] A systematic approach was taken, examining every tenth image on Flickr. This analysis focuses on visitors who have made a careful selection of photographs to publish on Flickr. While some visitors have uploaded over 200 images of their visit, indicating they are likely sharing every tour photo, for the purposes of this research photographs were selected if there were ten or fewer photographs published of their visit. The sample used for this research consists of 514 images contributed to Flickr by 87 visitors to Graceland,[2] which allows for a representative sample. The wide range of images provided from this sample also supports its representativeness, as every element of the tour is featured within this sample of visitor photos. This set provides a broad landscape of memorable tour experiences and the subsequent analysis provided evidence of tour components which resonate closely with visitors.

The first phase of analysis focused on the creation of content codes, which were derived from an initial review of the photographs themselves. These codes mapped the area where the photograph was taken, the central focus of the image, the people represented within the photograph (the visitor, Elvis, his daughter Lisa Marie, etc.) and its relationship with other photos in their Flickr set. This was a useful beginning, but did not seem to illuminate the complexities of images in terms of their ability to demonstrate how visitors connected with the site or their personal relevance.

An additional layer of coding was applied to the images in order to determine what visitors found most compelling during their visit. The "distance" of the shot was assessed based on the work of Kress and van Leeuwen (2006). The photographer can choose between a close-up, medium or long shot, which Kress and van Leeuwen equate to personal distance, ranging from "close personal distance", being the distance at which one can hold or grasp the other person, to "public distance", which is the distance between people who are to remain strangers (2006: 124-125). The authors suggest that there is a correspondence between the distance of objects and the relationship between that object and the viewer. While they are concerned primarily with commercial images and advertising, the idea that a close distance indicates an engagement with the object is transferable to the framing of visitor photographs. Composition of space inscribes spatial relationships of "closeness", placing objects within "touching distance". Barbatsis (2005: 342) elaborates that since "touching distances are experienced perceptually as personal and intimated, the spatial relationships in these images are potentially meant to be 'seen' as... intimacy". As visitors choose to frame images and zoom in to photograph certain objects, they are creating their own relationship with the space and objects being photographed. Throughout the Graceland tour there is almost always a physical barrier preventing visitors from fully entering the space, so by zooming to focus on particular objects in their photos, visitors are bringing the objects closer and composing a more intimately framed image.

The first step of this analysis was rooted in the content itself, examining what visitors select to photograph, while the second phase investigated the meaning of what was photographed. The material culture of homes has long been an interest in anthropology and ethnographic studies exploring the significance of objects within their context. The objects in our homes "appears as both our appropriation of the larger world and often as the representation of that world within our private domain" (Miller, 2001: 1). When visitors choose to photograph scenes and objects at Graceland they are capturing Elvis' world and in some ways appropriating it for them.

The objects that fill a person's home, from the mundane to the spectacular, all offer insight into the life they live. A person's home and belongings represent a greater understanding of that person, as "we extend our knowledge of a person when we look at his homes. We draw conclusions about his taste, aspirations, money and preoccupations. It is one of the ways in which he expresses himself" (Marsh, 1993: xiv). The objects at Graceland that visitors choose to photograph are ones that ostensibly allow the visitor to better understand Elvis, illuminating the relationship between the visitor and the significant elements of Elvis' home.

The objects in the home have their own intrinsic meaning and visitors add an additional layer of meaning when they photograph the object. Sociologist Stephen Riggins writes that the meaning of objects can only be understood through their relationship with people, as "objects are a cause, a medium, and a consequence of social relationships. Truly the only context in which artefacts can be observed is in their relation to humans" (1994b: 1). In historic homes these objects take on the significance of both the relationship between the original home occupants as well as the relationship between contemporary visitors and objects.

In order to assess what the photographed objects mean, a classification scheme is used to describe the contextual role of the object. The scheme used in this study is based largely on the work of Riggins (1994a), who framed a semiotic system of classification for everyday objects while conducting his "Fieldwork in the Living Room". Graceland is filled with everyday objects, alongside the objects of celebrity that celebrated Elvis' career, which requires a classification that focused primarily on the everyday that could extend to reflect his career. In his exploration of a typical living room Riggins identified a number of conceptual categories for objects found in most homes. Seven of the core concepts developed are applicable to objects found at Graceland, defining objects based on their use and significance. An "intrinsically active" object is intended to be used, whereas an "intrinsically passive" object is meant for contemplation or decorative purposes. "Status objects" are indicators of social status, rather intentionally or unintentionally displayed as such. "Esteem objects" represent either "intimate esteem", reflecting what an individual has achieved in private spheres of life such as parenthood or marriage, or "public esteem", which reflects public recognition. "Collective objects" demonstrate wider social ties, with affiliations to national or religious communities. "Occupational objects", reflect the occupation of the inhabitant. Figure 1 provides examples of how these categories can be applied to objects photographed at Graceland.

It should be noted that an object may fall into more than one category, as, for example, an object may be an intrinsically active object that also signifies intimate esteem. While this scheme addresses the meaning of the objects, it does not necessarily acknowledge visitor meaning-making. One of the most photographed objects from the sample set is the group of three televisions in the TV room, functioning as a status object

OBJECT CLASSIFICATION	GRACELAND EXAMPLE
INTRINSICALLY ACTIVE	Kitchen stove – the kitchen stove at Graceland is still accompanied by pots, a spoon rest and (now fake) vegetables indicating the act of cooking that happened almost around the clock for Elvis and his entourage.
INTRINSICALLY PASSIVE	TV Room Monkey – a white ceramic monkey sits in the middle of the coffee table in the TV room, typical of a 1970s decorative touch.
STATUS OBJECTS	Triple TV arrangement – in the TV room there are three TVs allowing viewing of multiple television stations simultaneously. This is reflective of his wealth and celebrity status.
INTIMATE ESTEEM	Portrait with Lisa Marie – this picture of Elvis with his daughter sits on his desk and is reflective of his relationship with his daughter.
PUBLIC ESTEEM	Gold records – the Hall of Gold in the Trophy Building contains the gold record awards Elvis earned, signs of his popularity and recognition of his work.
COLLECTIVE OBJECTS	Army uniform – when Elvis was drafted into the US Army he served his duty even though he could have used his celebrity to avoid being deployed. His uniform is an example of an object with larger patriotic resonance.
OCCUPATIONAL OBJECTS	Stage costumes – the costumes on display are objects connected with Elvis's stage performances.

FIG. 1: Conceptual categories for objects found in homes.

which is also intrinsically active, but more can be learned through the visitor captions and comments. These comments indicate that visitors are intrigued by how "advanced" the set-up was, how Elvis was inspired by the president and how much Elvis must have enjoyed television, which many people can relate to. Whilst the classification system provides a broad means of examining the semiotic relationship between the objects and visitors, the voice of the visitors must not be forgotten in the analysis.

The Graceland experience through the visitor's eyes

Tourists purposefully frame their photographs; they strategically place themselves for a position that will allow them to capture the "best" view and representation of their visit. They purposefully arrange frames for the images, which makes the length of shot the best place to begin considering how visitors represent the Graceland experience through photographs. The photos analysed indicated that the majority of images were panorama/public distance shots, with 45% of the sample comprised of these broad images, 22% being taken at the room detail/middle distance, and a significant 33% framed at an object/close distance.

It is not surprising, given the nature of Graceland's role as a tourist destination, that slightly under half the images in this sample are panoramic, where visitors have "snapped" an overall image of a space from a central viewing point (Figure 2). These images are designed to encompass as much of the room or view as possible from where the visitor is standing. The three most frequent panoramic views are of Elvis' grave, the front of Graceland, and the living room, all quite iconic

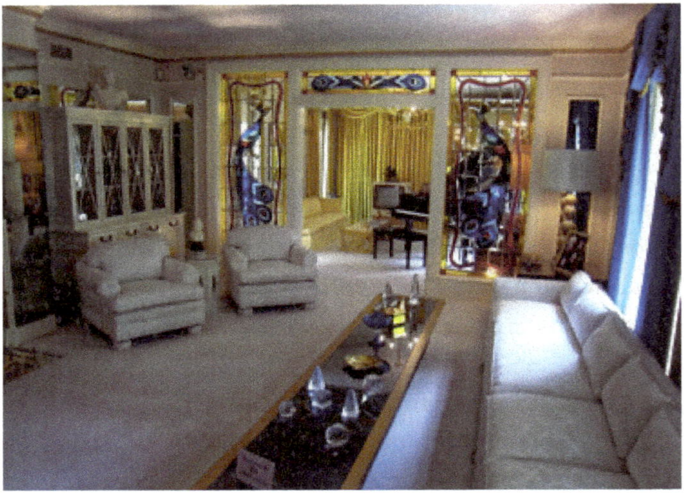

FIG. 2: Panoramic View: *The Living Room at Graceland Mansion*. 17 June 2009.
Photograph: Travel Shorts.

scenes indicating that these photographs act as "place images" for visitors. Place images are regarded as images that become "viewed as representative of the essential character of a place" (Thompson, 2006: 5). Visitors also frequently reproduce the images that they have seen in publications or on television to shape their travel, feeling that they must not miss seeing particular scenes.

Urry's work describes the tourist gaze as the product of visitors consuming destination images, taking photos of key site elements, reinforcing the gaze that has been created by the tourism industry and further perpetuating the iconic images of that destination. As one Flickr user noted in her caption of a living room photograph, "this is one of the first rooms you see upon entering Graceland. I had seen pictures of it in books and on TV prior to our visit: however, seeing it in person was pretty cool" (*dreaminofbeadin*, 12 October 2007). Visitors photograph iconic scenes because they have seen them before and they want to validate their visit by capturing the scenes that have been deemed important by others. These panoramic shots of Graceland retain a sense of visual distance, acting as concrete proof that visitors have seen one of the most visited homes in the world.

The notion that tourist photography is the reduction of tourist destination images, with sights becoming more important than the site itself, does not, however, appear to be substantiated by the Graceland Flickr data. Socially or intimately framed images, making up over half the overall sample, indicate a more authentic engagement in the mind of the visitor than the panoramic place images. Visitors taking more closely framed photographs focusing on a certain area or room feature make up a quarter of this sample. In selecting what to look at,

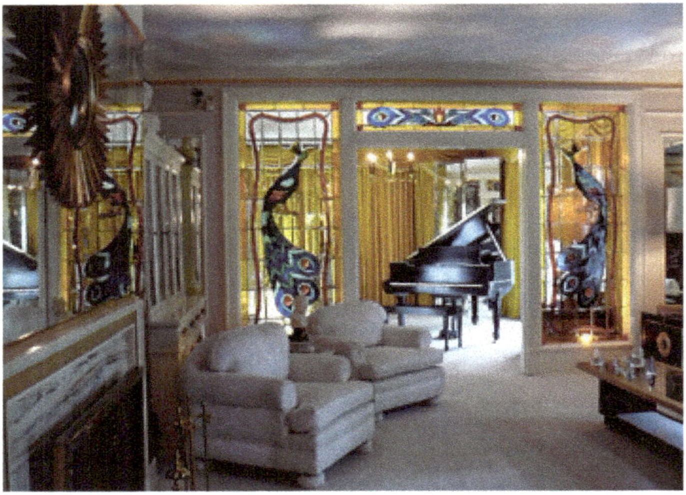

FIG. 3: Graceland Music Room: *The Light of Graceland*. 6 April 2008.
Photograph: fetchpics.

framing the scene with the camera, and recording them, visitors are expressing an enjoyment and engagement with that specific scene (Schirato & Webb, 2004). This level of framing requires visitors to select a portion of Elvis' world to capture, with the most common features being views of the music room, the waterfall and seating in the Jungle Room, and a corner of the living room incorporating portraits of Elvis and his parents.

The images which focus on the music room, at the far end of the living room, appear to attempt to connect visitors with Elvis as a musician, which is especially easy to imagine as the audio tour plays samples of Elvis and his parents singing along to a piano. This is one of the only places in the house which alludes to Elvis in a musical sense, with the piano providing an important reminder of Elvis' talents, but also affirming those talents as something appreciated and nurtured even in the small scale of his home. The photograph shown in Figure 3, is evidence of how carefully visitors frame their photographs of the music room. This is not a view that can be quickly and spontaneously snapped, it required the visitor to find a very precise location at the far perimeter of the viewing area and incorporate a view of the piano, making it a focal point of the image. If the number of images containing the music room piano in some framed context are combined, they constitute just under half of all social distance images in this set, proving how alluring this setting is for visitors. Captions of these framed images often reference the importance of the music room as it contains the actual piano which Elvis played. This space clearly evokes a level of authenticity and personal relevance which captures visitors' attention.

Beyond social or middle distance frames are the intimate,

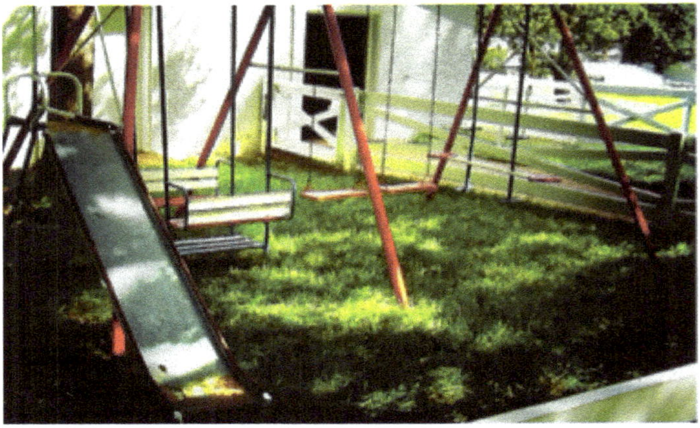

FIG. 4: Lisa Marie's Swing Set: *Gone are the Halcyon Days of Youth*. 19 September 2007. Photograph: Camera Obscure.

object-based photographs, constituting the second largest group of images in this sample. While the public and middle distance photographs fell into relatively few categories, as visitors photographed similar features, the variety of object photographs is quite wide, reflecting the visitor's own motivations and interests. Objects which appealed to many visitors included the Racquetball court costumes, the chair in the Jungle Room which Lisa Marie napped in, the bed from Elvis' wardrobe closet, Lisa Marie's swing set, the American Eagle cape from the *Aloha Special*, and even the kitchen stove.

Only twenty photographers did not include objects in their visit photos, meaning that just over 75% included an object image when publishing their visit experience. The importance visitors place on viewing objects, rather than on just producing iconic snapshots, is evidence of a desire to connect with the people who lived at Graceland on a personal level, examining more closely the objects which Elvis and his family used on a daily basis. As Baudrillard (2005: 14) notes when describing the purpose of house interiors, "the primary function of furniture and objects here is to personify human relationships, to fill the space that they share between them, and to be inhabited by a soul". It is perhaps this soul which visitors are attempting to capture when photographing the chairs that now sit empty, the swing set (Figure 4), now still and rusting after years of use, or the flamboyant costumes which gave Elvis so much life on stage now hanging lifeless in glass cases.

Object classification

After coding each of the objects photographed using Riggin's classification scheme, the largest proportion of

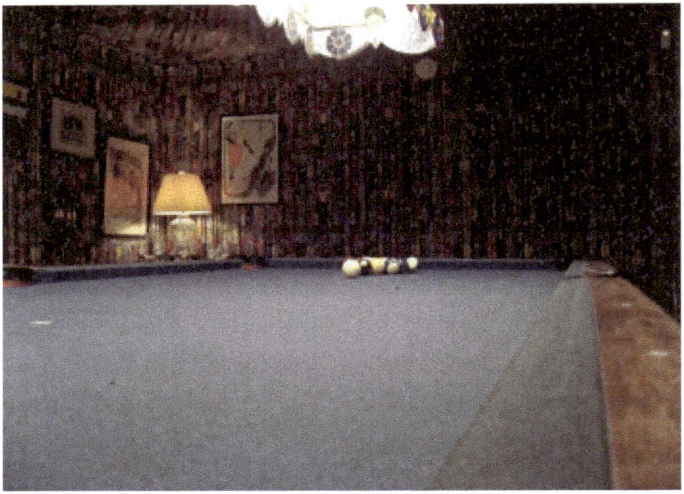

FIG. 5: *Graceland Billiards*. 14 July 2008. Photograph: edvoidswarranties.

objects photographed had an intrinsically active purpose. Visitors have chosen objects which Elvis or his family would have interacted with on a daily basis, many of which are similar to objects that visitors might find in their own home, from cooking utensils to televisions and telephones. The use of the ordinary and common experience to capture visitors' imaginations can be a particularly effective form of historic house interpretation, allowing visitors to understand the home's residents through objects that mean something to visitors and bear some relation to their own lives (Donnelly, 2002). Active objects appear more likely to build this resonance than those that are intrinsically passive.

Another important element in visitors photographing active objects is the ability to visualise Elvis actually using the objects, giving him a retrospective physical presence. A visitor who focused on the piano in the music room captioned, "This is Graceland. Elvis played this piano" (*kleepet*, 9 May 2006). This is not a prop or reproduction, this is *the* piano that Elvis actually played in his home. The focus on active objects photographed at Graceland represents the desire to envision Elvis in this space, whether playing the piano, reading and making notes in books, playing pool or riding horses. For example, two images in the group were photographed low on the edge of the pool table, including Figure 5, as if the photographers were about to join in a game of pool like one of Elvis' entourage. The Pool Room has been photographed in a number of ways, with many visitors snapping a panoramic shot or perhaps focusing on the ornate fabric hanging on the ceiling and walls. The active photographs, however, offer another glimpse into how visitors experience Graceland and engage with the collection more personally.

The second largest set of objects represents intrinsically passive and decorative objects. These are often items that inspire nostalgia amongst visitors, including the white monkey figurine in the TV Room and even a door in the Jungle Room, with visitors commenting that their parents had the same décor or it reminds them of an item in their home. The Jungle Room dominates the setting choice of visitors photographing decorative objects. It is no surprise that this now infamous room inspires great curiosity from visitors, as its decoration stands apart from everything else in the house. It has become one of the more iconic rooms in the house, reflected in the number of times it is photographed. The captions within many of these images of passive and decorative objects indicate that nostalgia and curiosity factors make them worth documenting and sharing.

The third largest group of objects photographed represent items reflecting intimate esteem. These mark achievements in the personal sphere of a person's life, such as marriage and parenthood. They most often focus on Elvis' role as a father to Lisa Marie. Her toy chest, swing set and photos with her father all appeal to visitors. Images of these intimate objects convey a revelation, moving him beyond a two-dimensional caricature to a beloved father who doted on his little girl. Despite the fact that there are no direct interpretive elements associated with the intimate objects photographed (they are not labelled or referenced in the audio tour), visitors conjure up a familial image of Elvis and his role as a father. Flickr captions proclaim this is "Elvis' swing set for Lisa Marie" (*that's* MR. POPLABS, 6 October 2006) and that "this was Lisa Marie's actual toy box and the original toys that Elvis bought her" (*RichM921*, 15 August 2006).

There is a familiarity in buying a swing set or toys for your child which captures the imagination of visitors.

The other setting which proves tantalising to visitors is Elvis' desk, brought down from his second floor office and covered with items which were significant to him, including books and photographs. While it remained on the general tour (it is now part of a specially ticketed tour), it was a popular source of intimate images. Figure 6 shows a very closely framed photograph of Elvis' desktop. The photographic frame is shared between Elvis' Bible, a picture of him kissing Lisa Marie, and a worn telephone book and telephone. The photograph portrays a vulnerable side to Elvis rarely seen as part of his public persona. A commenter, Freddie Phillips, concludes on Flickr that this image is "a really nice shot, a human touch to the legend." As one visitor reflected about seeing this side of Elvis, "you feel so close to Elvis' story here. He seems so vulnerable and sensitive" (Myers, 2010: D5). This is possibly the most intimate glimpse a visitor has of Elvis, with these objects which would be mundane if not associated with a celebrity. While visitors form emotive attachments with family images at Graceland, it is important to remember that what visitors perceive as readers of this image may not reveal the truth behind it.[3]

Objects representing Elvis' occupation and public esteem constitute roughly one quarter of the sample images. These objects, housed in the exhibit areas rather than the house itself, include gold records, awards and stage costumes. The costumes and awards in the Racquetball court are the most commonly photographed objects in this category, epitomising Elvis' flamboyant 1970s concert era. It is unsurprising that this setting appeals to visitors, as awards tower from floor to ceiling

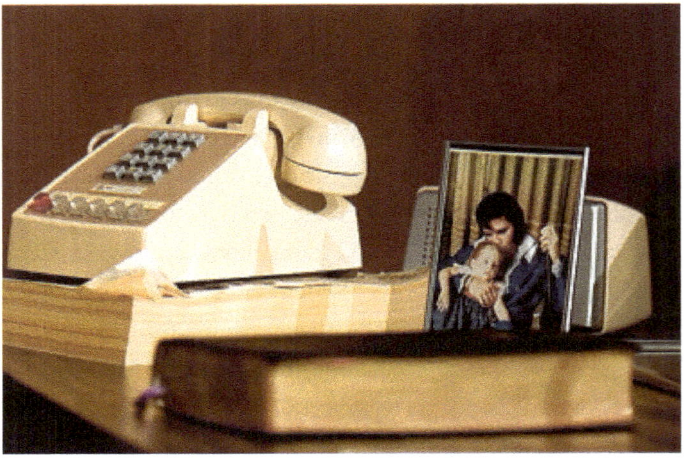

FIG. 6: *On Elvis' Desk*. 18 June 2007. Photograph: Carrie Musgrave.

in this massive double-height room, complete with rhinestone studded costumes and a large video screen production of *The Aloha Special*. It is an immersive encounter that mimics the excitement and enthusiasm of a concert, providing the only opportunity on the tour to experience Elvis the entertainer.

Despite the fact that Elvis was a wealthy celebrity, few visitor photos indicate social status at Graceland in this Flickr sample. The three televisions that play simultaneously in the TV Room most closely represent social status, with visitors commenting that Elvis was at the cutting edge of technology and must have been wealthy when even one television was often a luxury. Objects of social status are likely excluded from the photographs because there are actually very few objects within Graceland that reflect a higher social status. If anything, the objects at Graceland are decidedly middle class and rather commonplace.

Elvis' home is not an ostentatious show of wealth and the items most people associate with his celebrity, such as his extensive car collection and private airplane are across the street at the visitor plaza, are far removed from the intimate setting of his home. The data indicates that the number of objects they can relate to from their own family experience often surprises visitors. This is evidenced in the visitor photos, where everyday objects account for 20% of the images. In the online visitor reviews, sentiments such as "what comes across is that it's a cosy family home" (*JustPassingThrough*xx, 4 February 2012) continue to be expressed. There are no priceless antiques or masterpieces of art; Graceland is filled with objects that could be bought at local department stores or seen in the pages of catalogues, objects that do not act as wealthy status

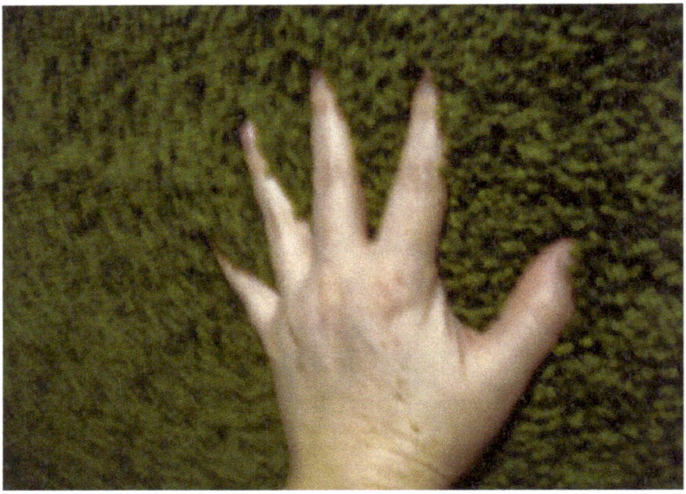

FIG. 7: A visitor's hand touches the wall at Graceland. 29 February 2008.
Photograph: Karen H.

symbols as much as they reinforce the idea that Elvis was a commoner who became "king" but never fully relished the trappings of his title.

Captured significance

The images shared on Flickr illuminate the range of memorable moments from the Graceland tour, providing evidence of how the objects and setting can produce its own affective presence. These images were introduced as a source of data to illuminate the visitor experience in a way that was un-mediated or dictated by a research agenda. The numerous photos that frame objects of intimate esteem at a close distance suggest that visitors are captivated by the personal world of Elvis, and the captions and social postings indicate that visitors routinely make connections between their own world and Elvis' home. This type of analysis proves useful for the study of historic site interpretation, where it is still too often the case that the personal and affective are obscured by architectural detail and object provenance. This set of photos indicate the need to understand what elements appeal to visitors in hopes of informing better interpretive practice.

These images provide evidence of the objects that fascinate, but also suggest the deep need for visitors to document their time in a place. Visitors share a vast number of documentary images proclaiming "I was here!" One (out of focus) image (Figure 7) shows a visitor's hand deeply embedded in a wall of shag carpeting in the Jungle Room, to which a viewer replied, "Ah, to commune with The King!" This style of image personifies the value of place and the ability for photographs to capture meaningful moments visitors want to share with others. Indeed the

Graceland experience is one embedded with ideas of communing with the past, which is rooted through the primacy of the physical place and rich personal collection.

The photographs offer a layer of understanding about the experience that could not have been captured in more traditional ways. Surveys and written evaluation do not offer the same window onto experience that is communicated through photographs. The self-selected images seen on Flickr allow a researcher to step into both the heart of the visitor and the experience itself. These images are indicative of the significant moments of the tour which express interest, resonance, and appropriation of place, serving as valuable tools to those trying to understand the visitor experience.

NOTES

1. Over 90,000 images were returned under a search for "Graceland", not all of them related to the home of Elvis Presley.
2. 500 was the limit which could reasonably be accessed due to the search return limitations of Flickr, after examining every tenth image and coding it only if it was part of a set of ten or fewer Graceland photos.
3. Personal pictures such as this can be "deeply unreliable, but it is in this very unreliability that their interest lies" (Holland, 2004: 118). Holland also suggests these can be the least readable of images, as they depend heavily on knowledge of the subject, on why the photo was taken and on its context. Priscilla reflected on a family portrait session where Lisa Marie cried constantly after leaving her nanny. As Elvis and Priscilla tried to coax a smile from her, Priscilla concluded, "That's when it hit me. My God, she's so attached to the nurse that she doesn't want to leave her. Now I knew I had to find more time to be with her" (Presley, 1985: 290). A sentiment such as this lends an entirely different dimension to the image on Elvis' desk.

REFERENCES

Banks, M. (2007). *Using visual data in qualitative research.* London: SAGE Publications.

Barbatsis, G. (2005). Narrative theory. In K. Smith, et al. (eds.), *Handbook of visual communication: theory, methods, and media* Mahwah: Lawrence Erlbaum Associates.

Baudrillard, J. (2005). *The system of objects.* London: Verso.

Crang, M. (1997). Picturing practices: research through the tourist gaze. *Progress in Human Geography*, 21 (3), 359-373.

Donnelly, J. F. (2002). Introduction. In J. F. Donnelly, (ed.), *Interpreting historic house museums.* Walnut Creek, CA: AltaMira Press, pp. 1-17.

Garrod, B. (2009). Understanding the relationship between tourism destination imagery and tourist photography. *Journal of Travel Research*, 47 (3), 346-358.

Holland, P. (2004). "Sweet it is to scan...": personal photographs and popular photography. In L. Wells, (ed.), *Photography: a critical introduction.* London: Routledge, Third ed., pp. 113-158.

Kress, G. & van Leeuwen, T. (2006). *Reading images: the grammar of visual design.* 3rd ed. London: Routledge.

Lester, P. M. (2003). *Visual communication: images with messages.* 3rd ed. Belmont: Thomson Wadsworth.

Marsh, K. (1993). Introduction. In K. Marsh (ed.), *Writers and their houses: a guide to the writers' houses of England Scotland, Wales and Ireland.* London: Hamish Hamilton. pp. xiii - xviii.

Miller, D. (2001). Behind closed doors. In D. Miller (ed.), *Home possessions: material culture behind closed doors.* Oxford:

Berg. pp. 1-19.

Myers, M. (2010). The Elvis enigma. *The Wall Street Journal*, 18 August. pp. D5.

Presley, P. B. (1985). *Elvis and me*. London: Century Publishing.

Price, D. & Wells, L. (2004). *Thinking about photography: debates, historically and now*. 3rd ed. London: Routledge.

Riggins, S. H. (1994a). Fieldwork in the living room: an autoethnographic essay. In S. H. Riggins (ed.), *The socialness of things: essays on the socio-semiotics of objects*. Berlin: Mouton de Gruyter. pp. 101-148.

Riggins, S. H. (1994b). Introduction. In S. H. Riggins (ed.), *The socialness of things: essays on the socio-semiotics of objects*. Berlin: Mouton de Gruyter. pp. 1-6.

Robinson, M. & Picard, D. (2009). Moments, magic and memories: photographing tourists, tourist photographs and making worlds. In M. Robinson and D. Picard (eds.), *The framed world: tourism, tourists and photography*. Farnham: Ashgate Publishing. pp. 1-38.

Schirato, T. & Webb, J. (2004). *Understanding the visual*. London: SAGE Publications.

Silverman, D. (2006). *Interpreting qualitative data*. 3rd ed. London: SAGE Publications.

Sontag, S. (1977). *On photography*. New York: Picador.

Thompson, K. A. (2006). *An eye for the tropics: tourism, photography, and framing the caribbean picturesque*. Durham: Duke University Press.

Urry, J. (1990). *The tourist gaze: leisure and travel in contemporary societies*. London: SAGE Publications.

Van Gelder, H. & Westgeest, H. (2011). *Photography theory in historical perspective*. Chichester: Wiley-Blackwell.

Waterton, E. & Watson, S. (2010). Introduction: a visual heritage. In E. Waterton and S. Watson (eds.), *Culture, heritage and representation: respect on visuality and the past.* Farnham, Surrey: Ashgate Publishing. pp. 1-18.

CHAPTER NINE

MY GRANDMA HAD THE SAME DOG: USER CAMERA STUDIES AT THE RIJKSMUSEUM

Johanna Barnbeck

WHEN I HAVE A CAMERA in my hand, I dare to walk in front of a painting. It's like having permission to crawl through the masses.
– Research participant.

The joint interest of the University of Amsterdam and the Rijksmuseum in researching how to link up analogue and digital cultural heritage, user-enabling technology and innovative research methodologies led to a collaboration called Augmenting Masterpieces. The term *augmenting* was used to refer to making "something greater by adding to it" (Oxford Dictionary). This chapter addresses the ways in which camera user studies can help develop new technologies such as digital interfaces, location-based communication, and augmented reality devices to offer different, additional access points to any exhibition.

As part of the Augmenting Masterpieces collaboration I undertook research examining the social aspects of a museum visit, with the aim of enhancing and supplementing the digital technologies used in the Rijksmuseum (Figure 1). The results of this study helped develop new digital interfaces in the museum which encourage visitors to engage with and experience artworks in new ways, enhancing their connection to masterpieces, and enabling active participation.

Methodology

A small-scale user camera study was used to explore the social aspects of a participant's visit. The study was based on the design-thinking approach by Stanford's Hasso Plattner Institute for Design, as introduced in their Bootcamp Bootleg (d.school 2011). In our case, I invited visitors to take photographs in the museum

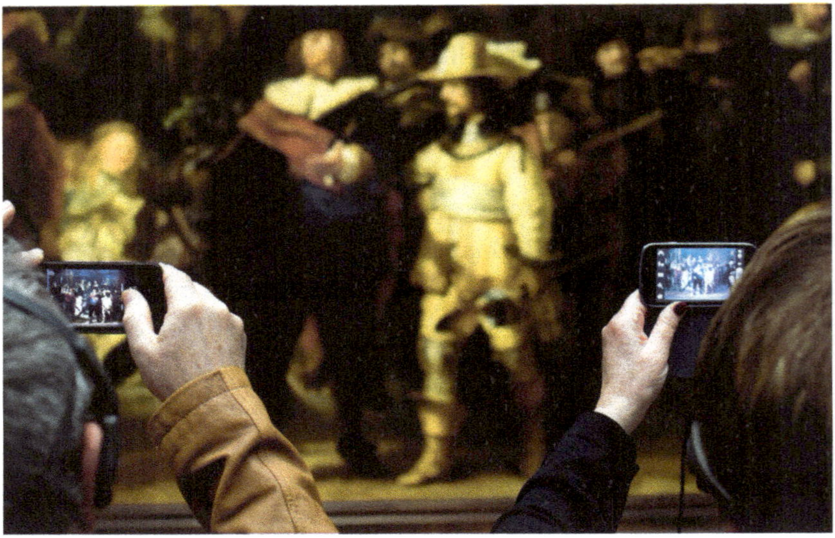

FIG. 1: A man and woman simultaneously take pictures of Rembrandt's *Nightwatch*, while listening to the multimedia guide. Photograph: Johanna Barnbeck, 2014.

and then talk about them with particular emphasis on the social aspects of their museum visit, and their interaction with the space, museum staff, other visitors and art objects.

The participants were selected based on the ways in which the Rijksmuseum segments its visitors for educational and marketing purposes. These segments are based on the visitor's main reason for coming to the museum:[1]

- Families with Kids: "A visit to a museum is fun and an educational way to spend the day."
- Cultural Tourists: "When you visit Amsterdam, you have to see a museum."
- Art Lovers: "I regularly visit museums and keep track of cultural events."
- Schools: "Visiting museums is in the school programme, [so the museum] should make it [the visit] as easy as possible [for me as a teacher]."
- Professionals: "This visit to the museum is part of my work in the arts/history/museum field."

The study included twelve participants: three cultural tourists, three art lovers, two professionals from the cultural sector, and four members of a family, a father with his three children, the youngest of whom was seven.

The study consisted of three phases. First, participants were given a compact digital camera and were instructed to walk through the museum and take pictures of anything that drew their attention. They could choose what to capture, how many pictures to take, and how much time they wanted to spend in the exhibition. The number of pictures which

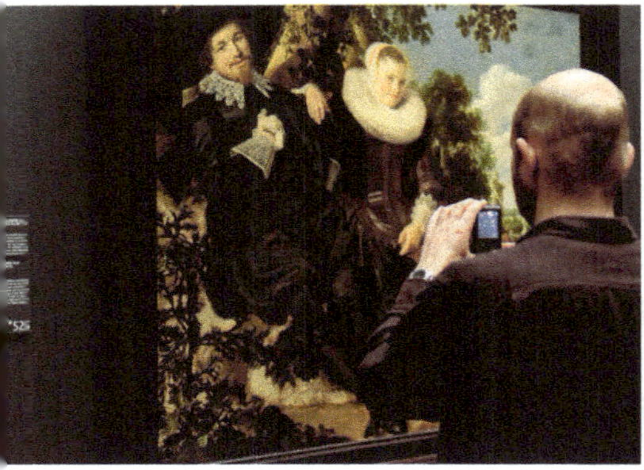

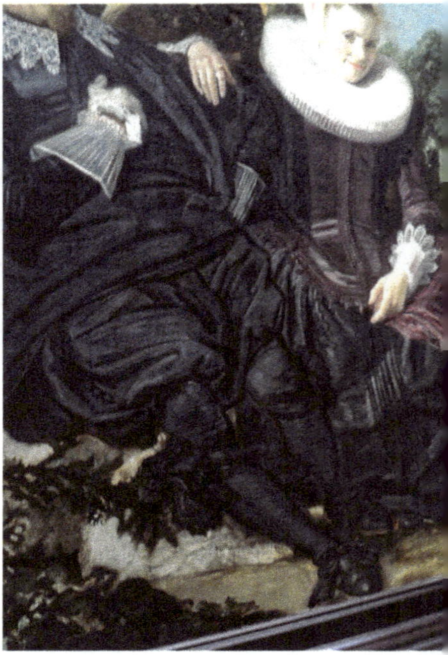

FIGS. 2 & 3: A participant in the camera user study takes a picture – and the picture he took. Photographs: Johanna Barnbeck; research participant, 2014.

participants took ranged from 38 to 169 images and the time spent in the exhibition ranged from 82 to 192 minutes.

Second, participants took part in a semi-structured, open-ended interview. The first part of the interview was designed to make participants feel as if they were showing their vacation pictures to a friend. For most participants their visit took place during their vacation or at least on a day off work, so the pictures *were* in a sense "vacation pictures". The interview questions were designed to elicit detailed and rich discussions around the circumstances of taking photographs in the museum and the meaning of the resulting photographs (Figures 2 and 3). The interviews also included questions about participants' sensual experiences in the museum *(What did you hear, smell, touch?)* and about the use of digital devices *(Which device did you use during your visit and what did you do with it?)*. While the first phase of this study encouraged visual storytelling, the second encouraged oral storytelling supported by the visual material they had produced (Figures 4 and 5).

Finally, the third phase of the study involved the analysis of the photographic material and its grouping into visual categories such as "social interaction", "painting", and "architectural components" (Figure 6). These were later cross-checked with the corresponding narratives from the interviews and, when necessary, complemented by additional categories based on the participants' descriptions of the images.

Results

All research participants mentioned pieces of information they gathered, in one way or another, about the collection. Having said that, more experienced visitors (Art Lovers and

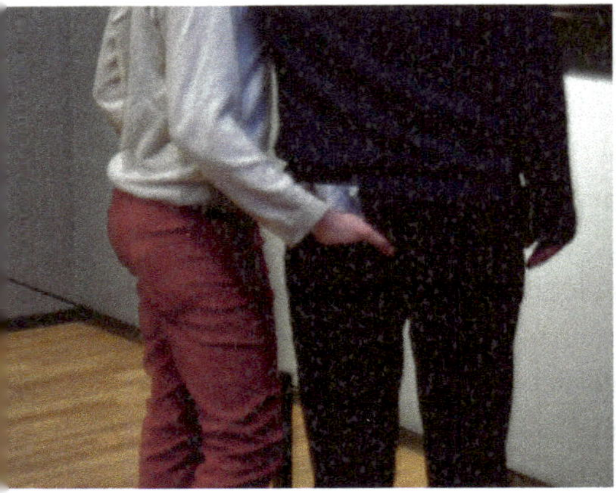
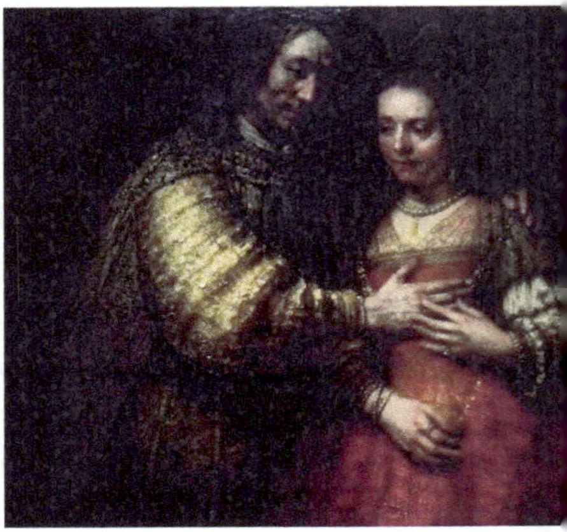

FIGS. 4 & 5: A study participant draws visual connections between what she sees in the museum and a painting: *"This woman had her hand in her boyfriend's pocket, almost like in this painting. Couples tend to cling to each other in museums."* Photographs: research participant.

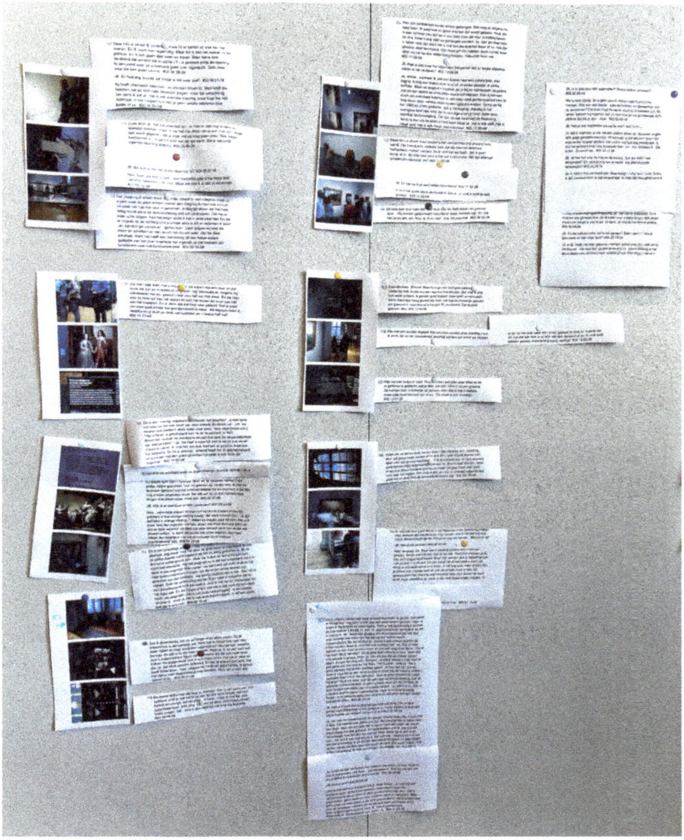

FIG. 6: Study participant photographs and interviews are prepared for analysis.
Photograph: Johanna Barnbeck, 2014.

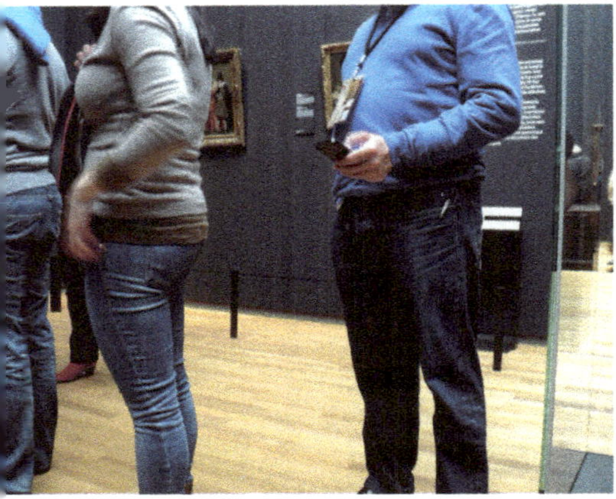

FIG. 7 [LEFT]: A participant describes his observation:
"This man was texting the whole time, only half listening to the tour guide. I think this is actually happening a lot." Photograph: research participant.

FIG. 8 [BELOW]: Participants describe their awareness of random flows of information: "I briefly listened in to the tour of a German tourist group... would have never looked at that painting otherwise." Photograph: research participant.

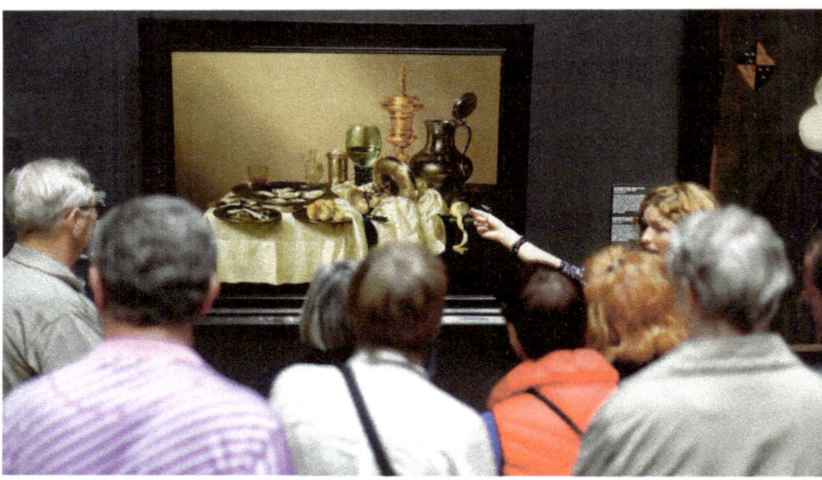

Professionals) were more willing to engage with the information provided by the museum in the form of labels and multimedia guides. Especially interesting was the fact that people listened in on conversations between other visitors and picked up information from what tour guides shared with their groups (Figure 8). The fact that they gathered this information serendipitously increased its value, even though one could have read this information on the official labels. Such information often led visitors to take pictures related to the information they gathered, as a way of remembering it. The interview data suggests that when visitors acquire information about an object unintentionally, their interest and the perceived value of that object increases. This is an important finding which was subsequently used to inform the design of additional features in the Rijksmuseum app.

Participants often captured the perspective of other visitors in their pictures. After overhearing a comment, or seeing what someone else had done, they took a picture from the same position and in so doing documented the other person's point of view. As Harper (2002: 23) suggests, such pictures encourage empathy for the other's perspective:

> Photographs appear to capture the impossible: a person gone; an event past. That extraordinary sense of seeming to retrieve something that has disappeared belongs alone to the photograph, and it leads to deep and interesting talk.

All the study participants were highly interested in social interactions within the museum space and in sharing narratives

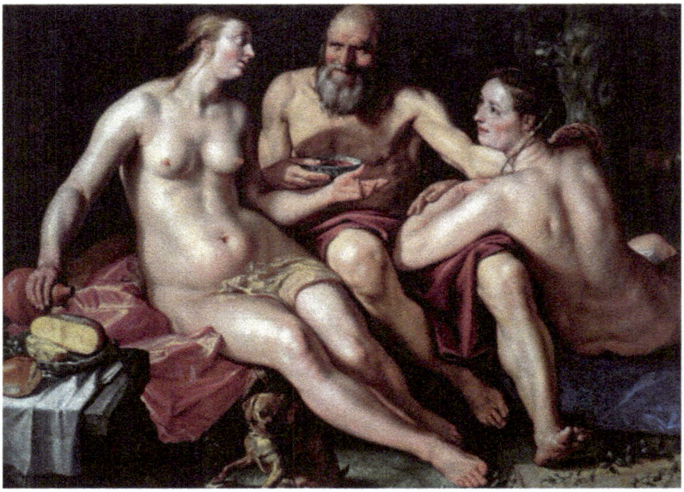

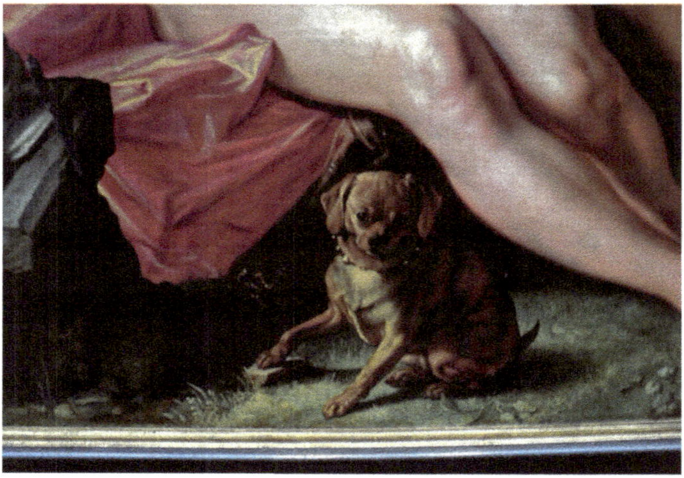

FIGS. 9 & 10: Two different participants capture their own perspectives on Hendrick Goltzius' painting, *Lot and His Daughters*. Photographs: research participant.

that were not necessarily about the artworks or about conveying art historical information. They seemed focused and relaxed when they were talking about social observations or when re-telling stories they overheard. As the literature suggests (see for example Packer & Roy, 2005) the social dimensions of a museum visit are very important.

All the research participants talked about carefully observing other visitors, listening to their conversations, or reflecting on their (own) (proper) behaviour (Figure 7). Most of them also described feelings of awkwardness which was, more often than not, linked to a perceived lack of knowledge.

These findings suggest that visitors influence other visitors through their overheard conversations. In an exhibit, visitors absorb an unpredictable flow of information supplied by people who do not realize they are providing it. When participants acquired information they found interesting, they seemed to particularly value it because of the serendipitous nature of the experience.

Some participants took pictures of the same artworks, but drew different meanings from them. Figures 9 and 10 show two participants' pictures of *Lot and His Daughters* by Hendrick Goltzius (1616). One took a picture of the entire painting and another of the corresponding label on the wall. During the interview she mentioned that the intense scenery and interaction between the three people drew her to the painting. However, after reading the label, which reads: *Because Lot's daughters were afraid of remaining childless – all of the men had perished – they got their father drunk and seduced him*, she was shocked. For her, the label completely changed the meaning of the painting, and she refused to look at the painting after that.

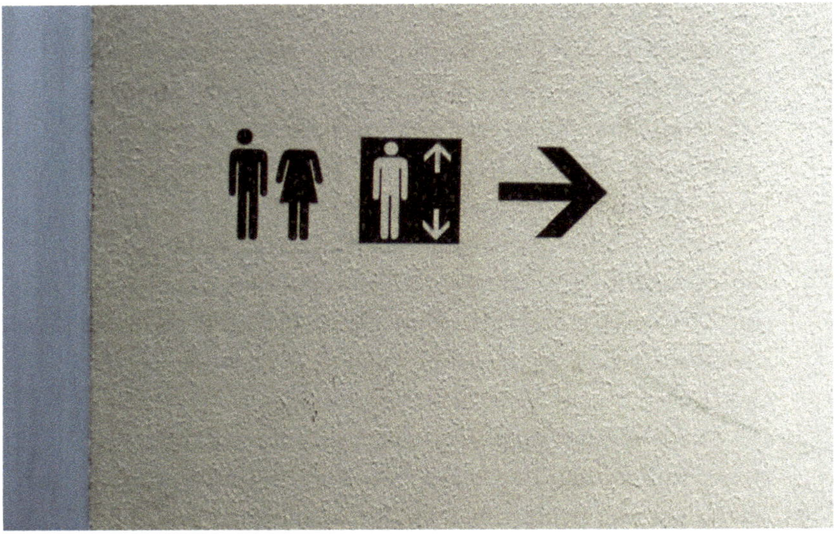

FIG. 11: Study participants pointed out details for improvement, describing their sense of feeling useful to the museum. Photograph: research participant.

The same painting had a different, very personal effect on another visitor. A 13-year-old girl took a picture of the dog in the foreground of the painting. She remarked during the interview: "My grandma had the same dog", and went on to talk about the dog's breed and characteristics. Furthermore, she mentioned that from that moment on, she set herself the goal to take pictures of dogs and similar animals throughout the museum, starting with the fox in the same painting. Recognizing a similarity to her grandma's dog from her everyday life helped her find an individual access point to the museum collection within the same painting which drove another visitor away.

As these examples suggest, visitor engagement depends on the narratives found in or around works of art, and meanings are as diverse as the very different backgrounds, knowledge, and states of mind of the observers.

Some participants brought back a photograph of a spelling error or a damaged navigation sign. One participant was not very excited by anything he saw in the museum. At first he talked about the exhibit in a very distant way, but then declared proudly that he found a mistake (Figure 11). He added that it took him by surprise to find an error in a place like the Rijksmuseum. He continued his visit searching for more imperfections (which he didn't find). However, this self-chosen mission was a way for him to engage with the museum, to look closely at objects, and to examine the museum's navigation system and the building in general. After the incident, he also took pictures of, and commented on, wall texts that he had read on his search for imperfections. Both his discovery of an imperfection and his mission to discover more, had the effect of putting this visitor at ease. He even asked me if I could report his

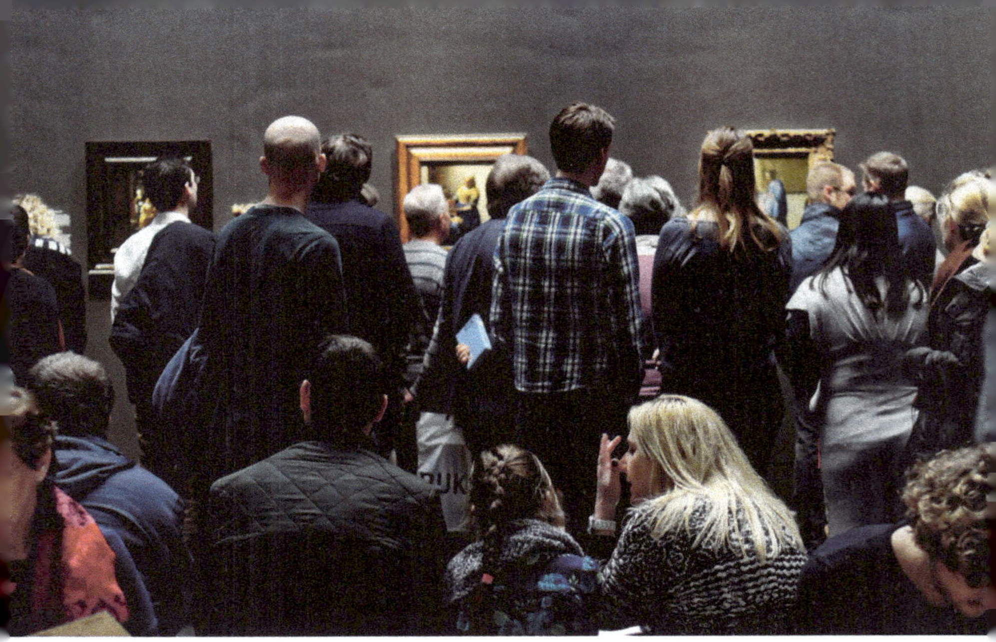

FIG. 12: I re-evaluated my own assumptions when one participant said, "I really like these parts that are crowded. If it's empty I wouldn't know how to behave." Photograph: research participant.

finding back to the museum in order to have it fixed.

To study these unusual perspectives and personal details before the ideation phase in the human-centered design process for new interactive features is a good way to get rid of one's own assumptions and gain new insights into the subjects being addressed. During one interview, I realized I had assumed most visitors would prefer a rather empty museum, with a quiet, contemplative environment ideal for experiencing artworks. This assumption, which reflects a traditional mind set, was challenged when a participant showed me the crowd in front of Vermeer's famous *The Milkmaid* (Figure 12). I expected her to start complaining about the crowd, but instead she described how the crowd made her feel comfortable. She explained that in empty museums she feels exposed and looked at, and therefore rushes through. I started asking other participants about their feelings about crowds, and others shared her preferences. They felt a vague pressure of having to "look at it in the right way" or not knowing how long to remain looking at a certain artwork. This insecurity, or "social awkwardness" accompanied many of the narratives of less experienced museum visitors, but even regular visitors had this feeling at times.

Implications and uses

The insights from this visual feedback method – as part of a larger set of studies – fed into the subsequent ideation process for Augmenting Masterpieces. The results led the research team to prototype social strategies which would allow visitors to engage with their surroundings in a playful way, as in the examples of the 13-year-old girl and the participant who

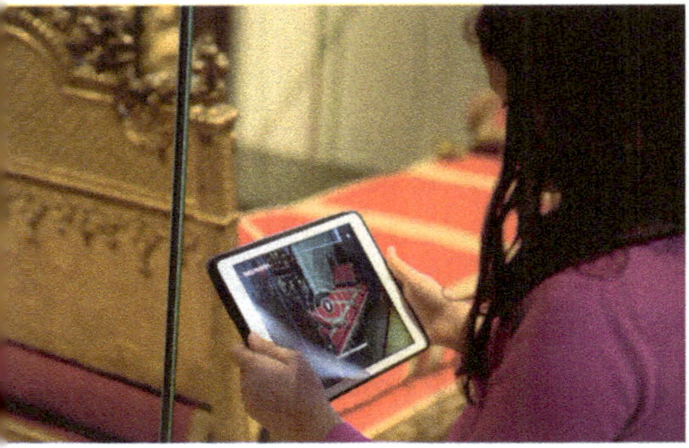

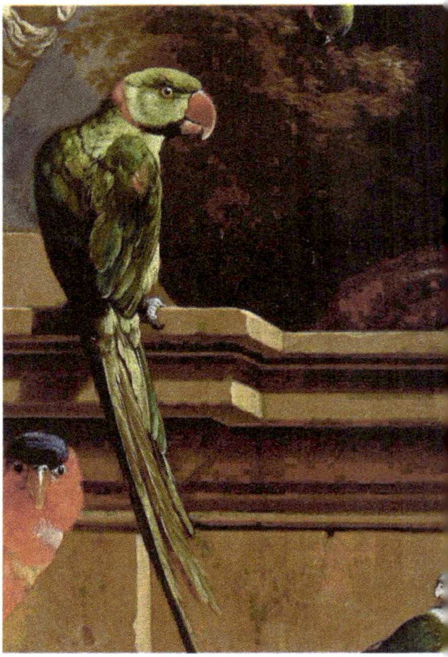

FIG. 13: Testing the *Hide Your Story* prototype on an iPad. Photograph: Floris de Langen.

FIG. 14: Melchior d'Hondecoeter, *The Menagerie (detail)*, c.1690. Photograph: Rijksmuseum Amsterdam.

searched for mistakes. Our aim was to enable engagement independently of someone's cultural capital in order to help visitors feel comfortable in, and valuable to, the museum. The main research findings used for the ideation and prototyping phase were that "random pieces of information" draw visitor's attention and are memorable. "Being on a mission" lessens social awkwardness and the feeling of not being knowledgeable. So the research team chose to work with mildly disruptive features which could be integrated into the existing Rijksmuseum app and which would complement the existing features in a meaningful way.

The team prototyped and tested three museum experiences which allow visitors to find individual access points to the exhibition. First, with the *Hide Your Story* feature, visitors can discover stories hidden by other visitors throughout the museum (Figure 13). Instead of following a route, visitors encounter stories coincidentally during their visit, using beacon technology to provide a random flow of information. They can also instantly record and add an observation themselves wherever they like. For example, *The Menagerie* (1690), a painting of green parakeets by Hondecoeter, reminded one visitor that the same birds are living in his backyard in Amsterdam (Figure 14). With the app feature, he recorded why these exotic birds live in the Netherlands, thus connecting the historic painting to contemporary city life. Through such recordings, visitors add a socially augmented layer to works of art which offer alternative approaches to the museum collections, alongside the art historical information provided by the museum.

Location-based beacon technology activates these stories

via bluetooth on visitors' devices when they are close to the work of art. In order not to swamp visitors with stories, the beacons react randomly, and the visit becomes a kind of treasure hunt.

Other surprises await visitors when using the *Trivia* feature. Also using beacon technology, visitors encounter multiple choice questions to answer. They can add their own trivia for other visitors and see how many of them give the same answer.

A third feature, *Improve the Museum*, allows visitors to directly submit suggestions for improvement. For example, when visitors encounter a broken sign or a spelling mistake, they can locate their spot, take a photograph with their smartphone and instantly submit a suggestion for improvement to the museum.

The results of a survey following the initial user testing of the features exceeded all expectations. Results showed that users very much enjoyed the social augmentation of the Rijksmuseum's masterpieces.

Directions for future research

The research study described here proved extremely useful in supplementing the Rijksmuseum's onsite multimedia applications. Nevertheless, future studies could benefit from some methodological improvements. For example, we found that sometimes participants felt frustrated because light conditions did not allow them to take sharp pictures, so future studies might use cameras which perform more effectively in low light conditions. Also, some participants found the small camera we provided difficult to use, as today most people feel most comfortable with their own smartphone camera, so future studies might allow visitors to use their own devices. Naturally, this will present some practical problems in saving the images centrally from multiple personal devices. It also means inviting participants to engage with their smartphones throughout their visit, causing additional distraction as they respond to incoming calls or messages.

Finally, the sample size used in this research project was small, since it complemented a larger set of qualitative methods. Future research might involve a larger group of participants and explore more aspects of the visit in order to collect comparable data. Giving visitors complete freedom to capture objects, settings and situations which catch their attention would – as well as providing in-depth comparisons of different perspectives of the same works of art – also allow an analysis of exhibition design and visitor flow within the exhibition space.

NOTES

1. Quoted from the Rijksmuseum's internal English-language documents, with reference to the Dutch-language version for clarification as necessary.

ACKNOWLEDGEMENTS

I would like to thank the initiators and coordinators of the project, Assistant Prof. Jan Hein Hoogstad from the University of Amsterdam and Annemies Broekgaarden, Head of the Public & Education Department at the Rijksmuseum. Thanks also to the staff at the Rijksmuseum (especially at the Medialab) for continuous support, the research team, our private sector partner UncInc. and everyone else who supported the research along the way.

REFERENCES

d.school (2011). *Bootcamp bootleg*. University of Stanford, Hasso Plattner Institute for Design Thinking. Available at: http://dschool.stanford.edu/wp-content/uploads/2011/03/BootcampBootleg2010v2SLIM.pdf.

Harper, D. (2002). Talking about pictures: A case for photo elicitation. *Visual studies*, 17(1), 13–26.

Packer, J., & Roy, B. (2005). Solitary vs. shared: Exploring the social dimension of museum learning. *Curator: The Museum Journal*, 48(2), 177–192.

Rijksmuseum FAQ (2013). Available at: https://www.rijksmuseum.nl/en/organisation/frequently-asked-questions/visiting.

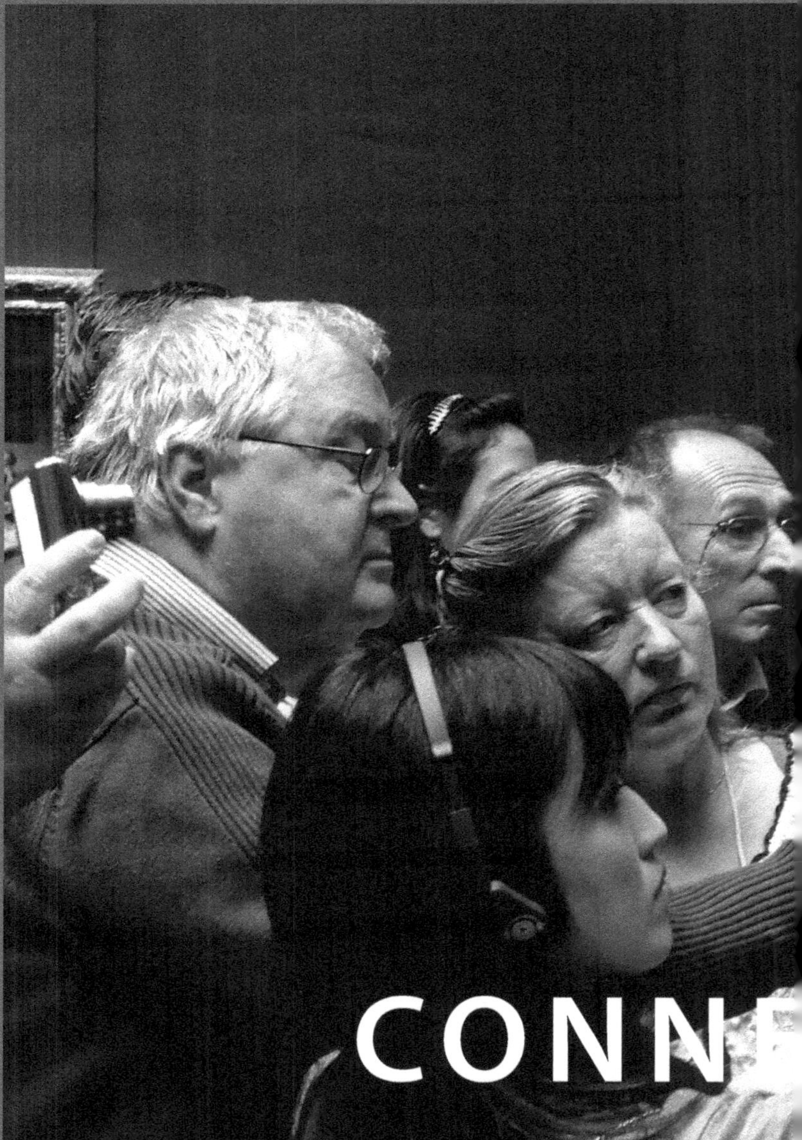
CONN

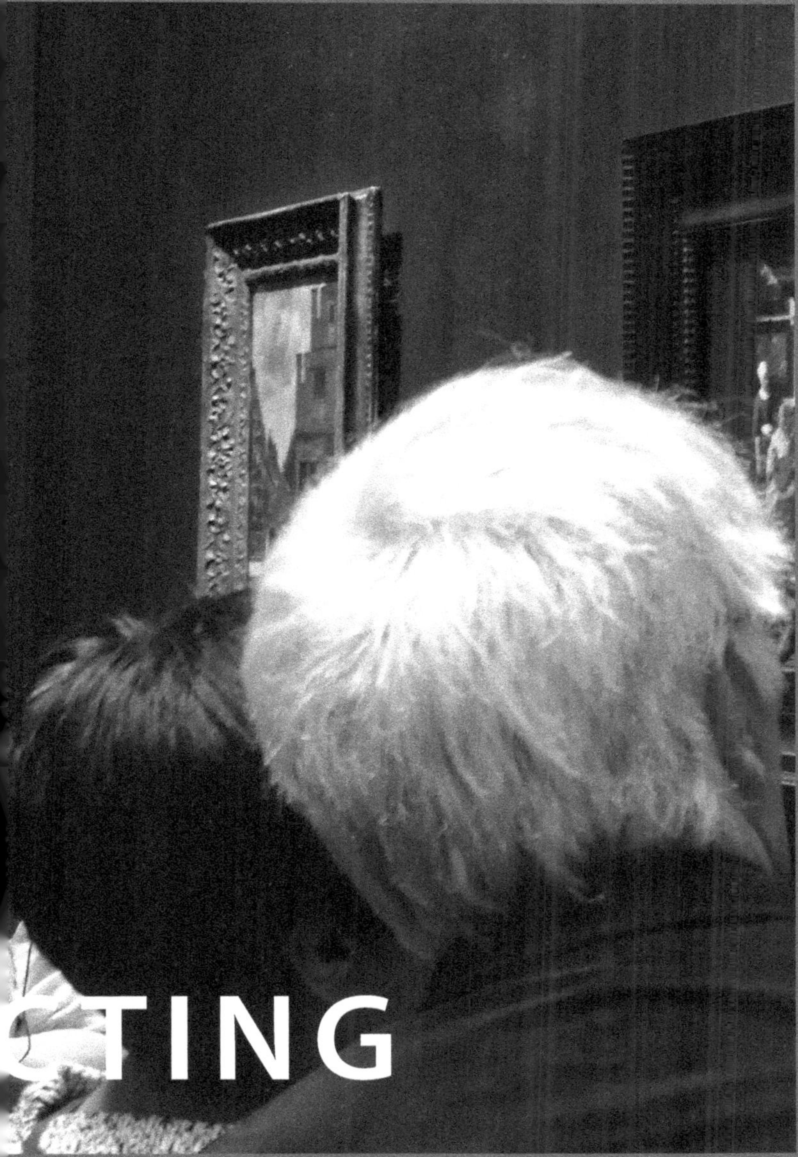
TING

CHAPTER TEN

VISITOR PHOTOGRAPHY AND MUSEUM MARKETING

Kjersti Lillebø and Kirsten Linde

EVEN THE MOST personal forms of experience and the tales we tell about ourselves are partly shaped by public imagery and publicly available narratives. These pictures become our pictures, these stories our stories. This is imagery in use. (Holland, 2004: 3)

In competition with TV and video games, shopping at the mall, health studios and walks in the park, history museums collect and display the old things which most people have long since thrown away. This is not an easy sell. So, what is it about museums that continues to attract? What is it about the museum that engages – for real? What makes people close their laptops, put down their tablets and go see an exhibit for themselves? The "museum experience" is wrapped in a veil of expectations, and we, as museum professionals, are trying to grasp, and then meet, the (often subconscious) dreams and desires which keep leading people back to the museum.

A general aim of the history museum is to educate and inspire participation by allowing visitors to engage with history first-hand. For the last few years, the visitor experience has been the foundation of MiA – Museums in Akershus' marketing strategy. But what do our marketing pictures tell us about the desires that we as museum professionals believe our visitors seek to fulfill? To investigate this topic we have to first look at *what* we picture and *how* we picture it.

We have analyzed marketing pictures used by MiA over the past ten years, up to and including the images that we produce and use today. These images have been published in the annual museum brochure and on the museum's homepage, as well as posted to the museum's Facebook and Instagram accounts.

All nineteen museums that make up MiA are represented, in highlights from our collections, events and activities. A formidable number of pictures have been published over the years, ranging from small, informal photographs made by non-professionals to more formal work made by professional photographers. Analyzing the composition of the marketing images used by the museum, we will explore how they reflect visitors' self-presentations and the portrayal of their museum experience online.

The changing role of the museum

MiA is a publicly-funded museum consortium consisting of nineteen affiliated museums, spread throughout the countryside surrounding Oslo, Norway's capital city. Some of the affiliated museums receive thousands of visitors annually, while some are only visited by a few hundred each year. The museums are devoted to a wide variety of topics: local and national history, artists' homes, farming, gardening, timber floating, traditional food, handicrafts, school life, and steam locomotives. Combined, the affiliated museums which make up MiA offer a unique window into Norwegian history, society and culture. As an institution, we seek to convey the unique stories told by our museums in a way that will ignite curiosity in potential museum-goers, and inspire them to want to come experience the exhibits for themselves.

Historically, one of the original functions of the museum has been to underscore what might be described as dominant narratives of power through the display of objects of significance. In the Norwegian context, the historical museum, rooted in formal academic traditions with strong ties to the political and cultural elite, presented artifacts in the service of implicit and explicit nation-building projects, ethnic-Norwegian perspectives, patriarchal values and bourgeois cultural mores.

Rapid cultural and social change following the end of the Second World War, however, resulted in a new role for the museum as institution. The post-modern deconstruction of history initiated by feminist and post-colonial theory, and an increasing focus on a subjective context and perspective have led to, among other things, a broader, more self-reflexive assessment of society and historical accounts (Ortner, 1984). By challenging the dominant historical canon, these new voices paved the way for multiple interpretations, and presentations, of times past.

Even more recently, the rise of the internet has confronted the museum with another set of challenges, through the liberalization and democratization of the flow of information. Once the exclusive prerogative of an elite minority, suddenly anyone with internet access could share their views with thousands of people around the world. As a result, academia, and by extension, the museum, has been forced to cede its exclusive authority over the dominant narratives of power, losing their ability to present history – and themselves – without challenge.

Reflecting high Scandinavian standards of living and Nordic enthusiasm for technology and digital media, the smartphone quickly gained a large share of the Norwegian cellphone market. By 2010, smartphones were on their way to dominating the cellphone market worldwide (Scoble & Israel, 2014). At roughly the same time, social media sites like Facebook, and online photo-sharing applications such as Instagram and Snapchat, created a revolution in the way people interact with one another and the world around them (Vaynerchuk, 2014). This new technological paradigm has inevitably led to major changes in the way in which people visit and interact with the museum. Today museums no longer only have physical visitors; they can also have digital and virtual guests as well. Social media allows (and encourages) visitors to draw on any number of experiences, museum-related or otherwise, to inform their online identities. As a result, this new technology allows people to take a more active part in defining what a museum and the museum experience is for the individual.

Reality and illusion: changing imagery

> A picture can pull a moment out from the passage of time and hold it static for our delight. It can offer us visions – of places we have never visited, people we will never meet, experiences we have only dreamt of, fantasies the more powerful for their seeming reality (Holland, 2004: 6).

Patricia Holland (2004) uses the term "imagery" to refer to that category of pictures which can stand for something both unique and universal at the same time. For example, a portrait of a boy named Johan sitting together with his parents on a bench depicts both a unique family, comprising specific individuals, while at the same time representing a general, abstract concept: "the family portrait" (Holland, 2004: 4). Advertisements and marketing images are, of course, designed to catch attention in public space, and routinely make use of imagery in order to communicate effectively to a broad segment of the population. These pictures remain with us, leaving lasting impressions. Their abstract and emotive messages are so powerful; a mere glimpse effects us, as we register their meanings at a glance. Holland suggests that these pictures at once offer the viewer both reality and illusion, using the term "desired pictures" to describe those images that illustrate objects of human longing (2004: 4).

Looking at the marketing imagery created by MiA over time, we can see that social, cultural and technological change has had a clear impact. Our research is based on 803 pictures from annual museum brochures and MiA's homepage in the period 2010-2014. We have also examined marketing pictures from a six-year period before 2010 – some 100 pictures, mainly in printed material such as brochures and posters.

Inspired by Patricia Holland's use of the term "imagery" we have searched for pictures representing a general abstract concept. Our aim has been to seek out typical representations of motifs telling us about MiA's attempt to promote itself to the outside world.

We find that the images can be grouped into a range of categories, according to motif and aesthetic expression, and positioned along a continuum defined by the tension existing between the museum's traditional institutional authority and the individual agency of the museumgoer. We have applied an empirical and inductive methodology to the marketing material, which has led to our defining seven categories. The analysis has been in part inspired by Weiner's (1992) and Urry's (2002) theories. Our categories are:

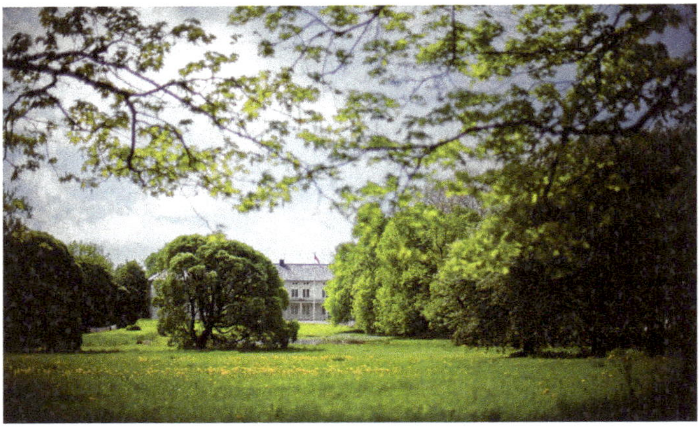

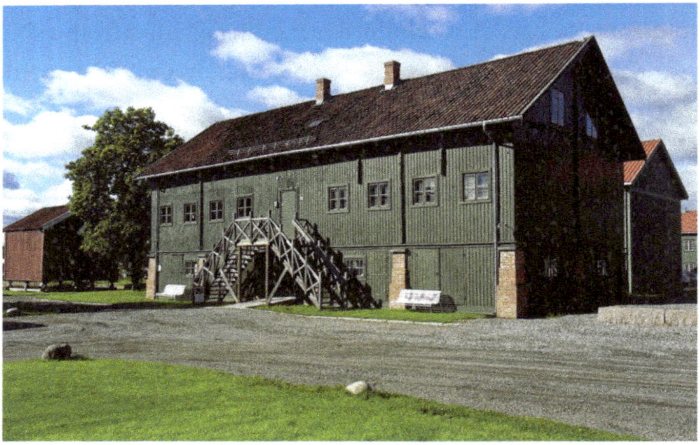

FIG 1: ABOVE | **Marketing image from 2013 showing the historic house museum, *Linderud gård*, hidden behind trees, promising experiences of old wealth and fantasy.** Photograph: Ingrid Aas.

FIG 2: BELOW | **Marketing image from 2005 showing, in a documentary style, the military warehouse at Ullensaker Museum.** Photograph: Kjetil Mortensen.

1. physical structures and objects as inalienable possessions;
2. the curator as an authoritative figure;
3. visitors viewing artifacts – "the tourist gaze";
4. visitors actively doing something;
5. behind-the-scenes;
6. the selfie-style informal amateur aesthetic;
7. food at the museum.

Most of the older marketing images we uncovered invariably fell into category 1, physical structures and objects as inalienable possessions. This category is characterized by the formal documentation of museum buildings, grounds, and artifacts. Through the sober compositions employed in these photos, the viewer senses the inherent authority embedded in the museum's very architecture. Photographs of physical objects within this category are presented as specimens, framed with little to no contextualization, lending the objects a sense of importance through the mere fact that they have been singled out and photographed. This imagery underscores the museum's authority through the implied scientific objectivity of the images themselves, often accompanied by lengthy texts, intending to further deepen the viewer's insight into the significance of these buildings or artifacts. This imagery draws on the object's status as artifact – something which belongs simultaneously to both the past and the present. Within the context of Norway's nation-building project, this imagery underscores a distinct, Norwegian past, informing – and legitimizing – a distinct Norwegian national identity in the present. Not unlike Annette Weiner's (1992) portrayal of an

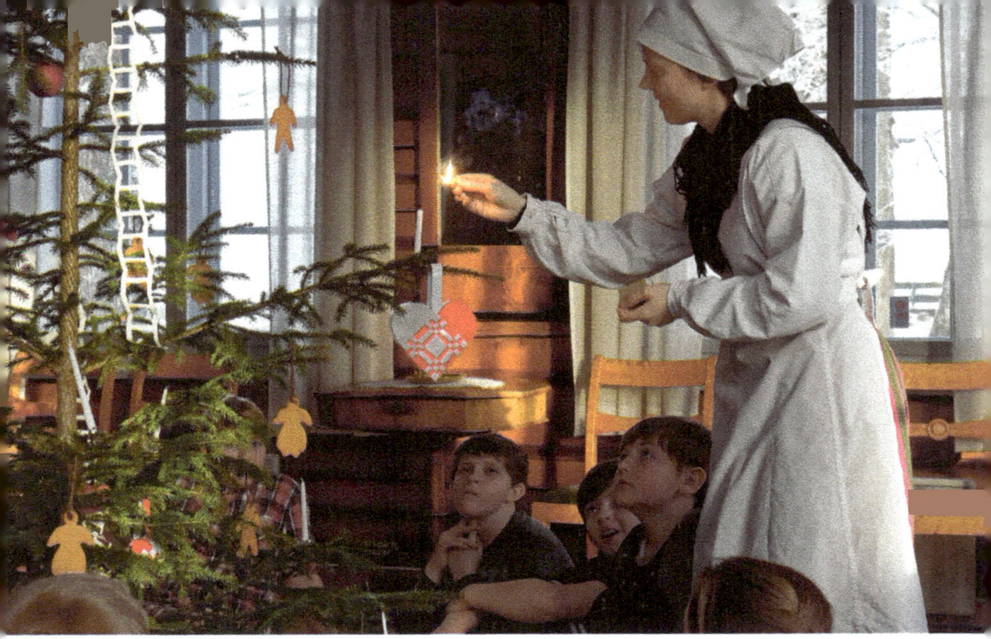

FIG. 3: Marketing photo from 2014 – young visitors watch a museum educator lighting Christmas candles at Skedsmo Bygdemuseum. Photograph: Øivind Möller Bakken.

intricate Trobriand relational exchange system of "keeping-while-giving" "inalienable possessions" where hierarchical and relational power is bestowed upon those who possess and define symbolically significant artifacts in society, these "special" objects serve as symbolic links between past, present, and future, conferring status on those who can lay a claim to them (Figures 1 and 2).

The second category, the curator as an authority figure, focuses on museum staff and volunteers authoritatively engaging a crowd of onlookers. In these images, the staff take on the role of expert – teaching, demonstrating, and symbolically embodying the authority of the museum as institution. We have a rather large number of images in this category and they recall a time when museums first and foremost were seen as keepers and teachers of historical knowledge and traditional skills. Imagery of this kind is still being used in today's marketing material, which may say something about the museum's own self-understanding and/or be an attempt to indulge visitor expectations about the museum experience (Figure 3).

The third category, visitors viewing artifacts – "the tourist gaze", is defined by representations of visitors looking at a variety of artifacts on display. For many, this imagery might be closest to what comes to mind when one thinks of what "going to the museum" entails. While engaged in what sociologist John Urry (2002) refers to as "the tourist gaze", the visitor nevertheless remains passively receptive to the authority of the artifacts themselves. While this type of image is widespread in museum marketing elsewhere, we found only a few images of this type in our material, most of which were at least ten to fifteen years old. This might be explained by the fact that

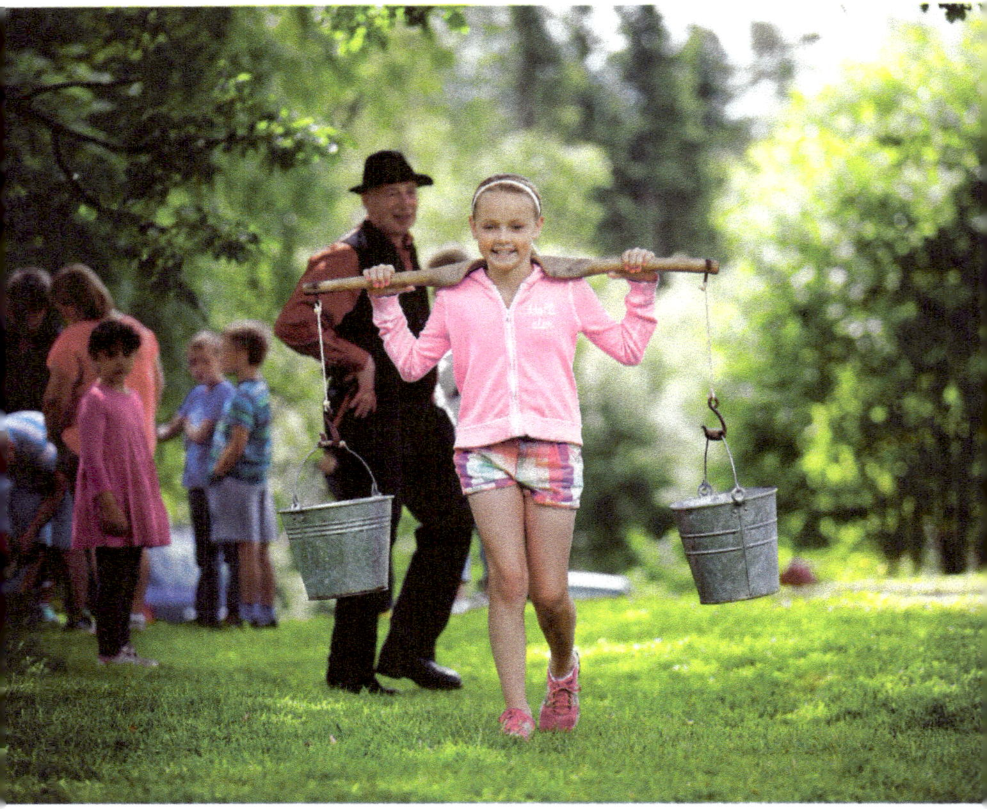

FIG. 4: Marketing photo from 2012 – a young girl enjoys an activity at Eidsvoll bygdetun open-air museum, with a traditionally-dressed volunteer in the background.
Photograph: Ingrid Aas.

very few objects in our collection have the kind of iconic status that would warrant "the tourist gaze". As a result, this imagery might not have been considered credible within a marketing context.

In the fourth category, visitors actively doing something, the roles are finally reversed – it is visitors, and not the museum or its institutional representatives, who are shown to have agency and the ability to influence their interaction with the museum. Whereas museum staff and volunteers were the active protagonists in category two, these images show visitors, many of them children, learning actively and joyfully, and engaging with their surroundings (the museum) as autonomous agents. One can read from the visitors' facial expressions that they are having fun or are doing something that requires their full concentration. This category forms a growing group of marketing images. Rather than being portrayed as a passive audience, visitors are now shown as active participants in the goings-on at the museum. Embedded in these pictures are also imagery of togetherness, fun and excitement (Figure 4).

Category five, behind the scenes, offers a post-modern glimpse into the workings of the museum. In this category, museum staff are shown performing tasks related to documentation, conservation, restoration and object display. This imagery asserts that museum staff are people "just like us", while revealing that exhibitions are consciously created, rather than simply unveiled. Rather than supporting the image of the museum as the purveyor of some objective, monolithic truth, this imagery alludes to the fact that multiple angles and perspectives make up the larger picture. These pictures are often taken by staff members themselves without any photographic

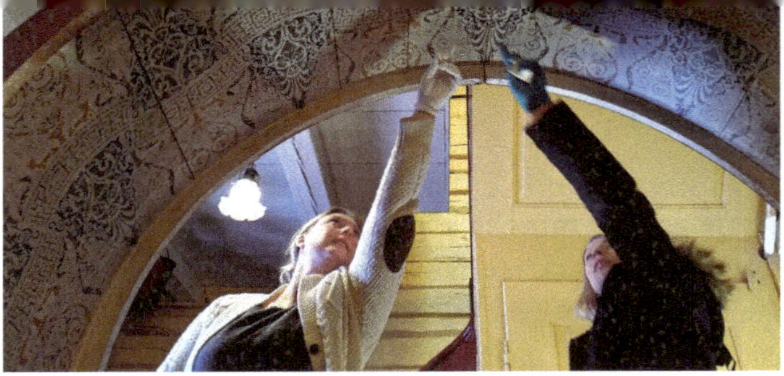

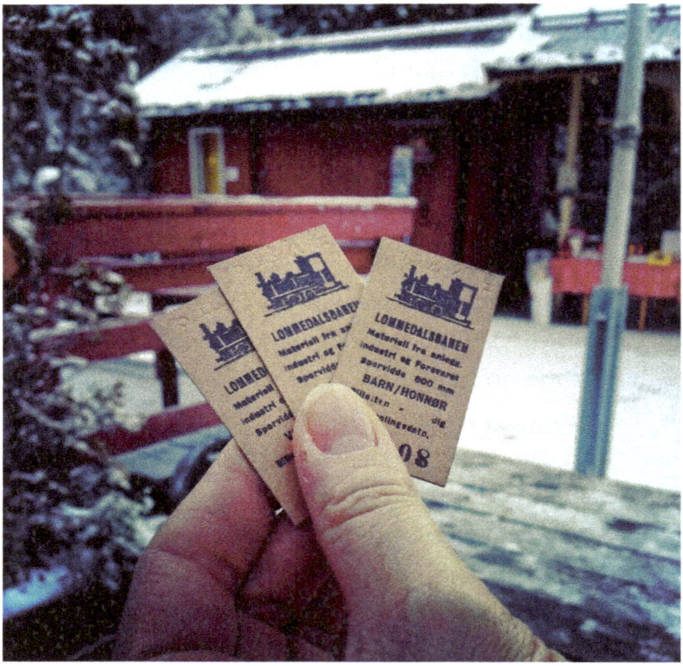

FIG. 5: ABOVE | The informal amateur-aesthetic used in marketing from 2014 onwards: behind-the-scenes with museum staff cleaning a bed canopy at the old farm museum of Gamle Hvam. Photograph: Kristine Draugedalen.

FIG. 6: BELOW | Train tickets selfie-style at the Lommedalsbanen railway museum, 2014. Photograph: Kjersti Lillebø.

training and, as a result, resemble the kind of private photos found on Facebook and Instagram. We noticed great interest among visitors in these glimpses "behind-the-scenes" of professional museum work and find it interesting that we are able to market our museum by simply doing what we do.

In the newest category (six), the selfie-style informal amateur aesthetic, the visitor takes center stage. This imagery is characterized by visitors staging and taking their own self-portraits with a camera phone. Here we see Instagram filters, Facebook and photo-sharing applications fundamentally changing the presentation of the museum experience. Here, too, we see irony and humor finding its way into the museum setting. We have now started using this informal amateur aesthetic in the promotional material produced by the museum. So far, our marketing material includes only a few selfie-style photographs, but we are increasingly experimenting with new ways of employing this aesthetic (Figures 5 and 6). One example is a marketing photo showing the photographer's hand holding up old-fashioned train tickets, selfie-style, using an Instagram filter. Another example is of museum staff members cleaning a bed canopy. This image was taken by a curator with a camera phone, recreating the same informal amateur aesthetic recognized from social media uploads. We predict that the use of selfie-style imagery will continue to increase and become a significant category in future marketing, especially in our efforts to appeal to younger audiences.

Posting pictures of oneself and others as selfies has rapidly become a regular activity, with the expanding access to mobile devices, and January 21st has quickly become established as international Museumselfie Day (see Dixon in this volume).

Clearly, many people enjoy expressing and sharing their personal perspectives of their lives with others. It is also a way to define and shape one's public profile. Photos provide protection from the fear that our dearest memories will fade away (Batchen, 2004). The fear of forgetting has been fought against long before the photography was invented – with keepsakes and souvenirs – but now everyone has the possibility to create a bridge to a previous reality by freezing the moment in a picture and sharing it with others.

Category seven, food at the museum, also borrows aesthetically from social media. This imagery is inspired by Instagram and Facebook users who share pictures taken on their smartphones of their food before eating it: a kind of object-based selfie. In our marketing strategy we consciously use this now-familiar imagery – because we enjoy it ourselves, but also because it promotes the museum experience of enjoying locally-produced, traditional food.

Our current advertising imagery closely reflects visitors' self-presentation on Facebook and Instagram. This is a fundamental shift away from imagery featuring historical artifacts and the museum itself, to museumgoers and their experiences. In 2012, a significant development in the museum's marketing strategy came with the founding of a communication department. The department made a conscious decision to focus on images showing activity in the museum, rather than just showing objects. As part of a wider trend in society of "reaching people where they are" the museum joined social media platforms, and participated using the same informal language and imagery familiar in these channels. While each social media platform has its own rules of conduct and use of language, what permeates them all is a focus on relevance, dialog, fast pace and the current: the use of real-time image uploads, and short and to-the-point language. The emotional, visual, and relational have become important factors in interactions.

Comparing the imagery in MiA's annual marketing brochure over the short timeframe of just five years, we see a significant change in the number of pictures featuring buildings and objects compared to pictures with visitors and museum staff engaged in different activities. In 2010, less than half (48%) of the images had people in them, while 52% where entirely devoid of people. In 2014, 73% of the brochure's images featured people, while only 27% were without.

It is interesting, however, to compare these print-media numbers with the images used in the museum's online marketing. Take, for instance, the website of the Gamle Hvam Museum, an historic farm museum which features popular exhibitions, gardens, events and activities. Looking at the museum's internet-based advertising of events and exhibitions in 2010, the proportion of pictures including people was 71% (increasing to 74% in 2014) while the images without people was only 29% (decreasing to 26% in 2014). Significantly, it was online, rather than in print, that the museum first began making significant use of more people-focused marketing imagery. This development is echoed in the imagery on the museum's Facebook page, with around two-thirds of imagery featuring people (71% in 2014 and 72% in 2013), compared to only one-third featuring buildings or objects (29% in 2014 and 28% in 2013). It is, however, not only the proportions which indicate a change in the way the museum is pictured. Differences can also be seen in the choice of themes and styles.

While marketing imagery featuring buildings and artifacts as primary subject matter continues to be produced, the new images are radically different to their predecessors. Buildings and objects were previously photographed almost exclusively from the front, in a formal documentary or scientific style, whereas in newer images the photographer frames the subject matter from a variety of different angles, highlighting the varied perspectives that might inform contemporary interpretation. Not unlike images found in contemporary interior design magazines, these more recent images present the museum in a more informal, accessible and, at times, playful light. Increasingly, we also see images featuring interior spaces or home furnishings, in which human presence, although formally absent, is nevertheless implied through lit candles or place settings. An otherwise "sterile" image of an empty room is transformed into an emotionally-charged vignette, contextualizing the objects and hinting at the human relationships once so intertwined with the artifacts. In a similar vein, images of well-worn pots and pans in a kitchen setting, or cultivated roses in an old garden, also serve to humanize history, offering a nostalgic glance at days gone by and lives well lived. There is a definite shift towards a visual imagery which blurs the line between objective reality and subjective fantasy, creating a longing for the past.

Telling stories in a noisy world: this is what we do

Borrowing the democratic aesthetic of social media, museums are now increasingly seen to engage in a subtle form of viral marketing, producing and presenting images which audiences might just as easily post themselves or find their friends posting on their Facebook feed. Some of the work with our marketing images is a conscious simulation of visitors' pictures that we see online, a recreation of universal "desired pictures", playing on people's emotions. Through our marketing images, we aim to portray feelings we see expressed at the museum by our visitors. We do not use professional models, but rather let professional photographers capture real-life visitors in real engagement and action. However, we have some concerns.

For our institution to thrive, we have to be seen as accountable and believable. The images we present must have more than a purely commercial interest. Is it all right for our pictures of objects and buildings to mimic the styles of social media? Are museum selfies just too silly to be used in museum marketing? Is the museum losing its academic standing when it incorporates emotion and nostaligia in our marketing images?

From information to imagination

At the turn of the millennium, futurist Rolf Jensen (2001) predicted a change in consumer mentality in the wealthy societies of the world with the emergence of "The Dream Society". Faced with an overwhelming over-abundance of consumer goods, consumers are less able to make informed decisions, turning instead from information to imagination in order to guide their behavior. Increasingly, consumers are drawn to those products connected with the most appealing story, and it is those products which most effectively tell a story that will win out in the marketplace.

Driven not only by the material quality of consumer goods, today's consumer is increasingly motivated by an interest in immaterial products and experiences. The currency of this marketplace satisfies a complex set of human needs. In the face of material comfort, the heart sets its sights on that which cannot be purchased directly: an "authentic" or "meaningful" experience.

Looking at visitor trends we can see a clear correlation between the consumer behavior described by Jensen (2001), and visitor behavior at the museum. Historical sites, exhibits, and events which have been linked to an interesting or compelling story do, in fact, attract more visitors than sites, exhibits, or events whose content has been communicated strictly in terms of objective, factual information.

Today, people are seeking adventure and experiences that can be shared with family and loved ones, fostering feelings of love and affection, security, care, and self-development. Within this context, the world of the history museum offers a multitude of arenas for such pursuits, while providing access to a rich well of stories to draw upon.

Many of Jensen's predictions about The Dream Society have proven correct, and are facilitated by the ease of information flow made possible by digital media (Flores, 2014; Scoble & Israel, 2014; Vaynerchuk, 2014). The ability to instantly share updates about one's life on Facebook, Instagram or Twitter offers today's consumer the opportunity to make even more visible the status-building behavior referred to by Thorstein Veblen (1994) as conspicuous consumption. Such updates are more powerful when accompanied by an image. Pictures are "like a mirror in which we see ourselves reflected, so that we seem to become part of the scene in front us" (Holland, 2004: 6). Photos that once were kept in albums and now are posted on

Facebook and Instagram are always filtered (Flores, 2010). Very rarely do we share pictures of boredom, sorrow, or arguments. According to Goffman (1984), people distinguish between front and backstage when managing their lives in complex social interactions. By posting striking images online, perhaps from a family outing to the museum, a person builds cultural capital (Bourdieu, 2010).

Just as the photo has become a proof of presence, people want to share their personal pictures with motifs from museum sites. Like the pilgrim – ritually having to prove to herself and others that she has been to the same places of interest as her peers – museum visitors today know that there are certain places that will confirm their identity and bestow success on themselves and others. The phrase "Picture – or it didn't happen" (Urban Dictionary, 2006) is a social media phrase referring to the fact that experiences are deeply connected with their visual representations. Not having a photo means a less valuable experience. These slightly cynical observations of consumer behavior are counterbalanced by Daniel Miller's theory of shopping. In his study of consumer behavior, Miller (1998) discovered that his subjects did not act motivated only by hedonistic and selfish desires, but mostly did their shopping as an act of love for their family. Consumption was interpreted as a way of providing what was necessary for the physical and mental health and welfare of one's loved ones.

Remembering the past, re-membering history

Although there may be many different reasons why people want to visit history museums, there are nevertheless certain activities people usually wish to undertake once they get there. A trip to the museum offers an opportunity to understand, relive, and perhaps also conserve the visitor's own history. At a traditional folk museum, we want to cook and bake, eat, sing, and learn how to make traditional handicrafts. At a coastal museum we want to learn how to row a boat, or set sail the old-fashioned way. We want to explore aspects of the past. Some people come to learn something completely foreign and exotic to them, while others want to learn something about their ancestors.

Museums act on many levels when it comes to preserving and transferring historical knowledge. Traditionally, they have been seen as warehouses of valuable material interpreted and contextualized by curators in exhibitions, books and lectures. Information about the past was mainly written. However, as Paul Connerton (1989) reminds us, historical knowledge and social remembering are transferred in many other ways besides the written word; memory about the past is conveyed and sustained by humans through their activities. By acting in certain ways in certain settings, people are able to relive and maintain elements from their past. Social life is made up of physical performances and bodily experiences. To act history is to preserve history.

In our museums, we see grandparents and parents bringing children in order to transmit old traditions to younger generations. When we use marketing images of joyful interactions between generations, we are also tapping into a deeply-felt longing that many people have about the transfer of historical knowledge, and, by extension, a sense of *identity*, from one generation to another. Not only the academic version of historical knowledge, but one's own, personal experiences and memories of the past. Images of children doing enjoyable things at a museum might also trigger a longing for a childhood long gone, a childhood that parents and grandparents want to reconstruct and reinvent for their loved ones – and themselves – through shared activities. What we offer is thus the emotional experience of a time gone by, yet recent enough that it is still within the grasp of memory. As a counterweight to the dominant historical narrative of larger-than-life heroes undertaking larger-than-life tasks, we are telling and sharing the little stories, stories of ordinary people's everyday life, of who people really were.

Our museums' advantage is that we allow visitors to engage in a history that is perhaps exotic for modern visitors, yet not so distant as to be completely unrecognizable. This allows for certain experiential overlaps between past and present, making remembering easier, and connecting people today across generations. Our objects are perhaps on their way to becoming iconic, but still part of our collective memory. Our museum offers a type of cultural space which is open to mainstream, as well as minority, cultural expressions, and where minority groups can join in, define and share common values in society. People thus take part in what Flores (1997) refers to as a "re-membering" where the use of minority cultural expressions allow members of mainstream society to "re-member" other, marginal, cultural values. By participating in rituals, rather than "everyday life", mixes of old and new customs come more noticeably to the fore, actively recreated and embodied by new actors. These physical activities can function as tools in the process of bridging the gap from being *outsiders* to becoming *participants* in what Renato Rosaldo (1997) called a "cultural citizenship". The museum offers such an arena for remembering and talking about the past. To pass on certain family

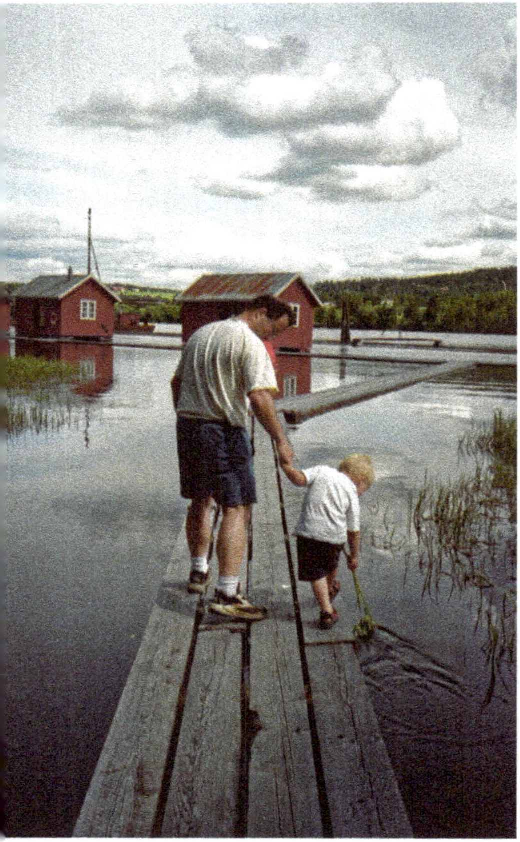

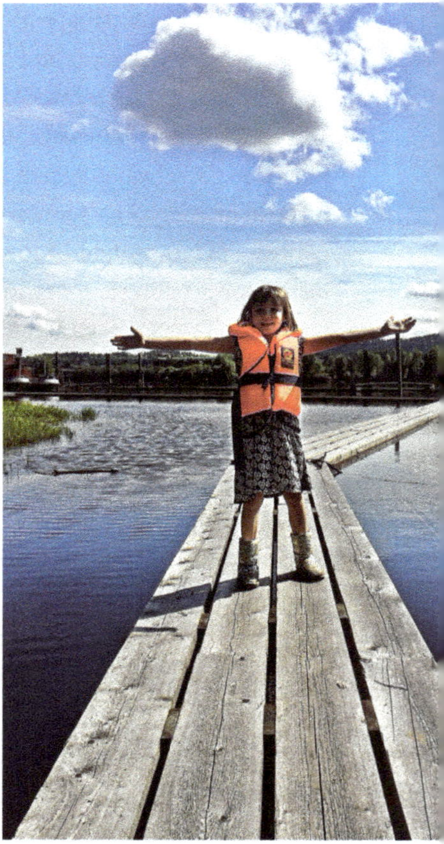

FIG. 7: LEFT | **A personal photo taken at the timber floating museum Fetsund lenser – a souvenir for a photo album (2003).** Photograph: Kirsten Linde.

FIG. 8: RIGHT | **A personal photo shared immediately on Facebook and in a blog (2014). Akershus Museum was allowed to use it to market the museum. Notice the little girl's correct use of a life jacket.** Photograph: Ninni Tranum.

remembering of the past creates value in present life, and a sense of belonging within a meaningful social construction, an "imagined community" (Anderson, 1991).

"Walk on water!" Engage, involve, act

The desire for both togetherness and the emotional sharing of values is well illustrated by an example from a campaign at the timber floating museum at Fetsund Lenser (Figures 7 and 8). A popular activity for many years has been "walking on water", by means of narrow walkways built of timber planks floating on the river, originally used by rafters to reach and hook timber sent down the river on its way to the sawmill. Today, as museum professionals we regard "walking on water" as a valuable experience of historical activity. Walking on the river is an extraordinary physical experience which brings our visitors close to the power of nature and the uniqueness of the site. While visitors have photographed themselves on the narrow walkways for years, this activity had not been the focal point of our marketing images. The timber floating museum had instead employed images detailing layouts of the impressive floating facilities, indoor exhibitions, or museum staff demonstrating the traditions of the rafters. After actively publicizing "walking on water" as an exciting activity to be undertaken in a family setting, through social media and a cinema commercial, we saw an increase in visitors coming specifically to experience this. We were also able to observe them taking their own pictures while participating in the activity.

Pictures are the language of our time

Our marketing strategies must always evolve in dialog with

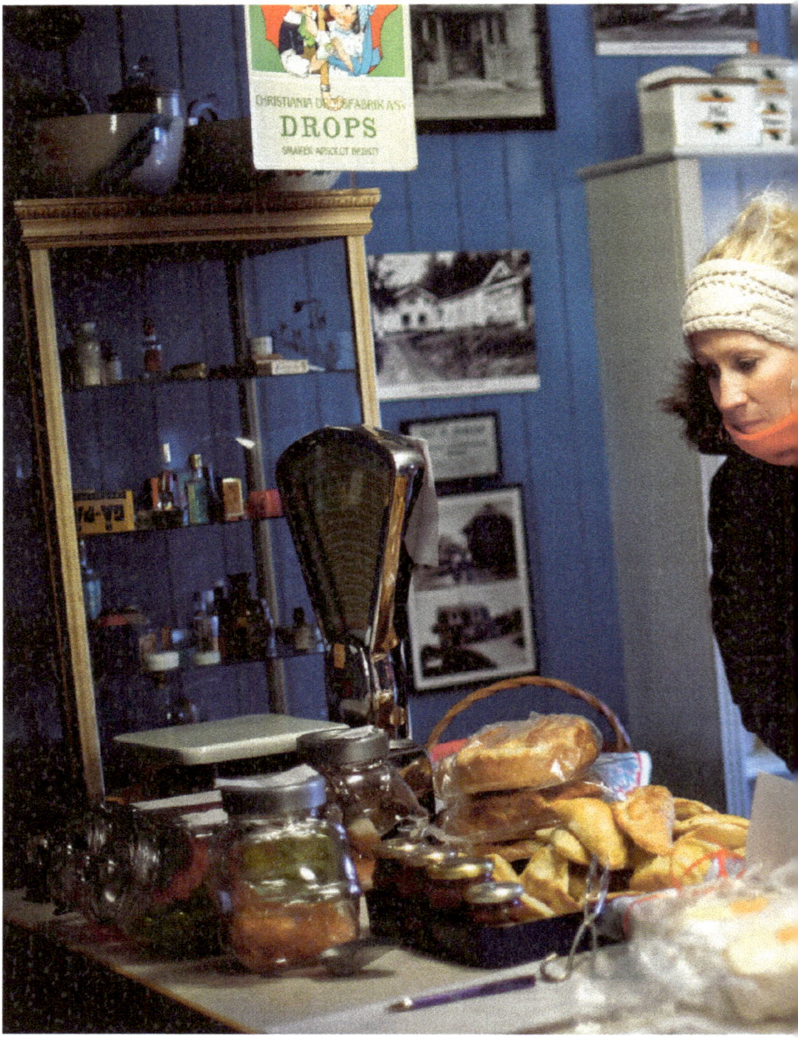

FIG. 9: A family experiences the old merchant shop at Rælingen bygdetun (marketing photo). Photograph: Ingrid Aas.

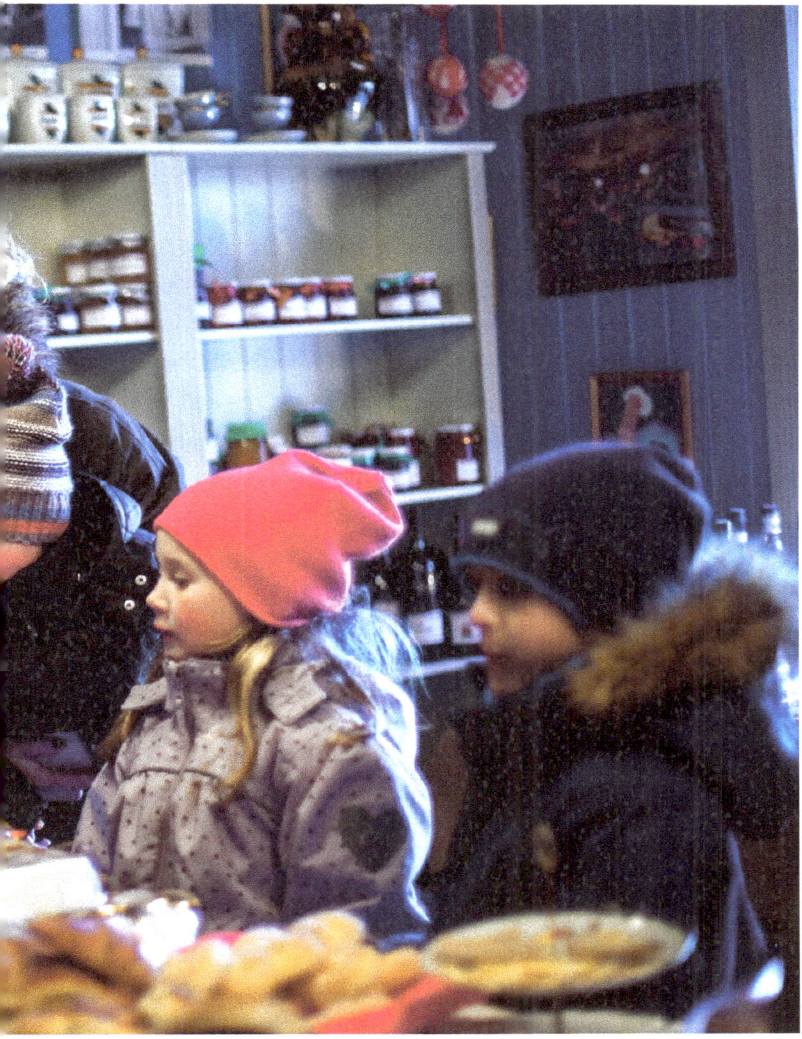

our physical and online visitors. When we come across good quality photos of the museum online, we always ask permission to use them in our marketing materials, allowing visitors' portrayals of their own personal experiences to expand and inform the symbolic representation of the museum experience in general. One such image created by a visitor, who subsequently gave permission for its use in our marketing, was posted by an American blogger in 2014 (Figure 9). The image of a young girl, excited, focused, and "in the moment" while "doing" our museum, was exactly how we wanted the museum to be pictured. There are, however, ethical concerns and legal parameters connected to using visitor's photos. We always obtain permission for use from both the photographer, and the legal guardian of the child, as well as consent in copyright release forms. On occasion, obtaining these permissions can be challenging, so we sometimes prefer to use our in-house photographers, and our staff's own children. The children soon forget the photographer, and immerse themselves completely in their activity.

Museums are not only selling a ticket to an exhibit, but a ticket to a lifestyle. And one which reflects values which your audience wants to be associated with, and which they can use via social media to broadcast to others that they find important, documenting their cultural capital (Bourdieu, 2010). These values may be sophistication, being historically aware, being intellectual, being a responsible parent educating and stimulating their children in the weekends. Ultimately, what we are selling in our marketing pictures is a ticket to an understanding of one's own place in the world and a feeling of belonging in history.

The museum today can contribute to an arena for cultural citizenship. We need to continually be figuring out innovative and creative ways of delivering this valuable content to new groups that might not otherwise look to the museum. This means talking the same language as the people we want to attract. And today's language is photographs and "desired pictures", shared over social media platforms. In a noisy world, it is all about getting your message across in a visually pleasing yet evocative manner (Vaynerchuk, 2014). The case above exemplifies the changing role of the museum and how visitors use the museum. From providing an historical and educational environment, focusing on indoor exhibitions and artifacts, the museum is now portrayed by visitors, as well as portraying itself, as a destination for family outings, of togetherness, activity and entertainment: "the museum experience". Visitors want to experience something unique while doing something together, and they want to share their experiences with others. Today, this is easily done through social media channels.

REFERENCES

Anderson, B. (1991). *Imagined communities. Reflections on the origin and the spread of nationalism*. London: Verso.

Batchen, G. (2004). *Forget me not: photography and remembrance*. Amsterdam: Van Gogh Museum.

Bourdieu, P. (2010). *Distinction: a social critique of the judgment of taste*. London: Routledge Kegan & Paul.

Connerton, P. (1989). *How societies remember*. Cambridge: Cambridge University Press.

Flores, R. (1997). Aesthetic process and cultural citizenship. The membering of a social body. In Flores, W. & Benmayor, R (eds.), *Latino cultural citizenship. Claiming identity, space and rights*. Boston: Beacon Press.

Flores, S. (2014). *Facehooked. How Facebook affects our emotions, relationships, and lives*. Tiburon: Reputation Books.

Goffman, E. (1984). *The presentation of self in everyday life*, Harmondsworth: Penguin.

Holland, P. (2004). *Picturing childhood: the myth of the child in popular imagery*. London & New York: I. B. Tauris.

Jensen, R. (2001). *The dream society: how the coming shift from information to imagination will transform your business*. New York: McGraw-Hill.

Miller, D. (1998). *A theory of shopping*. New York: Cornell University Press Ithaca.

Ortner, S. (1984). Theory in anthropology since the sixties. *Comparative Studies in Society and History*, 26(1): 126-66.

Rosaldo, R. (1997). Cultural citizenship, inequality and multiculturalism. In Flores, W. & Benmayor, R (eds.), *Latino cultural citizenship. Claiming identity, space and rights*. Boston: Beacon Press.

Scoble, R. & Israel, S. (2014). *Age of context: mobile, sensors, data and the future of privacy*. North Charleston: CreateSpace.

Urban Dictionary. (2006) *Pics or it didn't happen*. Available at: from: http://www.urbandictionary.com/define.php?term=pics%20or%20it%20didn't%20happen. [Accessed 15 January 2015.]

Urry, J. (2002). *The tourist gaze*. London: Sage.

Vaynerchuk, G. (2014). *Jab, jab, jab, right hook: how to tell your story in a noisy social world*. New York: HarperCollins Publishers.

Veblen, T. (1994). *Theory of the leisure class: an economic study in the evolution of institutions*. New York: Macmillan.

Weiner, A. (1992). *Inalienable possessions: the paradox of keeping-while-giving*. Berkeley: University of California Press.

CHAPTER ELEVEN

#CAPTUREPARKLANDIA: AN EXPERIMENT WITH INSTAGRAM

Kristin Bayans and Justin Meyer

OVER THE COURSE OF its run,[1] the Instagram project #captureParklandia empowered museum visitors and local residents alike to interact with the Portland Art Museum (PAM) in new ways and created a personalized experience through digital photography. Initially a public engagement project whose goal was to inspire museum visitors to explore Portland's parks, #captureParklandia ended up achieving much more. It expanded the museum's audience by forging new relationships with targeted, local special interest groups, identified the museum as a platform for discussing civic issues, and bridged, in part, the gap between traditional gallery and visitor-created content in PAM. The purpose of this chapter is to tell the story of #captureParklandia so that other institutions interested in Instagram-based museum visitor engagement may learn from the practical and theoretical issues that we,[2] the project's creators and managers, encountered.

Project goals

The name #captureParklandia conveys the initial project goal of encouraging Portlanders to capture personal moments in Portland parks using social media on a mobile device. We designed #captureParklandia as a project which would advance the education department's goals and the museum's strategic plan to increase digital capacity and cultivate targeted community partnerships.

As #captureParklandia developed, so did our expectations. Ultimately, the project used objects from the special exhibition *Art of the Louvre's Tuileries Garden* and Instagram photography taken by Portlanders as a catalyst to:

- increase Portlanders' awareness of the social history and

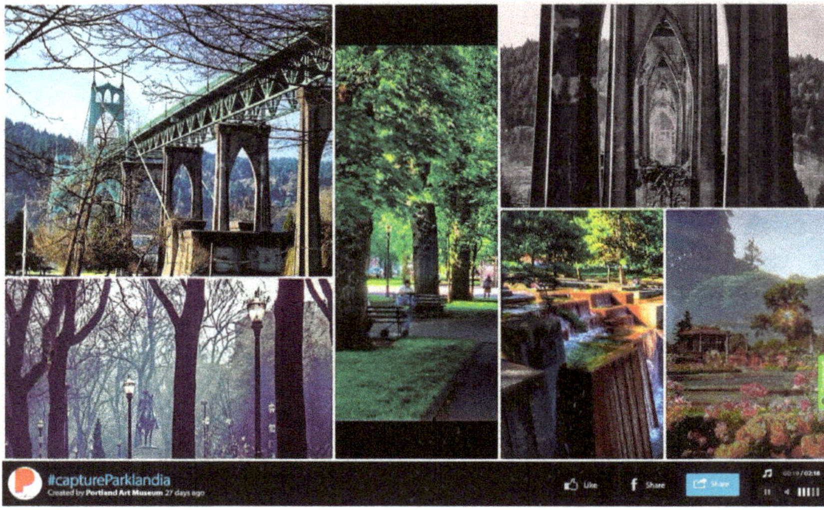

FIG. 1: #captureParklandia's Instagram gallery via the web application Slidely.

importance of their urban parks;
- enable Portlanders' to interact with PAM in new ways, both inside and outside the gallery;
- reach new audiences with diverse backgrounds;
- develop relationships and collaborations with new community groups;
- and build internal capacity for future social media projects.

How #captureParklandia began

#captureParklandia was one project in a suite of programs which Kristin Bayans proposed during the interview process for the position of PAM's Interpretive Media Specialist. During Spring 2014, the museum's education and curatorial staff communicated with Portland Parks and Recreation (PPR) and the Portland Parks Foundation (PPF) about designing a series of educational programs for the museum's 2014 summer special exhibition *The Art of the Louvre's Tuileries Garden*. The exhibition would illustrate the historical and social legacy of Paris' famous urban park. The museum saw this as an opportunity to expand on prior experience in social media[3] and draw parallels between the art exhibition and Portland's own civic resources through public programming.

The shared interest in implementing a community engagement project cultivated closer working relationships between the project directors and PPF and yielded a joint social media project. PPF wanted to use social media as a tool to make citizens aware of Portland's lesser known parks. They also wanted to increase awareness of an upcoming ballot measure which would, if passed, renew a tax-based funding source badly needed by Portland's parks. PAM's Interpretive Media Specialist, meanwhile, was keen to incorporate a place-based social media experience within the Tuileries to test new ways of interacting with repeat and first-time visitors to the museum.

Both the project directors and PPF wanted to use Instagram, which is popular among younger and ethnically diverse users,[4] groups which are traditionally not ones most likely to visit the museum.[5] The application is free to download and highly accessible to those with a smartphone, whose ownership is not as limited to higher income earners as it used to be – nearly half the U.S. population earning below $30,000 owns a smartphone. Using Instagram for the project meant there was a good chance to connect the museum to people beyond its usual audience.

Instagram is also unique in being primarily based on photography rather than text. It is also a hotspot for social interaction. Photographs are often annotated by the photographer with multiple descriptive hashtags.[6] Other Instagrammers can leave responses in the comments section of the photograph, as well as "like" the photograph by clicking on a heart icon. Together, these elements form a visual and written narrative of the photographic event being shared. These attributes, combined with the application's geotagging capability, made Instagram an attractive medium.

How #captureParklandia works

#captureParklandia was inspired by the community-sourced projects *Oh Snap! Your Take On Our Photographs* at the Carnegie Museum of Art[7] and *City of Memory* by CityLore (Zeitlin, 2012). #captureParklandia combines the collections-based, in-gallery components of *Oh Snap!*, with *City of Memory's* plotting of personal accounts on a city map.

In May 2014 the project managers initiated an open call for the public to share their Portland park experiences with PAM via Instagram. Initially, we sought out influencers within the Portland Instagram community to encourage participation in the project. PAM and the PPF promoted the call on their Instagram, Facebook, and Twitter social media channels, as well as on their websites, with pages dedicated to the project.

The project's entry points blended inside and outside museum experiences. Users could take a photograph on their mobile device anywhere in the Portland area with the Instagram application and tag it with the project's hashtag, *#captureParklandia*. All photographs with this hashtag were then immediately aggregated by the free web application Snapwidget[8] and plotted on an up-to-date geolocated map of Portland, all hosted on PAM's webpage dedicated to the Tuileries. A scrolling banner of the most recently captured photographs accompanied this map on the webpage.

Like the *Oh Snap!* project, #captureParklandia had an interpretive space inside the museum (Figure 2), located at the end of the Tuileries exhibition. Directly before entering the interpretive space, visitors encountered historic and contemporary photographs of the Tuileries Garden, and a timelapse video installation showing present-day moments in the famous gardens. These experiences primed visitors for the interpretive space's photography of present-day experiences in Portland's parks. #captureParklandia's in-gallery text panel described the project as follows:

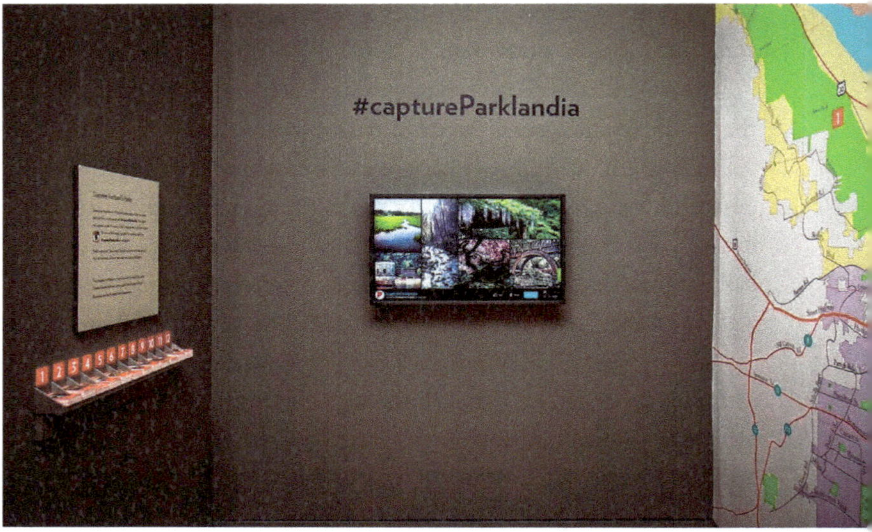

FIG. 2: The #captureParklandia interpretative space. Photograph: Cody Maxwell.

> **Discover Portland's Parks**
> Share your experiences of Portland's parks; capture them in a photo and post them to Instagram with *#captureParklandia*. Your photo may appear on the Museum's online Instagram feed and in this gallery. To view all the images captured this summer, search for *#captureParklandia* via Instagram.
>
> Need inspiration? Take a card, find the location on the map, and go. Visit old favorites, or discover new ones, and capture Parklandia.

In the interpretive space, 90 of the most captivating hashtagged photographs were rotated for display on a large monitor using the free web application Slidely[9] (Figure 1). The display was regularly curated by the project managers as new photographs were hashtagged.

Flanking the Slidely display were twelve numbered collectible Portland Park trading cards, representing twelve parks selected by PPF from among the hundreds in the city. Each numbered trading card featured an Instagram photograph of a Portland park (selected by PPF from the project contributions), the project's hashtag, several key facts about the park, and PPR and PPF standard visitor amenity icons (Figure 3). The cards were intended to help promote personal exploration of the selected parks. Visitors could collect these cards in the interpretive space, or at one of 120 citywide in-park events held by PPF. A wall map of the park system allowed visitors to match the parks on the cards with their numbered locations in the Portland area. The map also contained an icon orienting

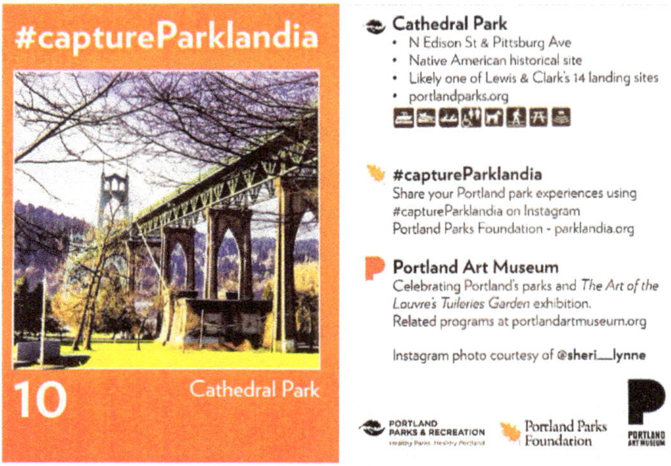

FIG. 3: Front and back of a #captureParklandia park trading card.
Photograph: Cody Maxwell.

visitors to the location of the museum in relation to the parks.

A second exhibition was designed in conjunction with the Tuileries and #captureParklandia, entitled *#captureParklandia: Experiments in Green Space*. This *Object Stories* exhibition shared five personal experiences relating to Portland's urban parks and green spaces. Launched in 2011, the *Object Stories* initiative displays personal perspectives and related physical objects on a single theme. The perspectives combine audio and still images into video interviews which are installed on iPad kiosks next to their corresponding objects in the *Object Stories* gallery. By honoring and collecting these perspectives, *Object Stories* aims to give the Portland community a voice inside the museum and make the museum more reflective of the community.

Experiments in Green Space helped illustrate the variety of ways Portlanders use public green space in the city, from producing fan-based *Star Trek* episode reenactments to building and maintaining an urban goat sanctuary. The *Object Stories* exhibition incorporated the #captureParklandia hashtag, and prominently displayed text mirroring the call-to-action found on the Tuileries interpretation space panel.

The digital museum experience

#captureParklandia is, in part, made possible by digital networks. Networks link people together in a community by common variables. As an Instagram project, #captureParklandia feeds into the community of local Instagram users, and into these users' individual online communities. By hashtagging a photograph with different tags, the Instagrammer can link to a variety of other users within their online community. For example, a photograph may be tagged *#captureParklandia*

#pdx #landscape, which users interested in Portland landscapes might take notice of, comment on, or repost. These tags might even lead a user to explore more about the project. Living among digital networks, #captureParklandia is similar to what Susan Smith Bautista (2014) describes in her book *Museums in the Digital Age* as a "place/experience." Engaging in the #captureParklandia project can be a process which happens between physically real spaces like PAM's building or online spaces such as a social network platform (Bautista, 2014). By connecting physical and online spaces, the museum has the capacity to become integrated into the fabric of a networked user's life. More importantly, however, this process has the potential to blend the museum's identity with that of the city, helping PAM to become a museum more *of* its place, and not just a museum *in* its place.

#captureParklandia also fits within the populist movement of viewing and creating art with a personal mobile device. Alli Burness (2014), museum selfie researcher and Digital Producer at the Museum of Applied Arts and Sciences in Sydney, states that these types of projects are visual evidence of the personal meaning making processes (popularized by Zahava Doering among others) conducted by visitors. Although Burness' statement refers specifically to selfies, the idea is not far removed from taking Instagram photographs of parks. #captureParklandia asks visitors for their interpretation of Portland parkspace to help make Tuileries a personally relevant experience.

Civic discussion

Portland residents who participated in #captureParklandia might not have been aware they were taking part in a civic discussion about urban parks. However, by sharing Instagram photographs of their Portland park experiences in the museum, they made digital, visual statements about how Portland's parks are used and what they mean to a variety of people. #captureParklandia created a democratic platform for this discussion by virtue of its accessibility and its inclusion of many voices.[10]

PAM, and museums in general, hold significant influence in cities, because of their function as custodians of material culture, as well as the political and social power held by their board members. This influence has been used historically to impart messages about national, ethnic, and civic issues through the museum's traditional authoritative approach to curation and exhibition (Coombes, 1988; MacDonald, 2003). Much criticism has been directed to the traditional collecting and exhibition functions of museums when they implicate social issues. While not quite as "high stakes" as an exhibition about a subject as sensitive as ethnic heritage, a unidirectional exhibition about urban parks, where a select few museum staff decided the content, would certainly not capture the full complexity of their meaning to Portland's residents.

The alternative to the unidirectional method of imparting knowledge is to design museums and their exhibitions as spaces for collaborative and constructive meaning making (Falk et al, 2006; Mason, 2004). The different uses of social media photography in #captureParklandia and its various paths of entry to participate make it accessible both to people who prefer digital interaction (tagging an Instagram to the project) and those who prefer more analog interaction (interacting with a printed wall map or collecting trading cards).

Accessibility to people with different learning styles allowed #captureParklandia to make its content more democratic by including diverse voices in the photographic conversation about urban parks. In political science and planning literature, the inclusion of as many constituent voices as possible in civic discussion invokes "communicative rationality", or an epistemology that claims that meaning is best discovered through the inclusion of as many points of view (and people) as possible (Alexander, 2000; Healey, 1993). Urban parks are used differently by different people and mean different things to different people. The accessibility of Instagram gives anyone with a smartphone the ability to communicate their experiences of the parks, and in turn, communicate what the parks mean to them through photography, giving viewers of the project's content a more complete picture of the importance of Portland's parks to its people.

Valorizing crowd-sourced content

What makes #captureParklandia particularly novel for an art museum is its melding of a constructivist space in a traditional gallery setting. #captureParklandia displayed photography of everyday Portland residents in the same exhibition as the highly venerated objects from the Louvre. Doing so might be perceived as putting #captureParklandia's crowd-sourced photography on the same symbolic level as the "traditional" artistic objects on display, a particularly controversial act for some in the museum field. While this was *not* the intention of either PAM or the project's authors, it does warrant some discussion.

Spaces already exist in many museums, including PAM

(such as the *Object Stories* gallery), where the visitor has the ability to interact with content and objects in a variety of ways and to join in meaning creation, but these spaces are often kept separate from the traditional galleries. This phenomenon, described as the separation of "temple" space and "forum" space (Cameron, 1971), is arguably the result of internal anxiety over museum authority since the advent of constructivist philosophy in museum education. This dichotomy of space symbolically maintains the superiority of the traditional gallery (and its messages) over the more constructivist gallery.

#captureParklandia was one of the first times at PAM that crowd-sourced social media was programmed in conjunction with a special exhibition, both conceptually and spatially. Though it did not fully bridge the symbolic gap between the Louvre's objects and crowd-sourced photography, displaying #captureParklandia in the same exhibition space as the Louvre's works did elevate the content of #captureParklandia more than presenting the crowd-sourced photography in another, self-contained gallery. The Instagram photography in #captureParklandia did not match the historical significance of the Tuileries objects, but PAM staff took great care to ensure the project's aesthetics matched those of its surroundings.

As mentioned earlier, Instagram is unique in that it is, first and foremost, a visually-based social medium. It has been a major influence in elevating social, digital photography through on-the-fly editing of photos, easy-to-use special effect filters, and instant access to a global network of hundreds of millions. This has empowered everyday smartphone owners to more carefully select and edit the experiences they capture and share with the world. It has also attracted artists and designers, especially in Portland, to share their work and market their services. Many of these artists (whom we met through the #captureParklandia project) depend on their Instagram accounts for most of their commissions, and consequently curate their Instagram photographs with as much care as they would a gallery exhibition. Thus, many photographs tagged to our project, #captureParklandia, were of a high aesthetic quality and could be easily displayed within the Tuileries special exhibition.

As is the case with any crowd-sourced and democratic project, there were inevitably photographs tagged *to #captureParklandia* that were not relevant to the discussion about city parkspace or aesthetically masterful. The free access of Instagram and use of our project's hashtag meant that we, the project's managers and PAM, could not control how it would be used by the public. Every so often, there were photographs tagged with the hashtag which contained content that either had nothing to do with Portland's parks, or were deemed potentially offensive to people. PAM, like many other museums, is not immune from the repercussions of potentially offensive material being shown in the galleries (those offended might stop visiting the museum or donating to the museum). To mitigate this risk, we curated the display of photography inside the interpretive space and kept the webpage feed uncurated. In this way, we could ensure the photography inside the interpretive space was relevant and had an appropriate aesthetic, but at the same time, we could also ensure that *everyone* had an opportunity to contribute to the project. This was a conservative move that still allowed space for photographs containing complicated or potentially offensive material to be shown, albeit outside the museum, in digital form.

One arts journalist and critic took issue with #captureParklandia's place alongside the Tuileries exhibition in her Arts Journal blog,[11] reigniting a familiar debate over whether traditional art museum exhibitions like the Tuileries really need engagement projects like #captureParklandia and whether museums should feel compelled to exhibit content created by the public. The Tuileries certainly would have attracted museum visitors without #captureParklandia, but would it have reached the same people which #captureParklandia reached? Would it have inspired the same visitor/museum interaction without #captureParklandia? The accessibility and crowd-sourcing of #captureParklandia's content attracted new visitors to the museum and did indeed initiate new museum/visitor interactions. Further, elevating crowd-sourced photography in the context of an art museum validated the voices and photographic work of community members and artists. This was indispensable in helping us cultivate new relationships between PAM and community groups.

Community collaborations

To jump-start participation in #captureParklandia, we sought out an Instagram superuser to seed the project using their social network reach. Through our education department director's connection with the InstaPDX social group, we met with two of the group's leaders, Jessica Selig and Paul Rudolph. According to its 927 member strong Facebook page, InstaPDX was founded in 2011, and is known as the first "Instameet" group in the world. The group brings together Instagram users in Portland, Oregon and the surrounding areas for in-person,

Instagram-related excursions at least once a month. Jessica Selig and Paul Rudolph are significant players in the group and artists by trade. Befriending Jessica and Paul meant legitimacy and access to the group; their stamp of approval gave our project some footing within the InstaPDX community, and allowed us to tap into the group's Instagram followers and their networks of tens of thousands of users. Jessica invited us to pitch our project in person at one of the group's meet-ups at a local pub. It was a bit awkward; we were essentially speed-dating people we had never met (at least in real life), describing the project and asking for their participation. Reactions to our pitch varied, but, within 24 hours of our appearance the project received hundreds of Instagram tags.

While interacting with our InstaPDX partners, we tried to dispel the stereotype of the art museum as an elitist and impersonal institution, and in doing so, reached more people. The way support for the project grew mirrored the way in which users normally communicate within their social networks. For example, formal modes of communication with our InstaPDX partners were replaced with more colloquial (and digital) forms. We communicated directly with our InstaPDX group partners via Facebook, Instagram, and in-person coffee meetings instead of through our PAM email accounts. Additionally, firm in our desire to cultivate a mutually beneficial and long-lasting relationship, we invited members of the InstaPDX community to submit photographs to be considered for the project's Portland Park trading cards. This opportunity was PAM's way of validating the expertise and artistic work of InstaPDX members. And since many of the members are artists, having one of their Instagrams chosen to be published as a set of 10,000 trading cards was a significant opportunity to get their work seen in a different medium and inside the venerated context of a museum. For those whose photographs were selected for the trading cards, we drafted formal contracts to ensure careful and respectful use of their work. We also provided the group with several behind-the-scenes press passes to the Tuileries, during which they, of their own volition, documented and shared the proceedings with their Instagram followers.

Did #captureParklandia achieve its goals?

Because #captureParklandia was an experiment for PAM, it was important to have some way of knowing whether the project was successful in achieving the goals we had envisioned for it. However, limited time (two months before the start of the Tuileries on June 13, 2014) and money precluded us from doing a thorough quantitative analysis to answer questions such as whether or not #captureParklandia increased the likelihood that museum visitors would take their experiences of the Tuileries exhibition with them into their own city.[12]

We did, however, gather quantitative data through participant observation and qualitative data through informal interviews to get an idea of who participated in the project and how they participated. With this information, we have evidence that #captureParklandia enabled new and diverse audiences within the community to interact with the museum in a new way, both inside and outside the gallery.

Participant observation inside the gallery took place an hour at a time on three days throughout the project: at the beginning, a week in, and near the end of the Tuileries exhibit and the #captureParklandia project. During each hour of observation, one project manager sat in a back corner of the last exhibition alcove, where #captureParklandia's interpretive space was located, and jotted down notes about the following characteristics of each group of visitors through observation:

- how many people were in the group of visitors?
- did any people in the group appear to be non-white?
- was the group diverse ethnically (containing more than one ethnicity)?
- did any people in the group appear younger than around 40 years old?
- did the group contain a diversity of generations (that is, younger visitors and older visitors)?
- did anyone in the group give at least a few seconds of attention to the park trading cards, looking at them, talking about them, or picking one or more cards up to take with them?
- did anyone in the group give at least a few seconds of attention to the digital display of Instagram pictures, looking at them or talking about them?
- and did anyone in the group give at least a few seconds of attention to the wall map, looking at it or talking about it?

The available human and financial resources (two project managers and zero budget) limited the number of days and times we observed project participants in the gallery. Also, judging age and someone's ethnicity by observation alone does not produce perfectly valid results. The small size of the gallery space and traffic patterns through it made in-person interviews, which would have allowed us to verify our observations of age and ethnicity variables, impractical.

Observation data of 174 visitors showed, unsurprisingly, that the majority of visitors to the Tuileries who also passed through the #captureParklandia interpretive space were white (90.2%) and belonged to an older generation (58.6%). There were, however, a handful of younger visitors (those who appeared younger than 40 years old), as well as visitors who were, by observation, ethnic minorities. Of the three components of the #captureParklandia interpretive space (the trading cards, the digital display of Instagram photographs, and the wall map of the Portland park system), the largest proportion of visitors interacted with the wall map (48.3%), followed by the digital display (35.1%) and the trading cards (31.6%). These proportions mirror those when controlling for white groups, where 45.9% of people interacted with the wall map, compared to 33.1% of people interacting with the digital display, and 26.8% interacting with the trading cards.

However, when looking at the gallery behaviors of ethnically diverse groups (groups of visitors with at least one "non-white" and one white visitor), the trading cards were more popular than the wall map: 78.6% of people in ethnically diverse groups interacted with the trading cards, compared with 64.3% who interacted with the wall map and digital display. The data suggests not only that the trading cards were more likely to appeal to ethnically diverse groups, but that ethnically diverse groups were more likely to interact with any component of #captureParklandia when compared to groups that were entirely white.

Controlling for age in our participant observation analysis produced similar results. People in older generational groups (where everyone in the group appeared older than 40 years old) had lower rates of interaction with components of #captureParklandia when compared to people in intergenerational groups. The wall map was the most popular among older groups, with 39.2% of people in these groups interacting with it, followed by both the digital display and trading cards with 28.4% each. People in young groups, surprisingly, had similar (and relatively low) interaction rates with the digital display and the trading cards to older generation groups. However, interaction among young people with the wall map was much higher relative to older generations (62.5% versus 39.2%). Interaction rates among intergenerational groups produced the most interesting results. People in intergenerational groups (groups with at least one young person and one older person) were around twice as likely to interact with the trading cards (50.0%) and digital display (65.6%) as people in exclusively younger and older groups. This data, first, challenges the assumption that younger generations alone would be more likely to interact with technology like the digital display, or even more playful elements like the trading cards, than older generations. Second, the data shows that the presence of both younger and older generations together in a group is more likely to lead to higher interaction rates with the digital display and trading cards.

While this data does not prove that #captureParklandia was necessarily responsible for attracting new audiences to the museum, these analyses suggest that the various methods of using Instagram photography in #captureParklandia encouraged more interaction among intergenerational and diverse ethnic groups than the predominantly white and older groups.

Informal interviews with several members of our community partner group, InstaPDX, revealed that many group members who came to the Tuileries and submitted Instagrams to #captureParklandia had never before been to the museum, confirming that the project did reach new audiences. Through discussions with these participants, we discovered that many first time museum visitors were attracted by the use of Instagram and the urban park subject matter of the project and Tuileries. Further, Instagrammers whose photography was selected to be displayed inside the #captureParklandia gallery invited family members and friends to see the Tuileries, #captureParklandia, and the museum for the first time.

We also analyzed Instagram comments on project submissions to understand how people used and were affected by the project. The data we collected and analyzed from Instagram comments was predominantly qualitative, so it cannot be used to draw conclusions about how many people were affected by the project in a certain way. However, this type of data evidences some of the ways in which the project gave museum visitors (including first time visitors) new ways of interacting with the museum and encouraged them to bring museum experiences outside into their own everyday environments.

For example, one Instagram user posted a photograph of a bronze sculpture of Teddy Roosevelt in Portland's South Park block with a quote from PAM's former chief curator Bruce Guenther: "As we walk the grounds of our parks, we walk on the bones of our past" (oregongirl_aroundtheworld, 19 July

2014). One of the key themes drawn out by PAM's former chief curator from the Tuileries exhibition was how urban parks are spaces in which much of a city's history takes place. This Instagram comment evidences a moment when the participant reflected on something she learned inside the museum while experiencing a place outside the museum. This Instagrammer even later added a photograph on Instagram of a past trip to Paris when she saw the Tuileries in person, indicating that she was reminded of her trip as a result of her museum experience.

#captureParklandia also successfully enabled community members to interact with the museum in new and informal ways. Inside the gallery, some Instagrammers narrated their experience of the Tuileries exhibition by posting photographs of their encounters with objects to the #captureParklandia project. One matched poetry to various objects they encountered in the Tuileries on Instagram. Another used Instagram's digital effects to dramatize Tuileries objects even further.

Outside the gallery, #captureParklandia gave PAM and members of the community equal opportunity to communicate with one another in a virtual public forum using comments and tags. The use of the museum's tag on Instagram, for example, does not require a special relationship between the Instagrammer and the museum. Instagram user everythingjence, who has no formal ties to the museum, communicated their appreciation of attending a preview of the Tuileries exhibition by tagging the museum in an Instagram. Another Instagrammer, ccfogarty, captured the moment when their picture appeared on the digital display inside the interpretive space, using this caption:

> It was wonderful to see one of my own shots on the #captureparklandia display at the Portland Art Museum's exhibit of "Art of the Louvre and the Tuileries Gardens" (sic). I love the way that the exhibit involves the local community and asks each of us to consider how we all interact with our own local parks. Masterful!

Also using the museum's tag, ccfogarty was able to speak not only to their followers/friends on Instagram about their experience of the Tuileries and #captureParklandia, but also to PAM.

Other, more anecdotal, evidence of #captureParklandia's success comes from conversations with many of PAM's senior education and public programs staff. They noticed that public programming which supplemented both the Tuileries and #captureParklandia had the best attendance of any summer program suite in recent memory.

Conclusions

Using Instagram photography as part of a museum exhibition revealed many practical and underlying theoretical issues. #captureParklandia required significant internal support from PAM's curators and marketing department to produce an in-gallery interpretive space, and support from PPR to produce the trading cards. Without the cooperation of our curatorial department and the lead curator, Bruce Guenther, we would not have been able to include #captureParklandia alongside the Tuileries. #captureParklandia made the representation of Portland's park space inside the museum more democratic, since anyone with the Instagram application had the freedom to use our project's hashtag and contribute their experience of a Portland park to the project. This freedom also meant that we needed to address contributions to the project that were less relevant and potentially offensive. While we allowed space on the project's website to display all contributions, we decided to curate the project content inside the interpretive space. #captureParklandia also required us to go into the community to recruit partner groups (such as InstaPDX) to jump-start participation in the project. The content of the project attracted interest from these groups, but because we engaged these community groups in their own space and in a down-to-earth way, we were able to form a lasting partnership.

For a museum to be of any value it must meet the changing needs of society (Weil, 2002). #captureParklandia pushed PAM past an internal tipping point of incorporating digital technology and social media to better reflect the personality and people of Portland. The museum is now, more than ever, moving towards generating a cohesive approach to digital and social media initiatives. #captureParklandia has increased PAM's internal awareness of social media, the value of using it on a large scale within exhibitions, and the need to reach out to our online and media-connected visitors. A cross-departmental and cross-hierarchical social media team has formed in large part because of #captureParklandia. This team will help integrate Instagram and other social applications more fully into future museum exhibitions and projects. #captureParklandia has also highlighted the importance of increasing staff digital literacy in order to negotiate experiences with new constituents and to have more ways to experiment.

The more than 2,000 Instagrams tagged to the project, the countless anecdotes of positive feedback, the continued use of the project hashtag by PPF,[13] and the new collaborations which have emerged from #captureParklandia, have, we believe, made it a successful experiment. However, the project was not without controversy – it reignited familiar debates about the value of public engagement and the use of new technologies like Instagram inside museums.[14] Despite this, our experience with #captureParklandia has made us even more confident that museums need to experiment and take chances in order to grow. Doing so makes us more likely to reach new constituencies, form new collaborations, and help to augment the important roles museums play in cities.

NOTES

1. Between June 13 and September 21, 2014 at the Portland Art Museum (PAM) in Portland, Oregon.
2. Kristin Bayans is interpretive Media Specialist at the Portland Art Museum and Justin Meyer is a PhD Candidate in Urban Planning at the University of Michigan.
3. One such example: the *China Design Now* special exhibition in 2009 reintroduced the Portland community to the museum, in part, by facilitating conversations about Chinese design between local community groups and businesses via social media.
4. The Pew Research Internet Project survey (http://www.pewinternet.org/fact-sheets/mobile-technology-fact-sheet/) shows that 58% of adults in the U.S. have a smartphone. This covers diverse segments of the population including (for example) 47% of people making less than $30,000 a year, 59% of African Americans, and 44% of people with a high school or less level of education.
5. Survey of Public Participation in the Arts, 2008, National Endowment for the Arts. http://arts.gov/sites/default/files/2008-SPPA.pdf.
6. A hashtag is a word or phrase preceded by the symbol #. It is usually a non-hierarchical keyword or phrase assigned to a piece of information (such as an internet bookmark, digital image, or computer file). This kind of metadata helps describe an item and allows it to be found again by browsing or searching. Tags are generally chosen informally and personally by the item's creator or by its viewer, depending on the system.
7. http://ohsnap.cmoa.org/.
8. http://snapwidget.com.
9. http://slidely.com.
10. Though not explicitly stating a desire to make its content democratic, one of PAM's missions is "to facilitate dialogue with diverse audiences."
11. http://www.artsjournal.com/realcleararts/2014/07/parklandia-stretching-striving-to-what-end.html.

12. Answering this question would have required a semi-experimental research design, where two sizable groups of random visitors (one group who interacted with #captureParklandia and one group that did not) would be studied before and after their visit to the Tuileries exhibition. We did not have the time to recruit research participants or to design the gallery in such a way to facilitate a control experience and an experience that included the #captureParklandia project.
13. Portland Parks Foundation extended the #captureParklandia hashtag for their own public engagement purposes. The hashtag also began to be used independently of the initial #captureParklandia project and the Portland Parks Foundation project.
14. Two examples of museums using Instagram for educational programming are: the National Gallery of Art's thematic Instameet series (#atnga_sculpture seen here: https://storify.com/ngadc/atnga-sculpture-instameet) and SFMOMA's initiative Play Artfully: https://www.sfmoma.org/exhib_events/playartfully. Debates about the use of mobile technology and social media in museums have been amplified, in part, by the need to relax gallery photography restrictions. For more see http://www.telegraph.co.uk/culture/art/art-news/11028015/National-Gallery-relents-over-mobile-phones.html.

REFERENCES

Alexander, E. (2000). Rationality Revisited: Planning Paradigms in a Post-Postmodernist Perspective. *Journal of Planning Education and Research*, 19, 242-256.

Bautista, S. (2014). *Museum in the Digital Age: Changing Meanings of Place, Community, and Culture*. Maryland: AltaMira Press.

Burness, A. (2014, November) Understanding the Museum-selfie. Panel session presentation at the Museum Computer Network Conference, Dallas, TX.

Cameron, D. (1971). The Museum, a Temple or a Forum. *Curator*, 14 (1), 11-24.

Coombes, A. E. (1988). Museums and the Formation of National and Cultural Identities. *Oxford Art Journal* 11(2), 57-68.

Falk, J. H., & Dierking, L. D., et al. (2006). Living in a Learning Society: Museums and Free-choice Learning. In S. Macdonald (ed.), *A Companion to Museum Studies*. Oxford: Blackwell.

Healey, P. (1993). Planning Through Debate: The Communicative Turn in Planning Theory. In F. Fischer & J. Forester (eds.), *The Argumentative Turn in Policy Analysis and Planning*. Durham, NC: Duke University Press.

Macdonald, S. (2003). Museums, national, postnational and transcultural identities. *Museum and Society* 1 (1): 1-16.

Mason, R. (2004). Museums, Galleries and Heritage: Sites of Meaning-Making and Communication. In G. Corsane (ed.), *Heritage, Museums and Galleries: An Introductory Reader*. London: Routledge.

Weil, S. (2002) *Making Museum Matter*. Washington DC: Smithsonian Institution Press.

Zeitlin, S. (2012). Where Are the Best Stories? Where Is My Story? Participation and Curation in a New Media Age. In B. Adair, B. Filene, & L. Koloski (eds.), *Letting Go?: Sharing Historical Authority in a User-Generated World.* Philadelphia: The Pew Center for Arts & Heritage.

CHAPTER TWELVE

#MUSEUMSELFIE DAY: A BIGGER PICTURE

Mar Dixon

@CULTURETHEMES IS A Twitter account which was created in March 2011 to promote museums and cultural venues worldwide (Dixon, n.d.). The idea is that once a month a friendly hashtag theme is conceived which museums can use to promote their collections in a fun, non-traditional-media way.

The process is relatively straightforward. Every month, as the creator and administrator of *CultureThemes*, I look around to see what is going on by listening to online conversations, watching trends and reading articles. From this research I go on to create the "theme". After checking that the hashtag is not already being used, is not too political and will ensure that as many institutions as possible can get involved, a write-up is created explaining the day and its theme. The theme is then shared and contextualized on CultureThemes.com (Dixon, 2011). The date and the theme are usually shared three or four weeks in advance.

In December 2013, The Oxford English Dictionary declared the word *Selfie* as word of the year (Oxford Dictionary, 2013). As a mom to an (at the time) eleven year old, I knew as soon as something became so popular it was mainstream, it meant its demise was imminent. Considering themes for CultureThemes and noticing there were a few projects online with museums encouraging people to take a selfie with an object (such as the Horniman Walrus) helped my hashtag choice for January (Horniman Museum, n.d.). This inspired me to make January 2014's theme #MuseumSelfie month:

> So this month we want you to share your #MuseumSelfie – whether you work in a museum, are a museum mascot or one of the lovely visitors – post your pictures using the tag on January 22nd! (Dixon, 2013.)

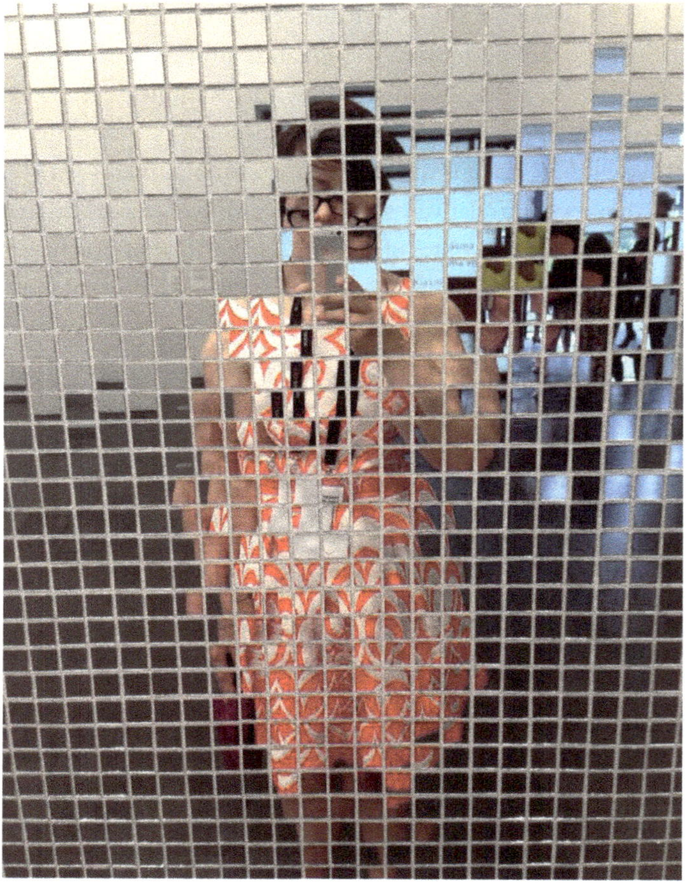

FIG.1: A #MuseumSelfie with Matti Braun's *Bali, 1998*, + @KiasmaMuseum #erc2014.
Photograph: Tracey Berg-Fulton (@BergFulton).

Almost as soon as the announcement was made, I knew it was going to be a popular one: I was seeing very quickly museums starting to plan how they could encourage their visitors to get involved and what they could do specifically on the day. However, as you can see from the write up, I never defined what the day should look like. For all themes (such as #AskACurator and #LoveTheatre) I try to leave the interpretation very open. When you are dealing with an international audience, it is impossible to structure these days to fit everyone's needs or understanding.

On January 22 2014, #MuseumSelfie was trending for most of the day in almost all parts of the world. The reaction was something I was not expecting. Museums were encouraging people to "come to the museum today and take your #MuseumSelfie!" (Birmingham Museums and Art Gallery, 2014). I witnessed many visitors trying to figure out if it was some elaborate joke, but then deciding that even if it was a joke they wanted to be part of it.

When I woke up the next morning I was overwhelmed... and speechless. By 7am I was being asked for numbers (you museum people and your stats!) I tried to capture what I was being told, by gathering data via a few sites which collect data from twitter use: 352 photos (Sharypic, 2014); 3,413 tweets; 2,045 contributors – different accounts taking part (Eventifier, 2014).

Now, I am not a stats or number person. I do not over analyse things, for me it works or it does not. If it does not work, the answer is obvious: change it. If it is not obvious: throw a rock in the pond and see where the ripples lead you, but do not force an answer that can sometimes be as simple as "just because". However, even I, after gathering some of the stats, was impressed.

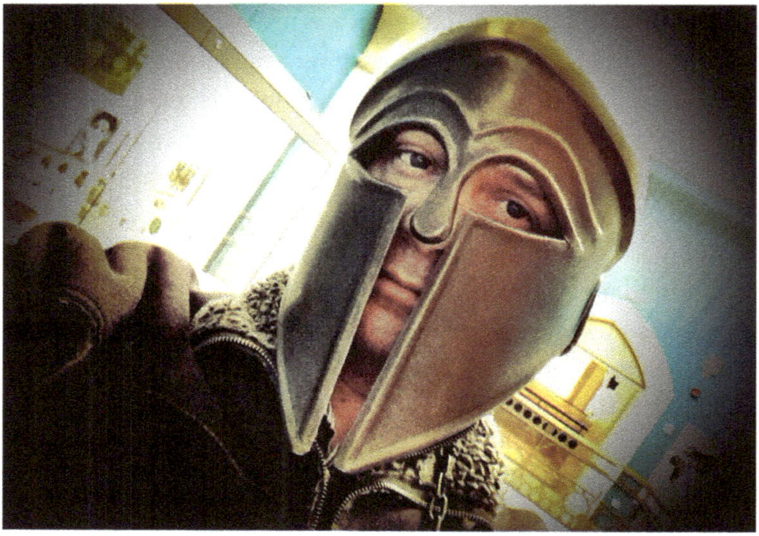

FIG. 2: #MuseumSelfie taken at the Royal Albert Memorial Museum, Exeter, 21 Jan 2015. Photograph: Steven Stewart.

Very quickly the whole theme gathered pace and it wasn't long before the *Telegraph* and the *Guardian* began to pick up on it (The Guardian, 2014; The Telegraph, 2014). Now keep in mind, I never stipulated what a #MuseumSelfie should look like; many decided however to self-police what a "selfie" is. I personally was happy for people to share their poses or selfies with the museum building, museum postcard or even a museum on a laptop in the background. The important thing was that people were sharing the advocacy that museums could be (and are!) fun.

By the end of 22 January 2014 the stats were: 3,791 photos; nine videos; 21,566 tweets; from 10,238 contributors (Eventifier, 2014; Sharypic, 2014).

#MuseumSelfie Day version 2.0

I decided that 21 January 2015 would be the next #MuseumSelfie day.

With the knowledge from the year before many more museums were preparing to be involved. That said, there were also some people who were not as positive about it, so I tried to prepare everyone by sharing the following message/guidance:

> **#MuseumSelfie day**
> (a) Yes it's a thing.
> (b) It helps get non-traditional visitors to museums.
> (c) It's a bit of fun – who cares that it's not a "true" selfie. Are they smiling & enjoying it? Good.
> (d) This will not solve any problems, stop analysing it.
> (e) Just enjoy it or mute it but don't complain, it's one day.

(f) The tag is #MuseumSelfie but if you use #MuseumSelfieDay or make up your own, it's all good. No one will scorn you.
(g) Just get involved.

This year, I was a bit more prepared, having talked about #MuseumSelfies throughout the year. On the actual day I was talking at a conference in Paris, but arranged to have private wifi access to ensure I could participate. My role within the day is quite straight forward, I retweet, ask questions and engage in conversations to help encourage participation and share the enthusiasm of those involved. Some people do have specific queries which I try to answer, but overall it runs very smoothly.

Sree Sreenivasan, Chief Digital Officer at the Metropolitan Museum very kindly tracked and shared hashtracking reports on #MuseumSelfie 2015, these were (from 1/1/2015 11:30 am to 1/31/2015 11:30 am): 31,321 tweets (with photos) and 183,772,793 timeline deliveries. Most of the publicity around the day remained positive, even CNN took the time to call me to understand the objectives behind the day and its success. (Imam, 2015; Vartanian, 2015).

If someone had told me three years ago that the Director of Boston Museum of Fine Arts would take a selfie, or that Rocky himself, Sylvester Stallone, would be involved in #MuseumSelfie I would have laughed (Boston Museum of Fine Arts, 2015; Philadelphia Museum, 2015). Even my mom took part and she still has no idea what a hashtag is (to her, it is still a pound sign)! And that is an important aspect: because there is no right or wrong, it is open for everyone to get involved and feel part of the day. What I love about these hashtag-days is how people make it work for them. I create these themes which in themselves are fairly generic, but due to their lack of specific boundaries it allows it to work for both the museums and the public that visit them.

As for photos in museums – I obviously am pro-photography. Not just for selfies, I rarely take them myself, but for photography in general. Allowing photography allows your visitors to become an advocate (Los Angeles Times, 2015). I travel a lot and love to take pictures and share. Many people have said I have taken them to museums or art galleries they would never have gone to themselves or never even heard of. Photographs also help me remember what I have seen and liked. Some people sketch or take notes, I snap the object and the label. That said, I acknowledge that there are times when not allowing photography makes sense. For example, Sir John Soane's Museum in London is a hidden gem of a townhouse filled top to bottom of architectural and other artefacts. It frustrates me that I am not allowed to take photos but completely respect and appreciate it while I am in there. It is quaint and full to the rafters. People stopping to take pictures would take away from the environment. My biggest statement is this: don't judge people who choose to take pictures and selfies. We all learn, process and make memories in our own way. But please, no selfie sticks!

ACKNOWLEDGEMENT

Thanks to Davida de Hond (@davidadehond) for assistance with this article.

REFERENCES

Birmingham Museums and Art Gallery. (2014). *Birmingham Museums and Art Gallery Twitter Account*. January 22 2014. Retrieved 9 June, 2015 from https://twitter.com/bm_ag.

Boston Museum of Fine Arts (2015). Director of Boston Museum of Fine Arts kicks off #museumselfie day. Retrieved 21 January from www.twitter.com/mfaboston.

Dixon, M. (2011). *CultureThemes*. Retrieved 16 March, 2015 from http://www.culturethemes.com.

Dixon, M. (2013). *CultureThemes*. Retrieved 13 March 2015 from http://culturethemes.com.

Dixon, M. (n.d.). *CultureThemes Twitter account*. Retrieved March 15, 2015 from http://www.twitter.com/culturethemes.

Eventifier. (2014). *Eventifier*. Retrieved 22 January 2014 from http://www.eventifier.com.

Eventifier. (2015). *Eventifier*. Retrieved 23 January, 2015 from http://eventifier.com/.

Hashtracking. (2015). *Hashtracking*. Retrieved 9 February, 2015 from https://www.hashtracking.com.

Horniman Museum. (n.d.). *InstaHorniman*. Retrieved 16 March, 2015, from http://insta-horniman.tumblr.com/post/114841124247/iya-bruv-vanduzzi-by-meganfinola-march-15.

Imam, J. (2015). Selfies turn museums into playgrounds for a day. [Weblog, 21 January 2015]. Retrieved 24 January, 2015 from http://edition.cnn.com/2015/01/21/living/feat-museum-selfie-irpt/.

Los Angeles Times. (2015, n.d). Museums embrace 'iconic

selfie moments' to drive younger visitors. [Weblog]. Retrieved 29 January 2015 from http://fw.to/8URPApM.

Oxford Dictionary. (2013). Oxford Dictionaries Word of the Year 2013 SELFIE is named Oxford Dictionaries Word of the Year 2013. [Weblog, 19 November 2013]. Retrieved 10 March, 2015 from http://blog.oxforddictionaries.com/press-releases/oxford-dictionaries-word-of-the-year-2013/.

Philadelphia Museum (2015). Sylvester Rockyter: Rocky at the Philadelphia Museum. Retrieved 21 January 2015 from www.twitter.com/.

Sharypic. (2014). *Sharypic*. Retrieved 23 January, 2015 from https://www.sharypic.com/.

Sharypic. (2015). *Sharypic*. Retrieved 9 June, 2015 from http://www.sharypic.com.

The Guardian. (2014). Museum Selfie. [Weblog, 22 January]. Retrieved 24 January, 2015 from http://www.theguardian.com/culture-professionals-network/culture-professionals-blog/gallery/2014/jan/22/museum-selfie-day-in-pictures.

The Telegraph. (2014). Museum Selfie day: your pictures. [Weblog, 22 January]. Retrieved 15 March, 2015 from http://www.telegraph.co.uk/culture/museums/10588960/Museum-Selfie-day-your-pictures.html.

Vartanian , H. (2015). The #MuseumSelfie Scourge Is Upon Us. [Weblog, 21 January 2015]. Retrieved 4 March, 2015 from http://hyperallergic.com/176347/the-museumselfie-scourge-is-upon-us/.

CHAPTER THIRTEEN

THE SELFIE FACTOR: DEVELOPING AND ENGAGING AUDIENCES WITH POPULAR SOCIAL BEHAVIORS

Jeffrey S Bowen

W

WE HAVE TO RECOGNIZE that a great many of our visitors don't know their way around and don't know much about art.
– Thomas P. Campbell (in Kennedy, 2011)

When I was a graduate student, I witnessed the dawn of the social media age. It was ten years ago. MySpace was still the most popular of platforms. Facebook was in its infancy, only available to a select few universities, including the one I was attending. Twitter and YouTube hadn't even been invented yet, and Instagram was still five years away from its launch. Use of social media was limited to PCs and laptops, so there was no posting and reading posts on the go. Needless to say, social media was not a topic of conversation when discussing audience development in my museum studies courses. In the seemingly short time since, social media has exploded, augmented by the rise of mobile technologies. The instantaneous sharing and receiving of digital content with hundreds of friends and acquaintances became possible from anywhere with little effort. Pictures, videos, and articles could go viral in a matter of minutes with the simple touch of a smartphone.

The explosion of mobile telephone use for ubiquitous social interaction certainly has its shortcomings. As a college instructor, I have witnessed a decline in the proper use of punctuation and grammar, as the abbreviated language of text messaging supplants higher standards of academic writing. As the manager of a university art gallery, I worry that shorter attention spans with ever more distractions from the virtual world will negatively affect physical attendance at our precious cultural institutions. Yet, this is the new reality we face as museum professionals, and as we struggle to keep our organizations relevant, we must consider all the various ways to reach our constituents. The quote at the head of this chapter, which appeared in a February 2011 *New York Times* interview with the then relatively new director of The Metropolitan Museum of Art in New York, addresses this very point. In the article, Thomas Campbell (Kennedy, 2011: C9) acknowledged that in the past the Met was primarily concerned with expanding the collection. Under his leadership, the institution would now focus on using technology to enhance visitor engagement in an attempt to "demystify the museum through digital means".

In this chapter, I suggest that one of the possibilities to bring in new audiences, specifically those of the millennial generation, is by appealing to the inherent social need in humans to leave a mark on the world, to prove our existence before our inevitable end. In the virtual realm, this is accomplished by the selfie. These pictures are often labeled with a hashtag, a keyword or unspaced phrase prefixed by the number sign that allows a user to electronically populate a list of similar posts and images within a social media platform. In what I am calling the "selfie factor," I argue that museums can adapt this popular social behavior into many different iterations in an effort to engage current audiences, help bring in new visitors, develop the institutional brand, and ultimately increase donations. There are many texts on the history, culture, and psychology of self-representation, and there is plenty of discourse on museum visitor engagement, marketing, and fundraising. However, typically these ideas are not juxtaposed in scholarly research. This chapter seeks to help fill that void.

Research is loosely divided into four sections. First, the history, psychology, and culture of self-representation; second, selfie culture within online videos, highlighting successful content created by and featuring supporters of charitable organizations; third, some of the ways museums and their patrons are using selfie contests and hashtags; and last, future possibilities for developing and engaging audiences by surveying a selection of institutionally-developed smartphone and tablet applications that use self-portraiture.

Selfie culture: from cave paintings to Kim Kardashian

In 2013, *selfie* was named Oxford Dictionaries Word of the Year, although the first use of the word began appearing nearly ten years prior (Fears, 2013). According to the Library of Congress (n.d.), the first self-portrait taken with any kind of camera is believed to have been shot by Robert Cornelius in 1839 (Figure 1). Unlike the quick snap of a phone's camera, daguerreotypes have long exposure times, so Cornelius would have had plenty of time to get situated in view of the lens. The parallels between the earliest self-portrait and the modern-day digital selfie are striking. The daguerreotype was one of the first methods of traditional photography, and the result was often quite grainy by today's standards. As the nineteenth century progressed, the technology would improve drastically. Similarly, although digital SLR cameras have become more powerful, many cellphone cameras still aren't able to achieve particularly sharp images, especially when held unsupported at an arm's-length away (selfie sticks can help with this problem, but this chapter does not delve deeper into this invention since they are prohibited at most museums). Add to that the fact that selfies are

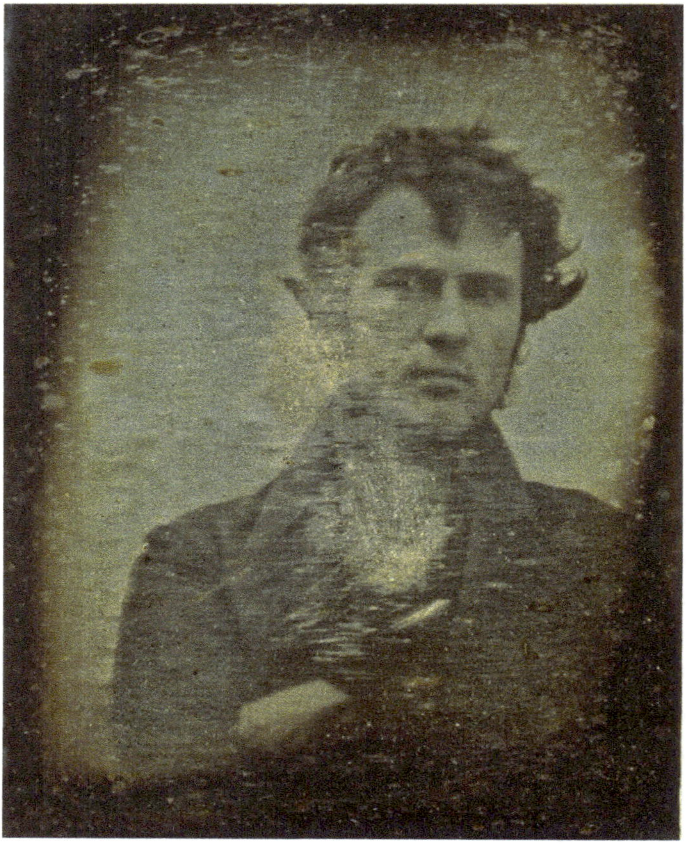

FIG. 1: *Self-portrait*. Robert Cornelius, daguerreotype, 1839.
Library of Congress, Prints & Photographs Division, LC-USZC2-4912.

often taken with the weaker (and lacking a flash) front-facing camera, used so viewers can see themselves on the display screen, selfies are characteristically coarse and slightly out of focus. While not desirable for a printed photograph taken by traditional means, this unpolished look gives a selfie its authenticity *vis-à-vis* the fleeting nature of the picture. If part of the goal of the self-portrait is for the subject to leave a mark during life's short existence, it's fitting that the digital result appears transitory.

Ages before the invention of the camera, Paleolithic hunters and gatherers painted deep within caves, most notably in northern Spain and southern France. Among images of prehistoric game animals, there was a propensity of artists to create negative stencils of hand prints by blowing pigment through hollow tubes. Blessing (2004: 19) noted that "Ancient handprints in caves, the first intentional gestures of marking by early humans, are indexes of individual existence". Initially believed to be men who painted the hands since it was argued that men did the bulk of the hunting, Snow (2013) has shown that the majority of these artists were in fact women. Juxtaposing Snow's research with modern cultural trends, Timpane (2013) suggests that a correlation can be made with the fact that statistically more women than men take selfies. Regardless, the hand prints are thought to have been a way for Paleolithic humans to show their existence or even connection with each other and the fauna around them, perhaps done as part of a shamanistic ritual (Hughes, 2013). Thousands of years later, artists began taking pictures of hands. Scores of hand photographs appeared in the Solomon R. Guggenheim Museum's 2004 exhibition, *Speaking with Hands: Photographs from The*

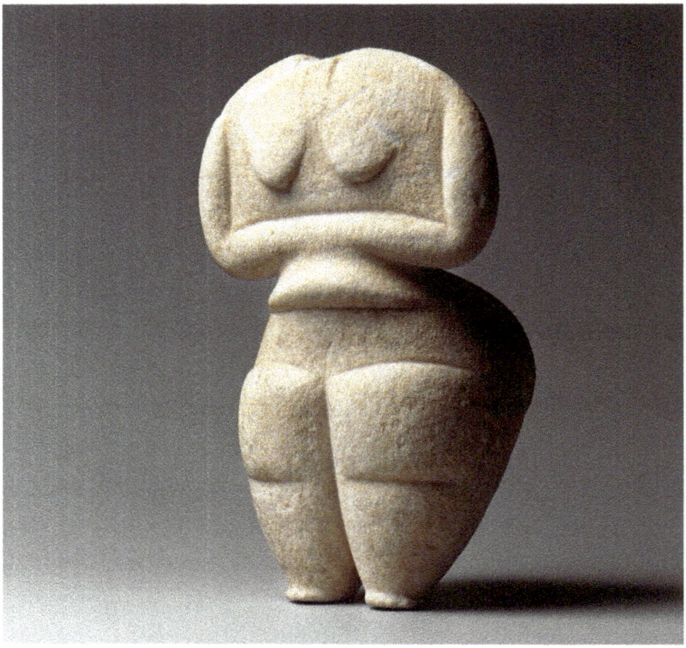

FIG. 2: *Steatopygous female figure*. Cycladic, marble, c.4500–4000 BC.
The Metropolitan Museum of Art, Bequest of Walter C. Baker, 1971. www.metmuseum.org.

Buhl Collection. Of particular note, Laszlo Moholy-Nagy's photograms of his hands convey the immediacy of the medium, and contextual comparisons can be made with prehistoric cave hand stencils. In the catalog, Blessing (2004: 18) addressed a motivation for taking photographs:

> So we fill albums with snapshots... in an effort to prove to ourselves that we really exist, that our loved ones will be with us always, that we are happy. The "reality effect" of the photograph, the sense that it scientifically proves existence through its insistent detail, serves to shore up our delusional beliefs... This seeming ability to stop time is appealing because of a pathetic fallacy, the desire to believe that the inevitable can be postponed.

W. K. Campbell (cited in Clements, 2014), stated that selfies are taken for three reasons: as a result of the inherent need in humans to create art, to find social connections, or to satisfy narcissistic tendencies. Using research collected from University of Georgia students, the author suggests that those who fall into the latter category overwhelmingly and over-abundantly snap pictures of themselves and post to social media. While this chapter does not specifically focus on this as one of the explanations for the selfie phenomenon, museums which are aware of this idea could use it to their benefit. On November 13, 2014, the Met did just that when it tweeted a picture of Cycladic female figure with the hashtag #breaktheinternet on its Twitter page. The post was a humorous affront to a recently published *Paper Magazine* photoshoot of Kim Kardashian, a reality TV star known for being an ambitious self-promoter who often posts selfies on the internet. The Met's photo even resembled a selfie. It wasn't particularly sharp, clearly a quick snap with a cellphone as opposed to a staged image taken by a professional photographer, such as the official collection record photo for the sculpture seen in Figure 2. The museum's tweet soon went viral, being retweeted over 1,000 times within the first hour of being posted (Perez, 2014). The story was soon picked up on a national level, receiving unanimous kudos for the post's creativity. Considering the news outlets it appeared in – NBC's *TODAY* Show, *New York Post*, *Huffington Post*, and the *Daily Mail*, to name a few – this one tweet yielded a significant return in earned media for the organization. While it's difficult to put an exact price tag on what that tweet was worth, let's examine just one of those outlets, *TODAY*. The morning news show's anchors talked about the Met's post for at least 30 seconds. Average viewership for each day that week was over five million households (Ariens, 2014). According to data from media agency TargetCast tcm, the average cost of a 30-second commercial spot on NBC was over $90,000 in 2012 (Friedman, 2013). Without taking into consideration any other national coverage or the amount of shares on social media, those few seconds of snapping a picture and posting to Twitter resulted in substantial earned media from one outlet. Further research would be needed to estimate the total value of earned media and to examine if physical attendance at the Met changed in the days that followed. Nevertheless, while still remaining academically focused – in the Twitter post the Met provided a link to learn more about the ancient figurine – it is an example of how a museum can use the selfie factor to garner free advertising and thus expands its brand to a wider audience.

And, this event certainly aligns with the director's philosophy of reaching broader audiences as discussed at the beginning of this chapter.

Later I will examine how other museums are intentionally using selfies to engage and reach out to new audiences. However, to find the most successful use of the selfie factor, which translated into record donations, we must begin by looking beyond museums.

Videos as "moving selfies"

In the summer of 2014, videos of the *Ice Bucket Challenge* swept the feeds of social networking sites, seemingly becoming a sensation overnight. The premise was simple: once called out by their friends or family on Facebook or Twitter, participants would either record themselves getting a bucket of ice water poured over their heads or be expected to donate $100 in support of the Amyotrophic Lateral Sclerosis (ALS) Association. A chain reaction was built in, since it was required that the newly doused individual then identify others to take the challenge. However, that alone would not cause it to go viral – something more profound was necessary. In essence, the Ice Bucket Challenge is a type of selfie. Though the file output is different (.jpg rather than .mov), videos are merely a continuous display of a series of still pictures with audio added. Since most Ice Bucket Challenge posts are focused on one person, captured with a mobile device, and shared on social media, they can be called "moving selfies."

A previous example of a viral video which promoted a cause was *Kony 2012*. Created by the nonprofit organization *Invisible Children*, it sought to raise awareness about war crimes committed by Joseph Kony, leader of the guerrilla group known as the Lord's Resistance Army. The video received instant success, receiving a record-shattering 100 million views within the first week of being posted (Grossman, 2012). Through online sales of tee-shirts and other ephemera, the video helped to raise $28 million for Invisible Children in 2012 (Taylor, 2014b). However, the initiative was soon labeled with the pejorative "slacktivism" or "hashtag activism," the idea that it raised awareness through social media but did little to incur significant action. As of December 2014, Invisible Children had laid off the bulk of its staff and began to wind down operations due to financial difficulties, despite the fact that Kony had not been captured (Taylor, 2014a).

In comparing the Ice Bucket Challenge to *Kony 2012*, the Challenge offered a stronger impetus for viewers to follow through with donating. By putting oneself in front of the camera, as opposed to simply reposting a link to a video, the individual became part of the solution, simultaneously leaving a stamp on social media. The results were astounding. According to a press release, the ALS Association received nearly $95 million in donations from 2.1 million new donors in August 2014. By comparison, the ALS Association only received $2.7 million during the same period in 2013 (Munk, 2014).

Museums have sponsored activities for users to create and share videos, though not to the overwhelming level of success achieved by the ALS Association. Chicago's Museum of Science and Industry (MSI Chicago), a 400,000 square-foot exhibit space in the nation's third largest city, received over 1,500 entries of 60-second video logs for its Month at the Museum contest in 2010 (Erdman, 2010). From roughly the third week of October through the third week of November, the contest winner would live and sleep in the museum and participate in science experiments, educational demonstrations, and other outreach events that simultaneously marketed the museum. In her video submission, Chicago native Kate McGroarty faced the camera and quirkily and endearingly argued why she thought she deserved the opportunity. It worked; the institution selected her as the winner of the inaugural contest. As of November 2014, her entry has received over 19,000 views, making it the fourth-most watched of the 84 videos listed on MSI Chicago's channel on YouTube (n.d.). The payoff in press was resounding. The program received local and national media exposure, including ABC's *Good Morning America*, and according to the magazine *Adweek* (2010), the museum doubled its Facebook followers and received a record number of website visits. Expect to see more programs like this. As video editing/publishing apps such as Vine and Instagram's new recording feature rise in popularity, contests like the one offered by MSI Chicago become even easier to host.

Selfie contests and hashtags

A simpler way to engage audiences are selfie competitions, where an organization asks its patrons to take a self-portrait and post it to social media using a hashtag. After a set period, people vote on – or the communication team picks – a winner. Small prizes are often awarded, although the biggest incentive is created by the sense of belonging (participation could also be driven by narcissism or the desire to produce art, as suggested earlier). Many museums have already hosted such events. Some are themed, such as the #LincolnSelfie contest

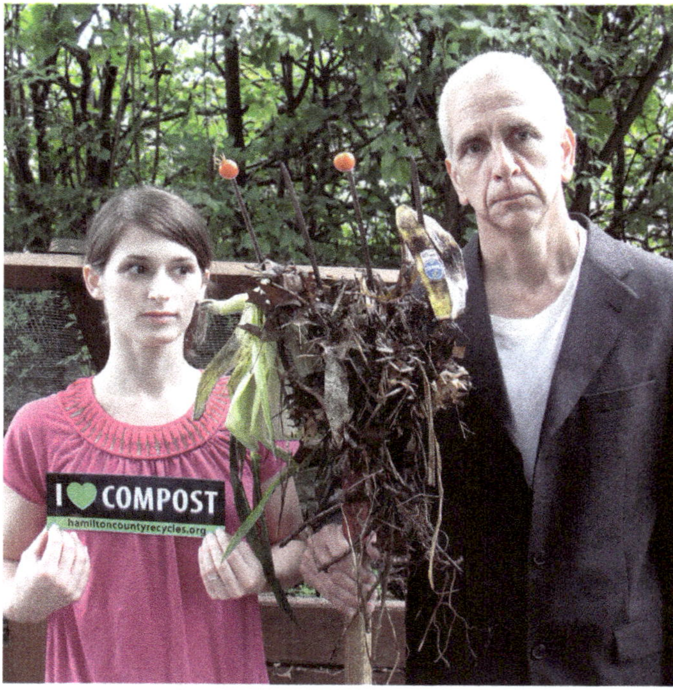

FIG. 3: Portrait of Michelle Balz and Brad Miller for the Cincinnati Art Museum's #CAMericanGothic contest.
Photograph: Belinda Bankes Frykman, Digital photo, 2014.

that the Abraham Lincoln Presidential Library and Museum in Springfield, Illinois presented in January 2015. Others are more general, whereby attendees simply find an artwork in the museum to pose with, like one at The Walters Art Museum in Baltimore, Maryland in the summer of 2014.

A themed competition was recently organized by the Cincinnati Art Museum in Cincinnati, Ohio, an institution that boasts 78,000 square feet of exhibition space and has a typical annual attendance of anywhere from 180,000 to 250,000 (Stringfield, 2014). On the occasion of a temporary exhibition of Grant Wood's *American Gothic*, on loan from the Art Institute of Chicago, the Cincinnati Art Museum invited its patrons to take a selfie inspired by the iconic 1930 painting. Participants were asked to upload the selfies to social media with the hashtag #CAMericanGothic, itself a creative fusion of the museum's acronym and the title of the painting to be imitated. In the two weeks the contest ran, over 50 photos were submitted. These were first narrowed down to three finalists, and then a winner was selected by the amount of likes on Facebook. According to Stringfield, the brainchild of the event, the "small prize" of a $25 gift certificate to the museum's café was not the impetus for the myriad submissions. Rather, participation was fueled by the fact that the contest was enjoyable and the artwork so recognizable. Plus, the contest had substantial buy-in from the museum's board of directors, who helped spread the word.

With over 250 likes from the organization's Facebook followers, the picture that won (Figure 3) features a composition mirroring Wood's famous painting, except that the pitchfork being held by the man at right is engulfed with biodegradable flora and foodstuffs, notably a banana peel and two cherry

ACTIVITY	AUGUST 2014	YEARLY AVERAGE	PERCENT DIFFERENCE
NEW FACEBOOK LIKES	955	654	46%
FACEBOOK INTERACTION RATE {(Post likes + Comments + Shares)/# of followers} x100	9.16%	5.54%	65%
NEW TWITTER FOLLOWERS	390	460	-15%
TWITTER INTERACTION RATE {(# Replies + #Retweets + # Favorites)/ # Followers} x 100	0.82%	1.03%	-20%
INSTAGRAM PHOTO LIKES	1266	514	124%

FIG. 4: Cincinnati Art Museum social media activity. (Stringfield, 2015)

tomatoes pierced on the tips of the farm tool's prongs. At left, a woman stoically holds a bumper sticker that reads *I Love Compost*. The woman and man are Michelle Balz and Brad Miller, employees of the Hamilton County Recycling and Solid Waste District and the Hamilton County Department of Environmental Services, respectively. It was taken by Belinda Bankes Frykman, also of the county's Department of Environmental Services, and so it is not technically a true self-portrait. However, most museums presenting such competitions are willing to look past this technicality so long as the photographs are composed in the same spirit of the selfie. As was the case with this example, selfie contests can present opportunities for cross-promotion with area businesses, government entities, and non-profits. Such competitions allow organizations to put a personal face behind their brand, simultaneously giving staff members an avenue to leave their stamp on social media. Museums should embrace these collaborative opportunities to expand their reach with new audiences.

Analyzing results from Bitly.com, in all of the owned sites with content posted in relation to the exhibiting of *American Gothic*, the link to the #CAMericanGothic contest announcement on Facebook performed better than any other link. For instance, it received 43% more clicks (185 versus 129 clicks) than the next most popular page, the exhibition webpage on www.cincinnatiartmuseum.org (Stringfield, 2015). This might surprise some, given that the exhibition page is where one traditionally goes online to receive pertinent information relating to a show. Furthermore, looking at social media activity stats provided by the museum (Figure 4), the month of August 2014 (which was when the contest was first announced and

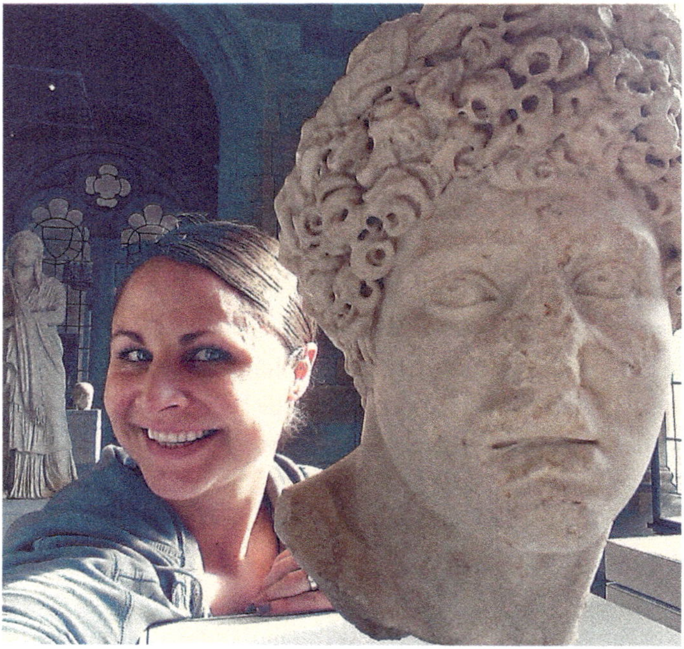

FIG. 5: Selfie with the Roman marble *Portrait of a Young Man, possibly an Olympic Athlete* at the Yale University Art Gallery.
Photograph: Christina Czap. Digital photograph with Instagram filter, 2015.

submissions were received) outperformed its yearly Facebook and Twitter averages.

There is no question that the Cincinnati Art Museum's selfie contest engaged its online audience on Facebook, which is where the voting took place. These pictures were reposted to Instagram, which explains the dramatic difference in August interaction compared to its yearly average. Interestingly, Twitter participation underperformed during the month of August. The contest was promoted on this platform, but links directed individuals to Facebook. Perhaps the lower interaction rate can be explained by social media cannibalization, the idea that the individuals with both Facebook and Twitter accounts ignored one because of more involvement with the other.

It will be interesting to see how museums continue to encourage its patrons to take self-portraits. In the future, visitor selfies might become a more effective marketing tool for the museum if arranged extraneously and on a national scale, the same way the Ice Bucket Challenge was organized at the grassroots level. An effort to this effect has already been started, spearheaded by museum enthusiast, blogger, power tweeter and fellow contributor to this publication Mar Dixon. After she launched the inaugural Museum Selfie Day on January 22, 2014, Dixon (2014) was able to determine that 23,778 tweets from 11,143 contributors used the #MuseumSelfie hashtag. In its second year, participation increased, with 29,365 tweets from over 14,807 contributors, resulting in a reach of nearly 60 million users (Dixon, 2015a; Dixon, 2015b). Even staff participated in the day, including Yale University Art Gallery's senior museum technician Christina Czap, as seen in Figure 5.

More specific to art museums, #artselfie was promoted

by the New York-based artists collective DIS, which gathered photos with this hashtag and reproduced them in a book published by Jean Boîte Edition; as of late October 2014, the number of posts tagged with that hashtag was around 13,000 (Akel, 2014). That number jumped to over 17,000 as of the end of January 2015 (Daniel, 2015). Helping the popularity of the #artselfie is the rise in famous individuals participating in the practice. One of the most influential celebrity couples did just that in a high profile trip to Paris. In the autumn of 2014, Beyoncé and Jay-Z, world-renowned moguls of the music industry, visited the Louvre and the newly reopened Picasso Museum, where they snapped self-portraits and posted them to Beyoncé's website and on her Instagram and Facebook accounts.

Both museum attendance and the culture of taking selfies at museums are on the rise. Citing a survey of over 4,000 individuals done by cultural advertising firm LaPlaca Cohen, Hakala (2014) notes that in comparison to 2011, in 2014 there was a significant increase in the number of Americans who attended at least one museum in the past year. The firm's study revealed that of those who used a mobile device, two-thirds of those surveyed used it to take a picture and nearly half used it to share a photo. By comparison, the next two most common reasons visitors used a mobile device in a museum – to browse a cultural organization's website or to use a search engine – was only done by roughly one-third of respondents (Hakala, 2014).

Are there drawbacks to museum selfies? Sure. There is a plethora of anecdotal stories that illuminate the downsides. For instance, after a recent trip to the Museum of Modern Art in New York, Martinet (2014) noted that, "Obsessive photo-taking might be somewhat self-centered in that there is no consideration about how it is impinging on the sight lines of others around them". However, she ultimately ceded that it is a "forgivable practice" since it is the goal of the photo taker to capture a moment in time with a culturally significant artwork. Considering the popularity of sponsored selfie contests, it appears that many art museums do believe that the engagement opportunities outweigh the drawbacks. Except where visitor photography is explicitly barred by copyright restrictions or could distract individuals performing in a live event, cultural organizations beyond just art museums should embrace this social behavior. Nevertheless, science museums seem to be slower at adopting selfie contests.

Fundraising opportunities for museums could present themselves by aligning selfies with giving campaigns, as evident by the success of the grassroots Giving Tuesday movement. Created by New York's community and cultural center 92nd Street Y in partnership with nonprofits including the United Nations Foundation, the Tuesday following Thanksgiving was selected as a nationwide day of charitable giving. It was done in an effort to thwart the rising consumerism of the holiday season. In its third year, there were 269,000 tweets with the hashtag #GivingTuesday (Twitter, n.d.), spurring individuals through social media to donate $45.7 million to nonprofits on December 2, 2014 (Goldberg, 2014). New to 2014 was the addition of the hashtag #UNselfie, which on Giving Tuesday received 7,000 tweets (Twitter, n.d.). In these posts, users pose in a similar fashion to a traditional selfie. However, individuals in the photographs hold signs that read – usually handwritten on an 8½ by 11-inch sheet – which organization they

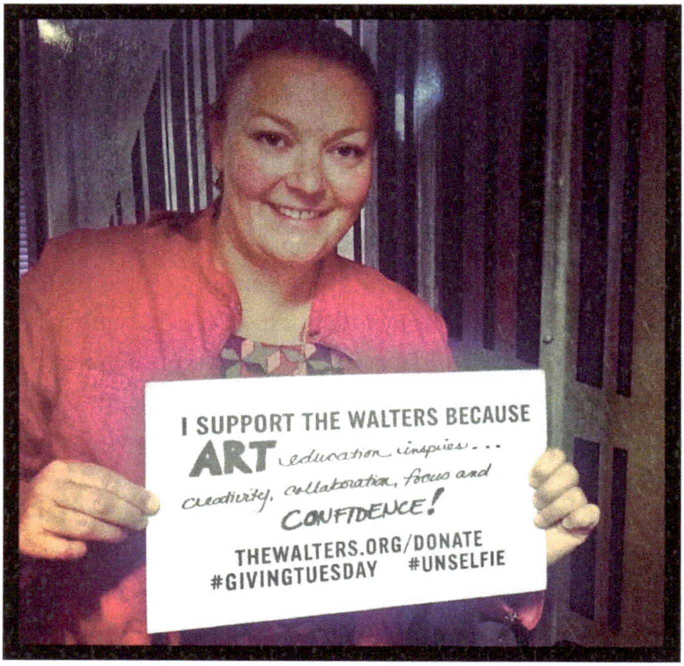

FIG. 6: Self-portrait with a #GivingTuesday/#UNselfie sign.
Photograph: Kelly Harris. Digital photograph with filter, 2014.

financially support. Kelly Harris, a member of The Walters Art Museum in Baltimore, Maryland, posted one such portrait to Twitter on Giving Tuesday 2014 (Figure 6). Many other samples found online show the sign covering the subject's face, further emphasizing the focus on the cause rather than the person.

Much like the Ice Bucket Challenge, the #UNselfie campaign appealed to individuals' need to leave a stamp on the world, make social connections, and contribute to a worthy cause. A quick Google search of *UNselfie* and *museum* showed that in 2014 many institutions did indeed promote the event to their constituents. One in particular, the Kohl Children's Museum in Glenview, Ill., even hosted an #UNselfie contest where winning photos would be featured in the organization's online and printed marketing ephemera (Kohl Children's Museum, n.d.).

Museum apps which focus on the self

Another museum which encouraged its patrons to post a selfie with the #UNselfie hashtag on Giving Tuesday 2014 was The Dalí Museum in St. Petersburg, Florida. For its first year of participation, the museum saw modest returns in social media engagement, which the museum hopes to expand upon in 2015 (Greif, 2014). The Dalí Museum is no stranger to innovative strategies that engage audiences using selfies. Reopening its doors in 2011, the institution's new $36 million, 66,000 square-foot facility (with 15,000 square feet of exhibition space) is about as old as when the word selfie entered the common lexicon. In early 2014, The Dalí Museum revealed a fascinating new smartphone/tablet application that takes a surrealist spin on the selfie factor. Created in partnership with the advertising

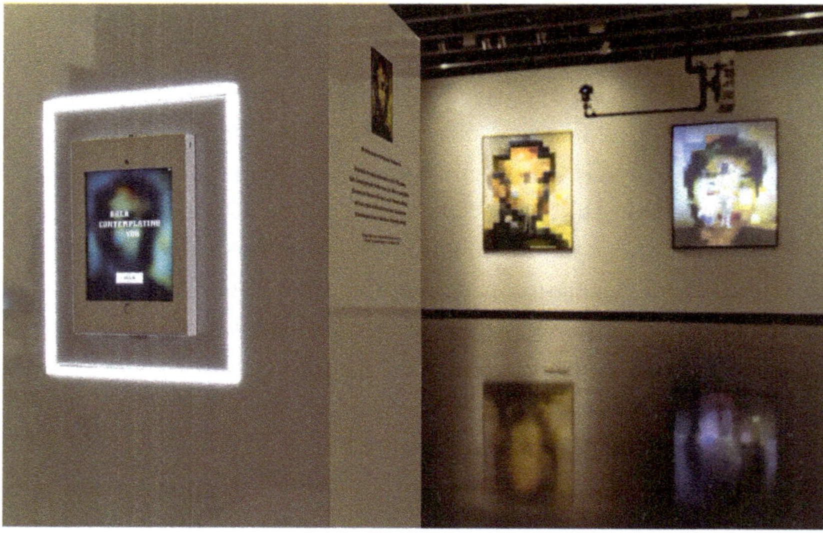

FIG. 7: Press photo of The Dalí Museum's *Gala Contemplating You* kiosk.
© Salvador Dalí Museum, Inc., St. Petersburg, FL, 2015.

agency Goodby, Silverstein & Partners, The Dalí Museum Staring Contest app pits the mobile device holder against Salvador Dali. To play, users hold their iPhone or iPad a few inches from their face. The device's camera shows a mirror image so that players can align their eyes to the appropriate spot. When ready to begin, one taps the screen, and the mirror image gets replaced by a photograph of the famed surrealist. The game is over when sensors detect a blink of the user's eyes. The catch is that while some aspects of Dali's portrait might change – such as the unfurling of his infamous mustache – he never blinks. After the contestant's inevitable loss, the app snaps a selfie and offers to post the results on Facebook.

The Dalí Museum Staring Contest app adeptly indulges our human social need to broadcast our existence. It was launched during the run of the exhibition *Warhol: Art. Fame. Mortality*, which according to the museum's press release, explored Warhol's "engagement with other artists through his own painting, how he constructed an approach to his image in terms of celebrity and fame, and his treatment of painting and image in terms of human mortality" (The Dalí Museum, 2014). Interestingly enough, the three themes explored in the exhibition – art, fame, and mortality – roughly coincide with the three reasons why we take selfies – to create art, to satisfy narcissistic tendencies, and to find social connections (i.e., before we die) – as discussed earlier in this paper. In addition to Dali, Staring Contest app users have the option of facing other opponents, such as a giraffe or one of Warhol's images of soup cans. As part of an integrated marketing campaign, the museum also placed decals on bathroom mirrors that encouraged visitors to play the staring contest against themselves. At least that result was never a loss, always a tie.

The Dalí Museum continues to update the Staring Contest application to keep users interested (Greif, 2014). Several months after its release, the museum introduced yet another concept that embraced selfie culture. On June 17 and as part of the exhibition *Marvels of Illusion*, the museum opened a kiosk with an iPad where visitors could have their selfies transformed into artworks on the wall. The snapped self-portraits were heavily pixelated and superimposed with the backside view of a nude Gala Dali, the artist's wife, appearing to examine it. The image was projected next to Dali's 1976 painting *Gala Contemplating the Mediterranean Sea Which at Twenty Meters Becomes the Portrait of Abraham Lincoln (Homage to Rothko)*, the artist's exploration of a *Scientific American* study which examined the minimum amount of pixels needed for the brain to recognize a particular human face (Elliott, 2014). As it appeared in the gallery (Figure 7), the visitor's selfie was in direct conversation with Dali's painting of a pixelated Abraham Lincoln. The installation was also a pro-bono endeavor by Goodby, Silverstein & Partners, and executive director Hank Hine estimated the project's value to be more than $100,000 (Elliott, 2014).

The development of the museum's Staring Contest app and Gala Contemplating You app/kiosk were created as "tools for engagement, not tools to drive attendance" (Greif, 2014). Yet, over the past few years, visitation rose on an annual basis. For instance, during the run of its Warhol exhibition, the organization saw a 40% increase as compared to the same period the previous year. Marketing Director Kathy Greif commented, "It's difficult to assess whether the experience drove the visitation or whether it was our ad campaign and other organic factors driving our [year-over-year] visitation increases."[1] While there's not enough data to show what impact, if any, the museum's innovative programming had on its attendance, I believe that at least part of the reason for the increase can be attributed to the app and kiosk, either through word of mouth or the national media coverage the museum received for these projects. Regardless, especially taking into consideration that both programs were pro-bono, they were a complete win for the museum.

Similar to the programs at The Dalí Museum, two institutions recently offered an in-gallery app as part of an exhibition. *Pointillize Yourself* was implemented by the Indianapolis Museum of Art (IMA) and created in collaboration with the software development firm E-gineering. The large regional art museum in Indiana hosted the app in conjunction with the exhibition *Face to Face: The Neo-Impressionist Portrait 1886–1904*, which was on view June through September, 2014. After viewing the show, museum visitors were invited to snap a selfie from a mounted iPad. The photo would then be converted to its pointillist version with either small, medium or large dots, and, as seen in Figure 8, the user could then adjust other filters such as color temperature and tint, add a digital signature, and then send the finished photo to an email address. Participants could also share their pictures on Facebook, but there were challenges setting up the Facebook application program interface, and so the institution will not include this step in further iterations (Sternbergh, Fantoni, & Djen, 2015). Completed pointillized selfies were also projected on a wall outside of the exhibition. Renamed *#NeoImpressed*, the technology was later shared with The Phillips Collection, a small private modern

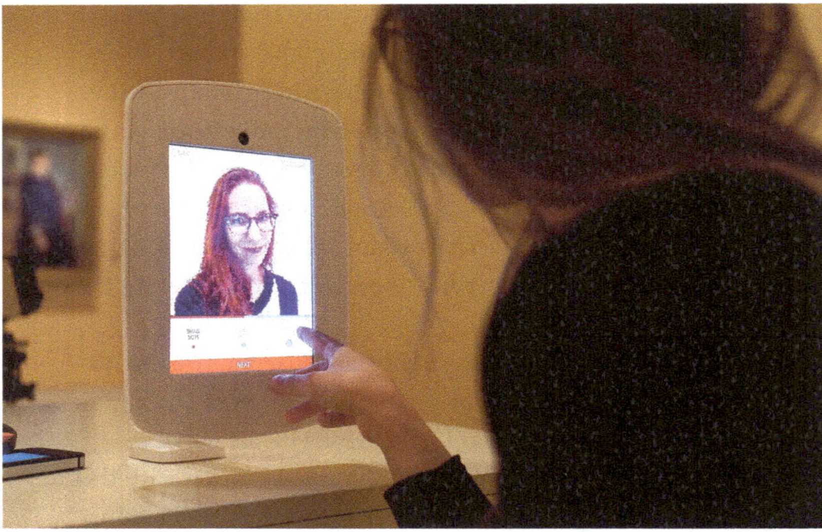

FIG. 8: Press photo of a visitor using the *Pointillize Yourself* app at the Indianapolis Museum of Art.
Digital photograph, courtesy the Indianapolis Museum of Art and The Phillips Collection, 2014.

and contemporary art museum in Washington, D.C. There, it was presented as part of the exhibition *Neo-Impressionism and the Dream of Realities: Painting, Poetry, Music*, which took place in September 2014 through January 2015. The Phillips retained most of the app's features, but since its exhibition displayed more landscapes than the IMA show, one of the main changes was that the participants at the Phillips were photographed in front of a mural of the Washington Monument (Figure 9) (Sternbergh, Fantoni, & Djen, 2015).

Both the IMA and the Phillips found that the application was successful in engaging audiences. For the IMA, the initiative was compelled by upper management's desire for exhibitions to become more accessible to visitors, especially those with little or no experience in art history. Based on data from Google Analytics, an estimated 13,000 portraits were created, of which approximately 9,000 were shared (Sternbergh, Fantoni, & Djen, 2015): "61% of visitors used the application, making this the most successful participatory tool the [IMA] has ever developed for an exhibition." For the Phillips, the path to introduce more in-gallery participatory experiences with technology was forged by a recently implemented strategic plan that emphasized public engagement. Of the 42,217 visitors to the exhibition, over 15% (6,752) submitted a portrait; furthermore, there were 919,461 impressions generated from 191 users on Twitter, Instagram, and Facebook (Sternbergh, Fantoni, & Djen, 2015). As museums become more interested in creating visitor-centric experiences, it would not be surprising to see an increasing number of institutions adopt applications like this for their larger exhibitions.

Considering that, from ancient handprints in caves to the

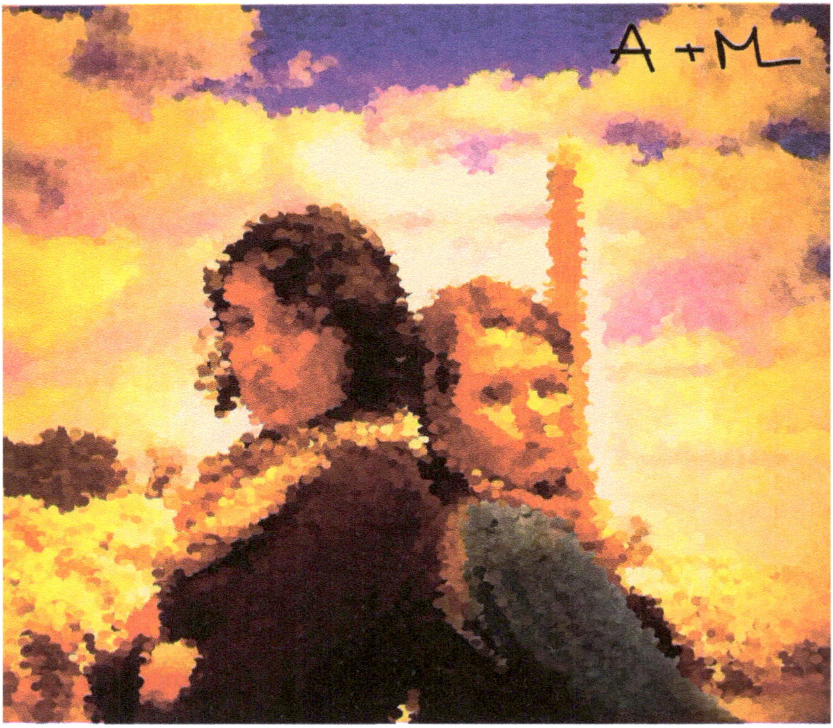

FIG. 9: ***#NeoImpressed*** **portrait at The Phillips Collection.**
Digital photograph with filter, courtesy the Indianapolis Museum of Art and The Phillips Collection, 2014.

first camera self-portraits, human beings have striven to leave their stamp on the world, I don't foresee a dwindling popularity of selfies. It has simply been a different means (coinciding with advancing technology) to achieve the same end (a captured moment in time). Several conclusions can be drawn on how museums can use the selfie factor to their advantage. Where copyright restrictions are not an issue, institutions should encourage their patrons to take selfies in front of their collections to help increase visitorship. This can be achieved through selfie contests or by promoting recognized museum appreciation days. A staff member should be dedicated to not just overseeing an organization's social media initiatives, but to run statistical reports to assess what is working and what isn't working. Smartphone and tablet applications can be expensive, and not everyone has the type of connection that yields pro-bono work. If this can be overcome, successful apps that appeal to the popularity of selfies can engage audiences and result in tremendous press coverage. The sharing of technology, as the Indianapolis Museum of Art did with The Phillips Collection, can reduce costs. In addition, selfies can help yield substantial funds for nonprofit organizations, as witnessed with the copious amounts of small gifts received via the Ice Bucket Challenge and the #UNSelfie campaign. Likewise, today's millennials – who are more apt to use smartphones and social media than older generations – are potentially tomorrow's big donors, so it is imperative that museums continue to cultivate them. It is human nature to want to leave a mark on the world, and selfies have significant power to affect positive change for museums.

NOTE

1. Personal communication, December 18, 2014.

REFERENCES

Akel, J. (2014). DIS canonizes the art selfie. *The New York Times Style Magazine*, October 27. Available at http://tmagazine.blogs.nytimes.com/2014/10/27/art-selfie-book/.

Ariens, C. (2014). Morning show ratings: week of November 10. *TVNewser*, November 20. Available at http://www.mediabistro.com/tvnewser/category/morning-show-ratings.

Blessing, J. (2004) Photophilia. In Blessing, J., Hoving, K. A., & Rugoff, R. (eds.), *Speaking with hands: Photographs from the Buhl Collection* (pp. 13-59). New York: Solomon R. Guggenheim Museum.

Clements, E. (2014). Are Kim Kardashian's selfies a form of art - or a sign of narcissism? Daily Mail, October 29. Available at http://www.dailymail.co.uk/femail/article-2813058/Are-Kim-Kardashian-s-selfies-form-art-sign-narcissism-New-study-aims-prove-selfie-takers-self-absorbed.html.

The Dalí Museum (2014). The Dali Museum releases staring contest app. January 14. Available at http://thedali.org/press-room/dali-museum-releases-staring-contest-app/.

Daniel, D. (2015). Did you know it's Museum Selfie Day? *Artnet News*, January 21. Available at http://news.artnet.com/in-brief/did-you-know-its-museum-selfie-day-226251.

Dixon, M. (2014). Going viral with #MuseumSelfie, January 26. Message posted to http://www.mardixon.com

Dixon, M. (2015a). #MuseumSelfie Day 2015 – press, stats and more! January 21. Message posted to http://www.mardixon.com

Dixon, M. (2015b) Personal communication, February 1, 2015.

Elliott, S. (2014). Thanks to ad agency, you're in the picture at museum exhibition. *New York Times*, June 16. Available at http://www.nytimes.com/2014/06/16/business/media/thanks-to-ad-agency-youre-in-the-picture-at-museum-exhibition.html?_r=0.

Erdman, S. (2010). Museum is home for a month for Chicago woman. *CNN*, October 25. Available at http://www.cnn.com/2010/LIVING/10/25/illinois.museum.month/

Fears, D. (2013). Oxford Dictionaries names 'selfie' word of the year. *Today*, November 18. Available at http://www.today.com/news/oxford-dictionaries-names-selfie-word-year-2D11603600.

Friedman, W. (2013). Trad 30-sec spot shines, costs up 5%. *MediaDailyNews*, March 13. Available at http://www.mediapost.com/publications/article/195725/trad-30-sec-spot-shines-costs-up-5.html.

Goldberg, E. (2014). Giving Tuesday raises $45.7 million, gives Black Friday a run for its money. *Huffington Post*, December 4. Available at http://www.huffingtonpost.com/2014/12/04/giving-tuesday-results_n_6264046.html.

Grossman, S. (2012). Kony 2012 documumentary becomes most viral video in history. *Time*, March 12. Available at http://newsfeed.time.com/2012/03/12/kony-2012-documentary-becomes-most-viral-video-in-history/.

Hakala, K. (2014). Museum attendance is at an all-time high, thanks to art selfies. *Nerve*, April 30. Available at http://www.nerve.com/entertainment/does-social-media-make-us-culturally-promiscuous.

Hughes, V. (2013). Were the first artists mostly women? *National Geographic News*, October 8. Available at http://news.nationalgeographic.com/news/2013/10/131008-women-handprints-oldest-neolithic-cave-art/.

Kennedy, R. (2011). The Met's plans for virtual expansion. *New York Times*, February 12. pp. C1, C9. Available at http://search.proquest.com/docview/1634221680?accountid=7108.

Kohl Children's Museum. (n.d.). #Unselfie Contest. Available at http://www.kohlchildrensmuseum.org/visit/calendar/unselfie-contest.

Library of Congress (n.d.). Robert Cornelius, self-portrait; believed to be the earliest extant American portrait photo. Available at http://www.loc.gov/pictures/item/2004664436/.

M.S.I. Chicago's 'month at the museum.' (2010) *Adweek*, November 1. 51(39), 13.

Martinet, J. (2014). Museum selfie-ishness. *Huffington Post*, November 24. Available at http://www.huffingtonpost.com/jeanne-martinet/museum-selfieishness_b_6213198.html?utm_hp_ref=arts&ir=Arts.

Munk, C. (2014). Ice bucket donations continue to rise: $94.3 million since July 29. *The ALS Association*, August 27. Available at http://www.alsa.org/news/media/press-releases/ice-bucket-challenge-082714.html.

Museums and the Web (n.d.). What's the "point?:" Two case

studies of introducing digital in-gallery experiences. Available at http://mw2015.museumsandtheweb.com/proposal/whats-the-point-two-case-studies-of-introducing-digital-in-gallery-experiences-2/.

Perez, C. (2014). The Met joins Kim's #BreakTheInternet in the best way possible. *New York Post*, November 13. Available at http://nypost.com/2014/11/13/the-met-joins-kims-breaktheinternet-in-the-best-way-possible/.

Snow, D. (2013). Sexual dimorphism in Upper Paleolithic cave art. *American Antiquity*, 78, 746-761.

Sternbergh, M. C., Fantoni, S. F., & Djen, V. (2015). What's the point? Two case studies of introducing digital in-gallery experiences. *MW2015: Museums and the Web 2015*. Available at http://mw2015.museumsandtheweb.com/paper/whats-the-point-two-case-studies-of-introducing-digital-in-gallery-experiences/.

Stringfield, J. (2014) Personal communication, December 23, 2014.

Stringfield, J. (2015) Personal communication, January 9, 2015.

Taylor, A. (2014a) Invisible Children, organization behind Kony 2012 video, to wind down operations. *The Washington Post*, December 15. Available at http://www.washingtonpost.com/blogs/worldviews/wp/2014/12/15/invisible-children-organization-behind-kony-2012-video-to-wind-down-operations/.

Taylor, A. (2014b) Was #Kony2012 a failure? *The Washington Post*, December 16. Available at http://www.washingtonpost.com/blogs/worldviews/wp/2014/12/16/was-kony2012-a-failure/.

Timpane, J. (2013). The meaning of the ubiquitous selfie. *The Philadelphia Inquirer*, December 29. Available at http://articles.philly.com/2013-12-29/news/45653437_1_selfie-instagram-oed.

Twitter (n.d.). #GivingTuesday: Encouraging and tweeting stories of charity. Available at https://media.twitter.com/success/givingtuesday-encouraging-and-telling-stories-of-charity-on-twitter.

YouTube (n.d.). Museum of Science and Industry, Chicago. Available at https://www.youtube.com/user/MSIChicago/videos?flow=grid&view=0&sort=p.

CHAPTER FOURTEEN

BEYOND THE MUSEUM SELFIE: BECOMING THE ART FROM AFAR

Leslie-Jean Thornton

SOCIAL MEDIA ABOUNDS with museum selfies, place-specific photos taken of one's self – usually at arm's length and with a cellphone camera – and then shared with others. They almost always include a work of art or distinguishing architectural view, such as the exterior of the Louvre (Akel, 2014; La Ferla, 2014; Palma, 2015). As a genre, these visitor records exist in multiple hashtags on multiple platforms. The hashtag #museumselfie on Instagram alone had more than 13,500 posts as of February 2015; #artselfie and #artselfies combined had more than 18,850. While automatically archived on Instagram, many are additionally curated in places such as Tumblr blogs[1] and Pinterest boards, ensuring wider distribution and longer life. A Pinterest keyword search on *museumselfies* returns hundreds of pins, many posted by museums where the photos were taken. Some institutions have collections – boards – dedicated to the genre. One, named #museumselfies and moderated by the Palazzo Madama of Turin, Italy, had 617 followers and 79 pins. The Walker Art Center, Minneapolis, Minnesota, had 3,789 followers of its Art Selfies board.

On January 22, 2014, and again 364 days later, museums worldwide declared a social media-fest #MuseumSelfie day, encouraging people to tweet, post and share photographs of themselves at museums in hopes of spreading appreciation of the various museums' holdings. Some venues monitored the results and republished them to encourage further visits. The Metropolitan Museum, for example, captured related entries in a Storify.[2] Major news organizations, including *The Guardian* and *The New York Times* reported on the event – an extremely successful international celebration (Dixon, 2014). In addition to abundance, there was variety: In a feature story,

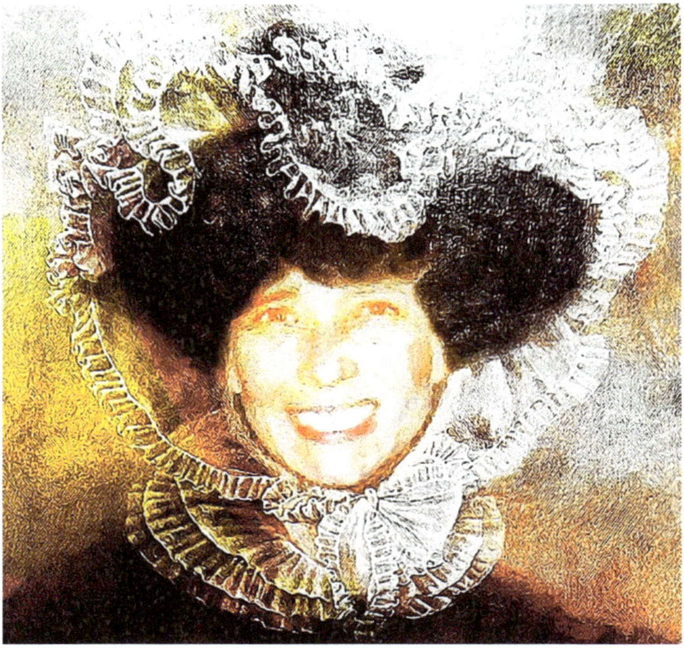

FIG. 1: Selfie. January 26, 2013. Photograph: @moosey1313.

The day's challenge: create an artistic selfie using a designated photograph of an oil painting by an anonymous nineteenth-century artist, then post it to #applifam26jan via Instagram to share with others. This one features the face of Applifam artist @moosey1313, Monica Wiley, in the painted headdress and hair of the portrait's original subject. The result: dozens of virtual visits in which artists interacted with art from the Musée Villa Montebello and whose works were published internationally.

New York Magazine reported finding nineteen different kinds of museum selfies, ranging from the cleverly composed to the blurry snapshot. According to the analytic tool Topsy, there were about 23,600 tweets tagged #museumselfie and 3,465 for #museumselfieday during the January 21, 2015 event

Museum Selfie Day, the creation of Mar Dixon,[3] is a mix of engagement strategy and fun, drawing on the public's growing involvement in shaping public history through event-sharing and documentation (Foster, 2014) and marrying it to entertainment and tourism (Caines, 2014). It fits well into a social digital world where visual communication was (and is) increasingly popular, particularly through mobile devices (Lunden, 2014). Instagram alone, launched in fall 2010 and acquired by Facebook in 2012, hosts more than 70 million photos and videos daily (Instagram, 2014).

There are multiple explanations posited for selfies' popularity (Day, 2013; Fausing, 2013), but one may underlie them all. We are designed biologically to react to faces (Bruce & Young, 1998), a trait that appears to hold up online as well as off. One research team, for example, found that Instagram posts with faces drew significantly more likes and comments than those without (Bakhsi, Chamma & Gilbert, 2014). And, they're fun. Museum selfies, in particular, put the visitor on an equal footing with great works of art. Not only can one attain greatness by association, one can interact, pretending to be part of a painting or that the statue is holding your smartphone and taking a picture of itself (with your help).

A so-far mostly unnoticed kind of museum selfie, however – one that takes more involvement than a snapshot (even if carefully and cleverly posed) – reaches another level of engagement entirely. It is born of a more abstract form of museum visitation – the virtual. In this expression, visitor-viewers are invited to download a specific image from the museum, transform it digitally, then share the result(s) to a common hashtag or venue, such as a Facebook page or Instagram feed. Early examples arose during collaborations between a regional art museum in France, the Villa Montebello, and Applifam, a global Instagram editing community founded in France in December 2011. Its creator, Johan Du Toit, was and is a prolific and popular photographer on Instagram, with 7,500 posts and 90,000 followers less than a year after Applifam's founding (Murray, 2012). Applifam (which, for its first six months, was Applified before a name change) rapidly attracted more than 10,000 followers (Thornton, 2015). An internal survey conducted in early 2014 showed that members represented 22 countries. The Electronic Social Art Forum, also founded by Du Toit, is a non-profit association registered in France to support this form of digital communication.

Each day, Applifam posts a photo cleared of copyright restrictions for its members to retrieve from a Tumblr site and edit.[4] Once done, they post the results to a date-specific hashtag on Instagram. Although suggestions are usually made for each challenge – to create something in a particular style, for example, or to honor an occasion – the artists are free to edit however they wish. One popular style is a Friday tradition: self-portraits incorporated into that day's challenge. When Applifam began offering work from the Musee Villa Montebello for editing in September 2013, it wasn't a stretch to think that selfies might be one of the editing styles used.

When in three of the collaborative 24-hour challenges the

artwork offered for editing was a portrait, it happened. One painting by an anonymous nineteenth-century artist yielded 74 transformed edits. In them, the digital artist inserted his or her self into the painting using an image (usually a selfie) or a symbolic placeholder such as a possession, or incorporated self-expressive artistic elements, such as changes in color, composition or style. The other anonymous portrait challenge resulted in 107 posts, with 127 posts for the third portrait, Claude Marie Dubufe's oil-on-canvas of the Empress Eugenie (Figures 2-11).

As of February 2015, Applifam had hosted 19 challenges incorporating images either from or of the Musee Villa Montebello. Not all were portraits, and not all were straight-on photos of paintings. Some incorporated the interior of the museum, visually inviting the visitor in. One rather unprepossessing photo of a room with a piano, a stool, and a wall-hung painting produced intriguing images during a week in which Applifam participants touched base with the museum daily, making it a virtual home of sorts. One artist, @haya_7, expressed that sense of identification, comfort, and extended sense of belonging by introducing a pixelated calico cat into the scene (Figure 12).

This visual visitation practice extends the realm of experiential aesthetics in potentially significant ways. Chiefly, one may explore original art from a vantage point that transcends physical proximity and allows viewers to, in essence, merge with what is being displayed. Museums valuing engagement afforded by museum selfies aren't dependent on people coming to the museum: the institution can effectively reach out. The edits themselves are artifacts referencing the contemporary

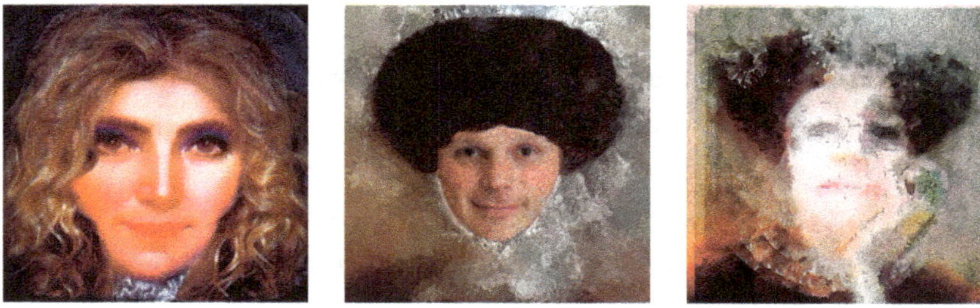

FIGS. 2-4: Selfies. January 26, 2013 (#applifam26jan). The center self-portrait is from Applifam founder Johan Du Toit. Photographs: @xaikia, @jvdt, @lolomah.

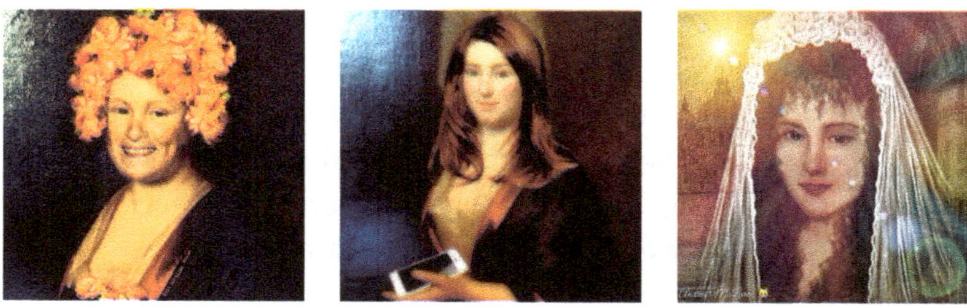

FIGS. 5-7: Selfies. March 8, 2014 (#applifam08mar). Note the iPhone held by the center figure. Photographs: @clopixe, @chonchies, @andrealuvsanimals_ud_fx.

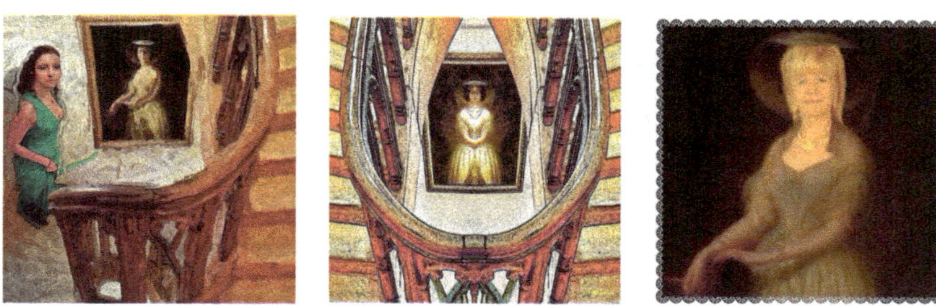

FIGS. 8-10: Selfies with the Empress Eugenie. December 13, 2014 (applifam13dec). The staircase and painting are at the Musée Villa Montebello. Photographs: @klimtt, @gardenart, @rossvii_fs.

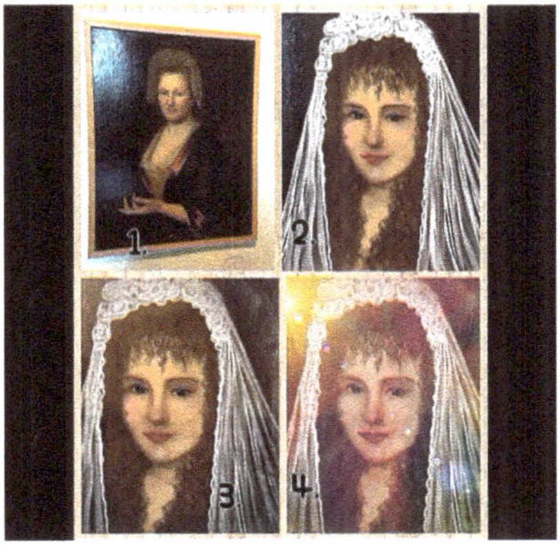

FIG. 11: Transformation process. March 8, 2014. Photographs: @andrealuvsar imals_ud_fx.

Artist Andrea McClaren showed stages (as an Instagram post) of the work she created using apps for smartphones and tablets. She began with the original Applifam post, then imposed that digital image over another one painted in Art Studio. The background was added in Phot to Lab; soft lighting was added in Jazz.

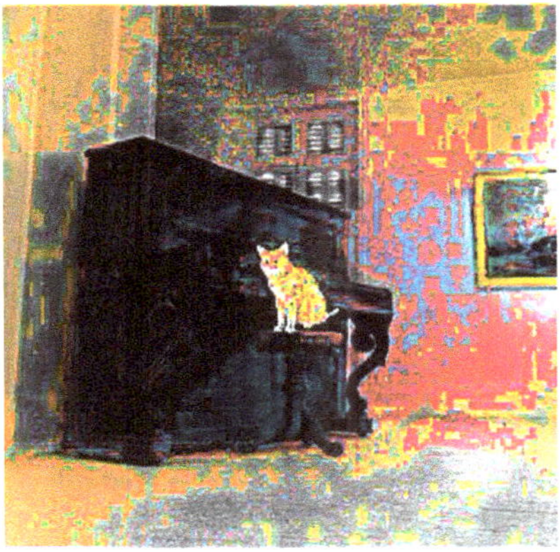

FIG. 12: Museum. December 12, 2014 (#applifam12dec). Photograph: @haya_7.

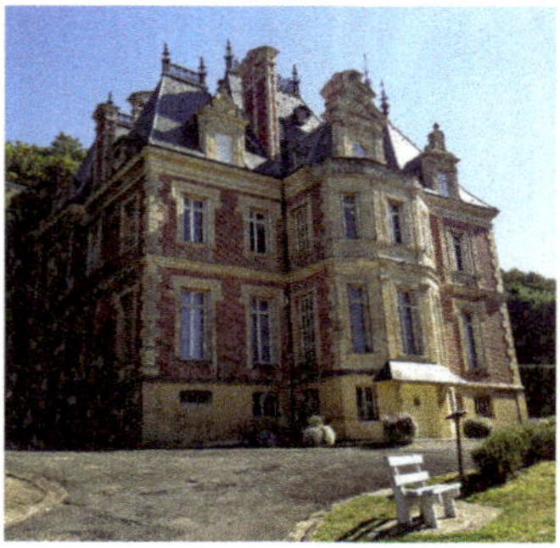

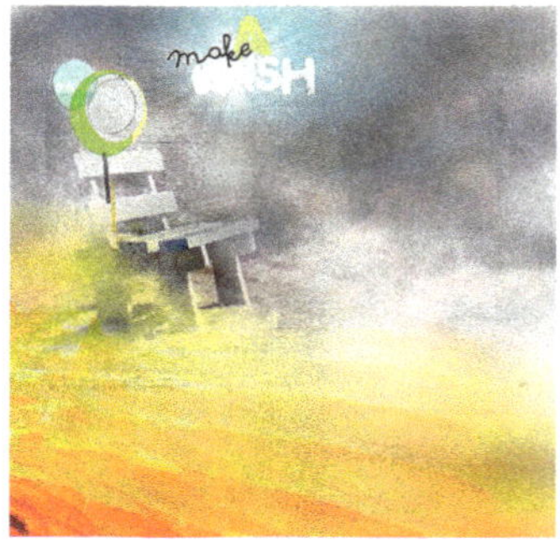

FIG. 13 (LEFT): Musée Villa Montebello. September 7, 2013. The museum made its first appearance in Applifam as an exterior view. The editing challenge results were tagged and posted to #applifam08sep. Photograph: Johan Du Toit.

FIG. 14 (RIGHT): Make a wish. September 7, 2013 (#applifam08sep). This flight of fancy from the original photo was, in part, a celebration of the first birthday of the Electronic Social Art Forum. Photograph: @casbury.

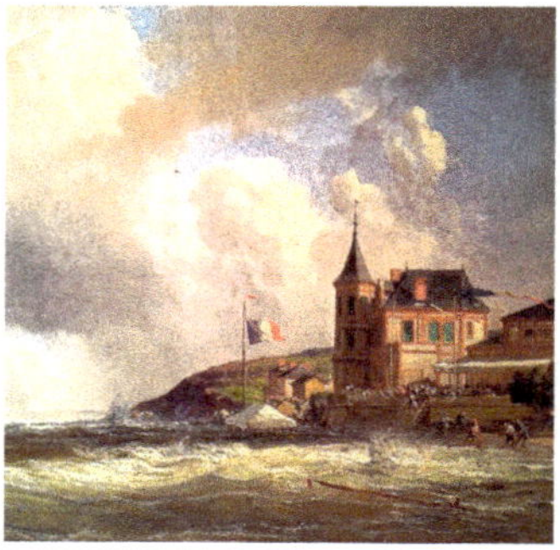

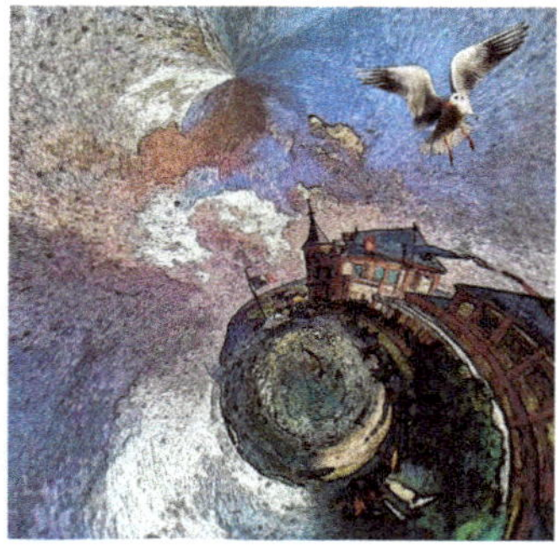

Image 15 (LEFT): Charles Mozin, *Beach at Trouville sur Mer at High Tide*. Oil painting, c.1850. This was the first image offered as an Applifam editing activity in support of Villa Montebello. The photo was taken and posted with the museum's permission.

FIG. 16 (RIGHT): Beach at Trouville sur Mer. November 9, 2013 (#applifam09nov). This and subsequent challenges featuring the museum's Mozin holdings spurred 494 posts to a separate tag, #montebello_mozin. Photograph: @jorgerionegro.

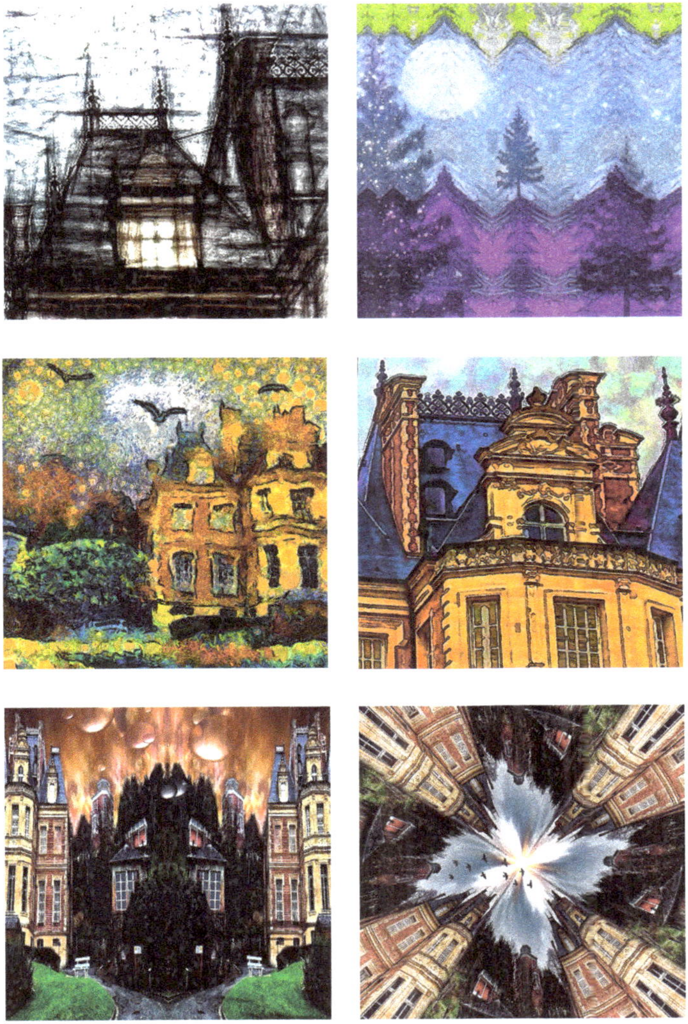

FIGS. 17-22: Interpretations of one photo of the Musée Villa Montebello. December 14, 2014. The edit by @rossvii_fs (Figure 19) was reposted by the @MulvaneArtMuseum account. There were 129 posts to #applifam14dec from this challenge. Photographs: @cyll, @ljthornton, @rossvii_fs, @giuseppemauriello74, @tikalight_fx, @jekillick.

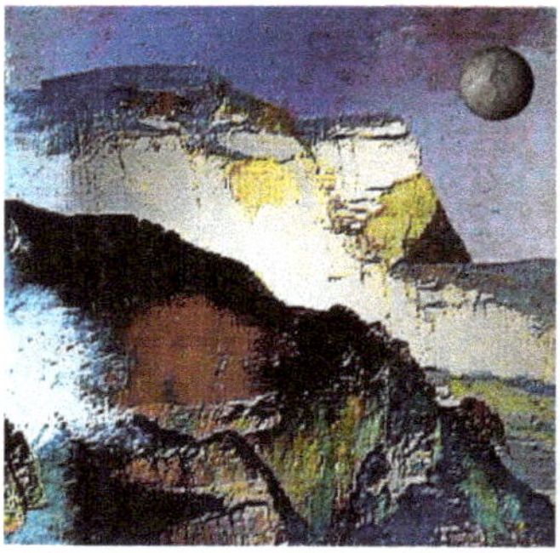

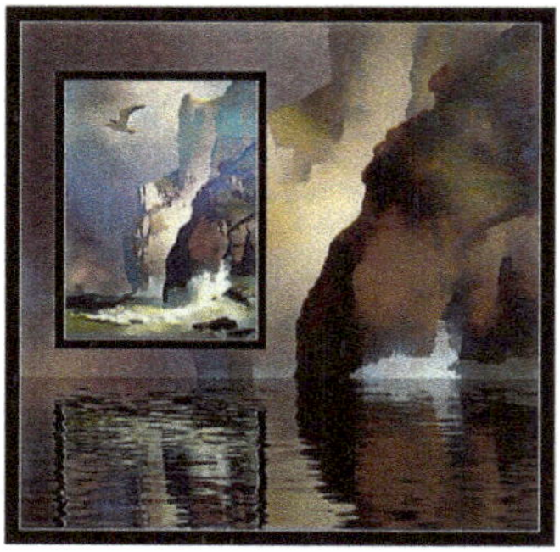

FIGS. 23, 24: After Mozin. December 15, 2013 (#applifam15dec). These were two of seven transformative edits posted by this Applifam artist; there were 99 posts overall for that challenge. A year later, the editing activity was inspired by an 1895 oil painting by Ferdinand Moutier, also on virtual loan from the Musée Villa Montebello. Photograph: @jostto.

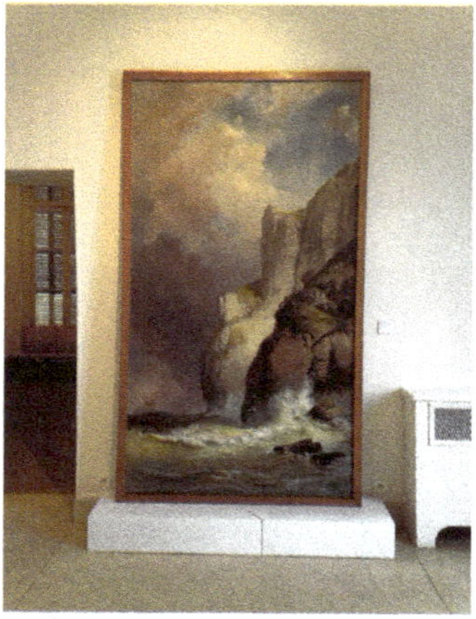

FIG. 25: Charles Mozin, *Falaise, Mer Agitée*. Oil painting; 1853. Photograph: Johan Du Toit.

art experience and emblematic, perhaps, of a social statement on the integral nature of art in everyday life. In the case of Applifam, the collaboration began outside the museum as a gesture of support, and as a way to spark discussion about art and artists. But it could easily start from within a museum, and could be the focus of interviews, curations, and teaching sessions as well as a vital web presence. More importantly, it forges bonds with practitioners of new forms of social media-inspired creativity (Hinton & Hjorth, 2013).

As museums grow in awareness of social media and their promotional possibilities, (Kidd, 2011; Padilla-Melendez & Rosa del Aguila-Obra, 2013; Weilenmann, Hillman & Jungselius, 2013), they might investigate an outreach to the general public and collaboration with the many Instagram editing communities, along the lines of Applifam and the Musee Villa Montebello's exploration. "As our motto for the @electronicsocialart forum is *To make art history happen*," Du Toit has written, "there is a natural move towards partnership and showing solidarity with museums and other guardians of art and cultural history."[5]

NOTES

1. Such as museumselfie.tumblr.com.
2. https://storify.com/metmuseum/museumselfie-day.
3. See Chapter Twelve of this volume.
4. The link – applifam.tumblr.com – is available on the Applifam profile on Instagram.
5. Personal communication, March 8, 2014.

REFERENCES

Akel, J. (2014). DIS canonizes the art selfie. *New York Times*, October 27. Available at: http://tmagazine.blogs.nytimes.com/2014/10/27/art-selfie-book/.

Bakhshi, S., Shamma, D. A., & Gilbert, E. (2014). Faces engage us: Photos with faces attract more likes and comments on Instagram. Paper presented at CHI2014, Toronto, Canada, April 26-May 1.

Bruce, V., & Young, A. (1998). *In the eye of the beholder: The science of face perception*. Oxford, England: Oxford University Press.

Caines, M. (2014). Museum Selfie day – in pictures. *The Guardian*, January 22. Available at: http://www.theguardian.com/culture-professionals-network/culture-professionals-blog/gallery/2014/jan/22/museum-selfie-day-in-pictures.

Day, E. (2013). How selfies became a global phenomenon. *The Guardian*, July 13. Available at: http://www.theguardian.com/technology/2013/jul/14/how-selfies-became-a-global-phenomenon.

Dixon, M. (2014). Going viral with #MuseumSelfie. Available at: http://www.mardixon.com/wordpress/2014/01/going-viral-with-museumselfie/.

Fausing, B. (2013). Become an image: On selfies, visuality and the visual turn in social media. Keynote address presented to Digital Visually, Rome, January 11. Available at: http://curis.ku.dk/ws/files/95157858/KEY_NOTE.docx.

Foster, M. (2014). Online and plugged in? Public history and historians in the digital age. *Public History Review*, *21*, 1-19.

Hinton, S., & Hjorth, L. (2013). *Understanding social media*. Los Angeles: Sage.

Instagram (2014). 300 million: Sharing real moments. Available at: http://blog.instagram.com/post/104847837897/141210-300million.

Kidd, J. (2011). Enacting engagement online: Framing social media use for the museum. *Information, Technology and People*, 24(1), 64-77.

La Ferla, R. (2014). Perfecting the art selfie in Miami. *New York Times*, December 12. Available at: http://www.nytimes.com/2014/12/14/fashion/perfecting-the-art-selfie-in-miami.html.

Lange, M. (2014). The 19 types of selfies at Museum Selfie Day. *New York Magazine*, January 23. Available at: http://nymag.com/thecut/2014/01/19-types-of-selfies-at-museum-selfie-day.html.

Lunden, I. (2014). Instagram is the fastest growing social site. Globally, mobile devices rule over PCs for access. *Techcrunch*, January 21. Available at: http://techcrunch.com/2014/01/21/instagram-is-the-fastest-growing-social-site-globally-mobile-devices-rule-over-pcs-for-social-access/.

Murray, Tonto. (2012). 50 Amazing photographers on Instagram. *HubPages*. Available at: http://tontomurray.hubpages.com/hub/photographers-on-instagram.

Padilla-Melendez, A., & Rosa del Aguila-Obra, A. (2013). Web and social media usage by museums: Online value creation. *International Journal of Information Management*, 33, 892-898.

Palma, K. (2015). 10 types of selfies you'll see today on

MuseumSelfieDay. *Boston Globe*, January 21. Available at: http://www.boston.com/travel/2015/01/21/types-selfies-you-see-today-museumselfieday/ev3NF02V9VPuFN-6TY8pPQL/story.html.

Thornton, L. J. (2015). The photo is live at Applifam: An Instagram community grapples with how images should be used. *Visual Communication Quarterly* 21(2), 72-82.

Weilenmann, A., Hillman, T., & Jungselius, B. (2013). Instagram at the museum: Communicating the museum experience through social photo sharing. *CHI '13: Proceedings of the SIGCHI Conference on Human Factors in Computing Systems*, 1843-1852.

PARTIC

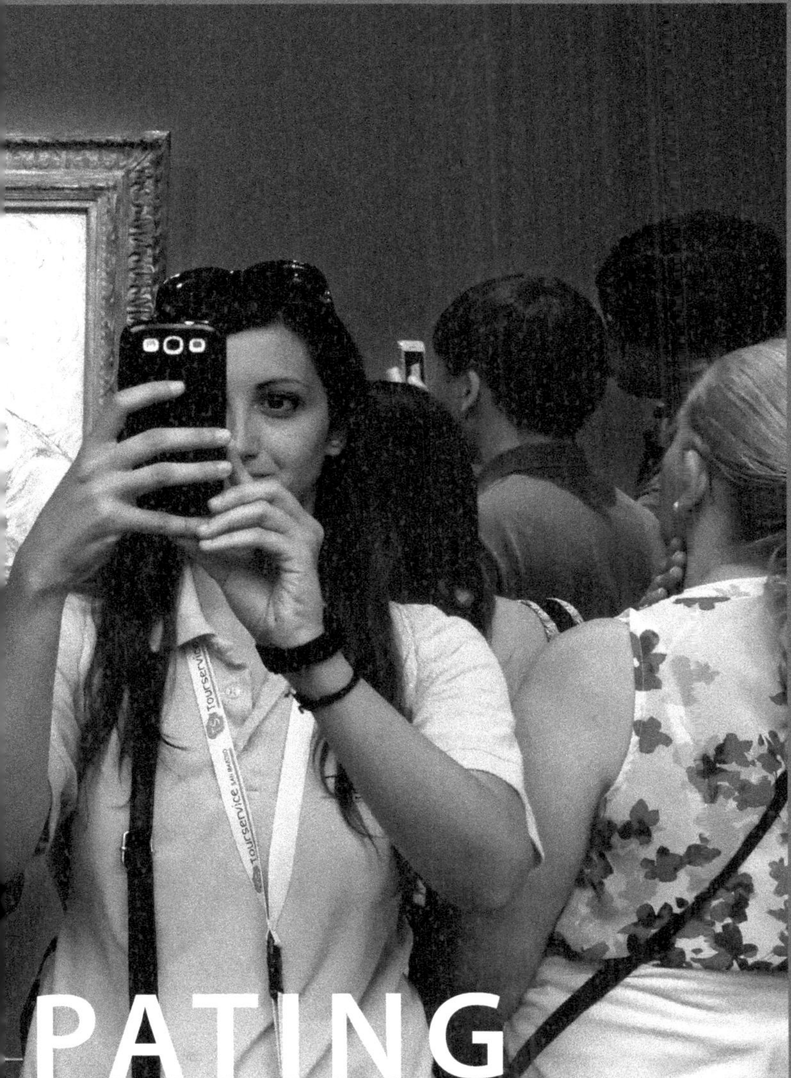

PATING

CHAPTER FIFTEEN

CURATING SOCIAL MEDIA PHOTOGRAPHY IN-GALLERY

Russell Dornan

IN 2014, WELLCOME COLLECTION mounted *An Idiosyncratic A to Z of the Human Condition (A to Z)*, a highly participative exhibition which ran from 24 June until 12 October. Half the exhibition was made up of historical objects from our collections and the other half displayed content generated by our audiences (both physical visitors to the gallery as well as online). We developed a way to include digital user-generated content in the exhibition: something we had not tried before; something exciting; and something to inspire our online audiences. Instagram, our newest social media channel, was the platform to do just that.

Aims

This project was an experiment and our goals were broad to reflect that. This chapter examines how we planned and executed a project to provide photographic content for the exhibition, whilst publicising our new Instagram account and reaching new audiences. The project also acted as a trial for future Instagram and photography ideas. Finally, using Instagram in this way allowed us to experiment with a new way to engage online, as well as in-venue, visitors.

Conception

The *A to Z* exhibition came about because of Wellcome Collection's development project. Running from 2013 to early 2015, this brought more areas of the building into public use, creating a new gallery for thematic exhibitions and doubling the capacity for public events. Our programme timings shifted slightly and left us with an exhibition-shaped hole to fill over the summer: we had about five weeks to come up with an idea

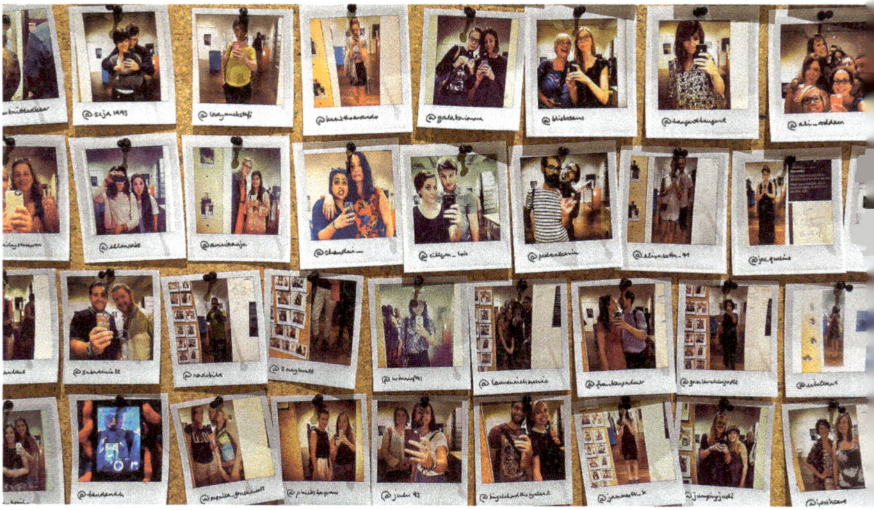

FIG. 1: Photographs submitted by visitors to the *A to Z* exhibition at Wellcome Collection, June 2014.

and execute it before opening to the public.

The curator, Danielle Olsen, decided to use parts of our collection to look at the ways our objects can inform what makes us human and, as fellow experts on the human condition, she wanted our visitors to be able to contribute to that inquiry. Since the show had to be designed and installed very quickly, the fact that the participatory elements were to make up 50% of the exhibition allowed us to maximise on the limited time available.

The exhibition

In *A to Z*, the alphabet ran along both of the longest sides of the gallery, each letter opposite itself; every letter stood for a theme (Figure 2). On one side, we presented a selection of our collection of historical objects for each letter. For example: B was for *Birthdays* and featured a horoscope dating from 1411; X was for *X-rated* and featured porcelain sex fruit.

The same themes were explored on the opposite wall using participatory activities in the gallery so that our visitors could engage with the themes directly, simultaneously contributing to the exhibition itself. For example: K (*Keeping up appearances*) asked people to draw a self-portrait; Q (*Quarantine*) prompted visitors to take part in a poll about whether forced quarantining was acceptable. Activities included drawing, writing stories, taking fortune cookies, leaving voice recordings, and marking your height on the wall. The outputs of these were then left to accumulate in the gallery for subsequent visitors to see and add to.

Themes

The curator approached the digital team at the beginning of the process about including social media elements in the exhibition

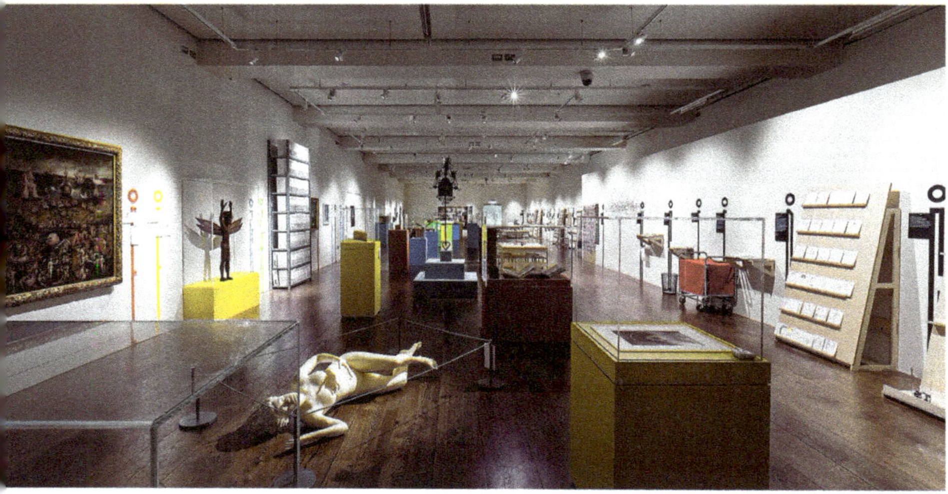

FIG. 2: *An idiosyncratic A to Z of the Human Condition* at Wellcome Collection, June 2014.

and we knew we wanted to use Instagram. It was great to be asked so early on; it meant our ideas were able to grow and fit together with the curator's as the exhibition took shape.

Out of the 26 themes on offer, we identified those we thought would resonate most with our audience, as well as those which would lend themselves best to Instagram/photography. To maximise the submissions received for each theme, we wanted their respective calls to action to be easy to take part in. Some of the themes weren't necessarily photographable (such as *Music* or *Philosophy*). Others were, but might strike the wrong tone (such as *Grief* or *War*). Then there was *X-rated*...

Some of the themes stood out in the right way *Skin Art* meant we could ask people for photos of their tattoos. *Individuality* would allow us to request selfie submissions. The chosen themes were: *Individuality*, *Natural Curiosity*, *Skin Art*, *Urban Living* and *Yawning*.

Development

We wanted to ask as little as possible of people to make sure the focus was on participating in and enjoying the project. Most of the chosen themes already had a built-in audience on Instagram (such as tattoos).

We intended to use social media to spread the word about the project. Our website provided full details about how to get involved, with examples for each theme, as well as background information and material from the collection, just like in the gallery. It was important for us that people from all over the world could get involved without ever visiting the museum, to bring in perspectives on the human condition outside of London and the UK. Just because someone may be unable to set

THEME AND #	SHARE YOUR PHOTO...	DISPLAY IN GALLERY
INDIVIDUALITY #HumanReflection	...of a selfie in the mirror in the exhibition	Large pin board (Figures 1 and 5)
NATURAL CURIOSITY #HumanNature	...of an interesting or curious thing you've seen in nature	Shelving (Figure 6)
SKIN ART #HumanSkin	...of your tattoo(s)	Photo album (Figure 7)
URBAN LIVING #HumanSardines	... evoking the sense of urban living and how we live together in such high numbers and in close proximity	Shelving
YAWNING #HumanExpression	...of any facial expression	Small pin board

FIG. 3: Theme setup and display.

foot in your building shouldn't necessarily mean they are unable to engage with, and contribute to, your themes and content.

Different options were considered for displaying the photographs: from digital screens capturing a live Instagram feed to covering a large expanse of wall with the printed photos. It needed to be a practical and sustainable solution: we had to be prepared for collecting and displaying images for over three months. The finished product also had to sit well alongside the other content and not look out of place in a museum exhibition.

Concept

We invited submissions using Twitter, Facebook and Instagram, directing people to our website for more information. People then submitted photographs via Instagram for their chosen themes, tagging each image with its respective hashtag. The photographs were printed out in a Polaroid style and displayed in the gallery and the digital images were displayed online on our Tumblr site.

Figure 3 summarises each theme's setup and how we displayed them. Photos for *Individuality* had to be taken in the exhibition itself: a mirror was fixed to the wall for people to take selfies in. This theme was unique in that the call to action was in the gallery only and not broadcast on social media. This standardised the photos for maximum impact, provided an in-gallery photo activity and allowed us to display photos of our physical visitors to the exhibition.

Process

We used social media to publicise the project, directing people to our website for more information. We also created a graphic

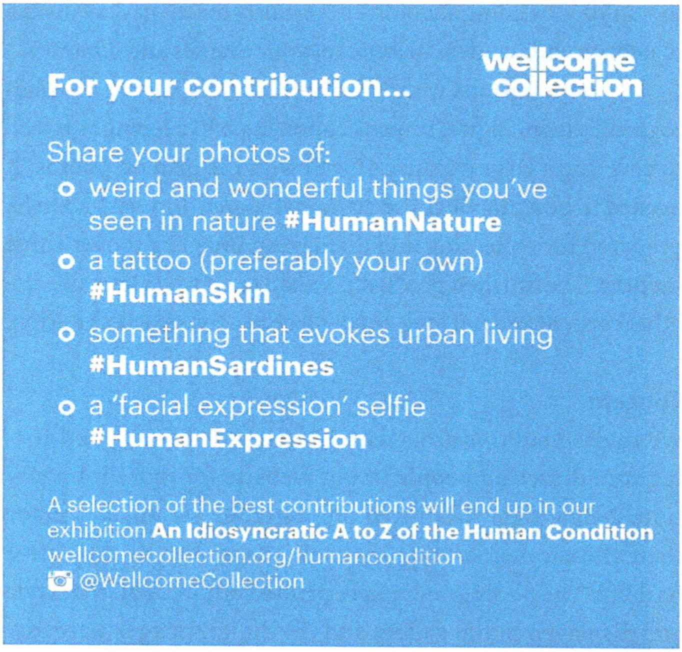

FIG. 4: Exhibition instructions graphic.

to attach to tweets and post on Instagram and Facebook, with details of the project and how to get involved (Figure 4). It meant that explanations within the tweet were unnecessary and that influencers on Twitter or Instagram could be tagged in without taking up space in the tweet itself.

We ran the social media elements of *A to Z* with assistance from our Visitor Experience team. The website IFTTT (If This Then That) was used to auto-aggregate the photos onto Tumblr as draft posts, incorporating the required hashtags. We went through the drafts, adding relevant ones to the queue to get published regularly throughout the day; irrelevant ones were deleted. We did this every few days over the run of the exhibition.

When printing the images, we used the website Collecto to browse photographs with each hashtag and then dragged relevant images individually from the browser to a Photoshop Polaroid template and printed them out, four per page. People's Instagram handles were written on the photos, which were then cut out and put on display (Figures 5-7). This was done every week throughout the exhibition to ensure the display was updated regularly. If any of the participants came in we wanted them to have a high chance of seeing their own photograph in the museum.

Outcomes

The project generated fantastic interactions across social media. Responses to seeing the photographic displays in the gallery were positive and people enjoyed seeing their own images on display; some even came in and photographed their pictures.

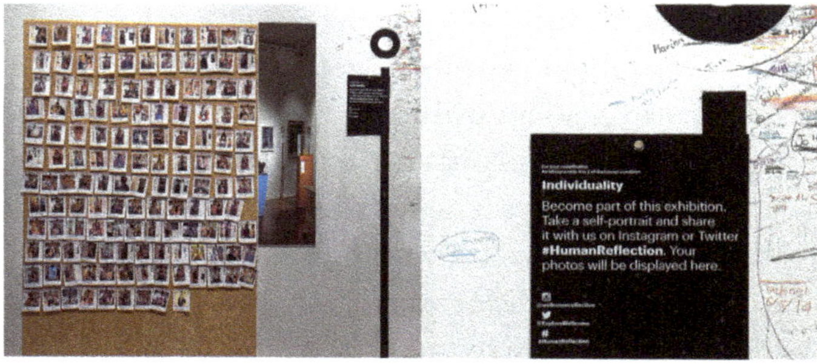

FIG. 5: The *Individuality* pinboard in the gallery (top left). The call to action features handles and hashtags (top right). Photographs: Wellcome Collection, June 2014.

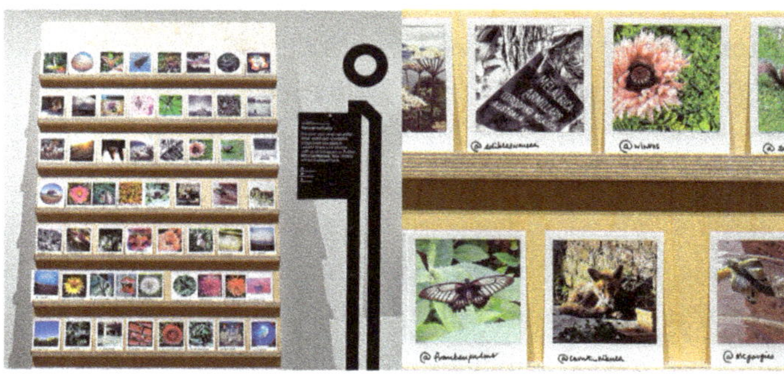

FIG. 6: The *Natural Curiosity* shelving next to its call to action (middle left). The Polaroid-style photographs (middle right). Photographs: Wellcome Collection, June 2014.

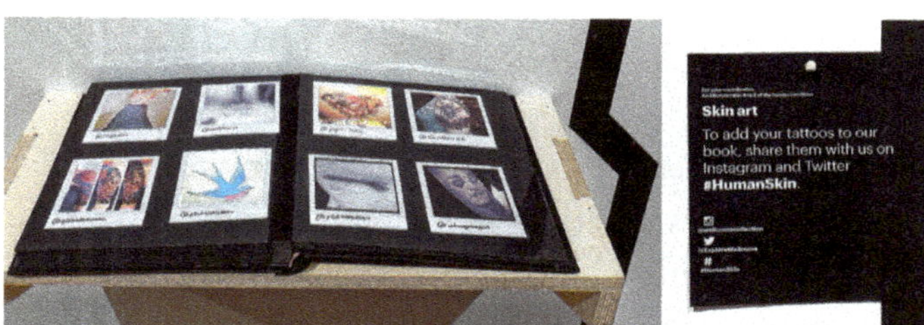

FIG. 7: Photographs of tattoos in a photo album are displayed in the gallery for Skin Art (bottom left). Again, the call to action features handles and hashtags (bottom right). Photographs: Wellcome Collection, June 2014.

Submissions

We received over 1,400 images across the five themes. The standard was high across the submissions so we displayed almost all of them. There were a number of individuals who submitted repeatedly over the show's run, leading us to develop relationships with them: they became great advocates for the project. Some people would submit as many as five to ten images in one go. In those cases, we chose a selection of them to make sure we could include as many people's as possible.

We had not used Instagram long at Wellcome Collection and were still growing our audience. Over the course of the exhibition, our Instagram followers grew by 217%.

One of the biggest successes of the project was an Insta-Meet we organised with the photography group, Instagramers London. Over 40 people came in for breakfast and a tour of the exhibition, before going on a photo walk to take pictures on Instagram using one of our hashtags. The following week, submissions for that theme increased substantially. It was useful to meet a network of local Instagramers who also spread the word about our project.

The submissions are still viewable on Tumblr and we have all the hard copies. We also commissioned blog posts to explore each theme further and used the submitted photographs to illustrate the articles. The *Individuality* post about selfies was very popular. We used the submitted photos on Facebook and Twitter to publicise the exhibition and project, and some images have been used on our website.

Challenges

Maintaining and requesting submissions for five themes at

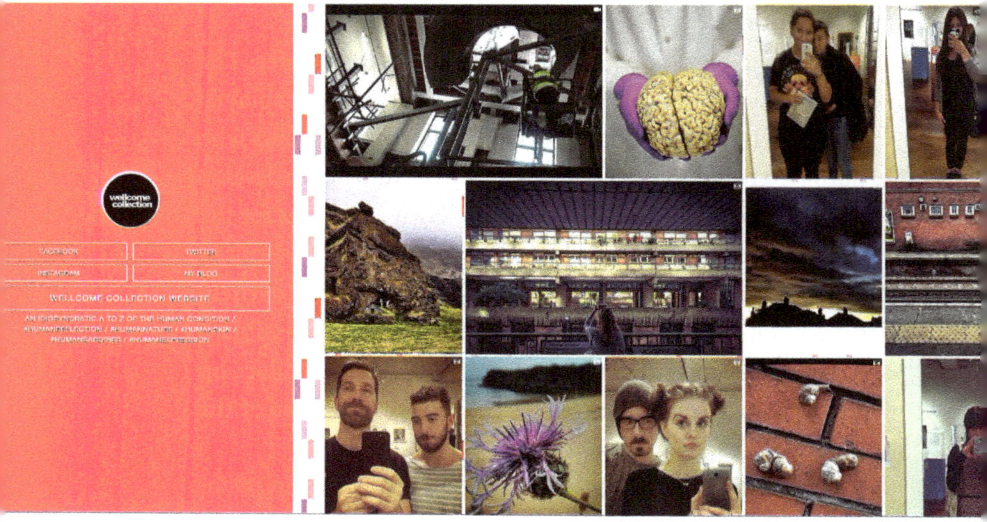

FIG. 8: Wellcome Collection's Tumblr website at the time of the exhibition.

once was time intensive. We had to make sure we devoted enough time to each one to get a balance of submissions. It was important to recognise which ones worked better (or not) and why so we could apply that to future projects. Going forward we will likely concentrate on one theme at a time.

Keeping up with submissions was a potential challenge; it was important to establish a sustainable workflow to keep the supply of photographs into the exhibition regular. We wanted people who had submitted their images to be likely to see them should they visit shortly after. Additionally, thanking all contributors on Instagram was impossible due to Instagram's spamming policy. After you've commented on a number of images, Instagram blocks your ability to keep doing so. In the end, we liked submissions as acknowledgement.

Learning points

Over the course of the project we learned a few lessons, either by doing something that seemed to work, or by realising we could have done things differently. Since our Instagram following was in its infancy, people could submit via Twitter too. We soon played down this participation method for several reasons: photos from Twitter could be any size and shape, making them difficult to fit the Polaroid template; IFTTT couldn't automatically pull them through to Tumblr, requiring a lot of extra effort; and they were of variable resolution. In the future, we will stick to doing a similar project exclusively on Instagram (the vast majority came via Instagram anyway).

I wanted to include our social media handles and hashtags in the design for the exhibition. Having faced resistance from designers and exhibition staff about this before, I successfully made a case for their inclusion. It was important for visitors to the gallery to be equipped to participate; including handles and hashtags on the panels near each theme's display meant there were fewer barriers preventing people from taking part. It also validated the contributions via social media as being as important as the others.

Choosing hashtags for each theme was challenging. We wanted to limit irrelevant noise, but also make sense in isolation. The exhibition's hashtag was #HumanCondition so we wanted *human* to prefix each theme's hashtag. This worked fine for all but *Natural Curiosity* (#HumanNature). Over the show's run, a new cosmetic range of the same name was promoted on Instagram; the anniversary of Michael Jackson's death in June added to the already high volume of images posted in tribute to him and Madonna (each has a song called *Human Nature*); and it's commonly used to express various sentiments. We accepted its common use from the start for the sake of hashtag consistency, but in the future we will try to avoid this.

While this project certainly grew our audience on Instagram, because we were just starting out it was difficult to be heard on the platform. We now have over 11,000 followers; next time we do something similar, we will be in a stronger position and the project will likely have a bigger impact. That is not to say a project like this is not a good idea in the early stages of joining a platform, but it is important to understand that without a critical mass of followers, progress may be slower and more time consuming than expected.

This project explored the human condition and the submitted photos covered aspects of our visitors' everyday life, their observations and their selfies. The lighthearted, participatory quality of the project has been beneficial for both ourselves and the public. The relatively simple call to action enabled our visitors to respond creatively and we were delighted to display such a wealth of photographic submissions as an intrinsic part of the exhibition.

CHAPTER SIXTEEN

DIGITAL SCULPTURES, DIGITAL VISITORS

Jenna C Ashton

THE MUSEUM *of Science and Industry (MOSI)* in Manchester features an astonishing digital sculpture – the *Chandelier*. The Chandelier is the first and last encounter between photography, visitors and the museum. Located just beyond the main entrance foyer, it is a dominant piece which informs the visitor experience upon entering and leaving.

Pulsating tubes of white-purple light drip through the Chandelier's core, with the twisting helix frame supporting brightly coloured images and key dates from Manchester's science and industry achievements – from 1781 and Arkwright's cotton mills to 2004 and the discovery of Graphene. Interspersed large screens punctuate the timeline, projecting the images of participating visitors (Figure 1). A textile piece was originally suggested for the space, but designers and curators settled on the concept of the Chandelier – an innovative digital sculpture looking towards new technologies to encourage image-making, computer interaction, and – importantly – visitor participation. Photography is used as the tool to initiate an experiment between the space of the museum and the personal space of the visitor. A place where art and technology collide, emphasis is placed upon the visitor's image as a key contributing element to this sculptural centre piece – testing creative interaction and visitor participation through the projected selfie.

A cluster of upright computer stations hover near the Chandelier. Visitors take their self-portraits through these computer screens, and in a few seconds the images are uploaded to the Chandelier. In its initial launch phase visitors were required to register a barcoded card, so they could revisit a personalised online scrapbook of their archived museum experience. However, after technical difficulties this system generated tensions

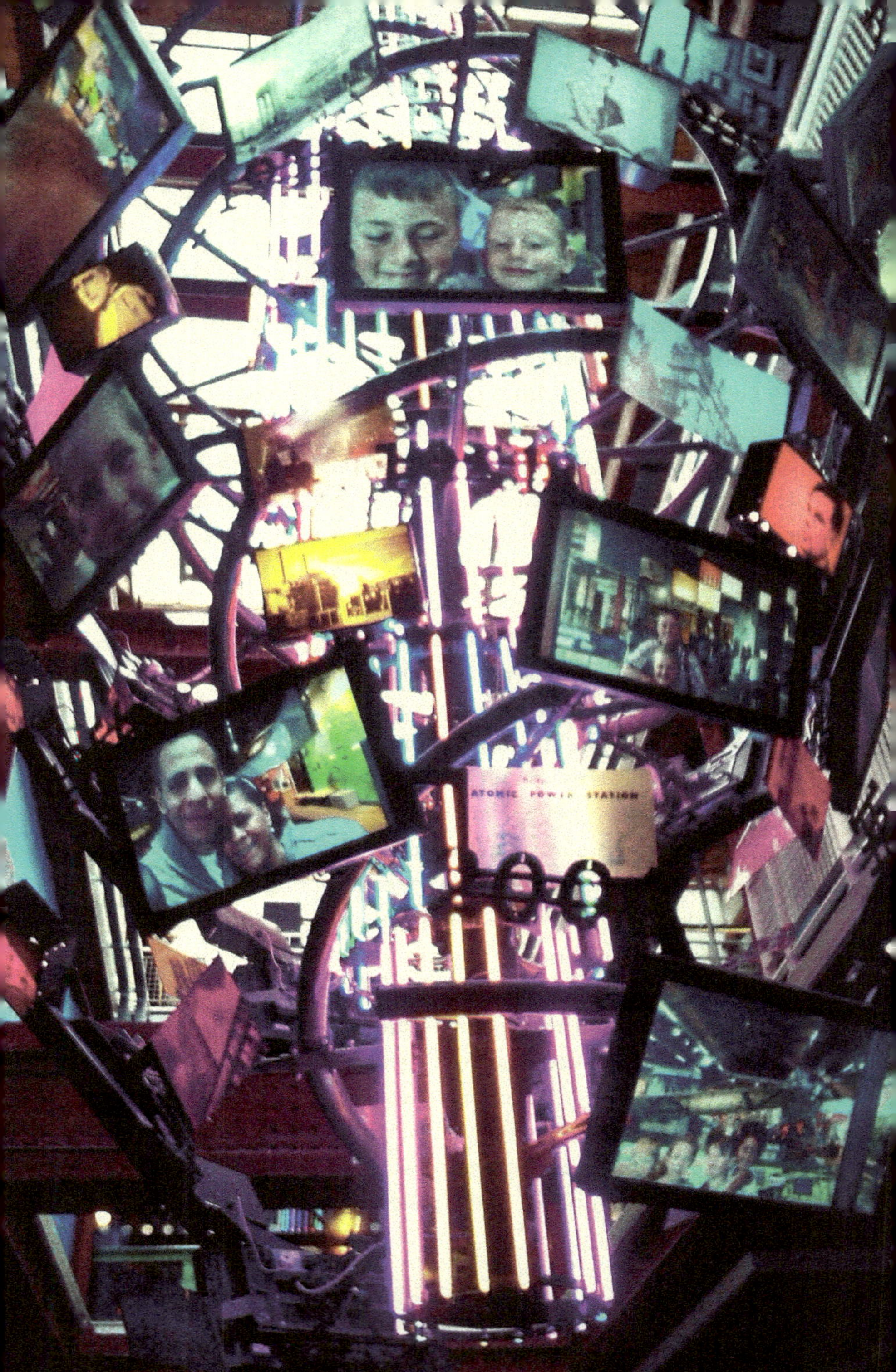

FIG. 1: MOSI Chandelier. Photograph: [illegible] C Ashton

and visitor dissatisfaction, so a touch-screen system evolved, connecting the images to the social network sites Facebook and Twitter. No individual website system exists for new visitors; instead the Chandelier feeds into people's existing digital and virtual spheres and links the material space of the museum with those personal and collective virtual spaces already overloaded with pre-existing selfies.

Curatorial responsibility for the Chandelier lies primarily with the nearby Visitor Services Team, who monitor that nothing inappropriate appears on the screens, simply checking the screens as and when the images appear. The public becomes part of the Revolution Gallery when their photo is displayed on the Chandelier sculpture.

Science and photography are intertwined bedfellows. Photography has historically found its own space halfway between industry and fine art – sitting in neither entirely comfortably, but straddling both. Its technology defines it, yet also betrays, restricting its easy categorisation. However, this makes photography the ultimate art-science, science in art, art of science. It is undefinable, always shifting (Wilder, 2009).

Daston and Galison (1992) chart the rise and development of objectivity in science and particularly the use of photography in constructing a notion of mechanical objectivity. They argue that moralising objectivity in the late nineteenth and early twentieth centuries is reflected in scientific image making which supposes that photography eliminated the dangers of human agency, interpretation and the scientist's own will (Daston & Galison, 1992). Followers of mechanical objectivity put their faith in technology to replace subjective modes of expression, such as spoken and written language. However, as is hotly critiqued by contemporary visual theorists, photography, like any medium, is by no means free from subjective influences, with its images (content, focus, intentions) a gesture of the photographer. As Daston and Galison emphasise, photographic techniques were not even hailed as specifically accurate (such as bad lighting, blurred images, fallen specs of dust) but a misplaced moralising believed photography would convey "truth", that "the machine stood for authenticity [...] miraculously free from inner temptation to theorise, anthropomorphise, beautify, or otherwise interpret nature" (Daston & Galison, 1992: 120). Any concept of mechanical objectivity is put out to pasture with MOSI's chandelier. In a context of a museum which celebrates scientific discovery and exploration, a sense of the curious and distinctly subjective emanates from the colourfully throbbing digital spectacle.

The name of the sculpture is itself evocative and heavy with associative meaning and contexts other than this museum space. Chandelier: an object of light, illumination; ornate and majestic, and a supporting structure. Photography, in its literal translation, is the writing of light. There is a sense of indulgence, of beauty and poetry; but what exactly does this infer about visitor photography in this context? Is the "poetry and beauty" of industry and science actually captured and conveyed? As Baudrillard (2000: 1) mentions:

> Through its unrealistic play of visual techniques, its slicing of reality, its immobility, its silence, and its phenomenological reduction of movements, photography affirms itself as both the purest and the most artificial exposition of the image.

It could be argued that through photography, *we* see nothing. Only the lens "sees" things. Photography is the dominance of technology and science over human intervention in terms of the actual *mechanics* of photography. The camera is a tool for capturing the spectacle, the object which stands before us. With the Chandelier, the Artificial Intelligence of the digital computer captures the visitor's image. Photography is a fiction; a continuous acting out, and play with reality. All that remains is the light. The original object, and context, has passed; the photograph is an impression. It is "irreversible, hence always nostalgic. The instantaneity of photography is not to be confused with the simultaneity of real time" (Baudrillard, 2000: 1).

The relationship between people and technology in this context is fairly muted, predictable, and passive. The visitor has little control over the style, technique, light. The job has been done, set, for them. The computers and their angles are immoveable and static. The visitor is not so much the photographer as a receiver of the photographic, as the computer reverses the view to focus entirely upon the face of the user .

In Winter 2014, MOSI hosted the Wellcome Image Awards 2014, displaying eighteen majestic photographs which are both, and neither, purely art or science. Capturing the minuscule or the hidden, these images were created using cutting-edge imaging techniques, and boldly steer clear of the ordinary in favour of revealing the extraordinary in nature as well as medical and human sciences. The technologically and aesthetically sophisticated Wellcome images radically contrast with those collated on the Chandelier: blurred shots; gurning or grinning faces; a thumbs up; loved-up couples; giggling families; the pouting and stern. The Chandelier does not take itself too seriously, and neither should the visitor. It does not look to creating innovative images, such as those collated by the Wellcome, but instead interjects a sense of the everyday – a snap (literally) of a face, for a few moments, in a place once bustling with the railway industry. These images are part of an archive of images, held somewhere in the museum's digital ether (although nobody could actually tell me where).

The Chandelier also intends to inform visitors about key names and dates in science and industry; however the photographic screens dominate, along with the computing apparatus used for taking the images. I would go as far to say that the viewer is not especially interested in the specific dates and heritage-images displayed on the Chandelier. It lacks any cohesive, meaningful narrative to draw people into its history of industry. This aspect of the Chandelier is a mere decoration, a space filler, until the visitor encounters the real "meat" of the exhibitions beyond. It is the photographic screens interspersed between the colourfully lit dates and historical material which offers real interest, and a certain drama. These images and performances of self and identity reject static histories in favour of participation and ever evolving sense of heritage.

Performance and identity in the museum

The Chandelier is a digital album of strangers' faces; a weirdly constructed family tree driven by a visitor rather than familial "genetics". The DNA helix-spiral is pertinent, perhaps even a little too obvious in drawing attention to the importance of human narratives to histories of science and industry. Visitors enact out a performance of the self in a space celebrating scientific and industrial experimentation. Photography becomes the tool through which visitors become exhibits. It is a rather strange event, watching someone watching themselves on a camera, to produce an image which others will continuously see. I watch people watching people; observing and scrutinizing each other's image making the final "product".

In that instant of image-making the museum becomes a little theatre full of comical, confused and excitable performances. Couples loiter in front of the screens, nervously aware that their image is soon to be uploaded – their "coupling" made ever more public. Small children get frustrated at not being able to reach the screens of the computers and hit away at the now obsolete keyboards – until an adult hoists them onto their shoulders or carries them closer. Individuals, trying to look discrete, go through a series of different facial movements, deciding on their best look before pressing the *take* button. All smile, as if on cue, then wait for thirty seconds. They then run around the Chandelier, checking all sides to see where their faces may emerge, which, once it does, results in mumbles, groans, laughter, squeals, and red cheeks. They walk away, glancing back now and then, and pointing. This performance is repetitive; some are quieter than others; groups and younger participants are raucous; elder users are gleeful when they easily work out the mechanics of the image-taking device.

Two different photographic histories come to the fore in the context of this museum – one of science imagery, and an ideal of mechanical objectivity; the other, self-portraiture. The portrait is a theatrical positioning of the self in space and time for a specific audience. The staged photographic self-portrait stretches back to the Victorians, and their distinctly non-objective experimentation with the new technology. The

MOSI self-portraits exist in the cultural context of an array of easily created digital imagery professing "we were here". The images enable the takers to stake a claim, to actively own and structure a small part of the museum experience.

Visual historian Amelia Jones (2002: 950) comments on those artists who interrogate the use of the photograph in identity construction:

> Exaggerating their own performances of themselves, these artists, then, explore the capacity of the self-portrait photograph to foreground the "I" as other to itself, the artistic subject as "taking place" in the future through interpretive acts that bring her or him back to life via memory or desire.

The acts of self-photography in MOSI also "foreground the I", projecting a performance of self into the museum space. At once both personal and collective, these images resurface both on the Chandelier and again in virtual time and space. From its opening, visitors have been encouraged to revisit this image taking, and re-engage with the museum virtually, the photograph acting as the go-between the physical museum and post-visiting experience. The photographs are intended to trigger feelings and emotive memories of the museum visit – but this personal interaction conflicts with an assumption that photographs are simply "carriers" of meaning, that new viewers will inevitably connect to the images once they are uploaded to the Chandelier. A shared sense of understanding is suggested here (the smiling faces, the enjoyed visit) – more in the vein of marketing techniques than a fine art use of photography.

Essentially, why should *we* care about these self-portraits? Who or what is revealed to us? Can any meaning or intention be read in these images, and if so, how are they positioned in relation to the museum? What, in turn, does the museum gain from such imagery? Photographic interactions occur in order to document, archive, experiment, represent, and capture. The portrait claims to effectively respond to such desires, but this promise – to be "revealed and documented" – is based upon a reading that with the photograph, "an indexical image of the 'real' is supposedly presented through the technological means of mechanical reproduction, tempting the viewer to turn to it as a document of truth of what Roland Barthes terms the 'that-has-been' before the lens" (Jones, 2002: 951). The Chandelier images attempt to capture the "real" visitor, to generate an archive of still-faces that collectively stand for an audience, of some kind. Visitors are lured by the curiosity to add to the collective, to generate yet more images; to be submissively compliant with technology that requests their contribution. Or perhaps there is no deeper motivation other than to simply "write with light"; a creative gesture which has no innate meaning or purpose, just the creation of the photograph for its own sake.

Notably, the heritage sequence displayed on the Chandelier reinforces the "male and pale" stereotype which circulates histories of industry and science – promoting those men of eminence from engineering, manufacturing, physical and chemical sciences. No women. No children. No ethnic minorities. A fleeting nod to the everyday is offered in the form of displaying fictional characters from the soap opera Coronation Street. Social histories and social politics are missing from the Chandelier's chronological, fragmented timeline. It attempts to offer a snapshot of Manchester's role as a powerhouse of industry and science, but it lacks initial acknowledgment of the workers' contribution to the realisation of the industrialists' dreams. The photographic screens which sit beside these other references add some much needed "difference" or "ordinariness" alongside those faces of the great and good.

The Chandelier glitters with all its cultural differences. Like a live DNA strand continuously evolving and transforming, the Chandelier offers light and life in the form of the photographic stills. The content is entirely unstable, as each new visitor potentially brings with them a new photographic self-performance, altering the mood and visual aesthetic of the Chandelier. Excitingly, there is no single author of the Chandelier's content; no curator deciding whose image should be displayed (images can only be removed once they have been displayed, even if fleetingly); what will be captured, and where images should appear. These curatorial decisions are wholly in the hands of visitors. Perhaps, then, it is more an experiment in curatorial control than photographic interventions.

I should acknowledge that as a visitor to MOSI and a spectator of the Chandelier, my interpretations are informed by my own visiting motivations and desires; my readings of photography; my understanding of sculpture in a wider context of science and art. Likewise, other visitors will bring their thoughts to the piece. The Chandelier thus encourages contemplation but does not demand definitive interpretation.

The digital interface between the virtual and real museum

The Chandelier is a physical rendering of the social media site ideology, where images are shared with people instantaneously.

The original concept for the Chandelier's virtual twin mimicked social media sites, with images finding a more permanent holding space to be shared with wider audiences, and for visitors to archive their museum experiences visually. However, due to management and technological difficulties – lack of staff to monitor and software problems – the interactive site in the museum and online is no longer active (although a "phantom" of it does still exist via the museum's website link, but visitors can no longer upload their own images – simply view a spiral of old uploaded images). Visitors instead can choose to upload their images instantly to Facebook or to their own Twitter pages, so the photographing experience becomes somewhat isolated from any sense of a "digital museum".

The Chandelier raises the curious question as to why visitors wish to have their images exhibited. The ideal of sharing experiences is a central drive of the Chandelier and yet experiences of the museum are neither captured nor projected. A series of self-portraits – or selfies – is offered, with no accompanying context or description. The images are fairly ambiguous in that viewers are simply left to contemplate the facial expressions of those in the photographs, and from this glean some form of response to the museum. The aim of capturing visitor experiences through this type of interactive photography fails in the sense of continuing a relationship with visitors outside the museum space; the Chandelier offers very little, aside from facial portraits. These images could have been taken in any space, anywhere; there is nothing in the content identifying them as specific to MOSI. If the images themselves are of little interest aesthetically, it is the process of participation (through photography) which is of interest – the selfie phenomenon creeping into other areas of cultural experience which, in turn, transforms how the visitor is perceived by museum staff, other visitors, and wider publics outside the museum.

The digital photographic selfie offers immediacy, improvisation; it is quick and informal, with short exposure times. Digital selfies contribute to an ever increasing archive of amateur photography which overloads all corners of the internet. Critics of such imagery argue it demonstrates ever-increasing cultural narcissism, vanity and self-absorption. Arguments in favour of the selfie argue, firstly, that the creation of self-portraits is nothing new, and this new accessible format emphasises its potential for self-expression and control of self-image, documentation, and playful interactions. In the museum space – one historically defined by strict taxonomical and hierarchical structures – the projected visitor selfie can be deemed anarchic. At MOSI modern technology is used to (literally) raise the image of the visitor to that of eminent scientists and industrialists such as John Dalton, Joseph Whitworth, Henry Moseley, and Nobel Prize winners Andre Geim and Kostya Novoselov. A tenuous connection is made between the historical importance and present significance, held together by technology.

Photography's meaning is created through its interpretation and context of viewing. The visitor's gaze is elicited on entrance to the museum. A forced visual negotiation has to take place. Meaning is only constructed once the image is looked upon; it is not inherent in the image itself. Thus the continued value and interest in the Chandelier is entirely dependent on new visitors and their interactions and participation. Once the visitor has taken his or her image, the participation ceases; the moment of image-making is fleeting. It is the continued interaction with the images post-taking which defines any future meaning or value as a document of the museum visit.

Photography as participation *and* spectatorship

The sculpture is an object of accumulation; an image-capturing machine with which visitors willingly participate to project their own image for others to view. The Chandelier is placed in the museum for visitors' consumption but it is an uncritical use of technology. The Chandelier itself has an overwhelming scale (we walk under it, not up to it); its parts are many and fragmented. Imagery and visual spectacle is fundamental. Its "success" is predicated upon visitors' desire to see their own image projected; the narcissistic seduction of the self-image.

Bishop (2011: 2) comments that in today's culture of "Self-exhibitionism (in Facebook, YouTube or Twitter) [...] we have a 'spectacle without spectators'". The Chandelier is caught between two ideals – that of self-exhibitionism, and also the aim of the museum to create an art piece in which everyone is a producer and participant in a "collective space of shared social engagement" (Bishop, 2011: 2). Through a curatorial co-authoring of imagery, the museum plays host to a new experiment to enable visitors to contribute to and construct experience, not merely absorb it. The Chandelier is participatory in term of content, with visitors responding to a series of instructions and guidance. However, there always lurks the threat of staff intervening to remove unwanted imagery, thus it is not entirely curatorially "free". The Chandelier's emphasis upon process rather than creative outcome leaves it open to selection criteria only known to the monitoring staff.

The Chandelier offers one type of model for visitor photography, however others which are led by both aesthetic and social criteria could be encouraged; where photography is applied critically and used as a tool for prising open the politics and collection histories of MOSI, not offering a mere seal of approval. Seemingly there is no political drive behind this photographic intervention other than an abstract method of "engagement". However, the visual involvement of visitors is significant in the existing political climate in which museums are required to justify any State funding received. MOSI is one of four museums in the Science Museum Group, which rely upon such funding. In 2013 the British government was forced to deny any plans of closures of its Northern museums. The Chandelier at its very basic level is a means by which to demonstrate visitor input and interest (although reflects nothing of impact or experience). The medium of photography (of happy, smiling faces) is a reduced to its simplest use in a system of marketing and fundraising agendas.

Crucially, MOSI is not an art gallery, nor claims to be interrogating the use of artistic practice in the context of science and industry, yet its star piece is a digital artwork that has never been thoroughly evaluated for its contribution or content.

The Chandelier is an attempt to move the experience of visiting from one of singularity to community, a bringing together of disparate group through the lone action of image-making. The Chandelier is a moment of participatory art, but with no lead artist this role is taken by a technological tool to facilitate these interactions. Participants are free to engage with other visitors in the same vicinity, taking photos through the computers. There is no central figure dictating how this three-way relationship should play out – between the visitor and computer, visitor-to-visitor, between resulting images with other visitors. However, this technological intervention seems not to increase interaction between visitors. The photo-taking may well link groups visually, digitally, through the display of their images, but the visitors they undertake their photograph-making in distinctly separate units: groups, individuals, families restrict their discussion and interaction between themselves. Of course this alters radically when large groups take over all the computers, and the photograph taking becomes one of genuine group activity – with individuals running to and fro between different cameras, with shared enjoyment and reflection when the images are projected on the Chandelier. However, the Chandelier fails to encourage spontaneous interaction and conversation between strangers. Technology, then, cannot replace the human mediator who enables photography to become a medium for narrative expression beyond the immediate act of taking and projecting.

Conclusion

As Jones (2002: 953) and many others have commented, the photograph is "an inexorable sign of loss and absence [...] While the taking of the photograph was surely motivated by the desire to retrieve or maintain the past in the present [...] the photograph will always fail at this task". The museum experience is thus lost in the process of image-making; the writing of light captures nothing other than an abstract and ambiguous portrait. Photography is not accountable to time.

However, the Chandelier is, in fact, the ideal analogy for

science: in-flux, ambiguous, fragmented, beautiful, and enticing – all captured through a technology which captivated the Victorians and continues to draw crowds when offering the opportunity to "play with light". Without light (and our own hovering solar Chandelier) our reality would be a thick suffocating blackness devoid of life.

The Chandelier is a creative intervention which requests visitors leave behind a little piece of themselves at MOSI – a little writing of light – which sets the tone for how future visitors will experience themes of science and industry in this space. The humanity of people combines with sophisticated technology to pose the question: where are the human stories of industry and science? The visitor adds their own image to the millions of unknown faces hidden within archives and histories.

The aim of the Chandelier was to generate a series of digital interactions between the museum and its departing visitors, but this initial agenda has been lost to one of photography (the selfie) as spectacle. The presence of photography through this medium – an installed piece of technology – does not facilitate conversations as it wished. However, this does not mean to say that interesting photography is not present in MOSI. Look hard enough and in every corner you will see image-making of a more significant kind, which is not being curated, directed, monitored or censored; image-making which captures *actual* interactions between visitors, each other and the exhibits on display, or with the museum staff. This somewhat raises a wider question as to whether the museum should abandon its selfie project via a static technological tool, and instead encourage a programme of photography truly informed by the visitor's photographic gestures.

REFERENCES

Baudrillard, J. (1999). *La Photographie ou l'Ecriture de la Lumiere: Litteralite de l'Image. L'Echange Impossible* (The Impossible Exchange). Paris: Galilee. (Trans. Debrix, F. *Photography, or the Writing of Light.*)

Bishop, C. Participation and Spectacle: Where Are We Now? Lecture, Creative Time's Living as Form, Cooper Union, New York (May 2011), 1-11. [Republished as Bishop, C. (2012). Participation and spectacle: Where are we now? In Thompson, N.,(ed.). *Living as Form: Socially Engaged Art From 1991-2011*, 34-45].

Daston, L., & Galison, P. (1992). The Image of Objectivity. *Representations. Special Issue: Seeing Science*, 40, 81-128.

Jones, A. (2002). The "Eternal Return": Self-Portrait Photography as a Technology of Embodiment. *Signs: Journal of Women in Culture and Society*, 27 (4), 947-978.

Wilder, K. (2009). *Photography and Science*. London: Reaktion Books Ltd.

CHAPTER SEVENTEEN

FOR THE PEOPLE, BY THE PEOPLE: PHOTOGRAPHY AND PUBLIC MEMORY

Divya Rao Heffley

HOW ARE OFFICIAL histories written, and who gets to write them? What makes some events rise to the top and define a culture for generations to come and others shrink into insignificance? *A People's History of Pittsburgh*, an online, crowd-sourced photography album created by and for the people of Pittsburgh, confronts these questions. This project asks us to consider how the personal histories captured in the photography of visitors and website users can offer more than just a sidebar to official history books and curated museum collections. Conceived by Pittsburgh artists Melissa Catanese and Ed Panar and implemented by the Hillman Photography Initiative at Carnegie Museum of Art, *A People's History of Pittsburgh* (*People's History*) invited the local community to share their most treasured photographs and stories of the city they call home. From 2014 to 2015, *People's History* grew into a digital archive of almost 1,500 images which celebrated everything from a childhood first kiss to a Tarantella-dancing grandmother (Figures 1 and 2). Founded upon multiplicity and personal narrative, *People's History* offers a collaborative and alternative local visual history from the 1890s to the present day.[1]

Background

A People's History of Pittsburgh is one of the projects of the inaugural cycle of the Hillman Photography Initiative at Carnegie Museum of Art (CMOA).[2] The Initiative was developed as a living laboratory for exploring the rapidly changing field of photography and its impact and role in the world. Early in 2013, the museum invited four external experts in photography, or "Agents", to join museum staff for an intensive planning process to identify the most pressing issues in photography and

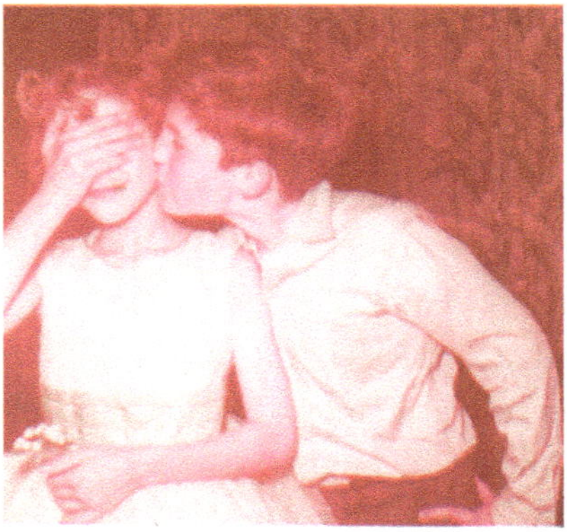

FIG. 1: *My First Birthday Kiss from Bobby Fry, caught on camera and I had a big crush!*
Photograph: Diane Lynn Lampenfield, 20 May, 1956. Digital scan of an original photograph.

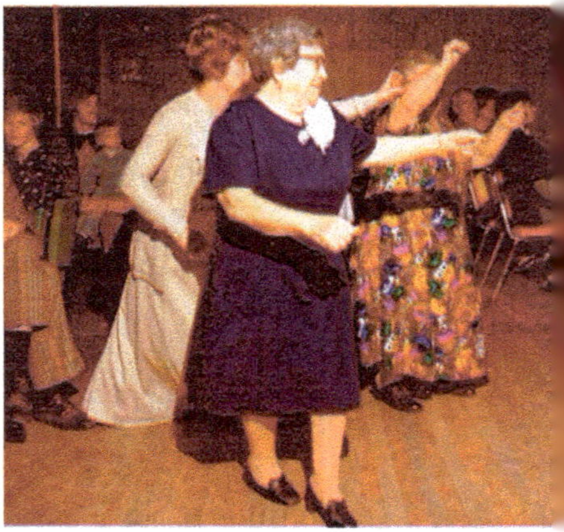

FIG. 2: *My Italian grandmother, Rachel Volomino Barone, dancing the Tarantella at my brother's wedding.*
My brother, Don Suley, was married on December 14, 1974. I remember taking this photo of my dear grandmother. She was in her eighties when this photo was taken. She came to America in 1903 from Southern Italy and was already married at that time. My grandmother had six children and family weddings always included the Tarantella… a rich family tradition. Great memories. A wonderful woman. She is the great-great grandmother of my only granddaughter, Bella Mae Suley. *Bella* means *beautiful* in Italian.
Photograph: Mike Suley 1974. Digital scan of an original photograph.

develop programming to explore those issues.[3] The Agents chose to focus on the unique ways in which photography travels, or follows a lifecycle from creation to transmission, consumption, storage, potential loss, and reemergence. They developed a series of programming concepts which the museum launched as five discrete projects on a custom-built website, www.nowseethis.org, in April 2014. Together, the projects investigated the boundaries and possibilities of photography in a culture of instant image sharing and dissemination.

One of these projects, *The Sandbox: At Play with the Photobook*, invited local artists Melissa Catanese and Ed Panar of Spaces Corners bookshop to curate and staff an onsite installation of photobooks which explored contemporary trends in the medium.[4] The artists proposed *A People's History of Pittsburgh* as a partner project to *The Sandbox*; if the latter explored the printed photograph in book form, the former did so through the personal photographic archive. The title was inspired by Howard Zinn's 1980 book, *A People's History of the United States*, which reconstructs the nation's history through the lives of ordinary people. As such, *People's History* was built to unearth and reconstruct the multiplicity of the city's narratives through the photographs and memories of its residents. Pittsburghers both past and present were invited to contribute their favorite images and stories to a dynamic, ongoing, and publicly accessible digital archive that included family snapshots as well as the occasional tintype or photobooth strip from the local theme park (Figures 3-5). At the end of the project in May 2015, the artists produced a photobook co-published by CMOA featuring submitted photographs and stories, bringing the project back to the medium

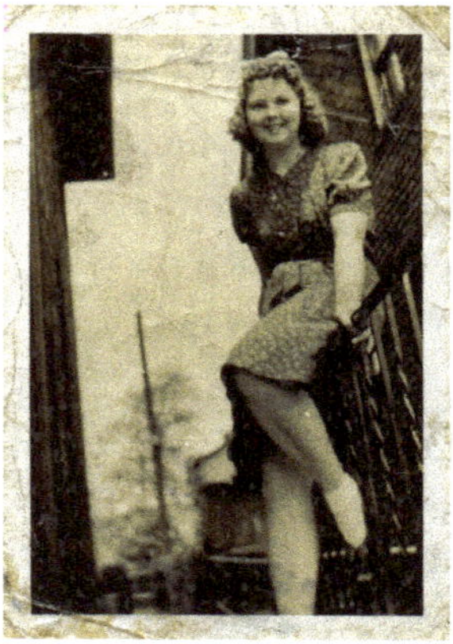

FIG. 3: *My mother, Ellen Kathleen Murray, at home.* She was the youngest daughter of John J. Murray and Mary Elizabeth Ward, who were immigrants from Galway, Ireland. They had 11 children, but only five girls survived. John Murray was a supervisor at Edgar Thompson Mill, although he had only gone to the third grade in Ireland. Ellen joined the Army at the age of 18, upon her high school graduation in 1942. She rose to the rank of Sergeant and served in Europe, based in Paris. Later, at age 27, she married John R. Hynes. Photograph: Patricia Hynes Ronallo, 1940. Digital scan of an original photograph.

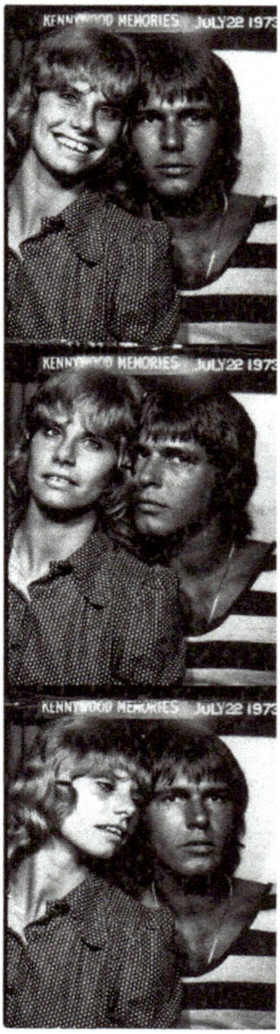

FIG. 4: *My parents, a few months before they got married. I have very few photos of them together.* Photograph: Lisa Toboz, July 22, 1973. Digital scan of a photobooth image strip.

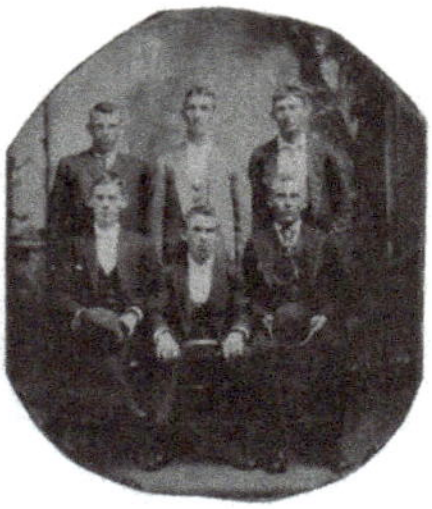

FIG. 5: *These are the six O'Donnell brothers: my great-grandfather James and his brothers.* Clockwise from back left: Richard, Anthony, Thomas, Charles, James, Harry. That is also age order, with Richard born in 1849 and Harry in 1872. Photograph: John W. Russell, 1890. Digital scan of an original tintype.

which inspired *The Sandbox* (Figure 6).

Implementation

When *The Sandbox* opened to the public in May 2014, it functioned as an artist residency. Catanese and Panar were onsite at regularly scheduled times to interact with visitors and discuss photobooks. Eager to forge an onsite connection between *The Sandbox* and the primarily online *People's History*, the museum and artists worked on a graphic strategy which incorporated the two. On the walls of *The Sandbox*, Catanese and Panar projected the most recent contributions to *People's History* in an ongoing loop (Figure 7) and displayed selected submissions on a long credenza at the installation's opening façade (Figure 8).

In addition, the museum hosted regularly scheduled scanning days in *The Sandbox* (Figure 9). On these days, the artists or museum staff were available to assist visitors with scanning photographs and adding stories to the growing online archive. Visitors who contributed to the project onsite received free admission to the museum. By encouraging visitors to incorporate unique photographic content to the growing digital archive, the scanning days strengthened the project's onsite-online connection and reinforced the project's local roots. The stories gleaned in-person from these participants were particularly memorable, like Johno Prascak's tale of purchasing an old trolley from the Port Authority over three decades ago and storing it in his front yard (Figure 10). After *The Sandbox* closed, Catanese and Panar continued to host scanning days at other sites in the city.

People's History was initiated and conceived primarily as a digital repository, with a dedicated page on the Initiative's website.[5] The digital interface was designed for ease of use,

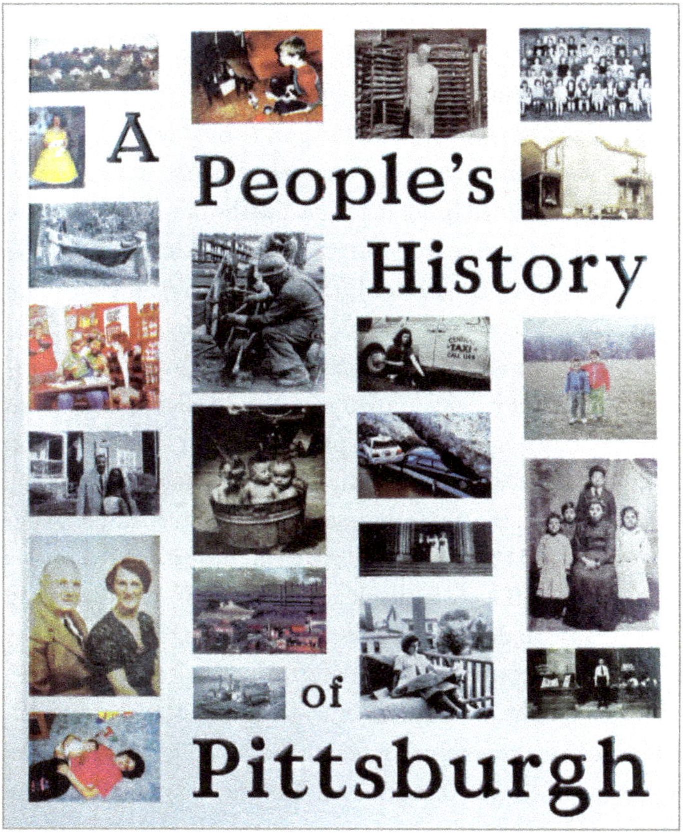

FIG. 6: Cover of *A People's History of Pittsburgh* photobook, edited and designed by Melissa Catanese and Ed Panar, part of the Hillman Photography Initiative at Carnegie Museum of Art. Photograph: Natalia Gomez.

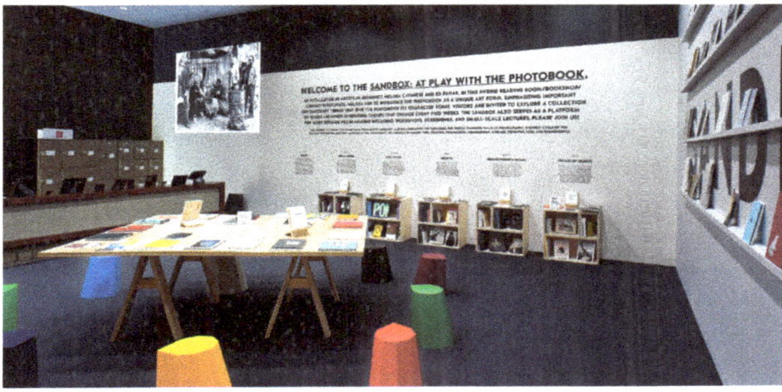

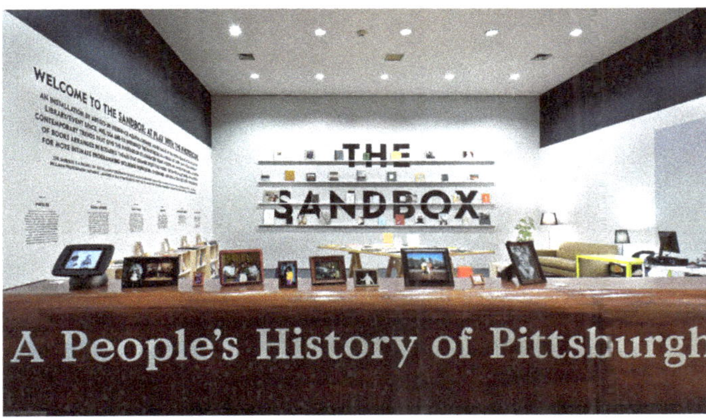

FIG. 7: [ABOVE] The ongoing slideshow of submissions to *A People's History of Pittsburgh* installed inside the *The Sandbox: At Play with the Photobook*, part of the Hillman Photography Initiative at Carnegie Museum of Art, May 3-July 28, 2014.
Image courtesy Carnegie Museum of Art, Pittsburgh. Photograph: Bryan Conley.

FIG. 8: [BELOW] Framed submissions to *A People's History of Pittsburgh* installed inside *The Sandbox: At Play with the Photobook*, part of the Hillman Photography Initiative at Carnegie Museum of Art, May 3-July 28, 2014.
Image courtesy Carnegie Museum of Art, Pittsburgh. Photograph: Bryan Conley.

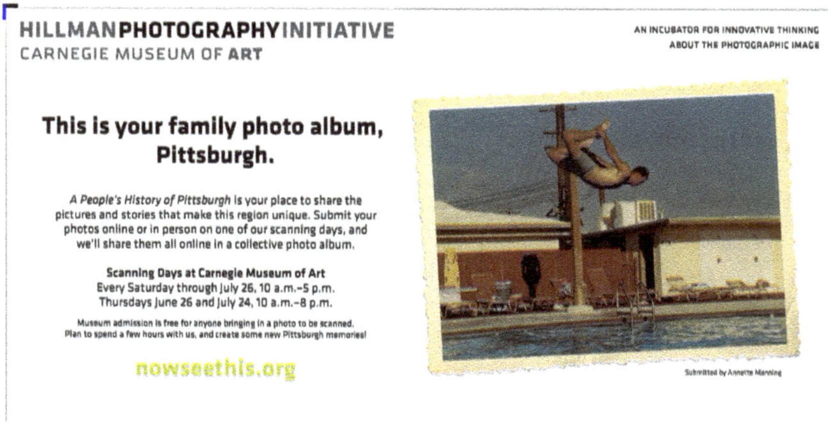

FIG. 9: Advertisement for *A People's History of Pittsburgh* scanning days in local Pittsburgh magazines and newspapers, Summer 2014

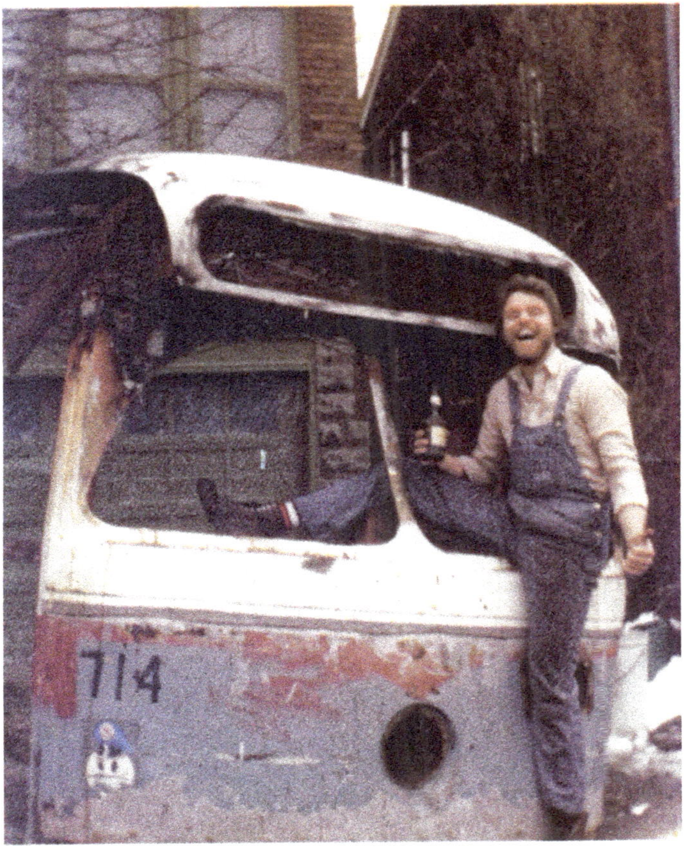

FIG. 10: *I bought this trolley for $10 from Port Authority on March 5, 1982.*
Photograph: Johno Prascak, 1982. Digital scan of an original photograph.

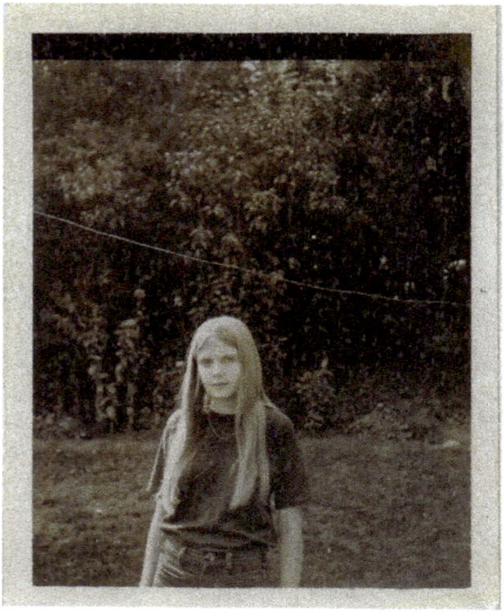

FIG. 11: *My mother as an aloof babe.* I love the smirk and the clothes line cutting across the frame behind her.
Photograph: David Oresick, 1974.
Digital scan of a silver gelatin print.

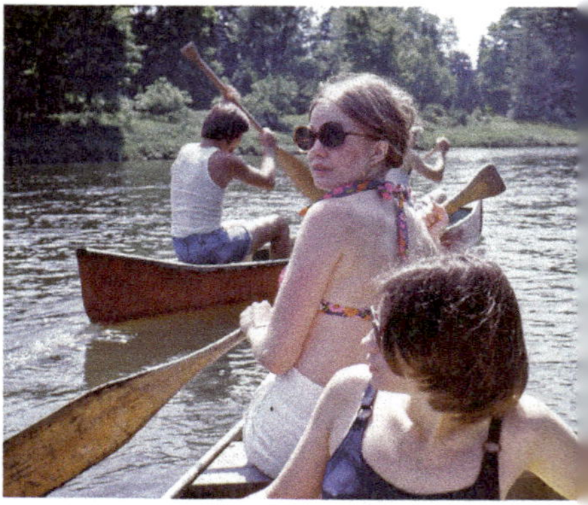

FIG. 12: *My dad took this photo of my mom canoeing on the Clarion River. This was two years before I was born. I can't get over how much my sister looks like my mom did back then.*
Photograph: Justin Visnesky, 1973.
Digital scan of a slide.

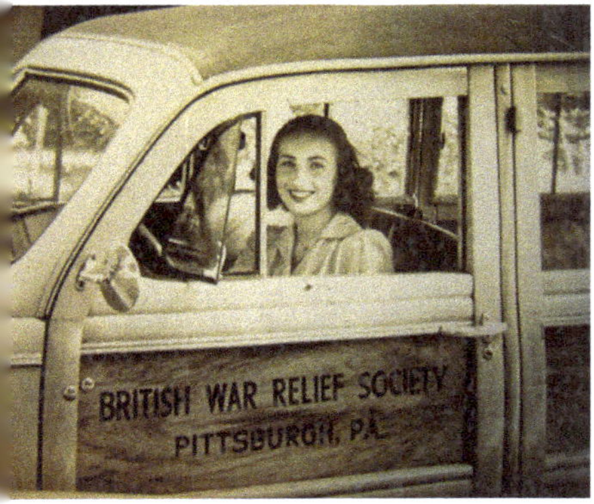

FIG. 13: *My mother, Mary Louise Myers, collecting donations in the woody wagon for the British.*
She collected clothing, medical items, household goods and food to be sent overseas. This was just the beginning of her many years of giving to others, something she instilled in all her children.
Photograph: Don Privett, 1943.
Digital scan of an original photograph.

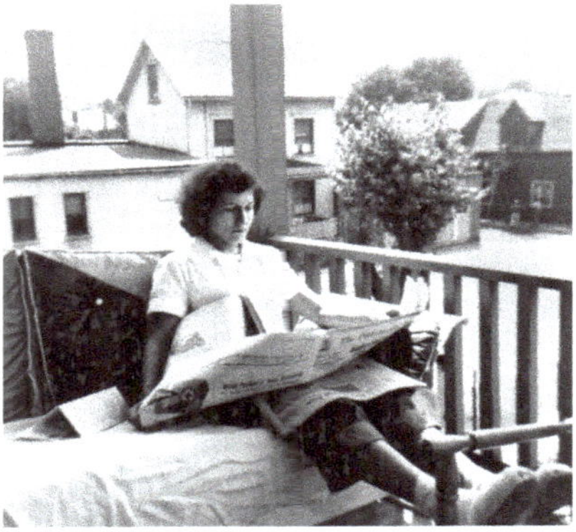

FIG. 14: *My mum on her mum's porch on the second story of the house.*
I love this photo because it tells so much about an ordinary day. In the background you can see the lonely chair on the other porch, the men working on the house and the hillside across the Allegheny. And then there's the fuzzy slippers and rolled up pants and the *Pittsburgh Press*.
Photograph: Toni Ferrante Niner, late 1950s.
Digital scan of an original photograph.

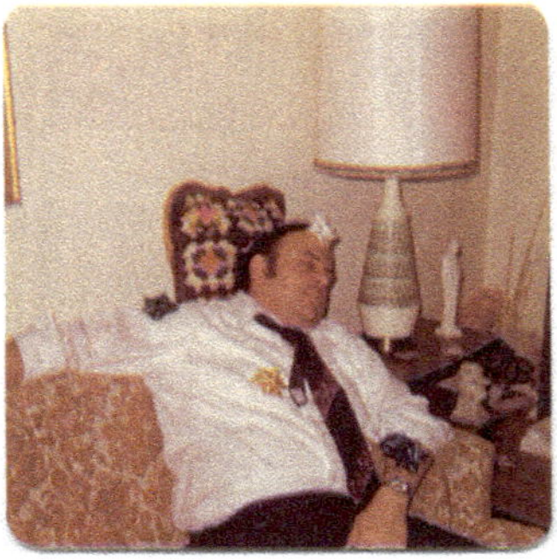

FIG. 15: *My grandfather does this every Christmas. He is still alive.*
Photograph: Dan Wetmore, December 1973. Digital scan of an original photograph.

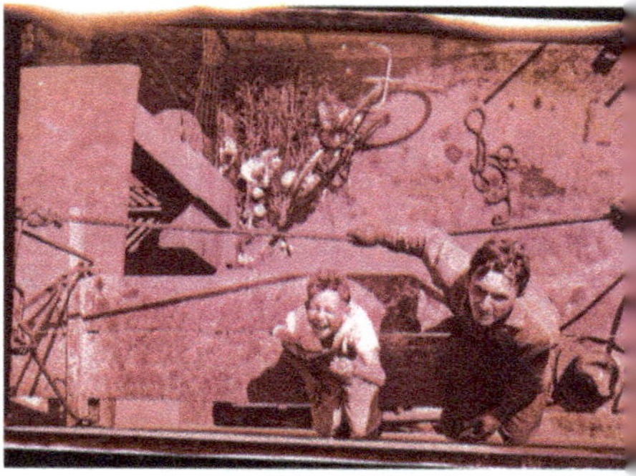

FIG. 16: *My grandfather, Charles L. Miklos, re-pointing his home at 1236 Columbus Ave. Skilio Gillott is the youth...*
Photograph: Frank Miklos, mid-1920s. Digital scan of an original photograph.

with streamlined steps to create online content. To submit a photograph, users were asked to create an account, a one-step process which required either submission of name and email address or authentication through Facebook, Twitter, or Google. Users were also required to accept the website's Terms of Use, which gave the museum permission to publish user content in print and online.

Users could then upload photographs, along with location and date information, and were encouraged to share accompanying personal anecdotes. Dates and locations were reviewed for consistency by project staff, a critical step that made the photographs searchable by decade and neighborhood via the website's timeline feature. As such, users could see their photographs alongside submissions from the same decade, same neighborhood, or both. Particularly striking were connections that surfaced during these searches between users celebrating their mothers. One user nostalgically described his mother as "an aloof babe" (Figure 11) while another was struck by just how much his sister resembled his mother in her youth (Figure 12). One mother was remembered for driving the "Woody wagon" down city streets for the local British War Relief Society (Figure 13) while another was heralded simply for painting a picture of everyday life, from her fuzzy slippers to her rolled up pants (Figure 14).

Engagement strategies

To generate public awareness of the project, the museum's marketing team developed a regional strategy which included paid, earned, and social media. Posters, postcards, and print and digital ads in local news outlets featured scanning days while *The*

Sandbox was open and then switched to generating awareness of the deadline for inclusion in the capstone publication (Figure 9). In December 2014, the museum instituted a paid social media strategy that targeted residents living within 50 miles of Pittsburgh with an interest in photography, which contributed to an exponential increase in both traffic and submissions to the *People's History* page of the website.[6] From the project's inception, it was consistently a top performer on the Initiative's website, with its landing page as the first- or second-most visited of the five on the site. *People's History* had a significantly higher conversion rate than *This Picture*, the only other project which invited user submissions. Most people who visited the *People's History* submission page ultimately uploaded a photograph.[7]

The results of our earned media efforts were evidenced by the number of stories which appeared in local news media outlets, including features on WESA radio's *Essential Pittsburgh*, and in the *Pittsburgh Tribune-Review*, the *Pittsburgh City Paper*, and Pop City. Popular city figures such as Rick Sebak were approached and asked to contribute photographs, which further increased awareness, particularly on social media. Many user submissions were highlighted on CMOA's Facebook page and Twitter stream. Dan Wetmore's photograph of his grandfather allegedly napping while covered in Christmas bows was a December favorite (Figure 15), while a personal favorite shows another grandfather in dizzying perspective, repointing his home in the 1920s (Figure 16).

Evaluation

Every month, museum personnel gathered to evaluate the project's progress and brainstorm opportunities for improvement, leading to several mid-course corrections. Our first two scanning days were poorly attended, garnering no more than three or four participants. When we increased the number and frequency of scanning days and moved them from Thursdays to Saturdays, we doubled participation, hosting eleven participants on our best-attended day. In an attempt to further strengthen the project's onsite presence, we asked the artists if they could provide us with a list of the users whose submissions were featured in *The Sandbox's* ongoing slideshow or printed photographic display. We surmised that a dual solution of emailing those users and offering them free admission to see their content in the museum might generate additional interest and strengthen the project's onsite identity. The artists, as part-time contractors, unfortunately did not have time to gather the names before *The Sandbox* closed. In this case, we had to recalibrate our expectations and accept that the artists were neither equipped with the resources nor required by contract to quickly implement a mid-project adjustment. Although this tactic for boosting onsite attendance was left on the drawing board, it could be successful in future if incorporated into our strategy from the outset.

We also attempted to implement several strategies to further increase online participation. In July 2014, we began publishing a monthly wrap-up blog post, titled *Snapshots*, which highlighted a handful of user photographs and stories and was publicized via an e-newsletter. Visits to the blog increased during this time period, although several other variables make it difficult to determine how much of that increase was due to our online strategies. Ideally, we would have liked to generate a personalized monthly email to registered users which drew

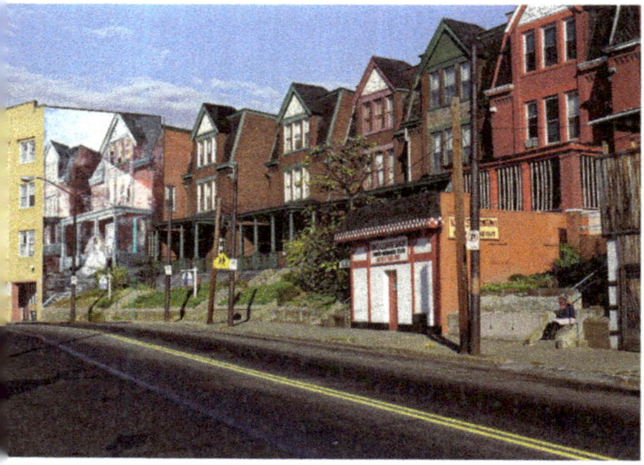

FIG. 17: *Long before the explosion of mural painting in Pittsburgh, there was Judy Penzer's trompe-l'oeil The Bride of Penn Avenue, painted in 1996, in the neighborhood where I have lived for over 15 years.* That summer, Penzer, a noted artist, died tragically with her friend, Jill Watson, when their airplane, TWA Flight 800, bound for Paris, exploded over Long Island Sound. One of the row houses next to the mural was recently gutted by fire. Kim's Coffee Shop and Chinese Restaurant was a beloved local eatery that closed a few years after this photo was taken. Friends of mine cried when they heard the news. Much change has occurred elsewhere along Penn Avenue, but this stretch looks much as it did in 1998. Photograph: William Real, 1998. Digital scan of a 35mm color negative.

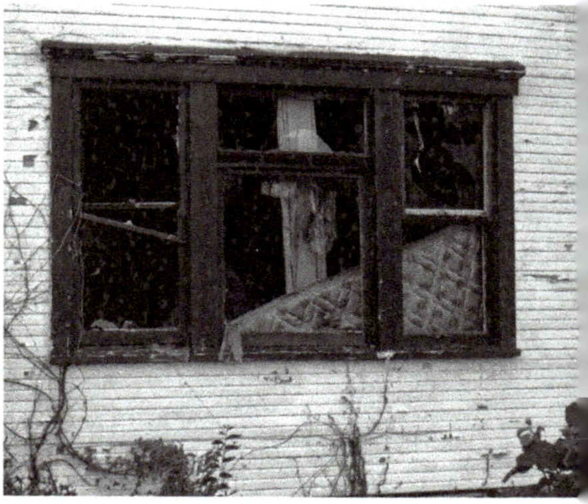

FIG. 18: *One of the sad things in the Pittsburgh region is the deterioration of some neighborhoods. This abandoned house is one of a number of deteriorating properties located in the same area.* The reason I didn't name the exact location is because there are different towns in the Mon Valley that are suffering the same plight. Organizations, city officials and citizens continue to work on the situation. In time, I hope all of the once-thriving steel towns can find solutions and be revitalized. Photograph: Vickie Babyak, June 2011. Digital photograph.

attention to the *Snapshots* post and the submissions it featured, but the complicated logistics of implementing this solution midway made it impossible to realize. Nevertheless, these monthly feature posts allowed us to document the project at regular points along the process and publicly reflect on user submissions on a monthly basis. Another strategy we employed was to more regularly rotate the Featured Selections at the top of the *People's History* landing page. Themes such as Sports, Bridges, and July 4th Celebrations increased the dynamism of the website, but did not generate any additional activity from users and was discontinued after several months.

In order to address the artists' goal of garnering submissions from all demographics and neighborhoods, the marketing department developed an outreach list targeting local councils and newsletters. The project did not generate significant interest as a result of those efforts, which could have contributed to the project's inability to accurately represent the city's diverse populace. Another related challenge was that of the users who occasionally flooded our site with photographs from the same family. In retrospect, restricting the number of photographs an individual user could submit could have guaranteed a more balanced representation among our contributors.

Finally, we ran into some issues with our content management system, a complex and custom-built solution intended to allow us to navigate the Initiative's multiple projects. The complexity made it difficult to organize, sort, and view user submissions for a single project, an issue that we did not foresee during the project's internal web development process.

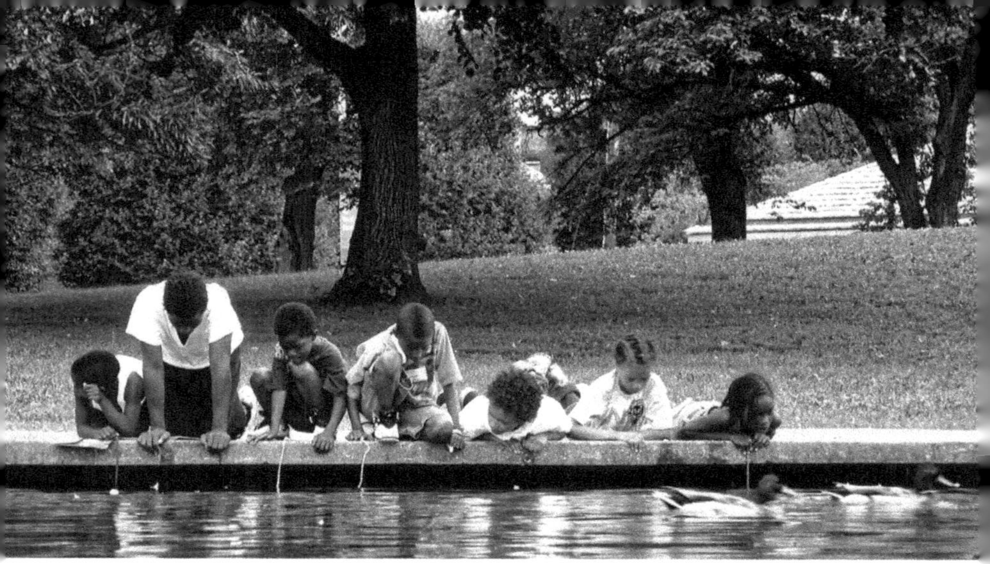

FIG. 19: *Walking through this beautiful park enjoying stunning views of the city skyscrapers reaching above the trees surrounding Lake Elizabeth, I noticed children intently looking into the water to see if any fish were approaching to bite at the lines they had submerged. As if on cue, a pair of mallard ducks paddled past, capturing the attention of one child just as I captured this nostalgic photograph!* Looking at this photograph takes me back to that carefree feeling of childhood where all we needed was a group of friends, our imaginations, and our zeal for exploration to lead us to some of the very best adventures!
Photograph: Linda Willhide, July 2009. Digital photograph.

Conclusions

The challenges we faced over the course of implementation served as opportunities for learning and have shaped our future thinking as a museum. Most importantly, we discovered that asking people to participate in an online project is an enormous challenge, especially when there is no constant, onsite presence for the project and the payoff for participation is not immediately apparent. Even when there are onsite events, such as scanning days, success is largely dependent on consistency and frequency; scanning days became more popular when the frequency increased and the messaging was simpler: *Every Saturday is scanning day!* If we attempt a similar project in the future, the onsite/online connection will be much stronger, specified in advance, and implemented consistently throughout the project. Similarly, the payoff for online participation will be more closely connected to the onsite presence and built into the messaging strategies from the beginning. The cyclical structure of the Initiative allows these lessons to be incorporated into our future programming. Every two years, a new group of Agents is invited to join the museum in planning the next round of programming for the Initiative. This iterative structure ensures a regular influx of new perspectives and allows us to address the most pressing issues in the field of photography. It also enables our learning from the first cycle of planning and programming (2013-2015) to be directly applied to the implementation of the second (2015-2017).

Despite the challenges we faced, *A People's History of Pittsburgh* exceeded the museum's expectations in terms of public participation and professional attention. The project has contributed to larger conversations about history and memory in a city with a rich and storied past, and has expanded the museum's engagement with the local community through the shared and increasingly universal language of photography (Figures 17-19). As an online, crowdsourced project, *People's History* occupies a digital public space that can be experienced and accessed from anywhere. Like the best of public art, it is simultaneously rooted in local context and global in reach and impact. *A People's History of Pittsburgh* builds a collective photographic story in a digital public space which invites and depends upon the contributions of this city's residents, whose prose and pictures are as beautiful, gritty, and nostalgic as the city they call home.

NOTES

1. Although the project asked users to submit photographs that were at least a year old, none of the submissions was disqualified based on date.
2. Support for the Hillman Photography Initiative is provided by the William T. Hillman Foundation and the Henry L. Hillman Foundation.
3. The first group of Agents consisted of Tina Kukielski, CMOA curator; Marvin Heiferman, independent curator and writer; Alex Klein, the Dorothy and Stephen R. Weber Program Curator at the Institute of Contemporary Art, Philadelphia; Illah Nourbakhsh, professor of robotics and director of the CREATE Lab, Carnegie Mellon University; and Arthur Ou, assistant professor of photography at Parsons The New School for Design.
4. The other projects are *The Invisible Photograph*, a five-part documentary series which investigates the expansive realm of photographic production, distribution, and consumption by way of the hidden side of photography; *This Picture*, which explores the meanings a single photograph can hold by inviting the public to

respond to a carefully-chosen photograph each month; and *Orphaned Images*, which consists of work commissioned by artists Antoine Catala and Shannon Ebner addressing questions raised within art practice by the increasingly widespread digital dissemination of photographs. These projects are archived and available for continued exploration on the Initiative's website at http://www.nowseethis.org.

5. The website was custom-built by Bearded, a Pittsburgh-based web design and development agency.
6. In December, 444 photographs were uploaded to *People's History*, more than any other month in 2014 and reflecting a 263% increase from November. This spike in participation likely reflects not only the changes in the marketing plan, but also the approach of the "due date" to be eligible for consideration in the artists' book.
7. A conversion rate on a webpage is the percentage of visitors to the page who take a desired action, in this case uploading a photograph. In 2014, there were 25,918 unique visits to the *People's History* landing page. During this same time, 1,304 unique posts were uploaded to the project, from a total 1,709 visits to the submission page. The average conversion rate was 76.3%.

CHAPTER EIGHTEEN

SCHOOL PHOTOGRAPHS: SUGGESTIONS FOR A PARTICIPATORY MUSEOLOGY

Marta Brunelli

THIS CHAPTER AIMS to introduce a different perspective on the possible social uses of photographs in museums, with a special focus on school museums and the photographic collections that these institutions often preserve. The objective is to examine how this material can be used to implement programmes of a social and participatory nature aimed at enriching the visitor experience in school museums – museums which preserve and present the history of an individual school (Meda, 2010, 2013).[1]

These museums have grown in number over the last three decades to the extent that Carreño (2008) talks in terms of an International Movement which – led by the Northern and Central-European countries, and inspired by new museology – expanded, first in Spain and then in Italy, in the late 20th and early 21st centuries (Meda, 2014). Alongside this drive for the preservation of educational heritage, international research has taken an ever-growing interest in the material culture of schools (Escolano, 2007) and in the "materialities" of schooling (Lawn & Grosvenor, 2005) examining, for example: school architecture (Burke, 2005; Burke, Howard, & Cunningham, 2013; Escolano, 2003; Kozlovsky, 2010;); the classroom (Braster, 2011; Grosvenor, Lawn & Rousmaniere, 1999; O'Donoghue 2010); school-desks (Herman, et al., 2011; Hnlica, 2010; Moreno, 2005; Müller & Schneider, 1998) and, finally, school photographs as demonstrated by the numerous publications and projects dedicated to this topic in the last fifteen years.[2] Thanks to this burgeoning of interest, school photographs now demonstrate their potential as complex but versatile sources through which we can explore as yet unknown aspects of school culture and open what historians have described as "the black box of schooling".

School photos can also be valuable means of communication and education in the museum environment. They can convey highly complex messages not only to historians of education but to any individual regardless of age, education, or origin. This is due to the immediacy and universality of their iconic language, whose communicative power goes beyond the objective data immediately recognizable in a photographic image. Photographs are no longer considered mere mechanical recordings of an objective reality, but rather a representation of it based on specific codes, and the result of multiple interpretive acts: the interpretation of the photographer, and the interpretation of the viewers who receive and contemplate the images (Dubois, 1983). School photographs are also a powerful visual synthesis of one of the first experiences of socialization and enculturation that anyone living in a society with widespread schooling has: the school experience (Escolano, 2002, 2011; Viñao Frago, 2010, 2012).

For these reasons, school photographs lend themselves to interpretation and narration. From photographs different situations, emotions and stories can be deciphered through, for example: the posture and discipline of bodies restrained by school-desks, standardized in school uniforms, regimented in lines or in fitness activities, or seemingly free in moments of recreation; the facial expressions of teachers, students and others; the proxemics emerging from images of classrooms, areas for recreation, sports and extra-curricular activities, and so on (Braster, 2011; Burke, 2005; Burke & Ribeiro de Castro, 2007; Comas Rubí, Motilla Salas & Sureda Garcia, 2012; Grosvenor, Lawn & Rousmaniere, 1999; Margolis & Fram, 2007; Moreno Gómez, 2013; Thyssen, 2007). Equally important is the contribution which individuals can provide by reconstructing narratives drawing on their own school memories and their "cultural arsenal" of ideas, practices and representations of education assimilated during the school experience. To explore how this communicative, evocative and narrative potential can be exploited, I will examine photographs as "social objects".

School photographs: social objects in school museums

The concept of social objects in the museum context appeared in Nina Simon's *The Participatory Museum* (2010). The concept is based on Engeström (2005), according to whom the most popular networks are not those offering users a generic or nebulous opportunity to meet other people, but rather those which provide opportunities to share specific interests focusing on specific objects (videos on YouTube, or photographs on Flickr). Social objects are those that facilitate connections between people, and are intended as a fulcrum of practices which people love to share, such as hobbies and common interests, but also memories of events or traditions in the family or community.

With the aim of transforming the museum from a static content authority into a platform provider where visitors can participate, create and/or share contents, Simon applied this approach to the design of museum environments where objects become social. To do this we need to look at objects not primarily in terms of their historic or artistic value, but rather for their social potential, their ability to attract people's attention and stimulate conversations. To be social, objects must possess four qualities. They must:

- be *personal*, i.e. able to arouse in visitors a personal memory, a shared history that becomes a potential topic of conversation (like a toy: the rocking horse for the older generations, or Lego toys for those born after the sixties);

- be *active*, i.e. capture the attention of visitors (by moving, lighting up, or imposing themselves in the physical space);
- be *provocative*, such as objects which visitors do not expect to find in the museum;
- be *relational*, i.e. be specially prepared for use by most people, like board games or interactive exhibits (Simon, 2010: 130-132).

It has been pointed out that "not all objects are naturally social" (Simon, 2010: 129). But what we see every day in a school museum is that objects such as school-benches, notebooks and nibs, vintage textbooks, punishment instruments and school photographs spontaneously elicit self-identification and the recollection of school memories.[3] As a consequence visitors themselves, when encouraged to freely act and (inter)act, equally spontaneously begin to tell stories, share memories, or make assumptions about the function of this or that lesser known object. The objects displayed in school museums do possess a strongly intrinsic social nature which we can usefully exploit, as educators and as mediators. One example of this kind of social exhibit can be seen in the museum at Macerata: The Dunce's Bench. The figure of the "rascal" is vividly evoked by an original untidy and scrawled-upon desk, two old notebooks full of errors, an arsenal of catapults and peashooters, and punishment tools such as a cane, chickpeas on which to kneel, and dunce's cap (a replica which can be freely handled). This evocative display has proved to be a social space in which all visitors – adults and children alike – gather to talk, to tell anecdotes and share memories of their own mischievous tricks in school and the punishments they received.

Online social practice mediated by school photos

The intrinsic social potential of school objects is clearly seen on the internet, where school photographs give rise to a wide variety of social practices: observations shared between users (with questions, hypotheses and comments on the objects and situations represented), the recollection of memories related to common experiences, and "appeals" to visitors and/or old classmates.

Photographs of school objects and situations, digitized and published online, become the social objects of Facebook communities such as *We who grew up in the 50s and 60s*,[4] or *Those of the film 'The Party'*, inspired by the 1980 French film *La Boum*.[5] Photos of old school-desks with an ink pot hole appear in albums of school memories or in dedicated posts (*Do you remember the bench with the 'hole'?*), and recall the first attempts at writing with nibs. These memories are vivid in the minds of older users:

> What chaos when writing with nib and ink, with the legendary blotter always among the notebooks.

> [T]he day the school caretaker filled the ink pots you dirtied your fingers, because the pot was deeper than the nib and if you didn't notice that it was full, you sank the pen to the bottom!

But also in the minds of younger users too, who recount the many "creative" uses that, more recently, have been made of this anachronistic desk, still in use in Italian schools:

> But what was the hole for? I never understood.
>
> ...due to lack of funds, our children still use them.
>
> We still have them in our classrooms... we opted to put a paper cup in the hole, and use it for pencil-sharpener scraps.[6]

The social use of school photographs is not limited to social networks, but is increasingly widespread on websites and blogs. The following important examples illustrate the social use and sharing of images and data about memories of a single institution, a local area or a specific community.

A combination of blog and forum, *Banchidiscuola*[7] aims to gather photographs and memories about schools in the city of Oristano, on the island of Sardinia. Visitors are encouraged to submit photos as well as comments, and to interact with other users by communicating asynchronously. The social object – mediated by photographs – is the school memory of the Oristano community, around which micro-communities of single schools, school years and even single class-groups are built. Informed by the same participatory logic – although based on Web 1.0 architecture – is the website which Paolo Cason has created to collect the memories of all those Italians who "like me, have left in Libya their past, their loved ones and their friends".[8] Though not specifically focused on schools, the website contains a School Memories section where one can find photos and information provided by Cason and by visitors. The last example, which confirms the importance of school memories as the foundation of community identity, is the website of Gianni Desti Baratta,[9] who has digitized old photos of Cerano San Marco (in the Veneto Region). Photos are categorized by topics and by significant community events, and once again school images emerge as an important theme (including Children, kindergarten and youth; Class groups; School photos). Carefully organized by theme and year, the photos recompose the puzzle of the visual memory of the community – for which Baratta asks the residents themselves to fill in the gaps, as in a virtual and digital family album that needs to be completed with the photos of the missing members.

As shown in these examples, school photographs are able to catalyse the interest of both individuals and communities. In these virtual collective photographic exhibitions, it is not difficult to trace the first seeds of real participative curation, the potential of which is still to be fully explored.

Photographs as the fulcrum of social practice in museums

Photographs can easily act as active mediators of social practices and interaction. In museums, however, the role of photography is normally limited to that of a passive iconographic aspect of exhibition design. To demonstrate the gap between these two different approaches, Simon (2010) has compared the "permitted" behaviour of visitors to a museum-based photographic exhibition, with the "expected" behaviour of users of a photograph-based social network such as Flickr. In the museum visitors are allowed only to observe photos, to read information about them and their authors, to leave a comment in the guestbook (if any), to buy reproductions in the bookshop (if available), or to take photographs (but only if permitted). On the contrary, Flickr users are expected to implement behaviour of an active and social nature: to add tags and communicate their comments to the authors; to ask authors to share their photos with other groups; to add photos to their favourite galleries; to contact other users; to create, participate in, or invite others, in discussion groups; and, last but not least, to add and share their own photos.

This telling comparison lets us imagine the communication and educational potential of museum objects if only institutions would embrace a social approach. From this viewpoint, school photographs have a double advantage: first, they are social since they refer to the social object *par excellence* as represented by the school experience; second, photographs are social by virtue of their very nature since – as highlighted by Edwards (2009, 2010) – they have been commissioned, created, forgotten in the darkness of a drawer, carefully preserved in a family album, annotated with signatures or dedications, owned or donated or passed down from people to other people, and ultimately been given to us. As tangible objects which are also reproducible, shareable and manipulable, photographs are particularly suitable for use in interactive exhibitions, educational programmes, intercultural workshops and in projects of collaborative curating.

Photograph-based activities in museums

In school museums, one of the most common activities within primary schools is the visit supported by a grandparent-witness. The witness recounts her school memories and accompanies the children through the discovery of the objects on display. The opportunity to interview the witness, makes it possible for children to have a learning experience facilitated by experiential and enquiry-based strategies. While not specifically centred on photographs, this programme has certainly revealed the social potential of photographic material, especially during post-visit work when students have collected the school memories of their relatives. As we have observed in the schoolwork produced,[10] invariably oral testimonies are accompanied by old school photos, which are not only important memory prompts for the adults, but also reveal their transactional power when they become the object of discussion in the class-group and, above all, the object of conversation within the family. Touched, photocopied, cut and drawn, photos not only translate a memory – unreal and faded by time – into tangible evidence but, at the same time, become a cognitive support with which to anchor the data and facts learned in the museum, as well as the emotional experience lived in the family.

In the museum of Macerata we have also implemented a hands-on laboratory of visual literacy for secondary schools. Specifically focused on school photographs, this activity aims to develop students' skills of observation, verbal description, historical contextualization and finally to aid the cataloguing of images (Brunelli & Meda, 2014). The laboratory relies on the research-based assumption that, despite the apparent conventionality of the scenes portrayed, school photographs actually reveal a complexity of structures, messages and functions (institutional-celebratory, propagandistic, educational

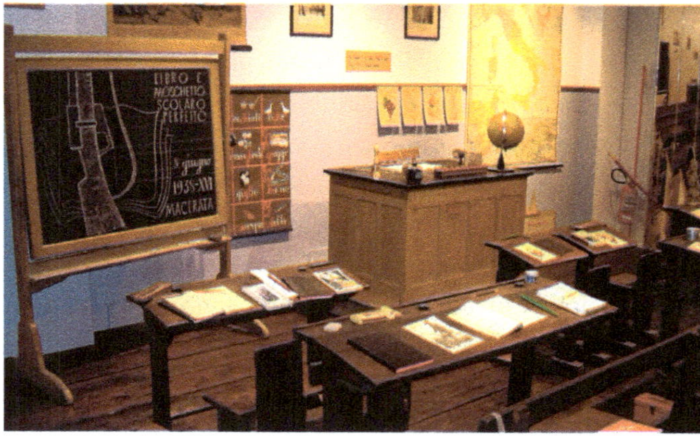

FIG. 1: The 1930s original multi-class environment recreated in the School Museum of Macerata. Macerata, January 10, 2015. Photograph: Marta Brunelli.

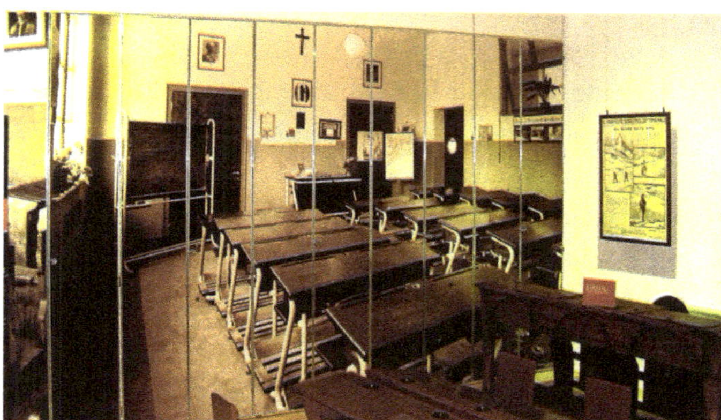

FIG. 2: Enlargement of a photo representing an Italian classroom of the fascist period, reproduced on the wall-shelving in the School Museum in Macerata. Macerata, January 10, 2015. Photograph: INDIRE Archive, Florence.

or documentary, or even personal and recreational) which can be identified only through a careful analysis, supported by a deep knowledge of the representational codes typical of this material (Comas Rubí, Motilla Salas & Sureda Garcia, 2012). After acquiring these interpretive tools, in the post-visit phase (i.e. back in the classroom) students continue their work on school photos from their families, in which they will be able to interpret the contents, collect contextual information from other sources (including oral and documentary sources) and deepen the analysis begun in the museum.

Careful observation of visitors' behaviour provoked by school objects and photographs has convinced us that in school museums enriched meaning-making processes can be developed through interaction not only between generations but also between different cultures (Brunelli, 2014). We have observed that school memories narrated by Italian grandparents stimulate in foreign pupils the recollection of educational practices heard from their parents, such as the use of corporal punishment at school (which frequently recurs in the memories of diverse Italian generations).[11]

Migrant children often find similarities between the material objects and practices of the Italian schools of the past, and the schools of their country of origin. During demonstrations of writing with pens and ink pots, some children have shown their ability in handling these tools (because "we too have ink pots and pens"). One young boy said his classroom was identical to the mixed-age class reconstructed in the museum (Figure 1), with the only exception being that school desks that were metallic "like in the photo" – indicating the photographic enlargement of an Italian 1930s classroom (Figure 2). Suddenly we realized that, not only the grandparents but also these children were able to teach their classmates something new, strange and magical like writing with pen and ink.[12] Such experiences confirm that school objects and photographs can prime a dialogue not only between the schoolchildren of yesterday and those of today, but also between children from different countries, who can recognize differences and similarities in a shared "grammar of schooling".

Collaborative curating: mashups of school photographs

An interesting prospect for enhancing the social use of historical school photographs is offered by the practice of the photo-mashup. Technically, the mashup is a website, or an application, which blends together contents from multiple sources on the web (such as data, photographs, maps, video and other multimedia objects) to give rise to new content. Here, we shall explore photo-mashups resulting from the alignment or overlay of historic photographs with a modern images taken in the same place, in the present time. An example of the appeal and of the great emotional impact of historical mashups is offered by Then and Now galleries – of which a spectacular example is the project Fade to 1906 by the photographer Shawn Clover who, in 2010, decided to overlay photos of the San Francisco earthquake with his photos of the modern city.[13]

Today one can find numerous websites such as Dearphotograph,[14] thematic projects like Ghosts of History (based on photographs of the Second World War),[15] or online communities such as the Flickr group Looking into the Past[16] based on such photo-montages and among them there are many based on school photographs.

Particular mention should be made of the photo-mashups on Detroiturbex,[17] a project of "urban exploration" of Detroit which shows the progressive transformation of the industrial metropolis severely hit by the economic crisis. Especially touching are the Then and Now galleries of old school buildings, including the former Cass Technical High School (abandoned in favour of a new venue, and then demolished in 2011). Created with found photos, the mashups show diaphanous figures of students – in the hallways, in the library, during sports activities or in school plays – which emerge from the recent past as ghosts to populate spaces now abandoned or demolished.

Whether the result of sophisticated digital photo editing, or of hand-made superimposition (as in Figure 3), a school-photo mashup can communicate a heart-breaking sense of loss which contrasts with the reassuring banality of the everyday school routine. This dissonance strikes all of us with a powerful message, at times moving and at times painful, but always forces us to "look with new eyes" at the places of our identity and to reflect on the meaning which buildings, spaces and landscape have for us, as individuals and as a community. In this regard, significant is the comment posted by a photographer about the school mashup (Figure 4) which he uploaded to Flickr: "I'm glad the images strike a chord. It's certainly caused me to look at the familiar streets of my town in a new light".[18]

These experiences tell us that the historic photographic heritage existing – and often "sleeping" – in our archives, libraries and museums, can come back to life thanks to creative and participatory practices. Citizens, in fact, can be involved

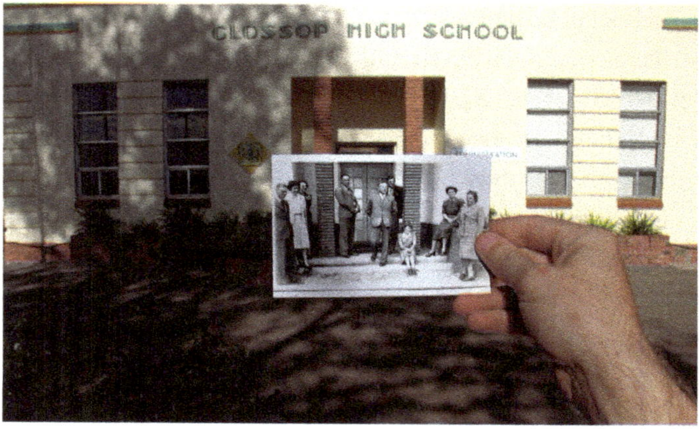

FIG. 3: Glossop High School, Now and Then, January 18, 2011.
Photograph: Ella Winnall. Retrieved January 15, 2015 from_ https://www.flickr.com/photos/58878745@N04/5397028598/. Creative Commons License.

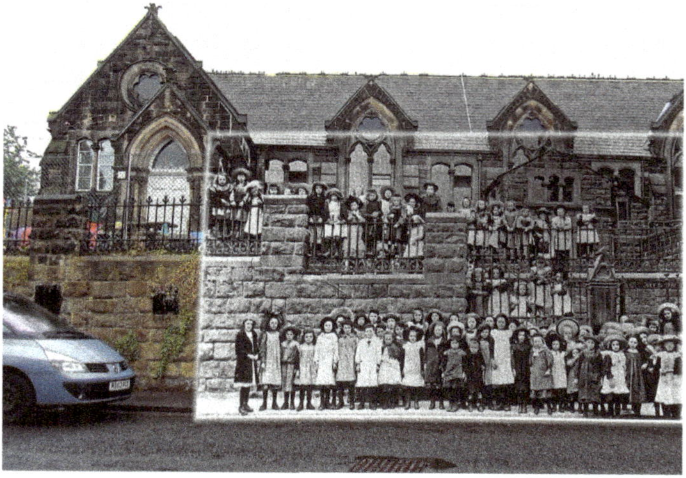

FIG. 4: Westgate School, Then and Now, August 6, 2008.
Photograph: Tom Blackwell. Retrieved January 15, 2015 from https://www.flickr.com/photos/tjblackwell/2738748279. Creative Commons License.

in photo-contests as in the case of the Then and Now Digital Photo Contest launched by the North Vancouver Museum & Archives in 2010;[19] or the project Libraryhack started in 2011 by the Australian and New Zealand libraries, which made their photographic collections available and encouraged people to use them in an innovative and creative way.[20] People were able to discover the history of their streets, neighbourhoods and buildings – including schools – and to connect the threads of their own memories with places of collective memory: "My old school! Awesome!"; "I see my uncle... top left."[21] At the same time, the photographic heritage preserved in the community archives has been rediscovered as a valuable resource accessible to everyone: "How can I access the photo archives remotely? Looking for 1953 to 1959...?"[22]

Similar initiatives can be realised based on the school photographs preserved by school museums, by school archives and finally by the students' families, teachers, or alumni. Mashups may be focused on images of school groups with the aim of retracing the history of people who have spent a significant part of their life in that school; but mashups can also relate to the school buildings themselves, documenting their survival, transformation, or disappearance,[23] and analysing how this affected the perception of these places as reference points for collective memories and community identities.

With this aim, digital photography workshops could be implemented in schools – in collaboration with museums – to engage students in the creation of their own mashups. And once realized, these could give rise to historical exhibitions curated by the students themselves, and mounted in the school, the museum and community spaces. In this way, the photographic act itself effectively becomes a cognitive and meta-cognitive process. Through its different phases – the gathering of visual sources, the recognition of places, the (re)construction of the modern photograph, and finally the montage of a "new" photo – the photo-mashup offers students a unique opportunity to identify themselves with the photographer of the past, to understand the choices she made and the visual conventions she adopted, and to learn and practice the art of seeing in a more reflexive and conscious way.

Conclusions

The visual turn also in the history of education has led to a shift of focus towards visual sources and the photographic in particular, offering historians of education new opportunities, but also new challenges (Dussel, 2013). Historians themselves, on the other hand, do not escape the evocative power of school photos, which never fails to arouse spontaneous processes of recollection and, in doing so, to raise questions which – going beyond the alleged factual objectivity represented – mobilize emotions and political responses, and open "a connection between the 'real past' of the photograph and the present of the viewer" (Rousmaniere, 2001: 111). The practice of mashups, in particular, appears to be a productive realization of the photographic montage and a powerful interpretive tool: through the decontextualization and the juxtaposition of different images (in our case: different photos of the same location in different epochs), the viewer is surprised and stimulated to make associations and create new narratives and meanings (Grosvenor, Lawn & Rousmaniere, 2000; Rousmaniere, 2001).

In this emphasis on the process not only of the production,

but also of the reception of photography, historiographic reflection meets the constructivist, critical-pedagogical and participatory approach reflected in contemporary trends in museology – indicated, among others, by Falk and Dierking (1992, 2012), Hein (1995, 1998), Hooper-Greenhill (1999a, 1999b), and Roberts (1997). In particular, the participatory approach proposed by Simon (2010) proves to be productive if applied to school museums, where the intrinsically social nature of school objects can easily provoke a variety of visitor behaviours and responses of social, conversational and collaborative character.

Like school objects, school photographs demonstrate an analogous social value, which is currently manifested through the social practices (encounters, conversations, sharing of memories and comments, or cooperative projects) which these photos are able to catalyse on the web. But photographs still have to fulfil their role as transformative agents. They have to be able to impact educational museum practices and improve the quality of the visitor experience. Within school museums, curators and educators can fruitfully exploit school photographs in order to implement innovative programmes and projects aimed at linking the museum with schools and with memories of people and places; so transforming the visitor experience into an uninterrupted dialogue with, and between, people across time, generations and cultures.

NOTES

1. Into this typology falls the Paolo & Ornella Ricca School Museum at the University of Macerata, established in 2009 within the Centre for Research and Documentation on History of Textbooks and Children's Literature, and officially opened in 2012. For the history of the Centre and the collections of the future museum see Brunelli (2009); for an overview of the first two years of museum activities see Ascenzi and Patrizi (2014). it is to this museum that we refer for the experience and the research presented here.
2. For some reviews of the vast historiographical literature produced on school photographs see: Braster, 2011; Comas Rubi, 2010; Pozo Andrés, 2006; Pozo Andrés & Rabazas Romero, 2012.
3. This is borne out by our experience in the Paolo & Ornella Ricca School Museum at the University of Macerata.
4. https://it-it.facebook.com/NoiCresciutiAnni50e60/posts/250779618293970.
5. https://www.facebook.com/pages/Quelli-de-Il-Tempo-delle-Mele/139482732755994.
6. Comments from the above websites were all retrieved on January 15, 2014.
7. Available at http://www.banchidiscuola.it/blog. The blog is managed by Roberto Pilia Nieddu and other collaborators.
8. http://www.paolocason.it.
9. http://www.destigianni.com/.
10. The schoolwork produced by class-groups is housed in the Educational Section of the museum in Macerata.
11. Testimonies are recounted in compositions such as *School in Egypt* or, in particular, *My Parents at School in Macedonia,* where you can read: "If [pupils] did not do home-work, or misbehaved, teachers beat them with a dried stick and made them leave the classroom." (Schoolwork. School year 2013-2014, Educational Section, Museum of Macerata).
12. The author of these lines collected these testimonies from Pakistani children

during a visit on November 27, 2014

13. http://shawnclover.com/projects/fadeto1906/.
14. http://dearphotograph.com/.
15. https://www.facebook.com/thenandnowghostsofhistory.
16. https://www.flickr.com/groups/lookingintothepast/. The group is created and managed by Jason Powell.
17. http://detroiturbex.com.
18. Comment by Tom Blackwell, retrieved January 15, 2015 from https://www.flickr.com/photos/tjblackwell/2738748279.
19. https://www.flickr.com/groups/northvancouverthenandnow/.
20. http://libraryhack.org/.
21. See the visitors' comments to the photograph Lynn Valley Elementary School THEN & NOW (1946 and 2010), submitted for the North Vancouver THEN AND NOW Digital Photo-Contest. Retrieved January 15, 2015 from https://www.flickr.com/photos/northvanmuseum/5015566353/.
22. Ibid.
23. See the evocative small series of mashups of nineteenth-century Australian rural schools, now disappeared, such as the Jallakin School (https://www.flickr.com/photos/25245971@N08/12582495265/), the Tooan School (https://www.flickr.com/photos/25245971@N08/12582955474) or the Boyeo School (https://www.flickr.com/photos/25245971@N08/12582496035). Retrieved January 15, 2015.

REFERENCES

Ascenzi, A., & Patrizi, E. (2014). A través del patrimonio cultural de la escuela: análisis y perspectivas de las experiencias didácticas realizadas en el Museo de la Escuela Paolo e Ornella Ricca de la Universidad de Macerata. In A. M. Badanelli Rubio, M. Poveda Sanz & C. Rodríguez Guerrero (eds.), *Pedagogía museística: prácticas, usos didácticos e investigación del patrimonio educativo. Actas de las VI Jornadas Científicas de la SEPHE* (pp. 179-193). Madrid: Universidad Complutense de Madrid-Facultad de educación.

Braster, S. (2011). Educational Change and Dutch Classroom Photographs. A Qualitative and Quantitative Analysis. In S. Braster, I. Grosvenor & M. M. Pozo Andrés (eds.), *The Black Box of Schooling. A Cultural History of the Classroom* (pp. 21-37). Brussels: P.I.E.-Peter Lang.

Brunelli, M. (2009). The Centre for the documentation and research on the history of textbooks and children's literature in University of Macerata (Italy). *History of Education & Children's Literature*, 4(2), 441-452.

Brunelli, M. (2014). Las fotografías escolares como objetos sociales. Primeras reflexiones sobre el uso educativo y social del patrimonio en el museo de la escuela. In A. M. Badanelli Rubio, M. Poveda Sanz & C. Rodríguez Guerrero (Eds.), *Pedagogía museística: prácticas, usos didácticos e investigación del patrimonio educativo. Actas de las VI Jornadas Científicas de la SEPHE* (pp. 203-217). Madrid: Universidad Complutense de Madrid-Facultad de Educación.

Brunelli, M., & Meda, J. (2014). *Dentro l'Aula "oscura". Laboratorio sulle fonti fotografiche per la scuola secondaria di I grado.*

[Teaching materials]. [Macerata: Museo della Scuola Paolo & Ornella Ricca].
Burke, C. (2005). Introduction In C. Burke (ed.), Containing the School Child: Architectures and Pedagogies (pp. 489-494). Special Issue of *Paedagogica historica, 41*(4-5).
Burke, C., & Ribeiro de Castro, H. (2007). The School Photograph: Portraiture and the Art of Assembling the Body of the School Child. *History of Education, 36*(2), 213-226.
Burke, C., Howard, J., & Cunningham, P. (eds.). (2013). *The Decorated School. Essays in the Visual Culture of Schooling.* London: Black Dog.
Carreño, M. (2008). Los Nuevos Museos de Educacion, un Movimiento Internacional. *Encounters on education, 9*, 75-91.
Colleldemont, E. (2010). La memoria visual de la escuela. *Educatio Siglo XXI, 28*(2), 133-156.
Comas Rubí, F. (2010). Fotografia i història de l'educació. *Educació i Historia: revista d'història de l'educació*, 15, 11-17.
Comas Rubí, F., Motilla Salas, X., & Sureda Garcia, B. (2012). Escuela y fotografia, entre el testimonio y la construccion del discurso narrativo. In P. L. Moreno Martínez, & A. Sebastián Vicente (eds.), *Patrimonio y Etnografía de la escuela en España y Portugal durante el siglo XX. [III Foro Ibérico de Museísmo Pedagógico : V Jornadas Científicas de la SEPHE* (pp. 405-417). Murcia: Sephe/Ceme Universidad de Murcia.
Dubois, Ph. (1983). *L'acte photographique*. Paris: Fernand Nathan.
Dussel, I. (2013). The visual turn in the history of education. Four comments for a historiographical discussion. In

Th. S. Popkewitz (ed.), *Rethinking the history of education. Transnational perspectives on its questions, methods, and knowledge* (pp. 29-50). New York: Palgrave Macmillan.

Edwards, E. (2009). Photographs as objects of memory. In F. Candlin, & R. Guins (eds.), *The Object Reader* (pp. 331-342). London: Routledge.

Edwards, E. (2010). Photographs and history: emotion and materiality. In S. H. Dudley (ed.), *Museum Materialities. Objects, Engagements, Interpretations* (pp. 21-38). London: Routledge.

Engeström, J. (2005). Why some social network services work and others don't. Or: the case for object-centered sociality. April 13, 2005. Retrieved January 15, 2015 from http://www.zengestrom.com/blog/2005/04/why-some-social-network-services-work-and-others-dont-or-the-case-for-object-centered-sociality.html.

Escolano Benito, A. (2002). Memoria de la educación y cultura de la escuela. In J. M. Hernández Díaz & B. Escolano Benito (eds.), *La memoria y el deseo: cultura de la escuela y educación deseada* (pp. 19-42). Valencia: Tirant Lo Blanch.

Escolano Benito, A. (2003). The School in the City: School Architecture as Discourse and as Text. *Paedagogica Historica*, 49(1), 53-64.

Escolano Benito, A. (Ed.). (2007). *La cultura material de la escuela. En el centenario de la Junta para la Ampliacion de Estudios, 1907-2007*. Berlanga de Duero: Ceince.

Escolano Benito, A. (2011). Más allá del espasmo del presente: la escuela como memoria. *História da Educação*, 15(33), 10-30.

Falk, J., & Dierking, L. (1992). *The Museum Experience.*

Washington, DC: Whalesback Press.
Falk, J., & Dierking, L. (2012). *Museum experience revisited*. Walnut Creek, CA: Left Coast Press.
Grosvenor, I. (1999). On visualising Past Classrooms. In I. Grosvenor, M. Lawn, & K. Rousmaniere (eds.), *Silences & Images. The Social History of the Classroom* (pp. 85-104). New York: Peter Lang.
Grosvenor, I., Lawn, M., & Rousmaniere, K. (eds.). (1999). *Silences & Images. The Social History of the Classroom*. New York: Peter Lang.
Grosvenor, I., Lawn, M., & Rousmaniere, K. (2000). Imaging Past Schooling: The Necessity for Montage. *Review of Education, Pedagogy and Cultural Studies*, 22(1), 71-85.
Hein, G. (1995). The Constructivist Museum. *Journal for Education in Museums*, *16*, 21-23.
Hein, G. (1998). *Learning in the museum*. London; New York: Routledge, 1998.
Herman, F., Van Gorp, A., Simon, F., & Depaepe, M. (2011). The School Desk: from Concept to Object. *History of Education*, 40(1), 97-117.
Hnlica, S. (2010). Schulbank und Klassenzimmer: Disziplinierung durch Architektur. In R. Egger & B. Hackl (eds.), *Pädagogische Prozesse zwischen vorprädikativer Situierung und reflexivem Anspruch* (pp. 141-162). Wiesbaden: VS Verlag für Sozialwissenschaften.
Hooper-Greenhill, E. (1999a). Education, communication and interpretation: towards a critical pedagogy in museums. In E. Hooper-Greenhill (ed.), *The educational role of the museum* (pp. 3-27). London; New York: Routledge.
Hooper-Greenhill, E. (1999b). Learning in art museums:

strategies of interpretation. In E. Hooper-Greenhill (ed.), *The educational role of the museum* (pp. 44-52). London; New York: Routledge.

Kozlovsky, R. (2010). The architecture of *educare*: motion and emotion in postwar educational spaces. *History of Education, 39*(6), 695-712.

Lawn, M., & Grosvenor, I. (eds.). (2005). *Materialities of schooling. Design, technology, objects, routines*. Oxford: Symposium Books.

Margolis, E., & Fram, S. (2007). Caught Napping: Images of Surveillance, Discipline and Punishment on the Body of the Schoolchild. *History of Education, 36*(2), 191-211.

Meda, J. (2010). Musei della scuola e dell'educazione. Ipotesi progettuale per una sistematizzazione delle iniziative di raccolta, conservazione e valorizzazione dei beni culturali delle scuole. *History of Education & Children's Literature*, 5(2), 489-501.

Meda, J. (2013). La conservazione del patrimonio storico-educativo: il caso italiano. In J. Meda, A. M. Badanelli (eds.), *La historia de la cultura escolar en Italia y en Espana: balance y perspectivas. Actas del I workshop Italo-Español de Historia de la Cultura Escolar (Berlanga de Duero, 14-16 de noviembre de 2011)* (pp. 180-193). Macerata: Eum.

Meda, J. (2014). La escuela del pasado y su conmemoración en los museos de la escuela italianos: tendencias y perspectivas. In A. M. Badanelli Rubio, M. Poveda Sanz & C. Rodríguez Guerrero (eds.), *Pedagogía museística: prácticas, usos didácticos e investigación del patrimonio educativo. Actas de las VI Jornadas Científicas de la SEPHE* (pp. 509-521). Madrid: Universidad Complutense de Madrid-Facultad de educación.

Moreno, P.L. (2005). History of school desk development in terms of hygiene and pedagogy in Spain (1838-1936). In M. Lawn & I. Grosvenor (eds.), *Materialities of schooling. Design, technology, objects, routines* (pp. 71-95). Oxford: Symposium Books .

Moreno Gómez, W. (2013). Fotoetnografía educativa: una ruta para comprender la cultura corporal escolarizada. *Revista Ibero-Americana de Educación*, *62*, 119-141.

Müller, Th., & Schneider, R. (eds.). (1998). *Das Klassenzimmer. Schulmöbel im 20. Jahrhundert*. München: Prestel.

O'Donoghue, D. (2010). Classrooms as installations: a conceptual framework for analyzing classroom photographs from the past. *History of Education*, *39*(3), 401-415.

Pozo Andrés, M. M. (2006). Imágenes e historia de la educación: construcción, reconstrucción y representación de las prácticas escolares en el aula. *Historia de la educación: Revista interuniversitaria*, *25*, 291-315.

Pozo Andrés, M. M., & Rabazas Romero, T. (2012). Las imágenes fotográficas como fuente para el estudio de la cultura escolar: precisiones conceptuales y metodológicas. *Revista de ciencias de la educación*, *231/232*, 401-414.

Roberts, L. (1997). *From Knowledge to Narrative. Educators and the Changing Museum*. Washington, DC: Smithsonian Institution Press.

Rousmaniere, K. (2001). Questioning the Visual in the History of Education. *History of Education*, *30* (2), 109-116.

Simon, N. (2010). *The Participatory Museum*. Santa Cruz, CA: Museum 2.0.

Thyssen, G. (2007). Visualizing Discipline of the Body in a German Open-Air School (1923–1939): Retrospection and

Introspection. *History of Education, 36* (2), 247-264.

Viñao Frago, A. (2010). Memoria, patrimonio y educación. *Educatio Siglo XXI, 28* (2), 17-42. Retrieved January 15, 2015 from http://revistas.um.es/educatio/article/view/111951/.

Viñao Frago, A. (2012). La historia material e inmaterial de la escuela: memoria, patrimonio y educación. *Educaçao, 35* (1), 7-17. Retrieved January 15, 2015 from http://revistaseletronicas.pucrs.br/ojs/index.php/faced/article/view/10351.

Van Dam, A. (2014). *To have, to hold, to share. A review of participatory curatorial practices in theory and practice in cultural institutions.* Amsterdam: Framer Framed/ Universiteit Leiden, 2014. Retrieved January 15, 2015 from https://www.academia.edu/7121970/A_Review_of_Participatory_Curatorial_Practices_in_Theory_and_Practice_in_Cultural_Institutions .

ABOUT THE EDITOR

THEOPISTI STYLIANOU-LAMBERT is an Assistant Professor at the School of Fine and Applied Arts at the Cyprus University of Technology and the founder and coordinator of its Visual Sociology and Museum Studies Lab. Her research interests include museum studies and visual sociology with an emphasis on photography. She is one of the founding members of the International Association of Photography and Theory and its current president. She holds a PhD in Museum Studies from the University of Leicester and an MA in Visual Arts/Museum Education from the University of Texas at Austin. Theopisti has published widely on museums and photography, is the author of *The Political Museum* (Left Coast Press) and the co-editor of *Re-envisioning Cyprus* (University of Nicosia Press), and *Photography and Cyprus: Time, Place, Identity* (I. B. Tauris). She has received several scholarships and awards including a Smithsonian Fellowship in Museum Practice, a Fulbright Fellowship (USA) and an Arts and Humanities Research Council Award (UK).

ABOUT THE AUTHORS

JENNA C ASHTON is an arts and culture researcher and curator, and is Creative Director of Digital Women's Archive North [DWAN]. She has multi-disciplinary research interests, including museums, collections, childhood, women's heritage and disability studies. Jenna is interested in exploring the intersections between arts, medicine, health and technology, and has collaborated with scientists and artists around these areas. Her PhD research applied Melanie Klein's theories to open up the childhood house of contemporary artist Rachel Whiteread and her methods of casting and collecting.
http://jcashton.wordpress.com
dwarchivenorth.wordpress.com

JOHANNA BARNBECK is an artistic researcher and creative consultant. She designed and collaboratively carried out the research project Augmenting Masterpieces at the Rijksmuseum Amsterdam. Based in Berlin, Johanna founded an agency for interdisciplinary research design, concept development and multimedia science communication. She holds two master's degrees in Cultural Analysis and Artistic Research from the University of Amsterdam. www.johannabarnbeck.com

KRISTIN BAYANS is the Interpretive Media Specialist at the Portland Art Museum where she produces interpretive media learning experiences – mobile, web, and in-gallery – for special exhibitions, the museum's permanent collection, and the *Object Stories* project. She is also the Co-Founder of Hive Cascadia, a Mozilla Learning Community. Kristin has served as the Senior Educator for the Vernier Technology Lab at the Oregon Museum of Science and Industry and as Assistant

Educator for the Smithsonian's Mobile Learning Institute. She holds an MA in Museum Studies from The George Washington University and an MA in Art History from the Courtauld Institute of Art.

JEFFREY S BOWEN runs the University of Houston-Clear Lake (UHCL) Art Gallery, where he has organized scores of exhibitions and public educational programs since joining the university in 2011. Among his major accomplishments, Jeffrey oversaw the gallery's first major renovation, overhauled its brand identity, including launching a new website, and introduced the space to interactive iPads. Before his position at UHCL, he managed the University of Houston Blaffer Art Museum's public relations, marketing, and membership initiatives. Prior to moving to Texas, Jeff worked in the membership department at the Nantucket Historical Association. In all three positions, Jeff gave each organization its first presence on social media. A native of Rhode Island, Jeff earned a Master of Arts in Museum Studies from Syracuse University and a Bachelor of Arts from Penn State University.

MARTA BRUNELLI is Lecturer in General and Social Education in the University of Macerata, where she runs classes in Heritage Education and Interpretation in the Master's Degree courses of the Department of Education, Cultural Heritage and Tourism. In the same university she is member of the Centre for Documentation and Research on the History of Textbooks and Children's Literature, and member of the Scientific Committee of the Paolo and Ornella Ricca School Museum where she has been nominated coordinator of the Education

Committee. Marta is the author of various articles and scientific contributions on heritage education and interpretation, and has a special interest to the field of historical heritage of schools and school museums as educational resources. Her recent books include: *Heritage Interpretation. Un nuovo approccio per l'educazione al patrimonio* (2014); *Manuale di formazione per interpreti museali* (2012), the Italian edition of the manual by Mary Kay Cunningham (*The Interpreter's Training Manual For Museums*). She is a member of the Italian Society of Education; the Italian Centre for the Historical-Educational Research; the European Association for Heritage Interpretation; and the Committee of Education and Cultural Mediation of ICOM Italia.

ALLI BURNESS is a Digital Producer at the Museum of Applied Arts and Sciences in Sydney, Australia. She turned to new media in the museum sector after exploring the visitor experience as part of an extensive independent travel and research project. She has tracked the evolution of the selfie in museums from early 2013, documenting the process with a popular website. Alli is now an advocate for digital museum audiences. She researches, writes and speaks about the value of creative digital expression as part of the museum visitor experience. She has created digital content for the National Gallery of Art in Washington, DC, The J Paul Getty Museum in Los Angeles and the Wellcome Collection in the UK. She holds an MA in Museum Studies from the Australian National Museum.

MAR DIXON is the creator of #MuseumSelfie Day and many other projects such as the Open Community Lab, MuseomixUK and MuseumCamp. She has fingers in many pies including culture, digital, publishing, wearables and tech sectors. Mar is the driving force behind acclaimed campaigns including #AskACurator, #MuseumWeek, @52Museums and #LoveTheatreDay. She speaks at many international conferences in addition to running workshops for small businesses and national museums and everything in between. www.mardixon.com

RUSSELL DORNAN is the Web Editor at Wellcome Collection. He is responsible for the content on the website, blog and social media channels and is always looking for ways to involve audiences in the work of the museum. Russell recognises the important role photography can play in museums, whether generated by the institution or its audience, and started Wellcome Collection's Instagram account. He developed the social media elements of their 2014 exhibition, *An Idiosyncratic A to Z of the Human Condition*, with a focus on audience participation, full integration of social media in the exhibition and the use of submitted images in the gallery. Russell also instigated the #MuseumInstaSwap project in 2015: a collaboration between ten London museums using Instagram to see themselves through a different lens. Previously, he used photography to document a project at the Horniman Museum and Gardens, resulting in a small photography exhibition to publicise it.

DIVYA RAO HEFFLEY is Senior Program Manager of Carnegie Museum of Art's Hillman Photography Initiative, an incubator for innovative thinking about photography. For the past five years, she has directed the collaborative and experimental process behind the Initiative to implement multiple public-facing programs. She received a PhD in the History of Art and Architecture from Brown University and a BA from Yale University in the History of Art. Drawn to the historic and contemporary relationships between artistic practice and scientific inquiry, Divya has research interests which span urban planning, architecture, photography, theories of spatial perception, and the evolution of imaging technologies. She has juried Photolucida's *Critical Mass International Photography Competition* and the Magenta Foundation's *Flash Forward Emerging Photographers Competition*, and has been an invited portfolio reviewer at CENTER Santa Fe's REVIEW Santa Fe. Divya's writing has appeared in *Design and Culture* and the Center for the Future of Museums blog and is forthcoming in *Museum Ideas: Innovation in Theory and Practice, v.2.*

LINDA HENKEL is Professor of Psychology at Fairfield University. She holds a PhD in experimental psychology from Stony Brook University and completed a postdoctoral fellowship at Princeton University. She specializes in research on memory errors and distortions in both younger and older adults, and has published over 25 research articles, with several focusing on how taking and viewing photos can shape people's memories of their experiences. Other areas of research include memory accuracy in eyewitnesses, false confessions, and collaborative remembering. Her work has appeared in journals such as *Psychological Science; Memory; Psychology and Aging; Journal of Memory and Language;* and the *Journal of Experimental Psychology: General.* She has received research grants from the

National Institute on Aging and from the Fairfield University Integrative Health Sciences Initiative, where she is currently conducting research on the role of photos and reminiscence activities on the cognitive functioning, well-being, and the quality of care for nursing home residents.

THOMAS HILLMAN is Assistant Professor of Information Technology and Learning at the University of Gothenburg. He is a trained industrial designer with several years' experience as an exhibition designer at museums in several countries. Thomas' research examines the relationship between learning and technology in a wide variety of contexts from schools to museums and online communities. His interdisciplinary research is done as part of *LETStudio*, the University of Gothenburg's priority research area on learning and media technology.

ELEE KIRK is a Researcher at the University of Leicester. In 2014 she completed her PhD at the university's School of Museum Studies, with a thesis, *Crystal Teeth and Skeleton Eggs: Snapshots of Young Children's Experiences in a Natural History Museum*. Her research made use of children's digital photography as a method for exploring the museum visits from their perspective. Her principal interests are in using innovative and participatory research methods with children, and children's engagement with science and nature in museums. Prior to rejoining academia, Elee spent eight years working in science museum education, first at Thinktank, Birmingham Science Museum, and latterly at the Thackray Medical Museum in Leeds.

MARIRUTH LEFTWICH currently serves as the Senator John Heinz History Center's Education Manager, overseeing school, teacher, early learning, and youth programs. Prior to joining the History Center, Mariruth served as e-Learning Officer at the Museum of London, where she developed one of the UK's first museum-based digital learning studios. Her work experience has also included museum teaching at the Atlanta History Center and tenure as Vice President for Education & Programs at the Charlotte Museum of History, where she built the education department and public programs with the opening of a new museum. Having worked in a variety of historic homes, Mariruth was inspired to research the visitor experience at Graceland, one of the world's most popular historic homes, which forms the basis of her doctoral work. She holds a PhD from the University of London's Institute of Education in the areas of museum education and heritage interpretation, an MEd focusing on curriculum design and instructional technology, an MA in history from Royal Holloway, and a BA in history with secondary teaching certification from Oglethorpe University.

KJERSTI LILLEBØ is Head of Communications at MiA – Museums in Akershus (Norway), where she oversees the museum's educational programs and MiA's social media and marketing profile. She holds a degree in Social Anthropology from the University of Oslo. Kjersti previously worked at the National Institute for Consumer Research (SIFO), where she was primarily engaged in research related to the construction of identity, migration, and new forms of regulation. Having conducted extensive fieldwork in the USA, the Caribbean and

Scandinavia, her research and work examines how different societal mechanisms are influencing human interaction and behavior choices, especially the constructions of belonging and the preservation of traditions.

KIRSTEN LINDE is a Curator at MiA – Museums in Akershus. She holds an MA in history from the University of Aarhus in Denmark. Kirsten has written about work migration and childhood care in the 18th century, and on topics of museology including object photography and museum history. Her special responsibility at MiA is documenting and collecting contemporary objects. She has undertaken many documentation surveys, on such topics as urban development, the decoration of houses, handbags in everyday life, and bread in supermarkets.

JUSTIN MEYER is a PhD candidate in Urban Planning at the University of Michigan, conducting research on the relationships between art museums, communities, and cities. He recently completed a certificate in Museum Studies at the University of Michigan, as well as a Masters Degree in Urban Planning as a Wallenberg Scholar. Justin holds degrees in engineering and environmental design from Stanford University and the University of Cambridge, respectively.

ELLIE MILES is Contemporary Collecting Curator at London Transport Museum. She was previously an Interpretation Officer at the British Museum, and worked on the redisplay of the Sutton Hoo and Early Medieval gallery. As part of the Interpretation Unit, she worked with curators and designers to increase visit engagement in galleries and to develop exhibitions. Ellie recently completed her PhD in cultural geography, which explored how city museums represent urban history, and she is also a visiting lecturer at the University of Westminster. Prior to her time at the British Museum, Ellie was the Museum of London's Digital Curator, collecting born-digital objects for the museum.

JONATHAN TADASHI NAITO is an Assistant Professor of English at St. Olaf College in Northfield, Minnesota. His research interests include twentieth- and twenty-first-century British literature, art, and culture, post-colonial studies, and museum studies. His current projects include an examination of the cross-pollination of visual art and literature in postwar Britain.

KATELYN PARISI is a graduate of Fairfield University with a degree in psychology, during which time she collaborated with Dr. Linda Henkel on research examining how reviewing different types of photographs shapes peoples' later memory. She has presented her research at the Association for Psychological Science annual conference, and has been inducted into Psi Chi, The National Honor Society in Psychology, and Sigma Xi, The Scientific Research Society. Katelyn currently works as a research assistant in the Aging Brain Center at the Institute for Aging Research at Hebrew SeniorLife, and plans on attending graduate school to obtain a PhD in Cognitive Psychology.

PATRICK VAN ROSSEM is Associate Professor of Modern and Contemporary Art at Utrecht University, Netherlands. He was Assistant Professor in Art History at Ghent University,

Belgium, from 2006 until 2008, having previously studied art history and communication science at Ghent University and curating at Goldsmiths College, University of London. Patrick obtained his PhD in Art History in 2006. He is the author of *Creation and Desire in the Encounter with the Audience: A Study on Bruce Naumans, Martin Kippenbergers and Anne-Mie Van Kerckhovens Self-Presentation* (Ghent University). His research interests include the performative turn in the visual arts, artist/audience relations since 1960 and the representation of spectators and audiences.

LESLIE-JEAN THORNTON is an Associate Professor at Arizona State University. Her research focuses on the acquisition, production, transfer, and meaning of information conveyed through journalism, mass communication, and social media. An enduring love of art is currently manifesting itself though an increased attention to visual forms and practices, particularly as they might relate to image use policies in a global environment. Leslie-Jean's work has been published in many journals, including *Visual Communication Quarterly*, *Journalism and Mass Communication Quarterly* and *Sex Roles*. She is currently working on a book about electronic social art. Instagram: @ljthornton.

CAREY MACK WEBER is Museum and Collections Manager for the University Museums at Fairfield University. She has over 20 years' experience working in museums and galleries. After graduating from Connecticut College with a BA in Art History, Carey spent a decade working in fine art galleries in New York City. At Fairfield University, she has helped bring twenty loan shows to the Bellarmine Museum and the Walsh Art Gallery. She has also been directly involved in the extensive programming and publications related to these exhibitions.

ALEXANDRA WEILENMANN is Associate Professor of Applied Information Technology at the University of Gothenburg, Sweden. Her research is concerned with the use of mobile communication and information technologies. The aim is to reveal how these technologies are brought into play as part of everyday activities, something which has involved exploring different methods for performing ethnographic work and user-centered studies. Previous fieldwork includes mobile technology use among hunters, journalists, airport personnel, professional drivers, teenagers and the elderly. Alexandra's recent work deals with social media and social photography practices in museums, science centers and zoological gardens.

ALSO FROM MUSEUMSETC

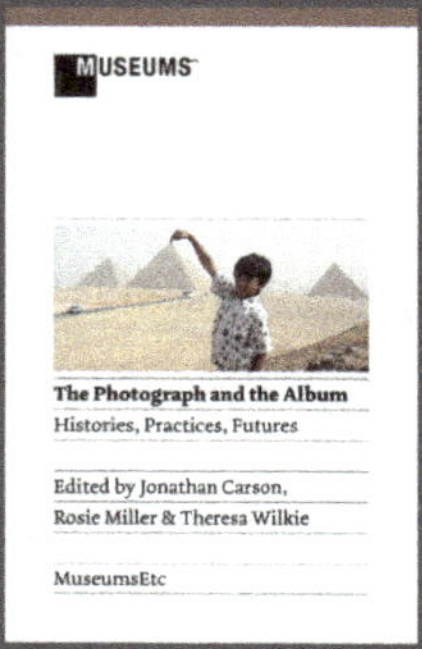

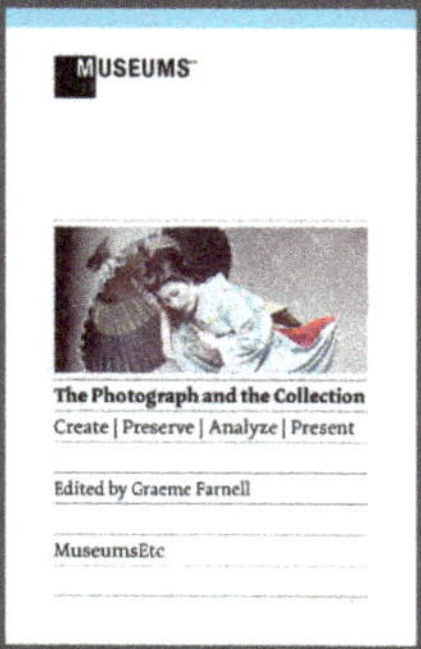

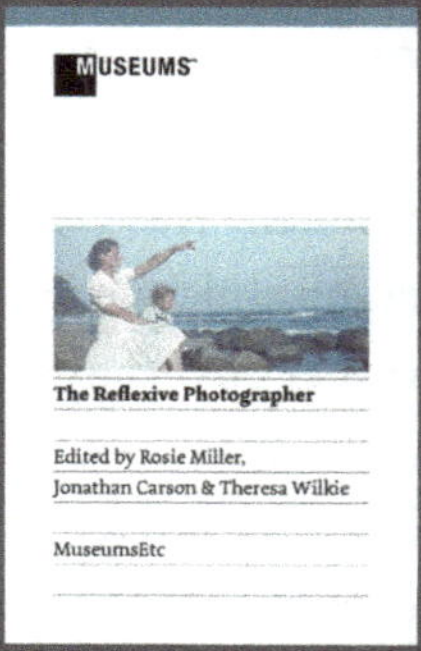

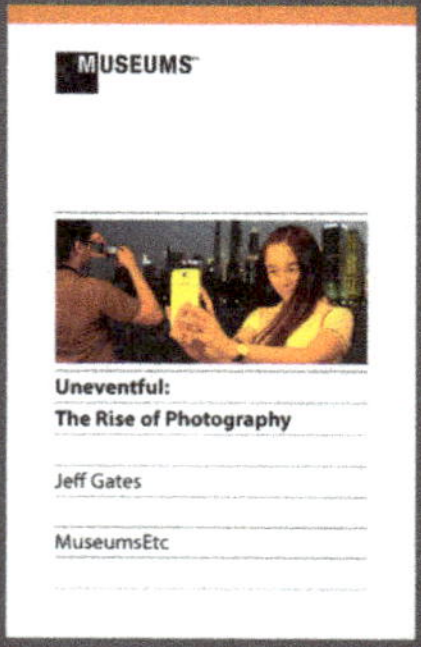

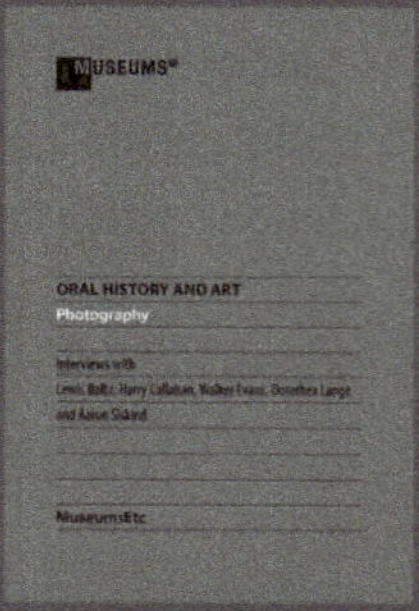

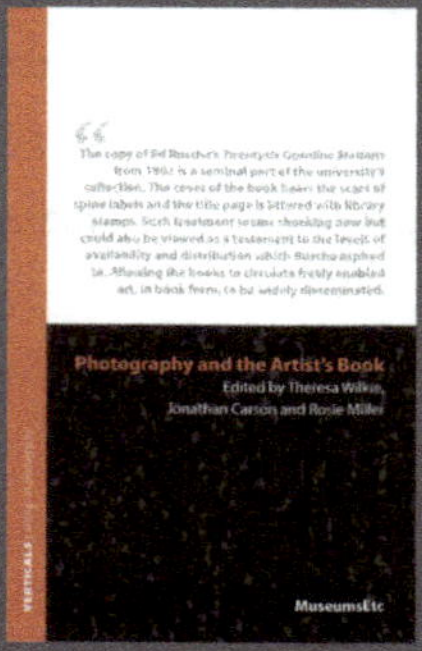

THE MUSEUMSETC BOOK COLLECTION

10 Must Reads: Inclusion – Empowering New Audiences

10 Must Reads: Interpretation

10 Must Reads: Learning, Engaging, Enriching

10 Must Reads: Strategies – Making Change Happen

A Handbook for Academic Museums, Volume 1: Exhibitions and Education

A Handbook for Academic Museums, Volume 2: Beyond Exhibitions and Education

A Handbook for Academic Museums, Volume 3: Advancing Engagement

Advanced Interpretive Planning

Alive To Change: Successful Museum Retailing

Contemporary Collecting: Theory and Practice

Collecting the Contemporary: A Handbook for Social History Museums

Conversations with Visitors: Social Media and Museums

Creating Bonds: Successful Museum Marketing

Creativity and Technology: Social Media, Mobiles and Museums

Engaging the Visitor: Designing Exhibits That Work

Inspiring Action: Museums and Social Change

interpreting the Art Museum

Interpretive Master Planning

Interpretive Training Handbook

Museum Retailing: A Handbook of Strategies for Success

Museums and the Disposals Debate

Museums and the Material World: Collecting the Arabian Peninsula

Museums and Visitor Photography: Redefining the Visitor Experience

Museums At Play: Games, Interaction and Learning

Narratives of Community: Museums and Ethnicity

New Thinking: Rules for the (R)evolution of Museums

On Food and Health: Confronting the Big Issues

On Sexuality - Collecting Everybody's Experience

On Working with Offenders: Opening Minds, Awakening Emotions
Oral History and Art: Painting
Oral History and Art: Photography
Oral History and Art: Sculpture
Reimagining Museums: Practice in the Arabian Peninsula
Restaurants, Catering and Facility Rentals: Maximizing Earned Income
Rethinking Learning: Museums and Young People
Science Exhibitions: Communication and Evaluation
Science Exhibitions: Curation and Design
Social Design in Museums: The Psychology of Visitor Studies (2 volumes)
Sustainable Museums: Strategies for the 21st Century
The Caring Museum: New Models of Engagement with Ageing
The Exemplary Museum: Art and Academia
The Innovative Museum: It's Up To You...
The Interpretive Trails Book
The New Museum Community: Audiences, Challenges, Benefits
The Power of the Object: Museums and World War II
Wonderful Things: Learning with Museum Objects

VERTICALS | writings on photography

A History and Handbook of Photography

Museums and Visitor Photography: Redefining the Visitor Experience

Naturalistic Photography

Oral History and Art: Photography

Poetry in Photography

The Photographic Studios of Europe

Photography and the Artist's Book

Street Life in London

Street Life in London: Context and Commentary

The Photograph and the Album

The Photograph and the Collection

The Reflexive Photographer

COLOPHON

Published by MuseumsEtc Ltd.
UK: Hudson House, 8 Albany Street, Edinburgh EH1 3QB
USA: 675 Massachusetts Avenue, Suite 11, Cambridge, MA 02139

www.museumsetc.com
twitter: @museumsetc

MuseumsEtc books may be purchased at special quantity discounts for business, academic, or sales promotional use. For information, please email specialsales@museumsetc.com or write to Special Sales Department, MuseumsEtc Ltd, Hudson House, 8 Albany Street, Edinburgh EH1 3QB.

A CIP catalogue record for this book is available on request from the British Library.
ISBN: 978-1-910144-74-9

The paper used in printing this book comes from responsibly managed forests and meets the requirements of the Forest Stewardship Council™ (FSC®) and the Sustainable Forestry Initiative® (SFI®). It is acid free and lignin free and meets all ANSI standards for archival quality paper.

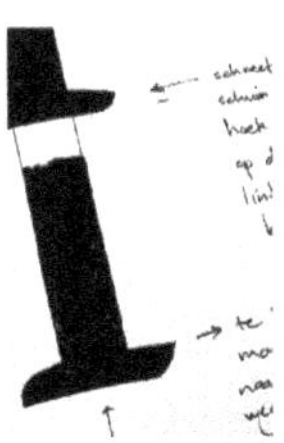

Dolly Pro, the typeface in which the main text of this book is set, is designed by Underware, a specialist type design studio founded in 1999 and based in The Hague, Helsinki and Amsterdam. The font is "a book typeface with flourishes", designed for the comfortable reading of long texts. The asymmetrically rounded serifs give the type a friendly but contemporary look - and it uses old-style numerals, which we love.

Myriad Pro was designed by Robert Slimbach and Carol Twombly for Adobe Systems and is the sans serif typeface probably best known as Apple's corporate font.

MuseumsEtc

Sharing innovation
in museum practice worldwide.